·旅游英语丛书·

四川

英语导游

(第2版)

Sichuan English Guide

四川省旅游局人教处组织编写

杨天庆　编著

Dr. Theodore Johnson 审校

旅游教育出版社

·北京·

责任编辑：晋小涵　丁海秀
图片来源：中国图片网

图书在版编目(CIP)数据

四川英语导游/杨天庆编著：四川省旅游局人教处组织编写.
—北京：旅游教育出版社，2003.12(2007.11)
ISBN 978—7-5637-1161-1

Ⅰ.四…　Ⅱ.①杨…　②四…　Ⅲ.导游—英语　Ⅳ.H319.9
中国版本图书馆 CIP 数据核字(2003)第 099108 号

旅游英语丛书
四川英语导游
(第 2 版)
Sichuan English Guide
四川省旅游局人教处组织编写
杨天庆　编著
Dr. Theodore Johnson　审校

出版单位	旅游教育出版社
地　　址	北京市朝阳区定福庄南里 1 号
邮　　编	100024
发行电话	(010)65778403 65728372 65767462(传真)
本社网址	www.tepcb.com
E—mail	tepfx@163.com
印刷单位	河北省三河市灵山红旗印刷厂
经销单位	新华书店
开　　本	850×1168　1/32
印　　张	17
字　　数	300 千字
版　　次	2007 年 11 月第 2 版
印　　次	2007 年 11 月第 1 次印刷
印　　数	1～5000 册
定　　价	29.00 元

(图书如有装订差错请与发行部联系)

出版说明

新世纪伊始，中国旅游业呈现出更加迅猛的发展势头。与此同时，各地的英语导游队伍也日益壮大。然而，有关地方旅游方面的英文资料十分匮乏，这无疑给英语导游、各大专院校旅游和英语专业学生的学习带来很大的不便。面对这种形势，我们本着提高导游素质、服务于地方旅游事业的宗旨，和地方旅游局人教处、培训中心一起，共同策划了这套“旅游英语丛书”。

本丛书经过精心组织与策划，具有三个特点：第一，语言通俗易懂。一方面，丛书作者尽量选择常用词、词组、语法结构；另一方面，专门聘请了外国专家审校，既保证了本丛书语言的规范性，又便于不同层次的读者学习。第二，知识与实践统一。丛书不仅知识丰富，而且为读者提供了模拟训练、领略实战的情景，在一定程度上减少了知识与实践脱节的矛盾。第三，有一定的文化含量。丛书并不是泛泛地介绍景区景点知识，而是尝试融入较深层次的地方旅游文化，有利于提高读者的整体文化素质。

《四川英语导游》为“旅游英语丛书”的第一本，是在四川旅游局人教处的组织下，由四川师范大学杨天庆教授编写完成的。杨天庆教授长期从事英语教学，语言功底深厚。为使本书更贴近实际，他与美国纽约州立大学 Dr. Theodore Johnson 多次进行试验与探索，共同走访了书中所述的大部分旅游景点。全书分为四川与成都、沿途导游、四川地区面面观、部分景点讲解词四大部分，资料丰富，内容翔实，不仅为读者提供了一般的景区景点知识，而且对四川的风土人情、旅游文化进行了较深层次的阐述。此次再版，为适应读者需求，第四部分增加了“乐山大佛”、“峨眉山”和“四川熊猫”等内容，使全文更丰富更详细；沿途导游部分增加了“成都—广安”、“成都—蜀南竹海”、“成都—广元”、“西昌—攀枝花”等线路。另外，“金沙遗址”和“碧峰霞”的内容也做了较大的调整。本书在编写过程中，得到了四川旅游界以及各方面的大力支持：Dr. Theodore Johnson 对全书进行了精心审校；电子科技大学外语学院的熊惠明副教授参与了第二、三部分的编写；四川师范大学旅游学院的刘小方、钱薇加同学提供了大量资料，且刘小方还独立完成了“接团注意事项”前期的英文写作；原光大国旅的李明经理对沿途旅游线路提出了宝贵意见，在此一并表示感谢。

本丛书既是旅行社英语导游必不可少的工具书，也是广大旅游英语学习者的良师益友。真诚地希望读者在使用中能够及时反馈不足，我们定会“从善如流”，使本丛书不断提高与完善。

Content
目 录

Section One:Sichuan and Chengdu
(第一部分:四川与成都)

Section Two:On-the-Way Tour
(第二部分:沿途导游)

Long-Distance Trips 长途旅游 /85

Farewell Speech 欢送词 /181

Section Three: Highlights of Sichuan Province (第三部分:四川地区面面观)

Sichuan Opera 看川剧 /187

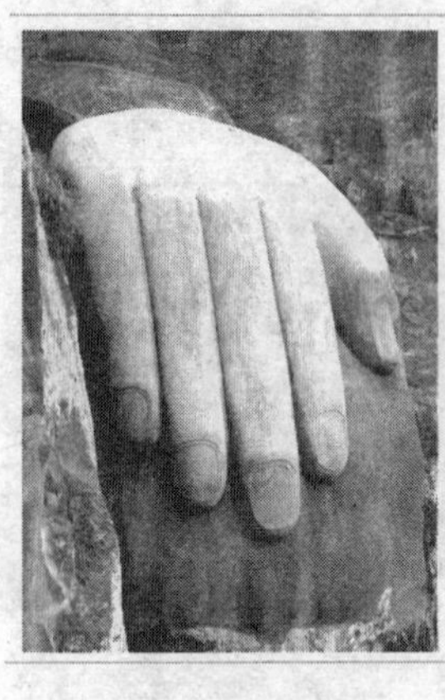

Section Four:Descriptions of Some Scenic Spots
(第四部分:部分景点讲解词)

River-Viewing Tower Park
望江楼 /334

Precious Light Monastery 宝光寺 /344

Sanxingdui Museum 广汉三星堆 /359

Dujiangyan Irrigation System
都江堰 /381

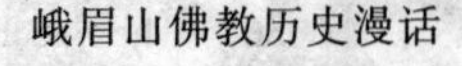

Pandas in Sichuan 四川熊猫 /511

Appendix 附录 /521

Section One :

Sichuan and Chengdu

第一部分：

四川与成都

Sichuan Province 四川省

Sichuan is the largest province in Southwest China. It covers an area of 485,000 square km and boasts the third largest population in China, after Henan and Shandong Provinces. It has 85 million people. Its population displays as much diversity as its landscape. The whole province is occupied by 53 Chinese nationalities. The main nationalities consist of Han(汉), Tibetan (藏), Yi(彝), Qiang(羌), Hui(回), Miao(苗) and others.

Sichuan adjoins the Tibetan Plateau in the West and the Changjiang in the East. The eastern section supports the densest rural population; the western section rises in giant steps to the Tibetan Plateau where the windswept grassland and deeper forests are home of Tibetans and Qiang.

The Chinese often refer Sichuan as the Land of Abundance. It refers to the province's abundance of natural resources and cultural heritage.

KEY WORDS & EXPRESSIONS 关键词汇及表达法

boast 以……为自豪;具有
diversity 多样性
landscape 风景,景色
abundance 大量,丰富
gain some insight into 了解

History and Legend
历史与传说

The first evidence of human habitation in Sichuan province

consists of simple tools and a skullcap. These objects date back to the Paleolithic (Old Stone) Age. During the Neolithic Period (approximately 8,000 - 2,000 B. C.), people in Sichuan areas used axes, pottery jars, bone needles, and crude weapons. However, the first major civilizations in the province were the Ba (巴) and Shu(蜀) peoples, who lived between 11th and 5th century B. C.. The Shu people lived on the Chengdu Plain; the state of Ba was in the center of Sichuan. Originally Ba referred to fish hunter or a person whose main food was fish; Shu referred to people living on the plateau. During your stay in Chengdu you will see the Shu and Ba relics in Sanxindui Museum and Sichuan Provincial Museum.

Scholars believed the ancestor of the early Shu people belonged to a tribe branch of the ancient Qiang nationality. These ancient people used to live along the areas between the upper and middle reaches of the Yellow River. Later they moved into Sichuan areas. They lived by hunting and farming in mountains and valleys on the upper reaches of the Minjiang River. Later their activities extended down along the Minjiang River and the Chengdu Plain. Can Cong (蚕丛) and Yu Fu (鱼凫) founded the Shu state. Du Yu (杜宇) taught the Shu people how to farm as he served as the king of the Shu state. Twenty-three hundred years ago, Kai Ming (开明), another Shu king moved his capital slightly east and named the new town Chengdu, which means "becoming a city". He hoped that it would one day be a metropolis. It is generally believed that the Ba and Shu states occupied Sichuan areas from the Shang Dynasty (1700 - 1027 B. C.) to the Warring States Period (770 - 221 B. C.).

During the Warring States Period, a Qin emperor conquered

the two states. The Qin emperor turned them into prefectures. He moved thousands of the Qin residents to the former Shu state in Sichuan. He hoped that this activity might help him secure his hold on the fertile land. Since then Chengdu became the government office center to manage affairs across the former Ba and Shu areas. Gradually Bashu became short for Sichuan. During the Three Kingdoms Period (220 - 280) Liu Bei occupied Sichuan. He claimed himself as the emperor of the Shu (蜀国). During the Five Dynasties Period (907 - 960) Wang Jian (王建) and Meng Zhixiang (孟知祥) established their own states in Sichuan. The former was called the Former Shu State, and the other the Later Shu State.

During the Tang Dynasty (618 - 907) Sichuan was divided into three major administrative regions. They were named the three roads,hoad means "daos" (道) in Chinese,it's also called sanchuan, "san" means "three" in English.

In the Northern Song Dynasty (960 - 1127), Sichuan was divided into four prefectures. They included Yizhou (益州), Zizhou (梓州), Lizhou (利州) and Kuizhou (夔州). They were named Chuanxiasilu (川峡四路). "Lu" was equivalent to "dao" in the Tang Dynasty. It means " Chuan Four Regions". People called the Chuan Four Regions as Sichuan for short. Si means "four" in English.

In the period of the Yuan Dynasty (1272 - 1368) when Sichuan formally became a province instead of daos or Lu, Chengdu was designated as its provincial capital.

Why do many people call Sichuan as the land of abundance or the state of Tianfu (天府)?

Tianfu was the official title. Its official responsibility was to take care of national valuable jewelry and other rare treasures. Tianfu also had an extended meaning relating to treasure storage. Later, people used Tianfu as a figure of speech to imply the fertile-land area where diversified products were produced.

Before the Qin emperor unified the whole China, the Tianfu area covered both the Chengdu and Hanzhong plains (汉中平原). The kingdom of Shu in the Three Kingdoms Period covered the most part of Sichuan and Hanzhong, which now is part of Shaanxi. However, the Tianfu area mainly referred to the Chengdu Plain because of the well-known Dujiang Irrigation System.

Ancient Sichuan mainly refers to the Sichuan Basin and the Hanzhong Basin. The two basins have fertile fields and mild climate. Particularly the Chengdu Plain in the Sichuan Basin has particularly benefited from the Dujiangyan Irrigation System since the Qin Dynasty (221 - 207 B. C.). Due to the irrigation system and natural advantages, local Sichuan farmers worked hard in the fields and yielded bumper harvests. There is an old saying: no serious flood or drought disaster ever occurred and local people had enough food to eat ever since the Qin and Han dynasties.

The Sichuan Basin is completely surrounded by high mountains. The ancient Chinese of central China were involved in many wars, and people suffered tremendously. The geographic location of the mountains had prevented the spread of the war disasters into ancient Sichuan, and local people in Sichuan were able to live in peace. Therefore, Sichuan was thought of as a good place to live in.

Besides, ancient Sichuan had a very important strategic position. During the Warring States Period, the king of the Qin

State occupied first the two states called Ba and Shu in Sichuan, and then he started his ambitious plan to establish his dynasty across all China.

Under the Qin Dynasty Liu Bang (刘邦) was a low official. Towards the end of the Qin he joined military attacks against the Qin Dynasty. Liu Bang successfully occupied the capital of the Qin and became the first emperor of the Han Dynasty (206 B. C. - A. D. 220).

Towards the end of the Eastern Han Dynasty (25 A. D. - 220 A. D.), peasant rebellions broke out. The warlord uprisings plagued the whole country. Zhuge Liang (诸葛亮), a well-known military strategist met Liu Bei (刘备). Liu Bei was one of the former Han generals and Zhuge Liang advised Liu Bei to take up the state of Shu in Sichuan and establish his own kingdom. Liu Bei accepted his advice. His army launched a series of hard attacks against the army from Shu, and finally Liu Bei set up his own kingdom in Sichuan, with its capital in Chengdu. The whole China was then carved up into the three kingdoms, ruled by the kings of Shu (蜀), Wei (魏) and Wu (吴).

Towards the end of the Three Kingdoms Period the army from the Wei in central China first destroyed the Shu. Afterwards the Wei's army marched down into the south of the lower reaches of the Changjiang where the Kingdom of Wu was located.

In the middle of the Tang Dynasty there were two serious war disasters. They occurred in central China. The emperors and their governments all moved away from the capital then located on the site of present-day Xi'an and took refuge in Sichuan.

In the Song Dynasty (960 - 1279) war disasters occurred many times in central China, but Sichuan found itself in peace.

During the Anti-Japanese War (1937 - 1945) the Japanese invaders occupied and brutally exploited most of China's major areas. Jiang Jieshe and his republican government withdrew from Nanjing and moved the capital to Chongqing in Sichuan where it remained until 1945.

In March 1997 the Fifth Session of the Eighth National People's Congress turned Chongqing into the fourth municipality after Beijing, Shanghai and Tianjin.

Since the founding of the People's Republic of China in 1949, economic development in Sichuan has experienced two important periods. The first period happened in the 1960s. Sichuan made up a large portion of the construction, which laid an important foundation for its economic development. The second period took place in 1978 when China started her domestic reform and opening-up to the outside world. Over the past two decades Sichuan's GDP has been at an average annual rate of 9. 3 percent. The agricultural and industrial production capacity has quickly increased; the people's living standards have significantly improved; infrastructure construction has made much great progress. All these factors have made Sichuan richer than before and become an economic power in west China. Sichuan still has much more to accomplish, and people in Sichuan are working hard towards developing a well-to-do life.

KEY WORDS & EXPRESSIONS 关键词汇及表达法

human habitation 人居;人迹

Paleolithic 旧石器时代的

Old Stone Age 旧石器时期

Neolithic Period 新石器时期

approximately 大约

the Chengdu Plain 成都平原
the upper and middle reaches of the Yellow River 黄河中上游
conquer 征服
valuable jewelry 珍贵的珠宝
rare treasure 珍藏,珍宝
diversified product 各种产品
tremendously 可怕地
warlord 军阀
uprising 起义,暴动
plague 使染瘟疫,使生灾祸
take up 占据
a series of 一系列的
take refuge 避难
economic development 经济发展
domestic reform 国内改革
opening-up to the outside world 对外开放
living standard 生活标准
infrastructure construction 基础建设

Geography and Environment
地理与环境

Sichuan province is located on the upper reach of the Changjiang. It is widely known as the land of abundance for its fertile land. Its east longitude extends from 97°21′ to 110°12′; its north latitude extends from 26°03′ to 34°19′. The province is about 1,200km from east to west by 900km from north to south. The annual average temperature is between 16° to 18° in the West, and 19° to 20° in the East. The annual rainfall is 1,200mm.

Sichuan is an inland province, and it ranks fifth in China for its vast territory size. Its area is 485,000 square km, and it encompasses landforms of great diversity. Sichuan borders on the Tibet-Qinghai Plateau in the West, the Three Gorges of the Changjiang in the East, the Qinling-Bashan Mountains in the North and the Yunnan-Guizhou Plateau in the South. It ranges from the Sichuan Basin in the East to the highlands and mountains in the West. The East of Sichuan ranges from 200m to 700m above sea level. The highlands in the West range from 1,500m to 3,000m.

The East of Sichuan resembles the structure of a basin on the surface. It covers an area of 162,000 square km as one of the five basins in China. The climate is mild, humid and subtropical. The area greatly fits diversified agricultural development. Traditionally it grows rice, wheat, and rapeseed and sweat potatoes. It also grows medicinal plants and herbs that are sold all over the country and to the world.

The West of Sichuan is subject to a cold continental climate except for the deep river valleys there. The Northwest of the highlands has comparatively lower level valleys. Its land surface remains extensive. There grass grows luxuriantly and offers favorite conditions to the development of animal husbandry. In the Southeast the highlands resemble different segments. They seem to be cut off by the typical land structure and many rivers that flow crosswise. The high mountains and deep valleys have vast forests and grasslands.

Sichuan has more than 1,400 rivers of different sizes. The Jinsha River (金沙江) is the upper section of the Changjiang. Yalong (雅砻江), Minjiang(岷江), Tuojiang (沱江), Jialing (嘉陵江) and Qingyijiang (清衣江) rivers in Sichuan are major tributaries of the Changjiang. Many of the rivers in Sichuan flow rapidly between hills, mountains and gorges, which make Sichuan the number one province in hydroelectric power potential. The estimated reserves of hydraulic recourses are 140 million kilowatts.

Sichuan also has rich mineral resourse. Sichuan is situated in a faultage zone and is known as the World Geological Museum. So far 130 kinds of minerals have been discovered. At present the reserves of 11 minerals rank first in China. They include vanadium, titanium, and lithium, silver and iron sulfide ore. The prospective reserves of natural gas stand at 7.2 trillion cubic meters. Panxi (攀西) is in west Panzhihua (攀枝花). It has concentrated ferrous, non-ferrous metals and rare earth. It contains 13 per cent of the country's iron, 69 per cent of vanadium, 93 per cent of titanium and 82 per cent of cobalt. It also has rich hydraulic, mineral and biological resourses.

Sichuan has innumerable species of biological resources. It is known as one of China's three major forest zones. Characteristically the Sichuan zone has large areas, concentrated distribution and enormous timber stock. Sichuan is also one of five big pasturelands after Inner Mongolia, Tibet, Xinjiang and Qinghai. Sichuan has fertile soil and pleasant climate. These natural conditions provide an excellent living environment for various kinds of wildlife. There are some rare tree species, which exist in Sichuan, such as metasequoia (dawn redwood) and larch. The redwood is known as a "living fossil". These rare tree species make up over one-fifth of the total in China. The medicinal plants account for 75 per cent of China's total due to the "land of traditional Chinese medicine". In Sichuan more than 50 rare animal species are under the protection at national level. They include the giant panda, the golden monkey and the white-lipped deer. In the past 40 years Sichuan has established 45 forest and wildlife nature reserves, covering an area of 2.8 million hectares. We will arrange for you to go and visit some of them.

KEY WORDS & EXPRESSIONS 关键词汇及表达法

annual average temperature 年平均气温
annual rainfall 年降水量
encompass 包围
landform 地形
plateau 高原
subtropical 亚热带的
medicinal plant 药用植物
comparatively 比较地
luxuriant 繁茂的
tributary 支流
hydroelectric power 水力发电
potential 潜势，潜力
hydraulic resource 水力资源
faultage zone 断层地带
geological 地质的
mineral 矿物，矿石
vanadium 钒
titanium 钛
lithium 锂
sulfide ore 硫化物矿
ferrous 铁的；含铁的
non-ferrous metal 有色金属
cobalt 钴

biological resource 生物资源
pastureland 草地
metasequoia 水杉
larch 落叶松
white-lipped deer 白唇鹿

Mountains and Rivers in Sichuan
巴山蜀水

Sichuan boasts a number of tourist attractions. Some of them are listed as the world natural and cultural heritages, and some listed as state -level scenic spots. Sichuan might well be one of the most attractive tourist routes in the world. A vehicle will climb over high mountain passes of the Qinghai-Tibet Plateau and cross big rivers. The road starts from the lower basin of Chengdu, and it ascends step by step to the highest plateau in the world. Along this way, multiple natural sceneries will be in your sight.

Jiuzhaigou National Park（九寨沟）**is the most beautiful region among them.** It is a deep valley of stunning natural beauty in the Northwest of Aba Tibetan and Qiang Autonomous Prefecture. It has also been admitted into the list of the World Natural Heritage. The name of Jiuzhaigou refers to the 9 Tibetan villages that are situated in the valley. Jiuzhaigou has a variety of natural scenery—lakes, waterfalls, snowy mountains and lush green forests. There are also more than 100 lakes of various sizes and shapes that sparkle with color in the flickering sunlight.

Huanglong（黄龙）is not far from Jiuzhaigou. It is known for its four unique beauties-colorful lakes, snow mountains, gorges and woods. In 1992 Huanglong was added to the list of the World

Natural Heritage. Huanglong covers an area of about 700 square km. Tibetan folk villages blend harmoniously into the mountains and sparkle like jewels.

Mt. Siguniangshan（四姑娘山，Four Girls Mountain）is in North Sichuan. It is a cluster of four peaks，which stand side by side like four sisters. Yaomei Feng（幺妹峰，the peak of the youngest girl）is the main peak，and rises to 6250m. Mt. Siguniangshan is honored as the "Queen of Mountains in Sichuan".

Leshan Giant Buddha（乐山大佛）is an enormous statue. It is carved into the side of Lingyun Mountain（凌云山）. The Buddha is over 71m（230ft）tall and is wide enough for more than 100 people to sit on its feet.

Mt. Emei（峨眉山）is one of the four most sacred Buddhist mountains in China. Local legend has it that the mountain was named after two peaks that face each other and resemble eyebrows. Lush forests and green bamboo cover the mountain in Southwest Sichuan.

Mt. Qingcheng（青城山）is located just to the southwest of Dujiangyan Irrigation system. It is also known as Green City Mountain. Dense forests of ancient trees cover the towering peaks，which are thought to resemble city battlements. Among the lofty trees are monasteries，temples and pavilions.

Southern Sichuan Bamboo Sea（蜀南竹海）is the bamboo

scenery. It is one of the 40 Best Tourist Attractions in China. The Sea is located in the southwest Liantian Mountains and covers an area of 120 square km. In its central region, big, tall and upright bamboo shelters ridges and peaks high and low. Bamboo grows in the fields, mountains and hills that stretch long and far, and is the reason for the name of "Bamboo Sea".

Tagong Grasslands (塔公草原) is in Western Sichuan. It is a vast expanse of green meadow. Snow-capped peaks are surrounded rising by its side. A Tibetan community lives in the midst. Tagong is also the place where an annual Horse-Racing Festival is held at the beginning of the 8th lunar month. This festival attracts thousands of local Tibetan herdsmen.

Sichuan has more than 1,400 rivers.

Jinsha River (金沙江) is the upper section of the Changjiang. It flows through Qinghai, Tibet, Yunnan and Sichuan. Traditionally, the Jinsha River is divided into upper, middle and lower reaches; the middle reach extends from Shigu city to the Yalong River Mouth (雅砻江口) in Panzhihua city of Sichuan, and the lower reach from the Yalong River Mouth to Yibin (宜宾) city of Sichuan. The Jinsha River formed "the most dangerous white-water section in the Changjiang" and the deepest gorge in the world. Mountains are more than 1,000m above sea level, and the Gorges stand magnificently facing each other. The Jinsha River has plentiful hydropower resources. They mainly concentrate on the middle and lower reaches from Shigu to Yibin. The total exploitable installed capacity is 59,080 MW. The middle and lower reaches enjoy the richest hydropower potential feasible to be developed. It also gives consideration to irrigation, water supply, flood control, wood drift and tourism.

Minjiang River（岷江）is a main tributary of the upper reaches of the Changjiang in Sichuan. The river has been developed over several thousand years. The upper reaches of the Minjiang River are located in the Northwest of the Chengdu Plain. The whole length is 735km. The steep peaks of Longmen Mountain（龙门山）and Qionglai Mountain（邛崃山）surround the upper reaches. There are many picturesque sightseeing spots along the river due to the natural and biological diversity.

Tuojiang River（陀江）flows into the Chengdu Plain. The whole length is 702km. It has ten tributaries. The main tributaries flow through the Sichuan Basin and some hilly areas where the climate is mild, and the production is rich. Also the areas have most important and elegant relics, which date back to the ancient Shu civilization.

Jialing River（嘉陵江）now ranks the first among all the branches of the Changjiang. The entire length is 1,120km. It flows through Guangyuan（广元）, Nanchong（南充）and Guang'an（广安）cities before it empties into the Changjiang in Chongqing. The Jialing River has many tributaries. One of them is called Pujiang（浦江）tributary. It flows through Mianyang city（绵阳）, Deyang（德阳）city and other areas. In Jialing River Basin are the largest and cultural relics groups dated back to the early Shu state and the Three Kingdom Periods in Sichuan.

I hope that the information I have given to you will stimulate your desire to visit as many of the tourist attractions in and around Chengdu and Sichuan if you have time. When you leave, I am sure that you will have many fine images and memories to share with your families and friends.

KEY WORDS & EXPRESSIONS 关键词汇及表达法

world heritage 世界遗产
flickering 闪烁的
resemble 像，相似
towering peak 高耸的山峰
battlements 碉堡上的城垛
expanse 广阔，浩瀚
meadow 草地，牧场
Horse-Racing Festival 赛马节
magnificently 显赫地
exploitable 可开发的
installed capacity 安装容量
give consideration to 考虑到
picturesque 如画的
stimulate 刺激，激励

Chengdu City 成都市

Chengdu is the capital of Sichuan Province and an important industrial, commercial and financial city in Southwest China. Chengdu is located in one of the richest agricultural plains, and it has an area of 12,300 square km. By rail, Chengdu is 2,048km from Beijing and slightly over 2 hours by air. It can also be reached by a less than 20-hour train ride with about 250km of tunnels. Chengdu has direct domestic and international flights from elsewhere in China and some countries. The population of Chengdu is about 10.03 million. They are divided among 7 districts, 4 outlying cities and 8 counties. About 1.4 million people reside in the city center.

KEY WORDS & EXPRESSIONS 关键词汇及表达法

outlying 边远的，偏僻的

History of Chengdu
成都历史沿革

In ancient times the Ba and Shu people lived in Sichuan and established their own states during the period of Xia(夏), Shang (商) and Zhou(周). Shu's center was on the Chengdu Plain. Sichuan has mixed itself into a Chinese multi-national family since the Qin annexed Ba and Shu. Even today some people still call Sichuan as Bashu.

Chengdu has a very long history. The ancestors of the Shu people lived in Chengdu more than 3,700 years ago. About 2,300 years ago, Kai Ming, one of the kings of the ancient Shu state moved his capital to today's Chengdu. It was said that at first Chengdu was only a county center; the second year it turned into a metropolis. It developed so fast that the city received the present name: Chengdu which literally means "becoming a capital". In the year of 311 B. C., the Qin people built a 25m high wall of approximately 6km around the city. It marked the formal establishment of Chengdu as a city. In 1985 an ancient building complex was unearthed near the western city gate. It has been identified as a palace of the Shang Dynasty, built more than 3,600 years ago. Some scholars have said that this discovery pushed Chengdu's recorded history back over 1,000 years.

During the past 2,300 years, Chengdu never changed its location despite many upheavals, and it has always remained the capital of Sichuan. Fortunately the Dujiangyan Irrigation System was constructed under the leadership of Li Bing (李冰). The Dujiangyan System brings the vast Chengdu Plain under irrigation and has protected it against droughts and floods for over 2,000 years. Because of this the Chengdu Plain has turned into the land of abundance with a mild climate and fertile soil.

In its course of development, Chengdu acquired many pleasant titles like "the Brocade City" and "the Hibiscus City".

During the Western Han Dynasty (206 B.C. - 24 A.D.), the brocade weaving and trade brought much prosperity to the local area. The government assigned Jinguan (锦官, an official in charge of brocade production) to manage the brocade production in Chengdu. The city became known as Jincheng (Brocade City). Another name was given to Chengdu during the Five Dynasties Period. Meng Chang (孟昶), Emperor of the Later Shu State loved hibiscus very much. He had those flowers planted atop the city wall. The hibiscus in blossom made Chengdu colorful for miles around. So Chengdu became called Furongcheng (Hibiscus City). The name is still used today.

Dated back to the Qin Dynasty (221 - 207 B.C.), Chengdu was a well-known business center. In the Han Dynasty, it was one of the five best major cities in China. The other four cities were Luoyang, Handan, Linzi and Wan. In the Tang Dynasty, Chengdu was as prosperous as Yangzhou (扬州), a big city located in South China. In the Tang and Song dynasties, the commerce and trade in Chengdu became overgrown. Traditional family workshops gradually developed . In Chengdu each month had its own typical commodity fair. January was for lamps; February flowers; March silkworms; April embroideries; May fans; June incense; July jewelry wares; August sweet-scented osmanthus trees; September herbs; October wines; November plumtrees and December peach wood charms; Besides, in the downtown areas, after-supper shopping markets flourished. Today, names such as the Business Street and the Button Fair Street are still used. It's a reflection of the city's historic commerce.

For over 2,000 years, Chengdu has been a city densely covered by rivers and dotted with bridges. Trees grow in great plenty, and flowers bloom all year around. Chengdu has remained a city of military importance in Southwest China. Gongsun Shu, king of the Western Han Dynasty, Liu Bei(刘备), emperor of the Shu Kingdom and Meng Zhixiang, king of the Later Shu State all founded their capitals in Chengdu. Later in the Yuan Dynasty, the Ming Dynasty and the Qing Dynasty, it remained as provincial government center at different times. On December 27, 1949, Chengdu was liberated and chosen again as the location of the provincial administration office.

The educational system in Chengdu is well developed. As early as 140 B.C., Wen Weng (文翁), head of the prefecture of the Shu started the first government-owned school. It is recorded that the school's enrollment had grown into 1,000 students in the Southern Song Dynasty (1127 - 1279). Chengdu led the way in China's papermaking technique as it was invented in the city around 600 - 1200 A.D.. During the Tang Dynasty workers produced jute paper named yizhoumazhi (益州麻纸) in Chinese. It was officially selected as the paper to print imperial decrees and edicts, as well as books for the State Library. Wood block printing is another great contribution. Some historians believe that it was also originated in Chengdu. The London Museum has preserved some of these Chinese documents. Among them is a woodblock-printed almanac. It was the earliest of its kind, produced in Chengdu around 220 A. D..

Traditionally Chengdu has been well-known for its many crafts: embroidery, lacquer ware, silver artistry, pottery, bamboo ware, silk weaving, jade and ivory carving. Between the Warring States Period to the Han Dynasty, lacquer wares enjoyed high popularity. Local embroidery and brocade are regarded as one of the top four fine silks in China. The local silk products were sold at home and abroad even in early ancient times. At present, near Du Fu Thatched Cottage is an embroidery factory where skilled workers stitch out with their needles silk paintings. The elegant designs are perfect to view from both sides of the fabric. In some other workshops, artisans at work carve intricate and elaborate objects of ivory and jade; they design precious silver articles, and weave bamboo into useful and beautiful pieces. Today these workshops are a part of the major tourist attractions as China opens up to the outside world.

In the past centuries, Chengdu saw the cultural development by contribution from first-class poets and top scholars like Sima Xiangru (司马相如), Li Bai (李白) and Su Shi (苏轼). They used to stay in Chengdu. The local culture nurtured them, and in return their excellent literary works enriched the local culture.

KEY WORDS & EXPRESSIONS 关键词汇及表达法

annex(to) 吞并

metropolis 主要都市

unearth 从地下掘出;发现

identify 认定,确认

upheaval 动荡

Brocade City 锦城

hibiscus 芙蓉树;芙蓉花
sweet-scented 芳香的
osmanthus 木犀属植物;桂花
peach wood 桃木
flourish 旺盛,繁茂
wood block printing 木刻印
embroidery 刺绣品,刺绣
lacquer ware 漆器
pottery 陶器
ivory carving 象牙雕刻
intricate 复杂的
elaborate 精心制作的
jute 黄麻

Chengdu Today
今日成都

Chengdu is the capital of Sichuan Province. It is mountainous in the northwestern area; it has plains and low hills in the southeastern area. Chengdu has a mild climate and abundant rainfall in the summer. Its average yearly temperature is 15.5℃/62 F degrees.

Chengdu is located at the junction of Tuojiang and Minjiang rivers. The two tributaries enable Chengdu area to be in the reach of the Dujiangyan Irrigation System. The main products in Chengdu are grain, rape seed oil, vegetables and other non-staple foods. The Pengzhou vegetable wholesale market sells tons of seasonal vegetables to other areas every year, making itself one of the largest vegetable distribution centers in the country.

Chengdu is advancing in various ways. It has already built up an industrial system. It consists of 38 industries and 100-odd sectors. They include electronics, information, machine-building, food, pharmaceuticals and the other leading industries.

Chengdu is also a national experimental trade and commercial center. It has more than 20,000 wholesale distributors and 240,000 retail outlets. A great number of wholesale markets have emerged in Chengdu, which now ranks No. 1 in Western China in terms of market size and capacity.

Chengdu has more than 2,000 domestic financial institutions and offices. The People's Bank of China has set up its southwest regional branch in Chengdu. Twelve foreign financial institutions have open offices in the city. They include Singapore's Overseas Union Bank, Britain's Standard Chartered Bank, Thailand's Bangkok Bank, Japan's Bank of Tokyo and Banque National de Paris.

Chengdu has over 2,000 scientific research and technological development institutions. It has 19 national and provincial colleges and universities. There are twelve national key laboratories, three national laboratories for special subjects, and nine state-level engineering centers. Chengdu has built a number of high-tech development zones. They include the Modern Agricultural Technology Zone, the Science and Technology Industrial Zone for the Modernization of Chinese Herbal Medicine and the Chengdu New and High-Tech Industrial Zone. Chengdu has made technological breakthroughs in several areas, such as the construction of the country's first magnetic suspension railway, and the giant panda relocation and protection project.

Chengdu is a famous Chinese historical and cultural city. Some of its scenic spots and historical sites are listed below:

Wuhou Temple（武侯祠）

The temple is situated in the southern suburb of Chengdu. It was built in memory of Zhuge Liang and other military heroes in the Three Kingdoms Period. It has halls dedicated to Liu Bei and Zhuge Liang. *The Romance of the Three Kingdoms*（三国演义）carries out the stories about these heroes. Reading these stories even in English translation is a great enjoyment.

Du Fu Thatched Cottage（杜甫草堂）

Du Fu（712－770）was a famous Tang poet who lived in Chengdu for a brief period of time. During his stay，he wrote over 200 poems. The original residence of Du Fu already disappeared. Don't expect to see anything in the cottage that belonged to Du Fu. What we see today is the reconstruction of the Ming and Qing dynasties. The cottage is located in the western suburb of Chengdu.

Sanxingdui Museum（三星堆）

Sanxingdui Museum is one of the most exciting new museums in China. It is built on the 3，000-year-old site of the Shu civilization. The museum houses interesting relics unique to the Chengdu area. The museum is located 38km from downtown Chengdu. The beautifully designed museum is worth a visit. Some world travelers have commented that this site reminds them of the South American Ancient Mayan Culture.

Chengdu Giant Panda Breeding and Research Base（成都熊猫基地）

Children and animal lovers enjoy this sanctuary. The base is a research center. It is located seven miles to the northeast of city. The goal is to breed pandas in captivity. So far 30 pandas have been successfully born here in captivity. The pandas at the center often roam across 80 acres of hills，forests and bamboo grooves. If you are lucky，you can find yourself a few feet away from a giant panda, sitting there and looking at you as he/she munches on bamboo shoots and leaves.

Precious Light Monastery (宝光寺)

The monastery is an enormous Buddhist temple complex. It houses a large collection of art treasures. It includes 500 Arhat statues, traditional paintings and a collection of contemporary works.

Dujiangyan Irrigation System (都江堰)

Dujiangyan is one of the world's first irrigation systems. It is located on the upper reaches of Minjiang River, west of Guanxian county. It was built between 306 - 251 A. D. by the local people under the guidance of Li Bing and his son. The project enables the western Sichuan Plain to become the land of abundance. In the visitors' center are pictures of many famous personages and world leaders who visited this engineering marvel over the years.

Chengdu is pleasantly laid out with broad streets and many public parks. However, some older parts of the city still have narrow streets and sculptured wooden houses. Local teahouses, snack bars and free markets are worth visiting. These attractions are still popular places for tourists where they can either taste the typical Sichuan cuisine, local wine, or tea. They may set out to shop for local products such as local embroidery pieces, bamboo-woven porcelain wares and lacquer wares. Sichuan opera is a distinct regional art form. This theatrical presentation features bright sets and costumes, plus a combination of music, dance and acrobatics.

Sichuan and Chengdu have been developing along with China's reform and opening-up. Its tourist industry also has made much progress. The local governments are working hard to speed up the construction of infrastructures and related facilities at the key scenic places. At the same time the governments will do their best to improve management and service in these places. Sichuan and Chengdu sincerely invite tourists from home and abroad to visit and enjoy local areas in the years to come.

KEY WORDS & EXPRESSIONS 关键词汇及表达法

GDP 国内生产总值
non-staple food 副食
machine-building 机器生产
pharmaceutics 药剂
manufacture 制造业
experimental 实验的
high-tech 高新技术
technological breakthrough 科技的突破
magnetic suspension railway 磁悬列车
the South American Ancient Mayan Culture 南美古玛雅文化
sanctuary 圣地
grove 树丛
munch 用力嚼,大声嚼
contemporary 同时代的人
personage 要人,个人;名流
sculpture 雕刻
theatrical 戏剧性的
presentation 表演介绍;陈述

Section Two :

On – the – Way Tour

第二部分:

沿途导游

Chengdu Shuangliu International Airport—Jinjiang Hotel 成都双流国际机场—锦江宾馆(欢迎词)

Good morning, ladies and gentlemen, welcome you to Chengdu, the capital of Sichuan Province. First, let me introduce myself. My name is Gao Ming and my English name is Turby, you may call me Gao or Turby as you like. I work for Chengdu International Travel Service Agency and I am your local tour guide today.

Now our tour bus is at the exit of the airport. Please take your handbags and follow me to our bus. Please leave your heavy bags to my assistants. They will load them onto a luggage car and transport them to Jinjiang Hotel where you will stay.

(***On the bus***)

May I have your attention, please. Our bus will leave soon. I'd like to say a few words before our departure from the airport. This is Chengdu Shuangliu International Airport. It is located in the southwestern suburb of Chengdu. It is only 17km from the city proper. It is the largest and most advanced airport in West China. The new building was been put into operation in October 2001. It has two spacious floors, and it is equipped with an up-to-date Siemon Category cabling system. The flow of passengers has reached 5 million. There are 204 straight flights, linking Chengdu with major cities in China, Hong Kong, Singapore, Bangkok and other international cities.

Now I'd like to introduce my colleague, Mr. Wang, our bus driver, working in the Chengdu International Travel Service

Agency for 15 years. I know you will feel relaxed and safe on his bus. Actually we will use his bus during our trips in Chengdu and other areas. Please do write down the bus number for your convenience, in case that you get separated from our group. The number is 23456. During your stay in Chengdu, Mr. Wang and I will be at your service. We will do everything we can to make your short stay pleasant and enjoyable. If you have any inconvenience, don't hesitate to let us know.

(***On the way***)

Ladies and gentlemen, we are now on the Airport Expressway. Transportation is convenient between the airport and downtown Chengdu. Buses, taxis and airport-buses run almost 24 hours a day. The expressway is a toll road, and it is about 11.98km in length. This expressway has been honored as the First Road in Sichuan. It takes only 15 minutes to go downtown from the airport. Perhaps you have noticed that the scenery expands far and wide. Around the expressway spread tiny strips of land, rows of trees and abundant greenery to please your eyes. They are fanciful in shape, color and design.

China adopted an official Tree Planting Day many years ago. Every year on March 12, people from all walks of life plant trees and grow grass in their residential areas and out in the countryside. Government officials and common people have come to realize the importance of a natural eco-environment and the sustainable use of natural resources. Our government at various levels has decided to plant more trees and grass along the denuded mountainsides and river valleys, and local people are encouraged to turn their areas into greenery. The natural eco-environment in Sichuan is suitable for tree planting and grass growing. This trip in Sichuan will offer you a great chance to enjoy the breathtaking natural scenery, mingled with local people and their customs.

Ladies and gentlemen, we are almost at the end of the expressway and are starting to approach the downtown of the city. Chengdu has many high-rise commercial and new residential buildings that may attract your attention. This has been a positive change for Chengdu and its residents. Many local residents lived for generations in narrow-spaced old buildings. However, Chengdu still retains much of its charm despite the dramatic change.

As you may know, Chengdu is the capital of Sichuan Province. Its abundance of greenery makes it an enjoyable place to wander on foot. It is also an important industrial, commercial and financial city in Southwestern China.

Chengdu was built in 316 B. C.. during the late Warring States Period. It boasts a 2500-year history, which is closely linked with art and craft.

You may ask me what Chengdu means. In the fourth century B. C. , the king of the ancient Shu moved his capital to this site and named it Chengdu. Literally it means "becoming a capital".

Chengdu has some other names. During the Western Han Dynasty, the silk brocade weaving and trade brought much prosperity to the city. The city became known as Brocade City, called Jincheng (锦城) in Chinese. Another name was given to Chengdu during the Five Dynasties Period. Meng Chang, emperor of the Later Shu State loved hibiscus, and he had those flowers planted on top of the city wall. When the hibiscus was in blossom, the flowers made Chengdu colorful for miles around. So the city name eventually shifted from Jincheng into Hibiscus City called Furong Cheng(芙蓉城)in Chinese.

Chengdu was one of the birthplaces of the ancient Sichuan culture. As early as 140 B. C., Wen Weng (文翁), head of the prefecture of the Shu started the first government-owned school. In the following centuries many first-class poets and top scholars came and stayed in Chengdu. They included Sima Xiangru (司马相如), Li Bai (李白) and Su Shi (苏轼), who made great contributions to the local cultural development.

Ladies and gentlemen, I know that you are looking forward to visiting some places of interest. The highlights of your trips will include Du Fu Thatched Cottage, Wuhou Temple, Dujiangyan Irrigation System and the Precious Light Monastery.

Du Fu Thatched Cottage was a place where Du Fu, the great Tang poet lived for some years and composed over 200 poems. These ancient-styled architectures, pavilions, pagodas stand among age-old trees and green bamboos. You will experience the tradition characterized by Du Fu's poems.

Wuhou Temple was originally built in the Tang Dynasty. It was built in memory of Zhuge Liang and other heroes from the Three Kingdoms Period. As you tour the temple, you will enjoy the tradition dated back to the Three Kingdoms Period.

We will also arrange for you to visit Dujiangyan Irrigation System. It is an ancient water irrigation project dated back to 250 B. C.. Apart from these spots, there are some more important attractions, and I will tell you about them as we arrive there.

Chinese cuisine is one of the delights of the world. I think few visitors have not tried Chinese dishes in their own country. This is due to the large number of Chinese restaurants in cities, big or small, throughout the world. Ladies and gentlemen, one of the highlights of your local trips is to appreciate the unique Sichuan food. Maybe you think it's numb, spicy and hot. I don't quite agree. I think you will enjoy a variety of flavors including a number of snack dishes and hotpot operations with meat, seafood and rich vegetables.

Teahouses are an impressive part of local culture in Chengdu. There are many teahouses in the city where people drink tea, chat or play cards and mahjong.

Ladies and gentlemen, if tea is the most popular drink in China, then beer must be number two. Local distilleries produce high quality beer. In fact, local people started to make and drink wine as early as in the Shang Dynasty (16th – 11th B. C.). The word "wine" gets rather loosely translated. Many Chinese "wines" are in fact liquors. Distilleries in Sichuan produce varieties of liquors, which are sold everywhere in China. I understand some of you never drink at home, but I sincerely suggest you to try the mild liquor. The liquors generally have a heavy fragrance and taste mellow and sweet. It does make you feel utterly refreshed soon after tasting.

Ladies and gentlemen, I'd like to remind you of shopping downtown. The local shopping is also one of your highlights in Chengdu. You may know that Sichuan is known as the land of abundance. Traditionally Chengdu has long been known for its crafts. They include Sichuan embroidery and brocade. Sichuan embroidery focuses on the needlework method and perfectly stitched patterns. The elegant designs are perfect to view from both sides of the fabric. The current brocade fabrics are mainly used for quilt covers, clothes and other decorative purposes. During your stay in Chengdu, I will surely take you to purchase some souvenirs in department stores or maybe you'd rather go on your own. Jinjiang Hotel is close to a number of shopping streets, where you can make an excellent purchase of the local products.

Now our bus is approaching to Jinjiang Hotel. It is a five-star hotel, where you will stay for a number of days. The hotel offers five-star services with good restaurants and shops. The hotel is located by the riverside. It is interesting to explore the local culture while walking along the river. If something strikes your fancy, get it written down in English or Chinese, and show it to me. I will help you find out its location.

Well, I'd like to take this opportunity on the bus to let you know our tentative schedule for the coming days.

D1/Aug. 7. That is today. We will start our tour in Chengdu at 1:30 this afternoon. We are scheduled to tour Funan River. We will view Hejiang Pavilion(合江亭) and the Living Water Garden. The landscape and newly built apartment buildings at either side of the river will impress you.

D2/Aug. 8. We will visit Du Fu Thatched Cottage, Wuhou Temple, Jinsha Village and the Tomb of Wangjian. On the way to the hotel we will go to the People's Park for tea drinking in a teahouse by the lake.

D3/Aug. 9. We will visit Wenshuyuan Buddhist Monastery and Chengdu Giant Panda Breeding Research Base. After dinner at the hotel, we will take a walk on Chunxilu shopping street to enjoy the magnificent night view of Chengdu.

D4/Aug. 10. We will visit Sichuan Provincial Museum and Sichuan University Museum. Great number of archaeological excavations will help you get to know more about the history of Sichuan. Afterwards we will go to the River-Viewing Pavilion Park.

D5/Aug. 11. On the 5th day we will start a long distance trip to Jiuzhaigou. On this trip we will view Dujiangyan Irrigation System and hike Mt. Qingcheng. We will stay in a hotel in Dujiangyan city. On the way to the Irrigation system, we can enjoy the green landscape and farmhouses amidst a green bamboo forest in the western Chengdu area.

D6/Aug. 12. We will continue our bus-ride. On the way we will arrive at Wolong Nature Reserve. We will visit the Grand Panda Research and Protection Center and make a journey into the forest in the mountain nearby.

D7/Aug. 13. We will leave Wolong Nature Reserve in the morning and arrive at Jiuzhaigou later in the afternoon. The bus ride takes about eight hours. We will eat lunch at Maoxian county center. On the way we will appreciate mountainous landscapes where the Qiang and Tibetan people live.

D8/Aug. 14. We will tour Jiuzhaigou Valley. It will be the highlight of this long trip. There are marvelous attractions in Jiuzhaigou, and we will enjoy the beauty of the nature in the Long Lake(长海), the Sword Cliff(剑岩), Nuorilang Waterfall(诺日郎瀑布), Shuzhenggou(树正沟) Valley, Zarugou(扎如沟) Valley and the Black Lake(黑水).

D9/Aug. 15. We will are scheduled to tour Huanglong Valley. It is wellknown for its "Five Wonders". The valley's colored ponds, beach flows, snow-capped mountains, and fascinating canyons and forests will overwhelm us as we walk into the valley.

D10/Aug. 16. We will return to Chengdu. We will arrive at the hotel later in the afternoon.

D11/Aug. 17. We will drive to Leshan Giant Buddha in the

morning. As we arrive there, we will take a ferry-boat across the river to view the Giant Buddha in a sitting posture. In the afternoon we drive to Mt. Emei and stay in a hotel at the foot of the mountain and visit some monasteries nearby.

D12/Aug. 18. We will drive to the summit of the mountain. It is one of "Four Famous Buddhist Mountains" in China. I know that you will get a longer view of the spectacular scenes. Whenever you come across a lovely waterfall and beautiful gorge, you should sit down by the waterfall and become content with the blessings of the nature. We drive to Chengdu later in the afternoon.

D13/Aug. 19. We will drive to Bifeng Valley for the landscape sightseeing there. Lunch will be at Tianquan town. Then we continue our bus-ride up to Hailuogou Glacier Park and stay in a hotel in Moxi town.

D14/Aug. 20. We will be sightseeing inside the nature reserve, trek up to see the magnificent glacier, and take a bath at the outdoor hot spring.

D15/Aug. 21. We will return to Chengdu after we have a short trip to Luding Bridge.

We will follow the above schedule in the coming days. Maybe we will do some adjustment based on circumstances. If there is anything we can do to make your trip more enjoyable, please do not hesitate to let me know. We take great pride in providing you with the utmost professional and personalized service.

Well, it is time to say something about the hotel you will stay. It is situated right in the heart of Chengdu by Funan river canal. The hotel is set in pretty and graceful gardens and has a very quiet atmosphere. The hotel is 17km away from the international airport and 7km away from the railway station. The hotel follows a guideline putting emphasis on high efficiency, prestige, and commitment to services. This striking building maintains 5-star luxurious standards throughout. I am sure you will enjoy your stay in the hotel. One more word:

1. Put your valuables in the safety of the hotel reception.

2. Do not drink the water from the water tap, the water may not be drinkable.

Well, welcome you to Chengdu again. You will find Chengdu is a perfect place for your trip. We are committed to exceeding your expectation. OK, here we are at the entrance of the hotel. Now please check your belongings and check-in at the reception.

KEY WORDS & EXPRESSIONS 关键词汇及表达法

category 种类,部类;范畴
cabling system 电缆系统
feel relaxed and safe 感到无拘束和安全
inconvenience 不方便之处
airport expressway 机场高速道路
toll road 收费路
fanciful 稀奇的;想象的
Tree Planting Day 植树节
residential area 住宅区
eco-environment 生态环境
sustainable 持续性的
denude 滥伐……上的树木
breathtaking 惊人的
retain 保住,留住
cuisine 烹饪;烹调风格
numb 麻木的

spicy 辣
snack dish 小吃
distillery 酿酒厂
heavy fragrance 浓香型
fabric 织品，织物
souvenir 纪念品
strike your fancy 引起好奇
tentative 暂行的，试行的
fascinating 迷人的，令人心醉的
canyon 峡谷
overwhelm 征服，压服
ferry-boat 渡船
spectacular 壮观的
be content with 满意的，满足的
adjustment 调整，调节
personalized service 个性化服务
efficiency 效率
commitment 许诺，承担义务
safety deposit 安全保管处
exceed 超越，胜过
mahjong 麻将

Inner City Tour 市区游览

Funan River
府南河

Hello, ladies and gentlemen, good afternoon. Please get on the bus. This afternoon we are scheduled to tour Funan River.

(***On the way***)

Funan River actually refers to two rivers: Fuhe (府河) and Nanhe(南河). These two rivers flow 29 miles through the city areas from Dujiangyan Irrigation System. Fuhe River flows south through the northern and eastern sections of the city. Nanhe River is also called Jinjiang River, and it flows towards the east. Fuhe and Nanhe rivers flow separately until they converge at Hejiang Pavilion. Now we are on the way to the pavilion. It only takes 10 minutes to arrive there. Actually our bus is moving along the Jinjiang River, which is more like a canal.

Do you know how Jinjiang River got its name? During the Han Dynasty brocade trade in Sichuan brought much prosperity to the area. Local people used to clean brocade products in Nanhe River before they were placed on sale. Gradually people called Chengdu as Jincheng (Brocade City) and Funan River as Jinjiang River.

Funan River provided clean drinkable water for the local people in the past ancient dynasty. The river benefited people in other ways: flood discharge, shipment and irrigation. The river also had rich aquatic resources. For over centuries it contributed to the development of the local economy and culture. Local people have been looking Nanhe River as their "Mother River".

Now here we are at Hejiangting Pavilion. Inside the pavilion is a model of the river's reconstruction. Some photos show the old appearance of the river and the changes through years. I'll explain the details about the river while your visting.

As I have just mentioned, Fuhe and Nanhe rivers converge here at the pavilion. Funan River continues to flow southward until it joins Minjiang River. Du Fu was a great Tang Dynasty poet. He wrote a famous poem, which vividly described the ancient picture of Funan River. It says:

Two yellow orioles sing in the tender green willow
A line of herons crosses the blue sky
When you open the west-facing window
The snow is framed on the summit of the mountain
And the boats that will sail east for Dong Wu
They lie at anchor in the sun-filled doorway

Before the 1950s, the water in the river was clean. Residents along Funan River used to wash rice, vegetables and clothes in the river. Traditionally there were a number of stone steps, which descended to the shore of the river. Every morning, women came to the river to wash rice and clothes. Every ordinary family had a pair of big wooden buckets. Adult family members were supposed to go down two or three times to fetch the river water for their daily water need at home. If families had a shortage of water carriers, they would have to hire somebody to fetch water from the river for them.

While the water in Funan River was drinkable at that time, local residents still had typical ways to filter water. They usually layered charcoal and fine sand in a pottery tub. A hole was made close to the tub bottom, and it was linked to another tub. The river water went through the charcoal and fine sand, and flowed out of the hole into the other tub. It is said that the filtered river water tasted a little sweet. Some families even used the water to cook rice and make tea.

This custom lasted until the 1960s. The local government helped residents install a water pipe system to supply water. Gradually local residents stopped going down to the river to fetch water.

Since the late 1960s the river water quality has become worse due to a number of facts. The local industry and agriculture advanced, the city expanded, and the population increased. People often say, "We used to wash rice in the 1950s in the water; the water quality declined in the 1960s; fish were killed in the 1970s, and no one washed their clothes there in the 1980s." Along Funan River bank, over 650 sewage pipes that discharged polluted water were installed. The statistics show that each day over 600,000 tons of the polluted water was discharged into the river through the pipes. The river developed detrimental elements and smelled foul. Flies and mosquitoes gathered. Residents complained, and the river became a nuisance to the city.

The first call to do something about the water pollution came from pupils at Chengdu's Longjianglu Primary School (龙江路小学). In 1985, the pupils wrote a letter to the then mayor, appealing for the "Return of the Clean Water"! The children appealed to all city residents to stop dumping garbage into the river and to treat industrial refuse before discharging it into the water. In 1987, the newspaper from Xinhua News Agency released the news saying that the pollution of Funan River was serious and had caused great harm to the local residents who lived along the river.

The city government immediately organized concerned departments to further investigate the condition of Funan River. In 1992, city government finally took a decisive measure to clean and refurbish the river. The project aimed to improve the water quality as well as urban infrastructure and environment.

As a big project, the reconstruction was much involved with the infrastructure along the banks. They included current flood discharge, environment protection, greenery, and resettlement of the local residents near the river.

The old houses, which stood along the river, covered an area of 540,000 square meters. Most of the houses were shanties. Some of them were made of bamboo shafts plastered with a mix of mud and straw. Many houses had no private water taps and toilet facilities. Dust and mud fell from ceilings as cats chased rats across roofs. During the rainy season the river rose. Local residents along the river couldn't eat or sleep well. They feared that sewer pipes might be blocked or the river would flood their old houses.

The concerned government departments had them demolished. Most of the residents from the old houses moved into 24 well-equipped living quarters. It is understandable that old houses held good memories because people had spent much of their lifetime there. However the local residents didn't complain about the houses that sheltered them for many years being demolished.

The water treatment was a tough job. The treatment project started in 1993. Factories along the river were closed down and moved away. About 478 others were ordered to update their waste disposal technology and facilities. A 16km river course was dredged, and the banks were rebuilt or enforced. A new 26km sewage pipeline has been placed beneath the ground near the river so that daily wastewater flows along the pipeline up to sewage treatment plants.

The project also included flood prevention, pollution control, greenery, housing reconstruction, cultural projects and others. Professionals use physical and biological ways to make the water clean. The purpose is to eliminate the suspended solids, the dissolvable, and organic matter. Now another sewage treatment plant is being constructed. The new plant will be much more helpful in treating wastewater before it flows back into the river.

Now, let's walk along the riverbank. Today Funan River has taken an entirely new look. The river water has become limpid. Fish, tortoises and other aquatic animals have returned. Visitors from home and abroad take tourist boats on the river to enjoy the beautiful scenery. Every early morning or late in the afternoon local residents take a leisure walk along the banks for fun or for physical exercise.

Please look at the new apartment buildings on your right side. Each building has its own style. They reflect the improvement of local living standards. Look at the bridge ahead. It is called the Anshun Bridge (安顺桥). Over 20 bridges have been set up crossing the river. Each bridge presents its own architectural style in harmony with the river. Our bus will pass Jinxiu Bridge (锦绣桥). Then we will continue our tour, following the curving river course, until we reach another bridge called Qingshuihe Bridge (清水河桥).

Look at the open space. We now plant trees and grow grass on the same sites of the old houses. Garden workers intentionally placed some white colored stones among the mowed grass. Do you know why? The placement is for a decoration purpose. Also it reminds people of environmental protection. You see. Some Chinese characters have been carved on them. Some say, "Don't hurt me"; some say, "Please protect me. I will protect you. We protect the Earth".

Ladies and gentlemen, Hejiangting Pavilion is a symbol of the convergence of Fuhe and Nanhe rivers. Look at the square construction across the river. It is a new music square, where symphonic orchestras or other art troupes sometimes perform for local people. There is a group of sculptures over there. Do you know who they were? The sculptures are dedicated to commemorate our ancestors who contributed to the local water control as well as the improvement of the local water canals. Among them was Li Bing (李冰. 250 - 200 B. C.). He was the local governor of the Shu State. During his tenure, he designed a dam for water control and irrigation in Dujiangyan and Chengdu areas. He even organized thousands of local people to complete the project. The next one was Wen Weng (文翁). He continued the water project and expanded the irrigation system in western Sichuan. The third is Gao Pian (高骈) who regulated the ancient city canals. The current inner city river remains more or less the same as the one he did.

Now please get on the bus and we will go to the other sights.

(***On the way***)

As we tour along the river, everything pleases the eye. The clean water, tidy dams, green lawns, tall trees, and newly set-up buildings are all a pleasant sight. Now local residents think that the Funan River resembles as a "green necklace" of Chengdu. The new riverside is open to tourists for sightseeing, and to residents for leisure walking and physical exercises. On summer evenings, you will see that many local people tend to gather by the river for fun. They practice shadow boning dance and chat.

Due to development strategy of Chengdu, the city plans to expand east and southwards. So the city government and construction teams have completed the construction of five trunk roads: the extension of the South People's Road, the construction of Chengdu-Longquanyi Road (成—龙路), Old Chengdu-Chongqing Road (老成—渝路), Chengdu-Luodai Road (成—洛路), and the third city ring road.

These projects have greatly helped Chengdu's development. At the same time the projects have relieved heavy traffic in Chengdu proper. Particularly the road along Funan River, and the second and third ring roads play an important role in relieving the city heavy traffic.

Ladies and gentlemen, please look at another group of sculptures in Mengzhuiwan (猛追湾) section. They are devoted to the history of the local Sichuan culture. Some sculptures there demonstrate the ancient relics unearthed in the area called Sanxingdui. This unique discovery proves that the local culture had reached an unexpected high level during the Bronze Age.

The third group of sculptures is near the Hundred Flower Pool Park called Baihuatan (百花潭) in Chinese. This group consists mainly of figure sculptures. They represent the ancient great men such as Sima Xiangru, Li Bai, Su Shi. The local culture nurtured them, and in return their excellent literature works enabled the local culture to advance. I am sorry to say that we have no time to view the sculptures there because I'd like to arrange a walk around the Living Water Garden (活水公园).

The garden was opened to us in April 1998. Since then it has become the most popular park in the whole city. The water in the garden is dynamic and always changing.

The project brings together art and science to promote new ways of understanding water's place in the global ecosystem. The Living Water Garden is a park on Funan River. It is 5. 9acres. The garden fully functions as a water treatment plant. It is also a giant sculpture in the shape of a fish that contains a multitude of smaller sculptures for wildlife and plants.

The project started in 1990. Betsy Damon, an American artist in St. Paul, Minnesota, initiated collaborations among artists, scientists and communities for this project. The purpose was to develop local awareness and educational solutions to local water-quality issues.

In 1995 in Chengdu, Keepers of the Waters brought together twenty artists from China, the US and others. In two weeks they created twenty-five public installations along the river. During the riverside art project, Betsy was introduced to Chengdu's five-year plan to clean up the river. The five-year plan involved moving 100,000 citizens, building the infrastructure for wastewater treatment, cleaning the river, rebuilding the flood walls, and creating 19km of parks along the riverfront. During her talks with local officials, she happened to suggest that one of the proposed parks should help clean the river and teach citizens about the environment. The officials instantly asked if she could do such a thing. Betsy said, "yes".

In March 1996, Betsy returned to Chengdu with landscape designer Margie Ruddick to present ideas for the park. After a meeting with Chinese officials, they were given the largest piece of riverside parkland. In three weeks Margie sketched a plan. Betsy stayed for ten weeks more to finish the design and build Chinese teams.

In February 1997, the Chinese officials gave notice to Betsy that the park would be built. She came back and completed the plan. Then Betsy, Chinese sculptors, experts and construction crews began working on this piece of land, which looks like a fish. The construction ended in 1998. Because of the natural shape, the construction team tried to exploit this shape and design the park in the pattern of a fish.

At the head of the park the river's floodwall has been converted into steps to make a "mouth". Water flow does not enter the mouth, but enters the park from pumps powered by waterwheels. The diverted river flow goes up a hill into a settling pond (the fish eye). In the center of the pond (the eye's iris) sits a water fountain. It is a green granite sculpture 13 foot in diameter. The sculpture resembles a living water drop. The water then burbles through an aeration system (the lungs), which is made from a series of sculptures called flow forms. The forms make the water move like a mountain stream, aerating it efficiently. After that, the water flows into the reconstructed wetlands. It is designed to resemble a sacred mountain with seven different water-purifying plants. Over the wetlands are boardwalks for strolling. The water then flows through two more sets of flow forms into ponds. The water meanders through the fish ponds (the fish's stomach). Sand and gravel filters clean the water further. The tail of the fish contains a rose-marble sculpture shaped after a chambered nautilus. It is a fountain to celebrate the cleaned water, and supplies a splash pond for young people.

People, walking through the park, can actually observe the water becoming cleaner and cleaner before it returns to the river at the end of the park. This is the combination of art, science, and education. In addition to demonstration of artful water purification, the park has a car garage under it, an environmental education center, a circular stone amphitheater facing the river for concerts and other activities.

Of course, the Living Water Garden cleans only 250 square meters of water a day, not enough to affect the river water quality. Its purpose is to teach and inspire. People can walk everywhere in the park, delighting in birds, butterflies and dragonflies.

Many overseas professional workers come and examine the great work. The United Nations has conferred to Chengdu People's Government several medals for its contribution to the benefit of the local people. One of the awards is the Best International Example of Human Habitat 2000.

Well, our tour of Funan River is coming to an end. I will give you 30 minutes to walk around and enjoy the park before we catch the bus back to the hotel.

KEY WORDS & EXPRESSIONS 关键词汇及表达法

converge 会聚
aquatic resource 水产资源
oriole 黄鹂
heron 鹭
anchor 锚
bucket 桶
charcoal 木炭
tub 桶，盆
discharge 放出排泄
statistics 统计学，统计表
detrimental element 有害成分
nuisance 讨厌的人或东西；麻烦事
appeal for 恳求
garbage 垃圾，废物
industrial refuse 工业废物
refurbish 整修
shaft 杆状物
plaster 涂以灰泥
demolish 拆除，除去
a tough job 棘手的工作
waste-disposal technology 废物，处理技术
dredge 挖掘，疏浚
sewage pipeline 污水管道
dissolvable 可溶解的，可分解的
limpid 清澈的
symphonic orchestra 交响乐队
be dedicated to 专注于，献身于
commemorate 纪念

tenure 任期
ecosystem 生态系统
awareness 知道,晓得
convert 使改变,使转变
divert 转向,转入
iris 虹膜
granite 花岗岩
aeration 通风
wetland 潮湿的土壤；沼泽地
gravel 沙砾；沙砾层
nautilus 鹦鹉螺
amphitheater 似圆形剧场的场所
dragonfly 蜻蜓

Tourist Spots along the Western Inner-City Route
市区西环线沿途导游

Good morning, ladies and gentlemen, please get on our bus. The bus will leave soon for the inner city sightseeing. There are three routes, and each time you will be on different route. The purpose of this sightseeing excursion is to give you a complete picture of the city and to help you explore the local culture and tradition. This morning we will go along the western inner city route. I will provide you with some guide-information as we reach key spots.

(***On the way***)

Now we are leaving the hotel. The wide street outside our hotel has several central lanes for cars, then a wide path for bikes on each side and finally sidewalks. Each lane is a nice arrangement. Due to so many bikes, it is a challenge to cross the bike lane. Bike riders pay a small fee to an attendant to park their bikes in a parking lot. All bikes in China are registered, and riders lock their bikes as they park them.

Now we are along Funan River. The water in the river looks clean and the dams are tidy. Green lawns, tall trees and newly erected buildings all please the eye. The present Funan River is a "green necklace" of Chengdu. The riverside is open to tourists and residents for sightseeing, leisure walking and morning exercises. On summer evenings many local people tend to gather by the river for fun. They dance, chat and practice shadow boxing.

In the late 1960s, the river water quality became horrible worse, the city government finally took a decisive measure to clean and refurbish the river in 1992. The project was expected to improve the general environment of the whole city. The treatment project started in 1993. Factories along the river were closed down and moved away. About 478 others were ordered to update their waste disposal technology. A new 26km sewage pipeline has been placed beneath the ground near the river. Now daily wastewater flows along the pipeline up to sewage treatment plants. The project also includes flood prevention, pollution control, greenery, housing reconstruction, cultural projects and others.

Please look at the new apartment buildings on your right side. Each building has its own style. It reflects the improvement of local living standards. Over 20 bridges have been set up crossing the river. Each bridge presents its own architectural style in harmony with the river.

Ladies and gentlemen, now we are approaching a bridge. It

is called the Old South Gate Bridge (老南门大桥). Its ancient name is Wanli Bridge (万里桥). Wanli means a 10,000 li in Chinese. Li is a Chinese unit of length, equivalent to 1/2km.

During the Three Kingdoms Period, the Han Empire had been carved into three kingdoms of Wei, Shu and Wu. The rulers of the three independent kingdoms struggled for the top power. Cao Cao and his son established the Kingdom of Wei at Luoyang (洛阳, 220). He actually controlled the North China. The two rivals soon proclaimed themselves emperors elsewhere. The Kingdom of Wu with its capital at Nanjing (南京) occupied Changjiang Valley. The Kingdom of Shu was created with its capital in Chengdu. It covered Sichuan and parts of the Southwest China highland.

Zhuge Liang, Prime Minister of the Shu planned to form a coalition with the Kingdom of the Wu against the ambitious Wei. So in 226, Zhu sent Fei Yi, his envoy to visit the Kingdom of the Wu to explore the possibility of allying with each other. As Fei departed, Zhu held a dinner party to entertain him at the bridge. Fei said, "My 10,000-li trip to the Wu will begin from this bridge (万里之行,始于此桥)." So the bridge was named the Wanli Bridge from the story. There is a couplet, which hangs on either side of the entrance to Du Fu's Thatched Cottage. It says, "The cottage is near the west side of the Wanli Bridge, and to the north of Baihuatan (万里桥西宅,百花潭北庄)." The Wanli Bridge also helps us locate where the cottage is.

Now we are on the Wuhou Avenue near the bridge. You will soon see red walls, which surround a complex of ancient buildings. It is Wuhou Temple. Du Fu, one of top Tang Dynasty poet composed a poem called *Prime Minister of the Shu Kingdom*

(蜀相). Two lines in the poem say,

"Where would I find the Prime Minister's shrine?
Somewhere outside Jinguan, in a dense cypress trees."
(丞相祠堂何处寻,锦官城外柏森森。)

Wuhou Temple is a famous historical site. It is dedicated to the memory of both Liu Bei (161 - 223) and Zhuge Liang. The temple was originally built in the Western Jin Dynasty (265 - 316 A. D.), and the present constructions date from the Qing Dynasty in 1672. An inscribed board on the top of the main entrance gate says, "Han Zhaolie Temple (汉昭烈庙)". *Han* refers to the State of Shu; Zhaolie was Liu Bei's posthumous title. The board indicates that the whole temple was built in honor of Liu Bei. Why do all the people call it Zhuge Liang Temple or Wuhou Temple instead of Han Zhaolie Temple? It is said that in the Ming Dynasty, a member of the royal family saw that there were many more visitors to Wuhou Temple than to Liu Bei's. He felt that was improper because Liu Bei was Zhuge Liang's emperor. So he demolished Wuhou Temple and moved Zhuge Liang's statue into Liu Bei's. However, the people did not like this arrangement. Instead of building a special temple for Zhuge Liang, they kept calling the combined temple Wuhou Temple instead of Han Zhaolie Temple. Gradually more and more people accepted the new name. In the people's view, Zhuge Liang has been immortalized into *the Romance of the Three Kingdoms*. His contribution is historically invaluable.

The whole complex faces the south direction. Liu Bei's hall is the highest and greatest one. The temple houses statues of 47 figures from the State of the Shu. The temple also has many inscribed stone tablets. Today Wuhou Temple is not only a museum for people to study the history of the Three Kingdoms, but also a good place for a general visit. Well, here we are at the entrance to the temple. Please get off the bus and walk into the temple.

(***On the way***)

Now we are on the way to Du Fu Thatched Cottage. We will pass several places of interest. The first one is Baihuatan Park (百花潭). It means "the hundred flower park". It is located in the southern suburb of Chengdu. The park used to be the Chengdu Zoo and housed many animals. In 1971 the animals were moved out, and the park began to grow flowers. The park especially focused on the development of potted landscape. At present, the potted miniature trees are the highlight of the visit to the park.

The potted miniature landscape is called penjing (盆景) in Chinese. In Japanese it is called bonsai. Bonsai first appeared in China over a thousand years ago. The main definition of bonsai is an outlet for both art and horticulture. Bonsai is a common practice to enhance our gardens and is viewed as a hobby that allows a greater understanding of nature.

Chinese bonsai comes from imagimny landscape. Overall, bonsai is something that is quite personalized. If you undertake it as a hobby, there are no strict rules to abide by. You will merely gain enjoyment out of your bonsai practice. Bonsai is obviously small in comparison to their huge life-sized brothers. So it requires a great amount of time, patience, skill and endurance.

Between 1185 and 1333, the Chinese bonsai was introduced to Japan. The exact time is debatable. However, once Chinese bonsai was introduced into Japan, the bonsai art rapidly spread around. Wherever you are in China, you will appreciate the traditional art of bonsai in parks, temples and even Chinese houses.

Now we are passing the Qingyang Gong Park (the Grey Goat Palace,青羊宫). It is on the east side of the city's first ring road. It is a Daoist temple. The compound is large, and it has many buildings. Its major structures include Lingzu Hall (灵祖楼), Hunyuan Hall (混元殿) and Bagua Pavilion (八卦亭). In the compound stand two eye-catching bronze goats. One goat actually is made of brass and is particularly popular. He isn't a goat, but rather a strange creature. It bears the ears of a mouse, nose of an ox, paws of a tiger, back of a rabbit, horns of a dragon, tail of a snake, mouth of a horse, beard of a sheep, neck of a monkey, eyes of a rooster, belly of a dog and bottom of a pig. People often line up to rub its nose. It is said that it has magic powers to protect visitors from evil.

Daoism is the native religion in China. Do you know anything about Huang Di (黄帝) and Lao Zi (老子)? We Chinese people often refer to ourselves as the descendents of Huang Di, the Yellow Emperor. At the beginning, Daoism worshiped both Huang Di and Lao Zi. Later, the Daoists shifted the emphasis of the worship to Lao Zi who was generally regarded as the founder of Daoism.

It is said that Lao Zi lived in the Zhou State for a long time. When he saw the state decline, he departed. According to an old story, Lao Zi rode a purple buffalo to the fabled land of the west. As he passed through the Hangu Gate, a guard said to him, "As you are about to leave the world behind, could you write a book for my sake?" Lao Zi did it. He wrote a book in two parts, setting out the meaning of the way and virtue (道德). The whole book has some five thousand characters. Afterwards Lao Zi departed. No one knew where he went.

Dao De Jing (道德经) is a prose poem full of philosophy. It has had an influence on Chinese thought. It is often referred as the Book of Five Thousand Characters. The book begins with the saying, "The way that can be spoken of, is not the constant way; the name that can be named, is not the constant name".

Daoism believes that human beings follow the Earth; earth follows heaven; heaven follows the Dao; the Dao follows only itself. What is the Dao? The Dao means the Way in English. What is the Way? The Way is impossible to define. Dao De Jing says, "The Dao begets one; one begets two; two begets three; three begets the myriad creatures." There are many philosophical sayings in the book, such as " Heaven is round and earth is square".

Well, on the way to Mt. Qingcheng, I'd like to tell you more about Daoism. Now we are along a stream by the name of Huanhuaxi (浣花溪).

Now please look at this side. The stream flows. Nearby is the Front Gate of Du Fu Thatched Cottage. The name of the stream is Huanhuaxi. Huan means "washing"; hua means "flower". There is a folk story of how the name was born.

A long time ago, a pretty young lady lived near the stream. It is said that she had a kind heart and often did something good for her friends and local people. One day a monk arrived when a group of ladies were washing their clothes by the river. The monk had a serious skin disease. He scratched as he walked towards the ladies. At the first sight of the monk, all the ladies ran away as quickly as possible. However, the pretty young lady kept doing her washing.

The monk had some clothes in his hand. Those clothes looked very dirty.

He said to the lady, "Would you like to wash my clothes?"

"Yes, I will do." said the lady. She took the dirty clothes from the monk and then put them into the stream.

Do you know what happened afterwards?

The young lady dipped the clothes into the water, and immediately lotus flowers grew and blossomed. There were many flowers, which covered everywhere in the stream.

"It's amazing." said the lady to herself. She turned to the monk, but there was no sign of the man. The local people came and watched the miraculous flowers. Since then, they named the stream Huanhuaxi or the Flower Washing Stream.

Well, that's all for the story. Across the road are walls. They surround the ancient style architectures, pavilions and pagodas, which are among old trees and green bamboos. The compound inside is the former residence of Du Fu.

In the year of A. D. 759, Du Fu fled the poverty and social upheaval in North China. He moved here from Gansu and built a thatched hut. During his stay of nearly four years, he composed more than 240 poems reflecting upon his life in Chengdu.

The original residence disappeared long ago. One hundred years after Du Fu's death, another thatched cottage was set up in memory of Du Fu. It has existed ever since. However, it was destroyed and restored many times in the course of the centuries. The present constructions date from the Qing Dynasty. Today, this cottage also contains teahouses and pleasant bamboo gardens, where visitors tend to wander and explore. Here we are at the gate. Please get off the bus and walk into the cottage with me.

(*On the way*)

Ladies and gentlemen, we are going to Chengdu Shu Embrodery Factory (成都蜀绣厂) and Shu Brocade Factory (成都蜀锦厂). The two factories are close to Du Fu Thatched Cottage. Actually they are within walking distance.

Shu embroidery is a kind of traditional craft in Sichuan. The silk needlework is fine and smooth; colors are simple and elegant; lines are graceful and easy. It has a unique feature of the traditional Chinese paintings. The factory has a store to sell various kinds of embroidered products.

Primarily, Shu embroidery was very popular among its people. It came into use on the basis of the skills of the local ancient crossstitch workers. In the old society, women in Sichuan, when they were young, started to learn how to stitch flowers. For the past hundred years women in Chengdu area have been skilled in embroidery needlework. Many women in the countryside nearby were mainly engaged in the silk stitching business as a means of maintaining their daily life.

During the reign of Emperor Daoguang (道光年间) of the Qing Dynasty, over 80 well-known handcraft workshops were set up in Chengdu's Goutou (沟头) and Kejia (科甲) lanes to produce embroidery products. Their main products were official clothes, gifts, dowries, as well as daily colorful clothes and necessities.

In 1949, People Republic of China was founded. Workshops began to employ young women. In present workshops or factories, more female workers are engaged in stitching works.

The modern embroidery has been much more improved. It tends to move towards an applied handicraft art, and it meets the demand of customers at home and abroad.

When we walk into the factory, we will go to the workshops to view how workers stitch patterns on the silk cloth, and then we go to the factory store to purchase embroidery products.

Chengdu Shu Brocade Factory is close to the Chengdu Shu Embroidery Factory. Shu brocade is one of the four best and most famous brocades in China. The others include Nanjing Brocade (云锦), Suzhou Brocade (宋锦) and Guangxi Brocade (壮锦). Shu Brocade is a kind of silk fabric. It was first produced in Chengdu during the Han Dynasty and flourished during the Tang, Song and Yuan dynasties.

Shu brocade has been in existence over 2,000 years, and it has several hundred patterns in use. Some patterns are so popular that they are shared as pattern models among the other three brocades. In Southwest China, some ethnic nationalities especially enjoy wearing brocade aprons and headscarves. The current brocade fabrics are mainly used for quilt covers, clothes and other decorative purposes.

When we arrive at the factory, we will go to view how two experienced workers manage a huge old style wooden loom, weaving colorful warp and weft silk threads. Afterwards we will go to some workshops where the brocade manufacture is under automatic control, and each jacquared loom is electronically equipped.

Here we are on Qintai Street (琴台路). The street keeps the style of the Ming and Qing dynasties. As you walk along, you will appreciate the old-styled buildings, which line the street.

They usually have two stories with glazed tile and curve shaped eaves.

Most visitors often encounter Chinese architecture of one type or another. It ranges from temples through gardens, mausoleums, pagodas, and imperial palaces to residential houses. The ancient Chinese buildings extensively used timber as a building material in addition to brick and tile. Timber was easily available, transportable and practical at that time.

The eaves are often slightly upturned. They seem to let the entire roof float above the building. Another way of achieving this floating illusion is the use of a double roof. A practical function of upturned roof is to ensure that enough light gets inside buildings.

Decorations for ancient Chinese buildings are largely of two types: colorful paintings and decorative sculptures. As the emperor's color was yellow, the roofs of palaces are covered with glazed tiles. Most ancient common houses have gray tiled roofs. The buildings here have yellow glazed tiles to display their different architectural style.

This street becomes well-known for an ancient love story between Sima Xiangru and Zhuo Wenjun (司马相如和卓文君). The story happened in a small town near Chengdu during the Western Han Dynasty. Zhuo Wenjun had good looks and real talent. Unfortunately she became a widow when she was quite young.

One day, Sima Xiangru came by and got acquainted with Zhuo. Sima Xiangru was a well-learned scholar. He fell in love with this lady. At a dinner party at Zhuo's home Sima Xiangru played a stringed music instrument. Intentionally he used a piece of music to express to Zhuo his sincere love. Zhuo understood the music, and fell in love with him, too.

However, Zhuo's parents didn't approve. So the lovers ran away secretly. They arrived at the western suburb of Chengdu where they managed a wine public house to make a living. It is said that Sima Xiangru sold wine; Zhuo Wenjun cleaned utensils and cups. Before long, Sima Xiangru went to Chang'an, the capital of the Han Empire for an imperial examination.

Sima Xiangru departed, and Zhuo remained in Chengdu. Sima Xiangru successfully got a good job in Chang'an after he passed the examination. However, his wife kept waiting for him in Chengdu. Her waiting lasted five years but unfortunately Sima Xiangru didn't come back for their family reunion.

One day, a letter came to Zhuo from her husband. She read the letter and realized that Sima Xiangru wanted to have a concubine from the capital city. Zhuo was completely depressed. She wrote back to Sima Xiangru. In her letter, she composed four pieces of poetry. After reading her letter, Sima Xiangru felt ashamed. He soon gave up the idea of having a concubine. Moreover, he himself drove a four-horse carriage back to Chengdu where he picked up his wife and took her away to Chang'an for their final reunion.

(***On the bus***)

Travelers, we are approaching to Jinsha Site Museum(金沙遗址博物馆), which was opened on April 16, 2007. Jinsha means "gold sand." It is located in Jinsha Village in the suburbs of Chengdu. It used to be known to very few people. This major archaeological discovery has put the village in the limelight nationwide.

Early in 2001, some construction workers from a local real

estate development firm were working at a construction site in Jinsha Village when they unexpectedly found ivory and jade artifacts amidst the mud. Archeologists went to the site upon hearing the news. When they started excavating, they found more than 1,000 precious relics, including gold, jade, bronze and stone-wares as well as nearly one ton of ivory. Most of the pieces date from the middle of the Western Zhou Dynasty(西周, 1050 - 771 B. C.) to the early Spring and Autumn Period(春秋战国, 722 - 481 B. C.).

The whole excavation includes 1,000m square palace area, religious ritual spots and residential and cemetery areas. Archeologists found out that the spot discovered by the construction workers was a ceremony ground where the ancient people offered sacrifices to the gods. After their ritual ceremony, they buried their ceremonial utensils in a pit. Some pits each contain at least 10 to 20 utensils, and some others have about 1,000 objects.

In the past years, archaeologists have kept finding out more relics, including gold, jade, bronze and stone artefacts, numerous pottery items and elephant tusks. At present, this 300,000m square museum exhibits the collection of the precious relics, and archaeologists consider the excavation as one of the most important discoveries in the history of this region.

Among relics there are over 30 gold artifacts including gold masks, gold belts and round-shaped gold ornaments. The unearthed jade items appear beautiful. Among these items is a well-carved jade piece, which appears octagonal in shape and has a round hole in the center. It is 22cm high and looks emerald green. In addition, more than 400 unearthed bronze wares have been unearthed including bronze standing figures, huge bronze rings, bronze dagger-axes, bronze bells, etc; 170 stone items, including stone figures, stone tigers, stone snakes and stone tortoises.

Many of the relics bear strong resemblance to those at Sanxingdui Site, 40km south of Chengdu in Sichuan. For example, a gold mask and a bronze statue of a standing figure might immediately remind visitors of the bronze masks and big bronze statues at Sanxingdui Ruins because of their similarity in style.

At present, archaeologists are not sure what the exact nature of Jinsha Site is. However, they guess that they might be the site of a workshop or sacrificial activities. After the sudden demise of Sanxingdui culture about 3,000 years ago, the Shu King likely moved to areas around today's Jinsha site in Chengdu. Jinsha site are most likely to have been the political and culture center.

Archaeologists believe that Jinsha excavation is one of the greatest archaeological discoveries after the exploration of Sanxingdui site, The site of Jinsha have offered important information and valuable materials for studies in local culture and history in ancient Shu.

Well, we are at the entrance of the museum. Please get off the bus. We will go and view the unearthed relics in the later years of the Shang Dynasty and the following Zhou Dynasty.

Now we are on the way to the Tomb of Wangjian, which is located in northwest of Chengdu.

Wang Jian (847 - 918) was the first emperor of the Former Shu Kingdom during the Five Dynasties and Ten States Period (907 - 960). His tomb has been designated as a protected treasure of the state.

The highlight of your visit to the tomb is to view a typical mausoleum and the carved musicians and dancers. In North China, most of the mausoleums are built underground. This mausoleum is built above ground. Why? Chengdu is located in Sichuan Basin. We always say, "You will get water if you dig a hole three feet deep beneath the ground in Chengdu." The ancient builders were afraid that the tomb might have been flooded if they had placed it underground.

The carved musicians and dancers remain the most valuable artifacts in the tomb. The music establishment looks very similar to the true portrait of Tang court music band. The carved dancers dance rhythmically with light steps; the musicians play their music instruments in a group. The carved stone figures have a highly artistic and cultural value. They are valuable objects to those who study music history and culture of the Five Dynasties.

Here we are at the entrance of the tomb. Please get off and walk into the tomb. At the same time I will continue offering you detailed information.

Now we are on the way to Chengdu People's Park. It is our last stop before we go back to Jinjiang Hotel for our meal.

The People's Park is in the center of Chengdu, just down the street from Tianfu Square (天府广场). It is a charming and very typical Chinese park. There are a number of places of interest. The monument and museum are dedicated to the martyrs of the 1911 Railway Protection Movement, and commemorate a people's uprising against officers who stole funds intended for the construction of the railroad between Chengdu and Chongqing.

The museum explains the history of the uprising and has a small collection of photographs and maps.

Chinese people like to go to teahouses just like western people like going to bars. The teahouse in the park is a great place to relax. It has many tables, all placed around a lake where you can hire pedal boats. The nicest way is just to sit at the teahouses to drink tea while watching shadow boxing, martial arts, or mahjong activities. You will see that local people wander peacefully in the park or sit in the bamboo chairs basking in the sun.

There are thousands of teahouses. They abound in this city. Local people, especially the elder usually go to teahouses to enjoy their pastimes. Some teahouses present performances like singing, local opera and story telling.

Well, we are getting close to the park. Please follow me after we get off the bus. We will all go into the park teahouse to sip tea as the local Chinese do.

KEY WORDS & EXPRESSIONS　关键词汇及表达法

excursion　短途旅行

lane　单行车道

take a decisive measure　采取决定性的措施

avenue　大街

prime minister　首相，总理

cypress　柏树枝

inscribe　记下；题记

invaluable　无价的

potted landscape　盆景

bonsai　盆景

outlet　通路；出口

abide by 坚持，遵守
in comparison to 比较，对照
endurance 忍耐(力)
debatable 可争辩的，值得商榷
eye-catching 引人注目的
philosophy 哲学
scratch 搔，抓
miraculous 奇迹般的
cross-stitch worker 刺绣工
maintain 维持
apron 围裙
headscarf 女人的头巾
warp 经；经纱
weft 纬；纬纱
jacquared loom 提花机
glazed tile 琉璃瓦
mausoleum 陵墓
transportable 可运输的
illusion 幻想
decoration 装饰
get acquainted with 结识
intentionally 有意地，故意地
livelihood 生计，谋生
concubine 妾，情妇
archeologist 考古学家
bear strong resemblance 很相似
mask 面具
limelight 引人注目的中心
demise 死亡

rhythmically 有节奏地
martyr 烈士
bask 晒太阳(享受温暖)
imperial examinations 科举考试
storytelling 评书

Tourist Spots along the Northern Inner-City Route
市区北环线沿途导游

Good morning, ladies and gentlemen, please get on our bus. We will continue our inner city sightseeing along the northern route. This time we will explore the local culture and tradition; I will give you some relaventinformation whenever it is necessary.

(***On the way***)

Now, we are on the South People's Road. It is the southern section of the main thoroughfare by the name of People's Road (人民路). People's Road runs north to south and consists of three parts: the North of People's Road (人民北路) from the North Railway Station to the Fu River, the Middle People's Road (人民中路) from the Fu River to Tianfu Square, and the South of People's Road (人民南路) from Tianfu Square to the South Railway Station. The South People's Road is wide and lined with trees. It runs from the city center and down past Jinjiang Hotel. Then it heads out to Railway Station of Chengdu South. The center itself is marked by a large, traffic flow around the grounds of the city's Exhibition Hall. The North People's Road heads east to Chengdu's entertainment and shopping district; the East People's Road points west towards Chengdu People's Park.

Many of the back streets around the People's Road have turned into fantastic markets for shopping. Maybe you think many local people only speak Sichuan dialect. That is wrong. The local people speak standard Mandarin. When they cater to tourists, they speak slowly so tourists can understand. The friendly local people often make an extra effort to try and chat with tourists.

Here we are at Tianfu Square. It is the center of Chengdu. Three roads encircle the city. They have been sensibly named as the First, Second and Third Ring Roads. On the square stand the statue of Mao Zedong(毛泽东) and the Exhibition Hall (展览馆).

The Tianfu Square used to be an imperial palace of the Ming Dynasty. It was called Shuwangfu (蜀王府), which means the Shu Royal Palace. Zhu Chun(朱椿)used to live in the palace. He was Zhu Yuanzhang's (朱元璋) son.

In 1644, Zhang Xianzhong (张献忠), one of the main peasants' rebellion leaders in the Ming Dynasty, had his residence in the palace. Later he had it burned down. At the beginning of the Qing Dynasty, the local imperial exam center was set up on the same site. People named it as the Imperial City (皇城).

In 1953,South of People's Road Square(人民南路广场)was completed. The square and the Imperial City stayed in harmony as the symbolic architecture in Chengdu.

In 1968, during the Cultural Revolution, the Imperial City was completely demolished. Instead, the Exhibition Hall and Mao Statue were established. At that time the hall was called the Exhibition Hall of the Longevity of the Victory of Mao Zedong Thought. The statue base is 7.1m in height, and the Mao statue is 12.26m in height. The former indicates the birthday of the CPC party; the later symbolizes the birthday of Mao Zedong. There are three stages leading to the statue of Mao Zedong. The stages symbolize the historic milestones from Marxism, through Lenism to Mao Zedong thought.

Pei Partnership Architects have presented the design of Tianfu Square. Upon completion, the square will restore its historic importance within Sichuan and elevate it among the world's celebrated urban spaces. Chengdu Museum, which will showcase the province's rich culture and traditions, will be located on the square's edge.

Now we are on Shuncheng Street (顺城街). During the Ming Dynasty Shu Royal Palace and its wall and moat were located here. There was a street that ran closely along the palace wall. So the street was named Shuncheng Street. Shun means "close to", and cheng means "city." The wall has disappeared for a long time, but the name of the street is still used.

Now, please look at the flyover, in America you call them overpasses. It is called Jade Belt Flyover(玉带桥). Actually there were some moat bridges outside the palace. Like Shuncheng Street, the name of Yudai Bridge is still used for the new bridge we see now. Some travelers may wonder where the moat is. Did it disappear? No, it is still existing. In 1969, the moat was turned into an underground air-raid shelter. At present, the shelter functions as a huge underground shopping mall.

Today, Chengdu still keeps using the old street names. The Business Street and the Button Fair Street reflect the city's historic commerce; the Local Governor Street and Generals' Offices Streets indicate the location of the Qing government and ministerial offices.

Now, we are on our way to Chengdu Bamboo Weaving Factory (成都竹编工艺厂), which is also a huge market for bamboo products. Bamboo is usually used to make covers and mats. But a special type of bamboo is used to wrap vases, teapots, porcelains and bowls. In the bamboo-weaving factory, you will view how the bamboo splits miraculously cover the surface of these pieces.

The bamboo weaving craft is very unique. At the end of the 19th century, Chengdu bamboo woven porcelain was displayed at the Panama International Exposition and won a silver medal. In 1975, a group of the local bamboo handicraft artists went to Japan for a visit. The artists demonstrated on the spot how to weave bamboo splits on porcelain products. Their performance amazed the Japanese audience. I know that your visit to the factory will be rewarding, and you will deeply appreciate the traditional craft.

Now, we are on the way to a Buddhist monastery in central Chengdu. It is called Wenshu Monastery (文殊院). It is dedicated to the God of Wisdom-Wenshu.

Those of you who study Buddhism know that it was founded by Sakyamuni(释迦牟尼), who was originally a prince of a small state in North India. Among his main teachings were the Four Noble Truths: (1) sorrow is the universal experience of mankind; (2) the cause of sorrow is desire; (3) the removal of sorrow can only come from the removal of desire; and (4) desire can be systematically abandoned by following the Noble Eightfold Path (the eight steps that should be taken).

Buddhism was first introduced into China at the beginning of the Eastern Han Dynasty. This had something to do with the opening of the western regions, which made travel between China and India easier than before. In 67 A. D., two Indian monks came to Luoyang (洛阳). Emperor Ming ordered the building of the White Horse Temple (白马寺) and asked them to translate Buddhist scriptures into Chinese. Other monks followed them from India and West Asia. At first, only members of the ruling class knew Buddhism. It was during the period of the Southern and Northern dynasties that Buddhism was spread among the ordinary people.

Do you know what Buddha, Maitreya or Bodhisttva is? Well, I'd like to give you some basic knowledge so that you will have a better understanding of our tour of Wenshu Monastery.

Buddha is the one who is perfectly enlightened and has entered Nirvana. In Mahayana Buddhism, there are many Buddhas in existence at the same time. Sakyamuni Buddha is respected as the past Buddha.

Maitreya (弥勒佛): Maitreya is also known as the Laughing Buddha. Buddhism predicts that when Sakyamuni's doctrines were going to become extinct, Maitreya would become a Buddha and preach Buddhist doctrines. In Chinese history, people respect Maitreya. Tradition has it that during the Five Dynasties from 907 to 960 A. D., a monk named Qici (契此) always carried a cloth bag. People called him a Cloth-bag Monk and regarded him as the reincarnation of Maitreya. Buddhism has it that Maitreya or the Future Buddha stands as a symbol to remind that everyone has the potential to be enlightened.

Bodhisattva(开士,大士): Bodhisattva is usually referred to as Pusa (菩萨) in Chinese. A potential Buddha in Mahayana(大乘佛教) was much favored in ancient China. Bodhisattva is one who has achieved perfect enlightenment and is entitled to enter directly into Nirvana. However, pusa renounces this. Instead, pusa is determined to salvage all suffering creatures before Pusa enters into Nirvana(涅槃). The best-known figures are Avalokitesvara (观音) Goddess of Mercy or Guanyin Pusa; Manjusri (文殊) Bodhisattva of Wisdom or Wenshu Pusa; Samantabhadra (普贤) Bodhisattva of Universal Benevolence or Puxian Pusa; Kistigarbha (地藏), Dizang Pusa.

Mt. Wutai in Shanxi province is the place where Wenshu Pusa performs the Buddhist rites. And Wenshu Monastery is devoted to Wenshu Pusa. It was founded during the Tang Dynasty. Most of the buildings date back to 17th century. The impressive collection in the monastery contains some intricate and beautiful art and architecture. There are five halls at the complex. All of them have pretty tiled roofs, carved eaves and beautifully painted ceilings. Wenshu Monastery is popular and busy. Many worshippers come for their visits. They buy incense, paper money and items at the entrance and burn them in front of Buddha statues inside the monastery for happiness and good blessings.

One of the highlights in the monastery is the vegetarian food provided by the monastery restaurant. Many visitors like to eat in the vegetarian restaurant after their tour of the monastery.

Vegetarian food is an important cuisine in the Chinese culture. In the Song Dynasty, the food was served as a popular food, and in the Ming and Qing dynasties the vegetarian recipes were much improved. The main ingredients are green leafy vegetables, fruits, mushrooms and bean curd products. Vegetable oil tastes delicious and is nutritious too. Some of the famous dishes include the Vegetarian "Chicken", Braised Vegetarian "Meat" with Bean Sauce, Vegetarian "Pork Tripe", Vegetarian "Ham", Hot-and-sour Beancurd Slices, and Vegetarian "Shrimps". The meat, pork and chicken of these dishes are actually made with vegetarian ingredients or bean curd products. However, they all look like real meat!

Now we arrive at the entrance to the monastery. The entrance is on a back-street. Part of the street serves as a market for funeral goods and services. Here one can find paper offerings of caps and hats, shoes and coats, furniture and even pets for the departed.

Now let's get off the bus, and we will start our tour in the monastery. Afterwards we will go to the Chengdu Giant Panda Breeding Research Base (成都大熊猫繁育研究基地).

(***On the way***)

Ladies and gentlemen, please look at the right side. It is the Chengdu Zoo, and is located 5km north of Chengdu. In 1953, the zoo was established on the site of the present Hundred Flower Park. Because the park was too small to house so many animals, in 1976, the city planning department moved the zoo to the present site. Besides, there are over 240 kinds of animals. On weekends, parents often take children to the zoo for fun. Children enjoy offering something to the greedy monkeys and bears, or view the lions and peacocks.

Next to the zoo is Zhaojue Temple (昭觉寺). It is also a Buddhist monastery. It was destroyed after being built in the Tang Dynasty and then rebuilt in the early Qing Dynasty. The tree-shaped temple remains quiet with less attractions than Wenshu Monastery.

Now we are approaching to Chengdu Giant Panda Breeding Research Base. It located 10km north of Chengdu, is one of the important giant panda conservation and protection centers. The base shows that the Chinese are determined to protect pandas and other wild animals. The base covers an area of 600-acre where bamboo grows in abundance, and birds fly around. Over thirty giant pandas and some other rare animals share the area. They include red pandas and black-necked cranes.

At the base is a museum called the Chengdu Giant Panda Museum established in 1992. It is a comprehensive museum that focuses on multi-programs: giant pandas' up-to-date information, scientific research projects, conservation and rescuing activities. It also demonstrates the variety of species and the importance of their protection by human beings.

Well, so much for my brief introduction to the base. Here we are at the entrance of the base. Many tourists at home and abroad enjoy coming to visit here. The main reason, I think, is that they are able to get close to the pandas in an ecological conservation environment. I know that you will experience the same excitement as you tour this place.

KEY WORDS & EXPRESSIONS 关键词汇及表达法

thoroughfare 大道，大街
fantastic 意想不到的，令人难以置信的
symbolic 象征的，符号的
symbolize 象征，用符号表现
longevity 长寿
milestone 里程碑
partnership 合伙；合股
elevate 提升；举起

showcase　展示;陈列橱
flyover　立体交叉路跨线桥
overpass　天桥，陆桥
moat　护城河，壕沟
air-raid shelter　防空洞
ministerial　部长的；部的
bamboo split　竹丝(片)
porcelain　瓷器
exposition　展览会；博览会
rewarding　有益的，值得的
universal　普遍的，全体的
systematically　系统地,有系统地
eightfold　八层的
Mahayana Buddhism　大乘佛教
reincarnation　再投胎,再生;化身
potential　潜能,潜力
enlighten　启蒙
nirvana　涅槃；圆寂
wisdom　智慧;才智
benevolence　仁爱心；善行
worshipper　崇拜者
incense　熏香；焚香时的烟或香气
paper money　纸钱
good blessing　祈福,赐福
vegetarian food　素食
recipe　处方
delicious　美味的
nutritious　营养的
braise　炖；蒸

pork tripe　猪肚子
shrimp　小虾
back-street　后街
funeral goods　祭品
breed　饲养；教养
greedy　贪吃的
peacock　孔雀
conservation　自然资源保护区
red panda　小熊猫
crane　鹤

Tourist Spots along the Southeastern Inner-City Route

市区东南环线沿途导游

Good morning, ladies and gentlemen, please get on the bus. It will leave soon. We will continue our inner city sightseeing along the southeastern route. I will give you some information whenever it is necessary.

(***On the way***)

Our bus is moving toward Chengdu South Railway Station (成都火车南站) along the South of People's Road. Please look to the right side on the corner of Renminnanlu and Binjianglu (滨江路), by Jinjiang Bridge. It is the location of a Sunday Evening's English Corner.

An English corner is a place where Chinese of all ages and occupations, meet at a specific time of a week to speak English with one another. Non-native Chinese speakers find it enjoyable and rewarding to interact with a relatively large group of Chinese in an informal and open setting. The English corner may be a perfect way for them to get to know the local culture.

At the English corner, local young people have an opportunity to better their English, and non-native Chinese speakers are guaranteed to meet people willing and eager to talk with others in English. Speaker will talk on a subject of his or her choice fluently. The form is questions and answers, and it requires participants to use their English actively.

Ladies and gentlemen, beyond the English corner is a sidewalk along the river. It is always busy in the early mornings and late afternoons with multi-outdoor activities. Many retired people often come out to the sidewalk to practice Chinese Shadow Boxing or Chinese Qigong exercises; some female participants enjoy performing in groups Chinese dancing or Western ballroom dancing. Some old men hang their cages of songbirds on tree branches and then sit down under trees to start a conversation with people around. The caged birds gather on the branches singing some chirp-chirp songs. In the afternoons, many neighborhood families and couples often come out for a walk along the sidewalk. They chat with friends, and enjoy the view of the sun setting over the river.

Ladies and gentlemen, we are passing the former West China University of Medical Science (华西医大). Please look to the right side. It is the university campus. At present, the former medical university has been merged with two other universities: Sichuan University (四川大学) and the former Chengdu University of Science and Technology (成都科大). The new merged university is called Sichuan University.

The former medical university had a long history. It used to be a comprehensive key medical university with well-known disciplines in dentistry, biomedicine, pre-clinical medicine, clinical medicine and stomatology.

Please look to the left side. There are several university hospitals: the Dental Hospital, the Hospital of Occupational Disease and the Hospital of Gynecology and Obstetrics. The three hospitals are the top-listed hospitals in Sichuan province.

Now, please look ahead on the left side. We will see the entrance gate of Sichuan College of Education. This is the largest provincial collage to train in-service teachers from elementary and middle schools in Sichuan. Opposite to the college across the South of People's Road is the College of Economics, which is under Sichuan Normal University (四川师大). Sichuan Normal University is a key provincial university in Sichuan. It mainly trains students to be teachers in elementary and middle schools as well as colleges. It also has a very good international program and co-operation with overseas universities in the United States, Britain, Australia, Japan and others.

Now we are approaching to Sichuan Provincial Museum. It is ahead of us on the right.

Sichuan has a long history and rich culture. "Shu" is Sichuan's old name. Thanks to a great number of archaeological excavations in Sichuan, people have the opportunity to learn more about their remote past in a number of museums across the province. These archaeological findings also provide interest and sightseeing for tourists. Sichuan is a new destination for archaeologists, museum-goers and tourists, who are keen on Chinese ancient history and culture.

Sichuan Museum

This is the largest provincial museum in Southwest China. It has more than 150,000 items on display, demonstrating the history of Sichuan. Exhibits include the skull of Ziyang Man from 30,000 B.C. and tiled murals and frescoes dating back to the Han Empire. Other collections are related to the ethnic minorities of Sichuan and the history of the Chinese Communist Party.

Chengdu Museum (Daci Temple)

This museum is on Dongfenglu Street (东风路). In past times, the temple was valued for its murals in the cultural relics exhibition hall. In the ancient temple you can appreciate the 1,215 Buddha statues or paintings in the dozens of halls, pavilions and pagodas.

Sanxingdui Museum

Sanxingdui Museum includes two large sacrificial pits. It boasts the most important archaeological discoveries for the past half century. A large number of excavated relics have made Sanxingdui Site well known to the world. The museum focuses on the display of the ancient town, ancient state and Shu culture. The Sanxingdui Museum also provides more than one thousand pieces of invaluable relics: pottery, jade wares, bone wares, gold wares and bronze wares.

Zigong Dinosaur Museum

The Dinosaur Museum is located in the eastern part of Sichuan Basin, Zigong City. Zigong Dinosaur Museum, the American National Dinosaur Park and the Canadian Dinosaur Park are three largest dinosaur museums in the world. About 150 million years ago, a large number of dinosaurs lived in the Zigong area. The dinosaur fossils are over 20m high. The unearthed dinosaurs include sauropodas, stegosaurs and pterosaurs. The Dinosaur Museum was built on the same site where the dinosaur fossils had been unearthed. The museum was open in 1987. It mainly displays rare fossil specimens and magnificent fossil burial sites.

The Salt Museum

The Salt Museum is also located in Zigong. In the Eastern Han Dynasty Zigong grew into a largest salt production district. Many local people engaged in the salt industrial production. There are over 130 different types of drilling tools on display used in the ancient Chinese well salt drilling industry. The museum also displays other historical well-salt relics.

Sichuan University Museum is worth your attention. I will tell you more about the university museum as we arrive there. Well, here we are at Sichuan Museum. Let's get off the bus and walk into the first hall where a museum tour guide will show you around. We will also go to the other halls related to the ethnic minorities of Sichuan and the history of the Chinese Communist Party.

Ladies and gentlemen, we are on Moziqiao Street (磨子桥街). People also call this street the IT Street or the Computer Sale Street. There are more than a thousand stores on the street, some line the street; some are in business buildings around the street. Computers of varied categories are all available. The stores on the street also sell computers' components and spare-parts.

In the Tang and Song dynasties, the commerce and trade in Chengdu grew to great size. Chengdu still uses some ancient street names such as the Business Street, the Salt Sale Street and the Button Fair Street. It's a reflection of the city's historic commerce. Today Chengdu is a host of commercial and shopping district: Dafa Electrical Appliances Market (大发电器市场) for Electrical appliances, Xiyulong (西御龙) Bicycle Street for bicycles, Taisheng Road (太升路) for telephones, beepers and cell phones, Hehuachi Market (荷花池市场) near the North Railway Station for home Accessories. People in Sichuan know where is the best place to do shopping for each category.

Here is Sichuan University. We will go directly to the university museum. The museum is the first museum founded in Southwest China, and in fact, it is also one of China's oldest museums.

In 1941, D. S. Dye, an American scholar, founded the West China University Museum. It was the predecessor of this museum. The West China University Museum became well known in China and abroad between the 1930s and 1940s. In 1952, the West China University Museum was renamed as Sichuan University Historical Museum. In 1984, the name was changed again to Sichuan University Museum.

Sichuan University Museum is a comprehensive museum. It has accumulated over 40,000-catalogued items in the fields of Chinese ethnology, folklore, traditional arts and revolutionary history. The museum also has collected nearly 2,000 items from over ten countries and regions of the world.

The ethnological exhibits of ethnic nationalities contain many Tibetan cultural artifacts as well as items from other ethnic nationalities. There are some precious items of folklore artifacts.

One of them is the sedan chair. Towards the end of the Qing Dynasty, bridal parties in Chengdu would hire the chair from the Sedan Chair Guild in Chengdu. There are some more traditional collections: stone carvings, Sichuan porcelain and pottery, paintings and calligraphy as well as over one hundred types of paper used for writing and painting throughout the ages. The museum also has a distinctive collection of the revolutionary history artifacts. They include materials from the Sichuan-Shanxi Base Area during the Second Revolutionary Civil War (1927 - 1937), particularly the Long March(1934 - 1936).

Well, here we are at the entrance. We will stay in the museum for one hour and then we will take the bus again and go to the River-Viewing Pavilion Park(望江楼).

(***On the way***)

Now we are on the way to the River - Viewing Pavilion Park. It is near Sichuan University. The park was built in memory of Xue Tao (薛涛), a female Tang Dynasty poetess. During the Qing Dynasty (1644 - 1911) Li Yaodong (李尧东), Chengdu governor arranged for construction workers to build several pavilions such as Yinshilou (吟诗楼, the Poem-Compose Pavilion), Zhuojinlou (濯锦楼, the Brocade-Washing Pavilion), Huanjianlou (浣笺楼, the Writing Paper-Washing Pavilion). In 1886, Chongli Tower (崇丽阁) was built. Since the buildings were set up along the Jinjiang River, it attracted visitors to ascend the buildings to enjoy the scene around them. This group of ancient buildings stands by the river as a symbol of the ancient culture and history in Chengdu.

In 1953, the park workers attempted to create some lively and charming atmosphere in the park. They started to grow bamboo, gradually the bamboo forest came to occupy the greater part of the park. There are over 150 varieties of bamboo from China, Japan and South-East Asia. They range from bonsai-sized potted plants to towering giants. At present, the park is well-known across the country mainly because the park shows a particular use of bamboo for multiple perspectives and illusions of scenery. Much like the People's Park, local residents enjoy spending their weekends in the park where they can drink tea in the park teahouse or to expose to nature by walking in the bamboo forest.

Now, here we are at the park entrance. We will stay in the park 40 minutes. Afterwards we will take our bus back to the city for a meal.

KEY WORDS & EXPRESSIONS 关键词汇及表达法

occupation 职业
specific 明确的；特殊的
informal 非正式的，不拘礼节的
guarantee 保证；担保
format 形式；格式
multi-outdoor activity 多项室外的活动
sidewalk 人行道
ballroom 舞厅
discipline 学科
dentistry 牙科
biomedicine 生物医学
pre-clinical 临床前的
stomatology 口腔病学
dental 牙齿的
occupational disease 职业病

gynecology and obstetrics 妇产科学
in-service teacher 在职教师
archaeological excavation 考古发现
museum-goer 参观博物馆的人
demonstrate 明白表现；显示
skull 头盖骨
ethnic nationality 少数民族
mural 壁画
dinosaur 恐龙
sauropoda 蜥蜴
stegosaur 剑龙
pterosaur 翼龙
artifact 古器物
drilling tool 钻具
component 部件
spare-part 零件
commercial 商业的，贸易的
accessory 附件
predecessor 前辈，前任
accumulate 积累
ethnology 人种学，人类文化学
folklore 民间传说
ethnological 民族的；人种学的
sedan chair 轿子
bridal 新娘的；婚礼的
guild 协会；行业协会
calligraphy 书法；书法艺术
distinctive 与众不同的；有特色的
in memory of 缅怀

compose 创作，撰写
atmosphere 气氛
multiple 多样的，多重的
perspectives 前景，远景
expose to 使受到……影响

Long-Distance Trips 长途旅游

Chengdu-Dujiangyan Irrigation System
成都—都江堰

Good morning, ladies and gentlemen, get on the bus, please. Today we start our trip to Dujiangyan Irrigation System and Mt. Qingcheng. First of all, I'd like to let you know the schedule today before our departure.

8:30 Departure for Dujiangyan Irrigation System.
10:30 Arrival at Erwang Temple (二王庙). We walk across Anlan Suspension Bridge (安澜桥) and view the ancient dam project.
12:00 Arrival at Dragon-Taming Temple (伏龙观).
12:30 Lunch at Dujiangyan City.
13:30 Taking the bus again to Mt. Qincheng.
14:00 Arrival at the foot of the mountain.
14:00 - 16:00 Hiking in the mountain.
16:30 Taking the bus back to the hotel in Dujiangyan city.

We will mostly follow the schedule throughout the trip. Sometimes we may also do some adjustment. If you have suggestions, please do not hesitate to let me know. I will do my best to help you and make your trip happy and enjoyable.

(*On the way*)

In the past days you have explored local culture and toured scenic spots in Chengdu. Chengdu is located at the junction of Tuojiang (陀江) and Minjiang(岷江) rivers. The two tributaries enable Chengdu area to be in the reach of Dujiangyan Irrigation System. Even in ancient times, Chengdu Plain had fertile fields and a mild climate. According to an old saying, no serious flood or drought ever occurred, and local people have had enough food to eat ever since the Qin and Han dynasties.

Now we are on Xiyanxian (西沿线) Street. This street is well known for a number of good restaurants, which line the street. I think Sichuan food may come into your mind as I mention Sichuan restaurants. However, Xiyanxian Street restaurants provide dishes for a variety of tastes. On this street you will have the opportunity to enjoy the exquisite regional dishes of China. Generally, there are the four basic gastronomic areas: Beijing, Cantonese, Shanghai and Sichuan. These designations have no specific geographical boundaries. The four regional cuisines influence one another, and each regional cuisine still keeps its own distinguished dishes as well as prevailing taste. Recently many exquisite hotpot restaurants have been opened on the street. The development of this particular hotpot cuisine with varied flavorings has been toned down for tourists. Maybe this is the main reason why the restaurants are busy in the evenings. Well, I think I will arrange a dinner in one of the restaurants here for all of you when we are back from our trip.

Now we are approaching the Chengdu and Dujiangyan

expressway entrance. As you may know, Chengdu has 7 districts, 4 outlying cities and 8 counties. Right now we are in Chengdu Jinniu District (金牛区). Jinniu means "golden ox" in English. There are at least two legendary stories related to the golden ox.

The first story is called "Golden Dung". In the state of Qin, King Hui prepared to attack the state of Shu. However, Qin's army couldn't move forward because there was no way to pass through the steep mountains and deep valleys between the two states. One day King Hui was told that the king of Shu was insatiably greedy for wealth. So King Hui had someone carve a large stone ox. Behind the ox, he placed gold, silver and other valuables. When everything was completed, the king claimed that this was a golden ox, and the ox produced golden dung. The king also said that he planned to present the stone ox to the king of Shu.

The king of Shu wanted to obtain the golden ox, and therefore he ordered his people to cut through the mountains and fill up the valleys. Then he sent five men of unusual strength to carry the stone ox back to his state. The Qin's army followed the five men all the way up to the state of Shu. As a result, the state of Shu was defeated. The king of Shu became the laughing stock of all the people in the world because he sought small profits and lost big ones.

The other story says that a long time ago, a cow herder and a girl weaver rode a supernatural ox and descended to the world. One day they arrived at this area. They began to teach local people how to plough the fields and weave cotton clothes. Soon this area turned into a vast expanse of fertile plains, and people had enough food to eat and clothes to wear. Finally the cowboy and girl weaver returned to Heaven. However they left the ox in the fields. The ox was asked to keep on working for local people.

The golden ox created a miracle in this area, didn't it? The local people use the image to encourage themselves to create more miracles in the fields of agriculture, economics, technology and science. The present Jinniu district is in the Northwest of Chengdu. The environment remains beautiful because this district has been designated as ecology and water resource reserves.

Please look at the scenes on the either side of the expressway. Here, strips of farmland and navigation canals crisscross and the farmhouses are scattered. Flowers offer multi-colors to the green landscape; farm houses remain dignified or simple in style; they stand amidst green bamboos; the wafting cooking smoke curls up above the endless green fields and the rows of trees and abundant greenery please your eyes. The scenery expands far and wide in fanciful shape, color and design.

Now we are in Pixian county (郫县) area. You may notice that on either side of the expressway many colorful flags are fluttering amidst farmhouses. Are you curious about this unique cultural fact? Let me tell you about it. Chengdu citizens like to spend weekends in the countryside. It is called the Weekend Vacation on a Farm. Citizens and their families in all walks of life depart from where they stay downtown and spend the weekend in traditional farmhouses in the beautiful surroundings. There they take part in some out-door activities. They play chess and mahjong, enjoy flowers and trees or do some fishing. Some doze off in their armchairs. The farmers are happy to open their houses to the visitors from the downtown city. They provide food and accommodation. Food costs are reasonable. The host farmers greatly contribute to the charm of the leisure weekend activities.

Ladies and gentlemen, we will soon arrive at Dujiangyan City. This is our first stop. The city is located in the Northwest of the Chengdu Plain. The area covers an area of 1,207 square km. The Dujiangyan area enjoys a mild subtropical wet climate. Its annual temperature averages 15.2℃ (62 F). A forest covers over 51% of the land.

Dujiangyan city owns both the ancient irrigation project and Mt. Qingcheng. It appears in harmony with its unique environment. On November 29th, 2000, the project and mountain were listed on the World Cultural Heritages by UNESCO. Besides, Longchi Reservoir (龙池) is a newly developed vacation spot. Longchi Reservoir means "dragon's pool". The reservoir has thick forest, clean water and fresh air, which please visitors at home and abroad. Now I'd like to take this opportunity to tell you the general facts of the ancient hydraulic project and the mountain.

The water project is in the middle reach of Minjiang River. Before Dujiangyan Irrigation System was completed, Chengdu Plain around Minjiang River was prone to floods. Around 250 B.C. during the Warring States Period, Li Bing served as governor of Shu in the Qin state. He and his son led the huge construction of Dujiangyan project. He separated the project into two main parts: the headwork and the irrigation system. The project effectively put the flooding waters under control. For over two thousand years the project has functioned perfectly. Besides providing a water source for irrigation, it provides a means to facilitate shipping and wood drifting.

The headwork is a large hydraulic water project. It consists of three main parts: the Fish Mouth Water-Dividing Dam (鱼嘴分水坝), the Flying Sand Fence (飞沙堰), and the Bottle-Neck Channel (宝瓶口). More details will be given to you concerning each part as we arrive at each spot.

On the way to the headwork, we will cross Anlan Suspension Bridge. It spans 500m over the river, right above the Fish Mouth Water-Dividing Dam. Tight steel chains reinforce the bridge. Some visitors, as they cross the bridge, catch hold of the steel chains and swing back and forth on the bridge for fun.

Not far from Dujiangyan Irrigation System is Erwang Temple Complex. It was built to commemorate Li Bing and his son. The two were granted the posthumous title of Wang (king). In the temple is a stone tablet, which is engraved with an six-character quotation from Li Bing. It says, "Where the river flows in zigzags, cut a straight channel / Where the riverbed is wide and shallow, dig it deeper."(深掏滩,低作堰) The temple is built near the mountaintop. It is a popular stopping place to enjoy a unique view of the most modern parts of the water conservation project.

The Dragon-Taming Temple is located on the top of a small hill called Lidui (离堆). Lidui means an isolated hill. A trunk canal cuts through the mountain and links up the inner canal for irrigation. Chengdu looks like a large bottle, and the trunk canal between Mt. Qingcheng and Lidui takes shape of the bottle neck. The Dragon-Taming Temple is our final stop at Dujiangyan Irrigation System, then we will take the bus and go to lunch in Dujiangyan city.

(*On the way*)

At 14:00 we will arrive at the foot of the mountain. So I'd like to take this opportunity to give you a brief introduction of Mt. Qingcheng. Daoism or Taoism is a Chinese native religion. It came into being among the Han nationality, and took shape during the reign of Emperor Shun Di (顺帝, 125 A. D. -144 A. D.) of the Eastern Han Dynasty (25 A. D. -220 A. D.).

Well, I hope you have enjoyed my brief introduction of Daoism and the mountain. The mountain entrance is at our right. In a few minutes we will arrive at the foot of the mountain. There are three main temples, which are worth attention. Each temple has its own statues and stories. I will describe them as we arrive there. So please stay in a group. If any of you have further questions, do not hesitate to ask me as we hike the mountain. Please pay attention to our schedule. Now, it's two o'clock in the afternoon. We will start our hiking very soon. I will accompany you all the way up to the mountain. Our bus driver will meet you at the entrance at 3:30, in case some of you come back earlier than scheduled.

KEY WORDS & EXPRESSIONS 关键词汇及表达法

hike 长途步行，向上运动
hesitate 犹豫
junction 交叉点，会合处
exquisite 优美的，高雅的
gastronomic 烹调的
designation 指定，选派
geographical 地理的
boundary 界面

prevailing 主要的，流行的
varied 各种各样的
flavoring 调味品，调味料
tone down 调和，配合
approach 接近，靠近
legendary 传说中的，传奇性的
dung （家畜的）粪
insatiably 不知足地，贪得无厌地
fill up 填补，装满
laughing stock 笑料
supernatural 超自然的，神奇的
image 偶像；形象化的比喻
navigation 航海；航空
dignified 有威严的，有品格的
waft 吹送；飘荡
curl up （使）卷曲
flutter 摆动；鼓翼
surrounding 环境
doze off 打瞌睡
accommodation 住处；膳宿
leisure 悠闲；安逸
subtropical 亚热带的
vacation 休假
facilitate 使容易，使便利
commemorate 纪念
mountaintop 山顶

Dujiangyan Irrigation System—Wolong Panda Protection Zone

都江堰—卧龙自然保护区

Ladies and gentlemen, yesterday you toured Dujiangyan Irrigation System and hiked Mt. Qingcheng. I know you all had a wonderful time in Dujiangyan area. Well, today we will go and visit Wolong Panda Reserve. Our bus leaves at 8:30. Before our departure, I'd like to let you know our schedule today.

8:30 We start to drive to the reserve.

10:30 We will arrive at the reserve and stay in the reserve guesthouse tonight.

10:40 We walk into the nature reserve, visit the Giant Panda Research and Protection Center, listen to the introduction given by a giant panda expert, and see the giant pandas.

12:00 After lunch, we will visit the Giant Panda Museum.

13:00 We will take a long hike into the forest in the mountain nearby.

16:30 We return to the guesthouse.

17:00 Dinner time.

(***On the way***)

Now we are on the road and will soon enter the high plateau in Northwestern Sichuan where Aba Tibeten and Qiang Nationality Autonomous region is located. On the right is Minjiang River. The river is a main tributary of the upper reaches of Changjiang in Sichuan. Minjiang River starts at Mt. Gonggangling (弓杠岭), Songpan county (松潘县), Aba prefecture. You see Minjiang River surges downward, thrusting itself into Dujiangyan canal. The whole length is 735km. The steep peaks of Longmen Mountain and Qionglai Mountain surround the upper reaches. A Forest belt has taken shape along the upper reaches of the river to prevent sand from drifting.

Mountains in Aba prefecture remain green all year around. River valleys are fully covered by trees. However, several years ago, workers in local forest companies kept cutting down trees in the mountains for multi-purposes. Due to the endless tree felling, some sections of the river valleys appeared bare. Since 1987 forest workers started planting trees and reforested the river valleys. In 1998 the prefecture government took enforcement measures to stop the felling of trees. Most forest workers have turned into tree planters, and their main responsibility is to take care of the forests in mountains and river valleys.

Well, please look at the huge construction site on the west side of the road down in the river valley. Do you know what construction site that is? It is Zipingpu (紫坪铺) Water-Control Project. It is a water resource distribution project, and it is listed as one of the key construction projects in China. It aims to improve city water supply and irrigation system. The other benefits will include power generation, flood-control, environmental protection and tourism. A huge reservoir will be constructed. Can you imagine how large it will be? It is said that it will be 100 times as large as the West Lake in Hangzhou city, Zhejiang province. The reservoir's storage capacity will amount to 1. 112 billion cubic meters (293 billion gallons), and its hydraulic power station will have an installed capacity of 760,000 kilowatts. The reservoir will greatly improve ecological water usage and enhance flood-control ability in the lower reaches of Minjiang River.

Now we are entering Aba Tibeten and Qiang Nationality Autonomous prefecture. I will give you some information about this prefecture.

Located in northwestern Sichuan, the prefecture covers an area of 83,000 square km, and the total population is 800,000. It has some of China's most imposing scenery-dense forests, snowbound valleys, and unforgettable views of mountain ranges rising up against crisp blue skies. The area also has a strong sense of history including monuments to the Long March during the 1930s.

Sichuan province has three autonomous prefectures. They are Yi Nationality Autonomous prefecture, Ganzi Tibetan Autonomous prefecture and Aba prefecture. The Aba prefecture boasts an ethnically rich population, including the Tibetan, Qiang, Han and Hui nationalities. You'll find the Han, Tibetan, Qiang, and Hui live together in harmony. Most noticeably, the Tibetan in Aba prefecture is the second largest Tibetan community in Sichuan province. You may ask me how the Tibetan people came and settled in Aba prefecture? Did they come from Tibet?

Well, in the 7th century the Tibetan Tubo regime (吐蕃王朝) became powerful and prosperous. During the Zhenguan Period of the Tang Dynasty, the army from the Tubo regime occupied the state of Tuguhun (吐谷浑) on the present site of northwestern Sichuan. Afterwards the king of the Tibetan Tubo regime garrisoned his troops in the state of Tuguhun, and moved a large number of Tibetan people into the Tuguhun area from the present Ali district in Tibet. The ancient immigrated Tibetan people resettled down here for generation after generation until now.

Now we come to the town of Xuankou (漩口). It is the industrial zone of Aba prefecture, where a number of factories and plants are located in and outside the town. In the town stands a tower at the end of a peninsula formed by a tributary to Minjiang River. It's a 9-storey tower, 20m in height, and believed to be over 170 years old. The tower looks fairly accessible from the road. The interior is open to the top, and light can be seen coming in from the windows at each level. The initial intention to build it was to harness the turbulent river when it passed through the peninsula.

When Zipingpu Water-Control Project is completed, the reservoir begins to store water. The water will rise up to cover the whole town and the tower. Local people living in the reservoir areas will be resettled to make way for the construction of the gigantic project. The town residents and farmers nearby will resettle down in the places in Dujiangyan area. The large-scale resettlement will be completed in the coming years. The local government will encourage resettlement by increasing business opportunities and ensuring stable incomes.

Ladies and gentlemen, we will soon come to another town by the name of Yingxiu (映秀), which is well-known for large hydraulic power stations. Aba prefecture is rich in water energy resources from Minjiang and Dadu rivers. Its reserves amount to 19.33 million kilowatts. Today Aba hydraulic-power industry is under rapid development. Taipingyi (太平驿) and Yingxiuwan

(映秀湾) Hydro-power stations in Yingxiu town are listed as two of the largest power stations in Sichuan.

Yingxiu town stands as an intersection with one road to Wolong Nature Reserve and Mt. Siguniang. Maybe I should share some basic facts of Wolong Natural Reserve since we are going to spend most of the time today there.

It is a four-hour bus ride from Chengdu to Wolong on a winding road that hugs sparkling and clean white-water rivers. The trip into Wolong takes you into some of the most spectacular scenery in China. You will see towering peaks, lush green vegetation, turbulent waters and the Tibetan and Qiang people.

China has several natural reserves set aside for about 1,000 giant pandas. Wolong Natural Reserve is the largest. It was set up in the late 1970s. It aims to protect 96 species of mammals, including the giant panda, red panda, snow leopard, musk deer, and golden monkey. Besides, 230 species of birds and scores of rare reptiles and butterflies are also (on the list of) protected species.

The United Nations has designated Wolong as an international biosphere reserve. About 100 pandas of the total number of about 1000 giant pandas live there. The area covers a space of 200,000 hectares, which abounds with an estimated 3,000 kinds of plants. It is especially rich in arrow bamboo and Chinese pink bamboo, the panda's favorite food. To the northwest rises Mt. Siguniangshan (6240m), and to the east the reserve drops as low as 155m.

In 1978, a research center was set up at Wolong. In 1980 the Wolong Nature Reserve was officially designated a part of the UN international network for animal protection. Both the Chinese government and the World Wildlife Fund cooperated to establish the first giant panda research center there.

In addition to research laboratories, the center has a breeding farm at the foot of the mountain. It is near bamboo groves and a stream flows by. Some pandas have been brought there. The scientists work out a diet for the pandas. The diet consists of bamboo, rice, corn, and sugar, and the pandas grow very well. The center has a nursery, quarantine quarters for adult pandas, a swimming pond and a 1. 5 hectare farm in a semi-wild state. It also includes some plots of enclosed land for keeping pandas penned up. In the center scientists do comprehensive research work related to the pandas' feeding, breeding habits, physiology and behavior patterns. Scientists keep detailed records on each panda's eating and sleeping habits, and her or his daily activities. The research work also includes pandas' necessary treatment, disease prevention and experimentation with methods of domestication and artificial fertilization.

In May 1994, the Ministry of Forestry and the Ministry of Public Security issued the PRC Wild Life Protection Law. The National People's Congress approved the Supplementary Regulation Concerning Punishment for Killing National Key Protected Rare and Endangered Animals. The local governments effectively enforce these legal documents to protect pandas and other rare animals. Local residents living in or around the reserves are not allowed to collect firewood or medical plants or to hunt wild animals. Besides, in the reserve areas forest workers have stopped their regular felling of trees. Instead, they plant trees and protect forests. Local residents have come to realize the truth, which says, "We humans have only one planet. However, the planet does not only belong to us but also to the animals as well. We should treat animals better and protect their environment".

Up to now, the number of giant pandas in the wild have remained stable at about 1,000. Their living environments are getting better.

Well, so much for my introduction about the reserve and pandas. We will soon get off the bus and start our tour in accordance with our schedule.

KEY WORDS & EXPRESSIONS 关键词汇及表达法

thrusting 有强大推进力
multi-purpose 多目的的
enforcement 执行，强制
responsibility 责任，职责
distribution 分配，分发
power generation 发电
storage capacity 储藏量，存储量
enhance 提高，增强
imposing 使人难忘的；壮丽的
unforgettable 忘不了的，令人难忘的
ethnically 人种上，民族上
noticeably 引人注目地，显著地
garrison 守卫，驻防
peninsula 半岛
accessible 可到达的
gigantic 巨人般的；巨大的
resettlement 再定居，重新安置
intersection 十字路口，交叉点
sparkling 闪烁的，闪闪发光的

spectacular 引人注意的，惊人的
mammal 哺乳动物
leopard 豹
reptile 爬行动物
biosphere 生物圈
decrease 逐渐减少
survivor 幸存者，残存物
stoutly 粗壮的；矮胖的
clumsy 动作笨拙的
socket 窝，穴
meat-eater 食肉动物
extinction 消失，消灭
genetic defect 遗传缺陷
nursery 托儿所
quarantine 检疫，隔离
enclose 关闭住，围住
pen up 装入，围绕
physiology 生理学
domestication 驯养，驯服
artificial fertilization 人工受精
degrade 退化
legal document 法律文件
felling 伐木
cycle 周期；循环

Yingxiu—Jiuzhaigou National Park

映秀—九寨沟

Good morning, ladies and gentlemen, did you have a wonderful time in Wolong Nature Reserve? Good! Now I'd like to let you know the general schedule for today. We will take a long-distance drive. We leave Wolong Nature Reserve at 8:00 in the morning and arrive at Jiuzhaigou later in the afternoon. We will have lunch at Maoxian county (茂县) seat, and stay in a hotel in Jiuzhaigou tonight. Along the winding road our experienced driver will drive very carefully. Maybe we will have to make some adjustment to our schedule due to the busy tourist road. I would very much appreciate your patience and understanding if that occurs. Now please get on the bus, we will leave at 8 o'clock sharp.

(***On the way***)

Ladies and gentlemen, now we are leaving for the reserve. This place is very remote and protects some fabulously rare wildlife. Fortunately you had a chance to see the pandas and other rare animals in their natural habitat. Wolong Nature Reserve provides the best ecological environment for rare animals. Frankly speaking, these animals are so rare that your chances of seeing them are very slim. However, you now have a good reason to revisit the reserve, trek into the forest and follow the panda tracks into the mountains. If you like, more excellent trips can be arranged to tour Mt. Siguniang from Wolong. The mountain with very beautiful scenery is situated in Xiaojin county (小金县), and is regarded as the Oriental Alps (东阿尔卑斯山).

Now we return to the intersection at Yingxiu town, and join

the tourist road up to Wenchuan（汶川）, Songpan and Jiuzhaigou. The weather is cool and the sky overcast. It is good weather for a long distance bus ride.

As our bus moves forward, you will notice that the area is becoming more and more Qiang and Tibetan in appearance. Occasionally you will see some village buildings made of brown rocks. Some of them are beyond the river valley where an old iron-chain footbridge straddles the river; some others are on top of impossibly remote mountain ridges. All these buildings look picturesque and blend in with the rest of the landscape.

Now we are approaching Wenchuan county seat. Aba prefecture has 13 counties under its jurisdiction. Wenchuan county ranks first among these counties in its population, and industrial output value. In 1985 Wenchuan county was listed as one of the first five Chinese counties to fully implement the first stage of electrification. In this town there is a college, which is called Aba Teachers College. This institution of higher learning trains students to be teachers in elementary and middle schools across the prefecture. There are some other intermediate schools in Aba prefecture. These schools recruit local young people to get more education.

Please look ahead at a section of wall on the mountain slope. It is called Jiangwei (姜维) City Wall. Jiangwei was a well-known general in the Kingdom of the Shu during the Three Kingdoms Period. Based on the historical book called Old Tang Book (旧唐书), Jiangwei conducted a western military expedition. When he arrived in Wenchuan, Jiangwei garrisoned his troops and had them build a city wall. During his stay here, he trained his soldiers with military exercises.

Well, we are on the way to Maoxian county from Wuchuan. Maoxian county used to be called Maozhou (茂州). In the county the Qiang nationality makes up 88.92 per cent of the total population. In 1958 the county was named Maowen Qiang Nationality Autonomous county. Later when Aba was renamed Aba Tibetan and Qiang Autonomous prefecture from Aba Tibetan Autonomous prefecture, this county was renamed Maoxian county.

Today the Qiang are one of the 55 ethnic nationalities in China. Its population is approximately 200,000. They all live in Sichuan province. The areas mainly include Wenchuan, Lixian (理县), Maoxian, Songpan in Aba prefecture, and Beichuan (北川) in Mianyang (绵阳) region.

The Qiang is commonly believed to be an ancient people whose history can be traced to the Shang Dynasty. At about 1300 B.C., people of the Qiang had already been recorded on the oracle-bone inscriptions of the Shang Dynasty. According to these inscriptions, they were a population living in the west. During the Later Han Dynasty the ancient Qiang people were widely distributed along the western frontiers of the Han Empire. Among them, the Qiang living in the upper Yellow River Valley in eastern Qinghai province are well known for their battles with the troops from the Han Empire.

During the Later Han (25 – 220) and Wei-Jin Periods (221 – 419), the Qiang people were widely distributed along the mountainous fringes of the northern and eastern Tibetan Plateau, from Kunlun Mountains and eastern Qinghai area, to southern

Gansu, western Sichuan, and northern Yunnan.

From the 14th to the 19th century, the terms Qiang rong (羌戎, Qiang barbarians), and zhu Qiang (诸羌, many Qiang tribes) or fan (番) and yi (夷) were still applied to a wide range of western non-Han people in a general sense, but only the Qiang living in the upper Minjiang River Valley and the nearby Beichuan region were recorded as Qiang, Qiang ren or Qiang min (羌民, Qiang civilians).

From the 16th century on, the Han people moved into the upper Minjiang River Valley and Beichuan areas. They were storekeepers, merchants, artisans, and civil or military officers. They lived in towns or villages. Many married native men or women, settled down and have lived there ever since.

The Qiang basic social unit is a fortress village, which is composed of 30 to 100 households. Two to five fortress villages make up a village cluster (村). The inhabitants of fortress villages or village clusters have close social contact. In these small valleys, people cultivate their crops along creeks or mountain terraces, hunt animals, collect mushrooms and herbs in the neighboring woods, and herd yaks and horses on the mountain-top pastures.

The houses in the fortress villages are built of stone and wood, standing two or three stories high. All the houses are built together for the purpose of defense. In some villages, all houses face inwards; the back walls are connected, forming the outer rampart. The symbol of a fortress village is its defense towers. These towers were built of stone. Each is about 15 to 20 feet across at the base, and becomes gradually narrower up to the top. Many towers exceed 100 feet in height. According to the natives, all these defense towers were built at least 80 years ago.

From a linguistic point of view, all modern Qiang people speak Qiang language, which is a member of the Tibetan-Burman linguistic family. However, they have close contact with the Han people, and many Qiang people also speak Chinese.

There is a long and abundant historical record concerning the Qiang in Chinese history. In 1949, People Republic of China was established. The equality and autonomous rights of all nationalities were guaranteed by the Constitution of the PRC. Until 1979, a total of 55 minority nationalities had been formally recognized by the state.

In this new environment, the history of the Qiang nationality became a focus of historical attention. During the 1970s and 1980s, many leading scholars became engaged in studies related to the Qiang from the Shang Dynasty down to the present. These studies also linked a wide range of northwestern and southwestern nationalities.

A folk story concerning a war between the natives and the Geji (戈基) people was adopted from the Qiang in the Wenchuan and Lixian areas. Scholars interpreted it again as evidence for the Qiang's southward resettlement. The story says that when the ancestors of the Qiang moved to the upper reaches of Minjiang River in Sichuan province, they came upon a strong enemy. The leader of the Qiang was instructed in a dream to overcome the enemy with white stones. Afterwards the leader and his people followed the instructions, and the Qiang defeated their strong enemy. The Qiang nationality therefore began to worship the white stone as a way of expressing their gratitude to the god who had appeared in the dream.

The Qiang people do not have a native writing system. In the mid-1980s after receiving the approval from the State Council, the Qiang scholars began to create their own writing system and to compile a dictionary of the Qiang language. They used a Romanized alphabet based on the standardized Qugu (曲谷) dialect. Since 1994, teachers have been trained to learn the standard Qiang language and the writing system. Afterward they are sent to teach in Qiang villages. Now the Qiang people are speaking the same language.

One of the highlights in the Qiang culture is the New Year Festival based on Qiang calendar. According to the native language, there are only two periods in a year, one equivalent to spring and summer, and the other, autumn and winter. The New Year Festival of the Qiang calendar starts on the first day of the tenth month. So the four Qiang counties—Maoxian, Wenchuan, Lixian and Beichuan—take turns hosting the activities of the day for all the Qiang people. During that day the Qiang people, especially young people enjoy the opportunity to sing and dance with their friends from different localities.

Guozhuang (锅庄) dancing is the most important activity in the New Year Festival of the Qiang calendar. It is a kind of group dancing. It is commonly believed that Guozhuang dancing is shared between the Tibetans and the Qiang people in Aba prefecture. In some fortress-villages (in northern Maoxian and southern Songpan), young people do Guozhuang dancing, elders perform Nisa dancing instead. It is another kind of group dancing with a more ritual or religious sense. Since 1989, both the standardized Guozhuang dancing of the Qiang and that of the Jiarong (嘉戎) Tibetans were gradually introduced to all the people. Guozhuang dancing now is widely practiced in every official or private celebration; it is not only a symbol of the Qiang culture but also a symbol of unification of the Jiarong Tibetans and the Qiang in Aba prefecture.

Ladies and gentlemen, my introduction about the Qiang people is over. We will arrive at Maoxian county seat very soon. We will stay there for lunch, and Qiang flavored dishes will be offered in the restaurant. I hope you will like them. Unfortunately, because of our tight schedule, we have only a short time in Maoxian county, otherwise we might go up to a Qiang village to experience local Qiang customs and appreciate their traditional arts.

(***On the way after lunch***)

Ladies and gentlemen, did you have a short nap on the bus after lunch? I saw that most of you did. Good! I think a short nap will greatly restore your energy for the bus sightseeing this afternoon.

Now we arrive at a place called Maoxian Ancient Drill Ground (茂县校场). This place is strategically located at the vital passage to Songpan pasture. In ancient times military strategists fought battles to control the passage. At present this place is peaceful and quiet. No military garrisons are here. Please look far left down the valley. There are two dammed lakes surrounded by hills. That place is called Diexi Earthquake Ruins (叠溪地震遗址). On August 25, 1933, an earthquake struck Diexi. It was an earthquake of magnitude 7.5 (on the Richter scale). The hills collapsed, and Diexi town moved over 40m southwards and sank several hundred meters in depth. The earth and soil from collapsed hills covered the town. At the same time the collapsed rocks blocked Minjiang River channel so that the river water formed the lakes we see today. Diexi Earthquake Ruins is one of the best-preserved earthquake ruins in the world, and many scientists come here to study the physical laws of earthquakes.

Ladies and gentlemen, we are approaching to Songpan county seat. As Songpan area is on the border region of the Qinghai-Tibet High Plateau, the area is becoming more open and flat in appearance. Mountains in Songpan area are not so steep, and rivers flow gently. We will arrive at Songpan county seat in 30 minutes.

Look, Songpan county is ahead within our sight. It is an ancient town, and it serves as a hub connecting Huanglong and Jiuzhaigou. In 1992, the seat was listed as a Historical and Cultural City of Sichuan. In 1379, during the Ming Dynasty people began to build the town. It took 60 years before the town was completed. It is said that the official in charge of the huge construction employed thousands of skilled workers from other parts of China. You will soon view the city wall, which is 10m high, 30m wide and 6,200m long. The wall is made of earth and bricks; each brick is 50cm long and 12cm thick. Each gate has ancient patterns and figures, which have remained unchanged for centuries.

In ancient times the town was well known for its prosperous business and trade. Businessmen established their own commercial firms, and there were hundreds of stores.

Ladies and gentlemen, we are passing a small town named Chuanzhusi (川主寺). Several years ago, the town was neglected. Now it serves as an important intersection, connecting tourist attractions in Songpan county. In the town are a number of hotels, shopping centers, bus terminals, as well as many restaurants, souvenir shops, stores, and trade centers. All the tourist buses and cars have to pass through this town before going to Jiuzhaigou in the north or to Huanglong in the east.

May I have your attention, please. There is a high-rising monument standing on the hilltop. At the foot of the hill is a memorial park. The monument construction started in April 1988 and was completed on August 25, 1990 in memory of Long March. The main monument is a triangle shape, symbolizing the strong unity and support among the First, Second and Fourth Front Armies of the Chinese Workers' and Peasants' Red Army. The carved Red Army soldier stands on the top of the monument. He stretches his hands upwards in a shape of 'V'. One of his hands holds a flower, and the other hand is grasping a rifle. His gesture symbolizes the victory of the Long March, which began in 1933 and took a year to be completed. The First, Second and Fourth Front Armies in the south made their way to Shaanxi in the north to join up with other Communist armies in Shaanxi, Gansu and Ningxia. Whenever tourists pass by, they can't help looking at the solemn monument, and admiration wells up in their heart.

Well, we will soon arrive at our hotel. Tomorrow we will tour Jiuzhaigou, and the day after tomorrow we will explore Huanglong. So I'd like to take this opportunity to offer you a brief introduction of these two natural attractions so that you will be able to fully enjoy them.

It is said that a long time ago that a male and female hill deities fell in love with each other. The man is called Dage (达戈) and woman Wonuo Semo (沃诺色嫫). They decided to reside in Jiuzhaigou because they deeply loved Jiuzhaigou's birds, animals, forests and mountains. Unexpectedly a devil called Shemozha (蛇魔扎) didn't want the male deity to live in Jiuzhaigou. Therefore the devil waged a war to drive the male deity out because he wanted to marry the female deity. During the battle, the female deity was snatched away by the devil. She dropped her precious mirror, given to her by the male deity, down to the ground. The mirror was broken into over a hundred pieces, which immediately turned into beautiful high mountains and lakes. The male and female hill deities finally defeated the devil and lived together in Jiuzhaigou thereafter as important deities to safeguard Jiuzhaigou.

Jiuzhaigou covers an area of 60,000 hectares. Its marvelous attractions include Shuzheng Waterfalls (树正瀑布), Potted-patterned Landscape Lake (盆景滩), Long Lake (长海), Sword Cliff (剑岩), Nuorilang Waterfall (诺日郎瀑布) and Five-flower Lake (五花海). Jiuzhaigou means Nine Village Valleys, named after nine Tibetan villages in Jiuzhaigou scenic area.

This fairyland remained unknown for thousands of years until the 1970s when some forest lumber workers accidentally discovered this scenic attraction. In 1982 it was under special state protection. Since then, endless visitors at home and abroad come and tour Jiuzhaigou to enjoy the beauty of the nature.

Literally Huanglong means the Yellow Dragon. Huanglong is called Se'ercuo in Tibetan language, which means Golden Lake.

A folk tale says that a long time ago floods frequently occurred in this area, and local people suffered a lot. Dayu (大禹)

is a legendary figure who was an expert in flood control. One day, he arranged for his people to come here for water control work. The Yellow Dragon also took a boat and arrived here. He helped Dayu to complete the water control system. After the system was completed, this area seldom had flood disasters, mountains and waters in this area became more appealing and colorful.

Another folk tale says that the seventh fairy maiden descended to the world and didn't return to Heaven. The Jade Emperor (玉皇大帝) became unhappy upon hearing the report of her absence. The emperor immediately sent down his troops to bring her back. The seventh maiden rode a horse and ran away. The troops chased her wherever she went. As she passed through Huanglong Valley, the troops were still after her. The solidiers' feet and horses' hooves disorderly trod the valley, then unexpectedly, turned into many colorful ponds and pools.

Do those two folk tales sound beautiful? Huanglong is well-known for its Five Wonders. They are colored ponds, beach flows, snow-capped mountains, and fascinating canyons and forests. Zigzagging streams flow their way through forests, and empty into eight pond groups. The streams resemble a golden dragon and the ponds look like dragon scales. In 1982 the State Council listed Huanglong among the first group of attractions at national-level. On December 14, 1992, Huanglong was added to the list of the World Natural Heritage.

Well, so much for the introduction to the two attractions. Here we are at the hotel in Jiuzhaigou. Please pick up your bags and check-in at the hotel reception desk.

KEY WORDS & EXPRESSIONS 关键词汇及表达法

fabulously 难以置信地；惊人地

track 路；踪迹
overcast 阴天的，阴暗的
occasionally 有时候；偶尔
straddle 跨越
impossibly 不可能地，无法可想
blend in 混合
jurisdiction 权限
electrification 电气化
intermediate school 中等学校
approximately 近似地
oracle-bone 卜骨
inscription 题记
western frontier 西部边境
fringe 边缘
tribe 部族，部落
civilian 平民
storekeeper 店主
artisan 工匠，技工
fortress 堡垒；要塞
village cluster 村落；建筑组群
yak 牦牛
rampart 垒；壁垒
linguistic 语言的；语言学的
equality 平等
autonomous right 自治权
constitution 宪法
interpret 解释；说明
gratitude 感谢，感激
alphabet 字母表

standardize 使符合标准,使标准化
calendar 日历
take turns 轮流
ritual 典礼;(宗教)仪式
unification 统一,合一
strategically 战略上
strategist 战略家
magnitude 震级
(on) the Richter Scale 里克特震级,里氏震级(共分 10 级)
terminal 点站,终端
triangle 三角形
thereafter 从那时以后
safeguard 维护,保护
accidentally 偶然地,意外地
tread 踏,践
hoof (hooves) 蹄

Chengdu—Leshan Giant Buddha

成都—乐山大佛

Good morning, ladies and gentlemen. We are on Chengdu-Leshan expressway, heading towards the Giant Buddha in Leshan. The expressway was completed in 1999, and the bus trip takes one and a half to two hours to reach Leshan city. The total distance is 160km. Before 1999 the trip took at least 5 hours over a rough road. Now the expressway provides a smooth and quick trip.

Ladies and gentlemen, we are in Shuangliu county (双流县). Please look at the green landscape on either side of the expressway. Plots of farm fields grow varieties of crops, irrigation canals crisscross and farmhouses stand amidst green bamboos. The scenery expands far and wide in fanciful shapes.

In ancient times Shuangliu county was called Guangdu (广都). The state of ancient Shui established its own capital in this area. At present the county is under the official administration of Chengdu Municipal Government. Shuangliu is an outlying county, which is geographically located lower than the other Chengdu districts and counties. During the rainy season each year, some sections of the county experience floods. There was an old saying, "Golden Wenjiang county, silvery Pixian county, and beggars come from Shuangliu county." (金温江、银郫县,叫花子出在双流县。)

Since the 1980s, a great change has taken place due to the policy of reform and opening up to the outside world. The county's annual output value has surpassed a billion Yuan. The Southwest Airport Economic Development Zone was set up in 1993 in Shuangliu county. It relies mainly on the service sector, which is only 6km away from Chengdu city proper and close to Shuangliu International Airport to the west. Now 208 enterprises have been established in the zone. Sixty are foreign-funded enterprises.

The local county government continues to make more efforts to push Shuangliu forward. One of their decisions is to offer a proficiency-training program to 320,000 Shuangliu farmers whose ages are between 20 and 45 years old. The training is free of charge, and it aims to help each farmer master a practical skill. The local farmers have come to realize that it is hard to have a good harvest in the fields without agricultural technology and skills; if they have no practical skill, it is hard to get short-term jobs downtown during the slack-farming season.

Shuangliu county is in the southwest of Chengdu. It has some tourist attractions. Chengdu citizens enjoy having excursions in the Shuangliu area. One of the main scenic spots is Huanglongxi (黄龙溪) town, 47km away from Chengdu. Huanglongxi is an ancient town with a history of more than 1,000 years. Huanglongxi means the Yellow Dragon Brook in English. Typical ancient Chinese architecture remains there. You will find that ancient streets, temples, and pavilions create fascinating scenery. On weekends visitors from Chengdu have a short stay and relax themselves in the town. They usually go boating, drink tea in teahouses and play mahjong.

Now we are in Xinjin county (新津县), 28km south of Chengdu. There are five rivers, which crisscross the extensive land in the county. The county is referred to as "Sichuan Venice".

In 1983, Xinjin county was transferred into the official administration of Chengdu Municipal government. Since then the county sped up its basic infrastructure, transforming the old county seat into the new one in accordance with the national level design. At present the county government uses three local market towns to develop a new way for the further expansion of its economy. The farmers in these three towns carry out the farming and planting of their choice in line with the local condition. They are also encouraged to build their houses in the towns to make room for the growth of new economic zones.

Xinjin boasts at least 20 tourist attractions. I think that one of the best is the ancient mural paintings in Guanyin Monastery (观音寺). The paintings were completed during the Ming Dynasty. One well-preserved mural painting is the 12 Pratyeka-Buddhas. It portrays that the 12 Buddhas in various postures, who have achieved their enlightenment, still take turns asking the principal Buddhas questions during their Buddhist practice towards the enlightenment. The painters used fluid and smooth lines to depict the various expressions of the figures. Each painted figure remains elegant and poised. The painting has a harmonious beauty with a strong decorative effect.

Now I'd like to offer you a brief description of the development of the ancient mural paintings in China. The mural painting developed in the Qin and Han dynasties. Apart from wall paintings in palaces and temples, there was a great number in tombs of that period. The earliest Chinese mural painting discovered was in the Han Dynasty tomb near Luoyang (洛阳), Henan. It depicts a buried couple ascending to Heaven in the company of immortals and mythical beasts. Han tomb murals have also been found in Henan, Shanxi, Shandong, Hebei and other places. The artistic value of paintings in the Han Dynasty can be appreciated mostly from its mural paintings.

During the Wei, Jin, Northern and Southern dynasties, Buddhism spread, and religious art thrived. This spread led to the practice of making cliff grottoes such as Mogao Grottoes (莫高窟) at Dunhuang (敦煌), Yungang Grottoes (云岗石窟) at Datong (大同) and Longmen Grottoes (龙门石窟) at Luoyang. These grottoes are furnished with sculptures and wall paintings of Buddhist images. Ancient mural painting reached its climax in the Tang Dynasty. The paintings in those years were realistic and well developed with easy flow of lines. Mural paintings had bright colors and broad setting, figures had vivid facial expression, and ladies had been painted with plump cheeks.

Down to the Ming Dynasty the mural paintings were much inferior to the ones of the previous dynasties. However, the mural paintings in temples advanced compared with the ones in tombs. The mural paintings are a reflection of both Daoism and Buddhism. The existing Ming mural paintings can be found in Fahai Monastery (法海寺) in Beijing, Shengmu Temple (圣母庙) in Shanxi province, and Lijiang Naxi Nationality Autonomous county (丽江纳西族自治县) in Yunnan province. In Sichuan the Ming mural temple paintings are in existence in Guanyin Monastery in Xinjin county, Longju Monastery (龙居寺) in Guanghan county, Juewan Monastery (觉宛寺) in Jiange county and others.

We are now in the third county named Pengshan (彭山). It is a small hilly land. In ancient times the county was called Wuyang (武阳) and was established during the Qin Dynasty. Pengshan county is well-known for its high grain production in China. Local farmers plant crop grains wherever it is possible. However as we pass by, green hills meet the eye on every side. Do you know why?

Several years ago the Chinese government began promoting the project of returning farmed land to grassland and forest in order to protect the forest belt along the upper and middle reaches of Changjiang. The local government encouraged farmers to return their farmed land to grassland and forest. The farmers warmly welcomed the project and intended to help restructure agriculture and accelerate the economic development in rural areas.

As a result in recent years, the hills have been covered with trees and grass. The forestation project progresses smoothly, and the forest coverage keeps increasing.

Pengshan county is well-known as a home of longevity. It is the hometown of Pengzu (彭祖), who was born in 1348 B. C. and died in 1210 B. C.. He lived for 130 years, which made him a symbol of longevity in China.

In the county is a mountain called Mt. Pengzu. It is the fairy tale mountain where it is said that Pengzu practiced his longevity exercises. Pengzu studied the relations between man and nature, food and health, martial arts and fitness, and proposed four techniques for maintaining good health. They are known as the absorbing technique, the food technique, the sexual technique, and the medical technique. According to an investigation, the percentage of old people over 100 years old in Pengshan county is much higher than in other places across the country.

In China, you can immediately identify long-livers, to be more exact, old people. They walk around, leaning on their canes. You can tell for sure that these old people are 90, 100 or older.

Perhaps I should tell you more about some traditional Chinese health exercises. One of the popular exercises is shadow boxing called Taijiquan(太极拳). It is commonly understood to mean "grand ultimate boxing". As far as old people are concerned, it is superior to other forms of Chinese martial art. The open and close movements of Taijiquan reflect the Chinese philosophical concept of an endless cycle. Taijiquan practice restores vigorous health, improves digestion, and raises one's spirits. The practice further emphasizes that it has the ability to improve the circulation of blood and energy throughout the whole body.

There are many other ways for the possible achievement of longevity in China. Some elders do Qigong exercise, some stick to diets, others walk backward. The teaching of longevity and immortality emerged in ancient China. It was an important component of Daoism. Daoists developed some respiration methods to increase the life span. For instance, one can breathe as a tortoise or any other animal, which lives longer than man.

Well, we are in the fourth county by the name of Meishan (眉山). The county was called Meizhou in ancient times. Meishan is known for being the hometown of Su Xun (苏洵) and his two sons: Su Shi (苏轼) and Su Zhe (苏辙). The three men were noted writers of the Northern Song Dynasty. Their home residence was converted into a temple during the early Ming Dynasty and further renovated in the late 19th century. Today, the mansion and pavilions serve as a museum for the study of the writings of the Northern Song period. At their residence complex, some 4,500 items of historical documents are on display, including relics of the Su family, writings and calligraphy.

Su Shi, also known as Su Dongpo (苏东坡, 1037 - 1101), was remarkably accomplished in ancient Chinese literature. After he passed the imperial examination, he came in third as a chinshin (进士) 1061, Su was appointed notary in Fengxiang, but his official career was marked by a series of political setbacks. In his forty-year career as a government official, Su Shi experienced three periods of political exile. His third and final exile on Hainan Island lasted three years, from 1097 until 1100. How did Su Shi manage to survive three years on Hainan? Most officials banished to the island never returned because living conditions there were primitive, harsh, and extremely difficult. Indeed, banishment to Hainan in the Song period was considered a death sentence. And yet, despite Hainan's hostile environment, Su Shi survived and eventually returned to the Central Plains. Unfortunately, he died on his way home.

Su Shi is known for his Song Dynasty lyrics, ci-poems as we called (宋词). The Song Dynasty lyrics is a type of poetry. Their lines are in unequal length and set to music. Most of the poems do not even have their own title, but they are named after an original melody. Composers and writers used that melody to write a new poem. The original melody is a tune pattern, in Chinese it is called cipai (词牌). There are more than 800 tune patterns. Famous patterns include Butterflies Love Blossoms, Die Lian Hua (蝶恋花), Scent Fills the Hall, Man Ting Fang (满庭芳) and Lady Yu, Yu Mei Ren (虞美人). Poems written based on a certain melody or tune pattern are ci poems. The ci-poem genre emerged during the Tang Dynasty, and reached its full development during the Song Dynasty, and it is a major achievement of Song literature.

Song Dynasty ci-poems may be divided into two groups. One is known for delicate restraint (婉约), and the other for heroic abandon and vigor (豪放). The vigorous ci-poem type is represented in the works of Su Shi of the Northern Song and Xin Qiji (辛弃疾) of the Southern Song. Under the influence of the great writer Su Shi, the ci-poem began to free itself from its musical background and became primarily a literary creation. The poet does not know the underlying melody of the poem. Ci-poems again became very popular during the Qing Dynasty.

We now are in the fifth county. Its name is Jiajiang (夹江), which is well known as the key production place of Xuan paper (宣纸). Ladies and gentlemen, you may ask me what Xuan paper is and how it is used.

Well, Xuan paper is a kind of writing paper for Chinese painting and calligraphy. It is mainly produced in two places. One is in Jiajiang county, and the other in Jing county (泾县), Anhui province. During the Tang Dynasty Jing county was under the official administration of Xuanzhou prefecture (宣州). Jing paper had to be transported to Xuanzhou center before it was distributed to the other places. So this painting paper was named Xuan paper.

The paper absorbs ink well and shows clearly the lines and strokes. The paper has tensile strength, and it retains its quality a long time. Artists prefer using Xuan paper mainly because on the Xuan paper their paintings and calligraphy can last many years.

According to Chinese historical accounts, Cai Lun (蔡伦) of the Eastern Han Dynasty invented paper. He used the inner bark of a mulberry tree and bamboo fibers to mix them with water, and pounded them with a wooden tool. He then poured this mixture onto a flat but coarsely woven cloth. The water from the mixture dipped through the cloth, leaving the fibers on it. Once the mixture became dry, Cai Lun discovered that he had created a good quality writing paper. This kind of paper was easy to make and lightweight. Cai Lun also used some other materials for various papers. They included tree bark, remnants of hemp, linen rags, and fishnets.

During the Tang and the Song dynasties, varieties of paper were developed for different purposes. The varieties include the hemp paper, the hide paper, and Xuan paper. Song Yingxing (宋应星) of the Ming Dynasty summarized the technology of papermaking in his book: *Exploitation of the Works of Nature* (天工开物). The book also has an account of "dipping paper" as used in Jiajiang county.

Today many ancient papermaking workshops in Jiajiang are well-preserved, and some of them continue to make paper in small quantities. Due to the rich bamboo resources, more than 40,000 Jiajiang farmers are engaged in papermaking. The workshops amount to about 3,000, and varieties of paper are produced. The high-quality Xuan paper is sold both at home and abroad.

Well, ladies and gentlemen, we are in Leshan area now. In 15 minutes we will arrive at the entrance of Lingyun Hill (凌云山), where the 71m height Giant Buddha sits. Leshan is the National Grade A City of tourist value. It's well known for the Grand Buddha and Mt. Emei. Besides, it has other attractions, including Wuyou Temple (乌尤寺), Mahaoyan Tomb (麻浩岩墓) and so on. I will continue offering you more information about these places of interests as we tour the Giant Buddha.

KEY WORDS & EXPRESSIONS 关键词汇及表达法

crisscross 在……交织;纵横

administration 管理

municipal 市政的,市立的

annual output value 年产值

surpass 超越,胜过
foreign-funded enterprise 外企
proficiency 熟练,精通
free of charge 免费
practical skill 实用技能
slack farming season 农闲季节
fascinating 令人心醉的
Venice 威尼斯(意大利港市)
transform 转变,转化
in accordance with 和……一致;合作
expansion 扩展,扩大
posture 姿态
elegant 优雅的,优美
poised 泰然自若的
harmonious 和谐的,协调的
immortal 不朽者,名声不朽的人
appreciate 欣赏
thrive 兴旺,繁荣
climax 高潮,顶点
plump 圆胖的,丰满的
be inferior to 下级的;差的
green hills meet the eye on every side 青山满目
forest belt 森林带
restructure 重建构造;调整
accelerate 使加速
forestation 造林
absorb 吸收,吸引
long-liver 长寿者
vigorous 精力旺盛的;有力的

digestion 消化
circulation of blood 血液循环
diet 饮食，食物
respiration 呼吸
renovate 革新；刷新
on display 展示，展览
remarkably 非常地；显著地
accomplish 完成，达到
notary 公证人
setback 顿挫，挫折
exile 放逐；充军
survive 幸免于，幸存
banish 流放，放逐
eventually 结局地；最后地
lyric 抒情诗；歌词
original melody 原始曲调
genre 类型，式样
restraint 抑制，制止
under the influence of 在……影响下
underlying 基本的
stroke （绘画等）一笔
mulberry tree 桑树
pound 连续重击，连续敲打
coarsely 质地粗糙地
remnant 残余，剩余；零料
hemp 大麻纤维
linen 亚麻布
hide 兽皮
well-preserved 保存好的

mural　墙壁上的

mural painting　壁画

Chengdu—Hailuogou Glacier Park

成都—海螺沟

Good morning, ladies and gentlemen, we are scheduled to leave Chengdu at 8:30 after breakfast at the hotel. We will drive to Bifeng Valley (碧峰峡), do some sightseeing there and then have our lunch at Tianquan town (天全镇). Afterwards we will drive to Hailuogou Glacier Park(海螺沟冰川原始森林) and stay in a hotel in Moxi town (磨西镇). Tomorrow we will continue our sightseeing to trek through nature reserve, later we will take a bath at the outdoor hot spring. The day after tomorrow we will return to Chengdu. We will follow this schedule throughout the trip, but sometimes we may also make some adjustment. If you have suggestions, please do not hesitate to let me know. I will do my best to help you make your trip happy and enjoyable.

(***On the way***)

Ladies and gentlemen, lovely weather today, isn't it? The temperature has climbed to 30℃ (86°F) in Chengdu. The weatherman predicts that there will be a shower this evening. Tonight we will stay in Moxi town. The temperature in Moxi will be 20 - 25°C(68 - 76° F).

We are now on the Second Ring Road, driving towards the entrance to Chengdu-Yaan Expressway (成雅高速公路). Recently Chengdu has greatly improved its transportation network. This extensive network includes the First, the Second and the Third Ring Roads, and the Outer City Ring Road (市外环

路)，Chenglong Road，Old Chengdu-Chongqing Road，as well as Chengdu-Chongqing Expressway (成渝高速公路). Before the Third City Ring Road and the Outer City Ring Road were completed，the Second Ring Road had very heavy traffic，particularly during rush hours when vehicles moved very slowly. At present the situation is different. We won't have any traffic jams as we pass these ring roads.

Nearby the Second Ring Road is Chengdu High-Tech Industrial Zone，where many well-known high-tech companies have set up their headquarters. Chengdu has over 2,000 scientific research and technological development institutions. It also has built a number of high-tech development zones. Apart from the above-mentioned zone，there are the Modern Agricultural Technology Zone，the Science and Technology Industrial Zone for the Modernization of Chinese Herbal Medicine and others. These zones and companies have greatly enhanced Chengdu in science and technology.

Now we are entering the entrance of Chengdu-Yaan Expressway. The total length is 120km，and it takes about one hour to get to Yaan (雅安) city.

In 1876 a French missionary discovered pandas in Yaan，Sichuan. Since then，Yaan gradually became known to people at home and abroad. In 1999 this expressway was completed and has greatly shortened the distance between Chengdu and Yaan.

Traditionally Yaan is known for its Three Wonders，Yaan Rain (雅雨)，Yaan Fish (雅鱼) and Yaan Women (雅女). The Yaan Rain means that it rains a lot all year around in the Yaan area. The Yaan Fish refers to a very tasty local fish. The Yaan

Women mainly refers to pretty young ladies in Yaan.

The total population of pandas in China is about 1000, but almost the half are in Yaan as their habitat. Therefore the government department under the Ministry of Forests plans to build the second largest panda research center in Yaan. The largest Panda Research Centre is the Wolong Nature Reserve.

Yaan has many attractions. One of the highlights is Bifeng Valley, which lies 8km north to Yaan city. It is said that a legendary figure by the name of Huanglong (黄龙) used to stay in the valley. During his stay Huanglong became immortal, and his body began to grow wings.

Bifeng Valley is one of the best-protected reserves for plants and animals. The area includes a visitors' center, an ecological zoo and Ya'an Base of China Giant Panda Protection and Research Center. The whole scenic area consists of two gorges, one stretching 7km and the other 6km. These gorges are 79m at their widest and 200m at their highest. The scenic spots in the valley include Nuwa's Hand(女娲之手), Guanlongtan Waterfall(观龙潭瀑布), Bifeng Temple(碧峰寺), Nuwa Pool(女娲池), Shenying Peak(神鹰峰) and others. Steep cliffs, odd stone edifices, thick wood forests, clear water and cool breezes from waterfalls overwhelm visitors as they discover themselves in a fairy kingdom amidst sky-touching cliffs and unique beautiful flowers. The ecological zoo consists of three areas. One of these areas is the Wild Beast Zone. By taking a sightseeing bus, visitors can get close to animals such as tigers, lions and bears. The panda base was opened on December 2001. In September 2003, 16 pandas came here from Wolong Panda Protection Zone. Scientists and base staff are working hard, preparing everything to make sure that these pandas that are ready to return to the wild.

Well, we are approaching to Yaan city. We will go about a dozen kilometers to a turn-off and then drive directly to Bifeng Valley. It takes only 25 minutes. The tour of the valley will be one hour and thirty minutes. May I make a suggestion? When we are in the valley, we should stay in a group so that we are able to catch the bus and depart on time for lunch in Tianquan. After our walk I am sure we will all be hungry.

(***On the way after lunch***)

Now we are on the way to Erlangshan Tunnel (二郎山隧道), leaving Tianquan county behind. Tianquan county is located at the foot of Mt. Erlangshan, which is about 172km from Chengdu. Tianquan county has many natural resources. It is abundant in forests, animals, precious plants, hydropower, etc. This morning you were on Chengdu-Yaan expressway and enjoyed the view of the scenic countryside in Western Sichuan. After lunch in Tianquan town you will enjoy a bus-view of scenic Mt. Erlangshan.

Erlangshan Tunnel is 4162. 17m long. We will drive in a green valley along Qingyijiang River (青衣江). Of course, the best is always the hardest. We have to get over the first natural barrier—Mt. Erlangshan. This mountain was a major barrier between Sichuan and Tibet in the past years because of its high altitude and zigzagging road. But now, with the opening of Erlangshan tunnel, the former barrier has become an easy way. At present, Erlangshan pass is open for traffic only in one direction at a time. Every twelve hours it reverses, and it is the other side's turn to wait.

As we climb the mountain higher and higher, the fog clears,

and you will be rewarded with views down to small rivers and towns thousands of feet below. You can look down at the turbulent white and gray river surging forward.

When we get over Mt. Erlangshan, we will enter Sichuan Ganzi Tibetan Autonomous Prefecture (甘孜藏族自治州). Now I'd like to tell you some basic facts about the prefecture.

Ganzi Tibetan Autonomous Prefecture is one of the three autonomous nationalities prefectures in Sichuan Province. It was the first autonomous prefecture established in 1950 and covers an area of 153,002 square km. Kangding (康定) is its capital. The city is a very famous city all over the world. It used to be the most important market of the Tea-horse trade when in the past the Tibetan people came here to exchange their animals or animal products with the Han people.

In 2000, the prefecture held a festival ceremony to celebrate the 50th anniversary of its founding. The prefecture is situated at the edge of Qinghai-Tibetan Plateau. The climate varies in different altitude, much like that of Qinghai-Tibetan Plateau. Low temperatures, long winters, and abundant sunshine characterize the prefecture. Therefore, its economic activities vary due to its geographical landforms. Some local people mainly make a live by farming on the plains and in river valleys, some others focus on animal husbandry in the highlands.

The prefecture has three main tourist natural attractions due to its geographical landform: the wonderful sceneries, the local custom and the unique Kangba culture (康巴文化). The trip to Ganzi prefecture would be so successful and special with the local culture. Traditionally, local Tibetans usually present you a hada (哈达) to express their respect when you visit them. Their generous hospitality will make you feel welcome.

Now we are on the way to Moxi Old town where we will stay tonight. It is located in the mountains 50km southwest to Luding county. Moxi is a peaceful township shared by different ethnic nationalities. They include Han, Yi, Tibetan, and Tujia. There are some old, traditional wooden buildings at the bottom of the town, which gradually climbs its way up a hill. If you follow the town road up to a small pagoda, you will get a view of the surrounding scenery. In 1935, the Red Army troops arrived at Luding county, Chairman Mao and the Central Committee stayed in the town.

Tomorrow we start our tour of the glacier. Now the most popular way to ascend the mountain is by mini bus. It departs at the park entrance. You should wear warm clothes and bring sunglasses.

Actually Hailuogou National Glacier Park is part of Mt. Gongga (贡嘎山), which has an elevation of 7,556m. It is the highest peak in Sichuan Province as the King of Sichuan mountains. Snow remains on the mountain all year around. The glacier park rests in the valley that stretches down from Mt. Gongga. For roughly 1,600 years this ice wall has been creeping and carving its way down to the forests below and towards Moxi town. The park is the lowest glacier in Asia. The glacial melt has created the Dadu River (大渡河) and continues to alter the landscape further down the valley.

The glacier is about 30km inside the park. The mini bus and cable car are a short and quick way to take you to the viewing area. The climb is from about 2,000 or so meters to 3,200 at the top. As you gain elevation, the fog becomes thicker, and you hope to get high enough to be above it. The green, dense and tranquil scenery grows more and more beautiful.

Camp No. 3 lies at 2,940m. From the camp you have a 3km walk. From the top you will eventually be able to take a cable car over the glacier to the glacier base. On route to the base is the Glacier Waterfall Viewing Platform at 3000m. At the glacier-viewing stand are several beautifully constructed bamboo walkways, and if you are lazy, you can hire porters to transport you and your bags up.

At the viewing station you can see the Glacier Tongue to the left and to the right the No. 2 Glacier. The massive glacial field stretches out and disappears back into the clouds. At its densest, the glacier is 200m thick.

At Camp No. 4, you are close to the end of the glacier. It stretches 14.7km down from the slopes of Mt. Gongga. The ice extends 6km into the forests below, and finally tapers out near Camp No. 3.

As you take a short walk down into this amazing landscape, you will notice that the glacier surface is fractured with splits, holes, crevasses, and rivers disappear down one hole to pop up again hundreds of meters away. Everywhere is shattered rock and bluish ice, snow and mud. Further ahead is the summit of Mt.

Gongga at 7,556m. A local tour guide will walk with you and keep you away from deep crevices and melting points. The local tour guide will also point out wind tunnels and name mountain peaks.

Well, so much for the brief introductory information about the glacier. Tomorrow morning before our departure for the glacier, the local guide, the driver, and I will agree on a return time with you, and the bus will wait for you at Camp No. 3.

The day after tomorrow we will return to Chengdu. On the way back we will stop at Luding county. Luding is regarded as the most glorious moment of the Long March. It took place on the Luding Bridge over the Dadu River. I think it is worth a brief stop.

Luding Bridge was built in 1707 according to ancient historical accounts. It is an iron-chain bridge over Dadu River. It is 103. 7m long and 3m wide. There are 9 huge chains on the bridge floor and another 4 on the bride railings. There is a 20m high abutment on both sides of the river. All the 13 chains are fixed on the iron columns on the abutment. It is the bridge that functions as a gateway to Ganzi Prefecture.

On May 1935, the Red Army arrived at Dadu River and was ready to cross it. However, the number of available boats was inadequate, and Luding Bridge was the only alternative for the Red Army to move further to North China. So on May 29, 1935, the troops of the Red Army vanguard unit reached the bridge. The soldiers discovered that the Kuomintang (KMT, forshort) Army units at the opposite end had removed two-thirds of the planking, the remaining flooring had been set on fire. An advance unit of 22 men was ordered to take the bridge. They inched their way over the chains under the enemy's fire. Finally they successfully reached the other side and utterly defeated the KMT troops. Eighteen of the 22 survived the crossing. After another two hours, Luding Bridge was securely in the hands of the Communist Party and the Red Army. This crossing allowed the Long March to continue before the main body of the KMT forces could catch up with them.

The crossing of Dadu River during the Long March was a truly heroic feat. the glorious feat has been written into the Chinese revolutionary history. Chairman Mao wrote the great feat in his poem by the name of *the Long March*, "The waves of Golden Sand buffet the towering warm cliffs; the iron-chain bridge spans the Dadu River with cold stiffs".

After the founding of the People's Republic of China, the Central Committee built Luding Revolutionary Relics Showroom and a monument in commemoration of the Red Army's Long March in Luding county. Before the monument, two bronze statues of the Red Army solders are rising straight up; one soldier throwing a hand grenade, the other one is firing at the enemy. In 1961, Luding Bridge was listed by the State Council as one of the protected treasures of the state. The crossing of Dadu River contributed greatly to the Long March, and over the years, many movies have been made to memory the soldiers' heroism.

Well, so much for my introduction today. In 20 minutes we will arrive at our hotel in Moxi. Do you have anything to ask me? I will be pleased to answer your questions concerning the accommodation for tonight and the tour tomorrow, or about anything I just told you.

KEY WORDS & EXPRESSIONS 关键词汇及表达法

trek 做艰苦的旅行；泛指旅行
predict 预言
network 网络，网
jam 交通拥挤
headquarter 指挥部，总部
modernization 现代化
herbal 草药的
meditation 沉思；冥想
calmness 平静，定静
sky-touching 摩天的
barrier 栅栏，屏障
altitude 高度
zigzagging 曲折的
turbulent 狂暴的；吵闹的
surging 汹涌的；澎湃的
autonomous 自治的，自治权的
hospitality 热情的款待
glacier 冰川
sunglasses 太阳眼镜
creep 爬行
tranquil 安静的
porter 行李搬运工
fracture (使)破碎，(使)破裂
crevasse 裂缝
shatter 打碎，使散开
bluish 带蓝色的
crevice 裂缝
melting point 溶化点

abutment 桥台
columns 圆柱
alternative 可供选择的
vanguard 前锋，先锋
planking 木板
an advance unit 先遣队
heroic feat 英雄壮举
grenade 手榴弹

Chengdu—Guan'an
成都—广安

Good morning, ladies and gentlemen. We are scheduled to leave Chengdu at 8:30 after breakfast at the hotel. We will drive to Guan'an(广安). On the way we will pass Suining(遂宁), Nanchong(南充)and Bazhong(巴中), where we will stop for some sightseeing. I believe you all will have a wonderful time while visiting each place, sometimes we may make some adjustment. If you have suggestions, please do not hesitate to let me know. I will do my best to help you make your trip happy and enjoyable.

Well, Now we are on the Chengdu—Nanchong Expressway. The total length is 214km, and it takes about two hour to get to Nanchong city. Before the completion of this expressway, the bus drive usually took at least 5 hours between Chengdu and Nanchong along the old road. This expressway greatly helps speed up transportation.

(***on the way to Suining***)

Now we are approaching Suining where a number of scenic spots will amaze you, including the Salt Lake or the Dead Sea of China(中国死海)in Daying county(大英县), Guangde Monastery

(广德寺) and Lingquan Hill(灵泉山).

According to the geological studies, 150 million years ago, Daying area was once under the shallow water ground, which was surrounded by sea. A large amount of salt deposited because of the long-term sea ebb and flow, and the shallow water therefore had the high density of salt. Due to the twice movement of mountain formation and upheaval, the shallow water area had been imbedded 3,000m beneath ground; and it gradually turned into an underground salty lake. At present, this salt lake keeps a large reserve of salt water up to 4,200 million tons. It is called "dead" because the high salinity prevents any fish or other visible aquatic organism to live in its water. As every 4km contains 1km of salt in the water, the high density of the water causes a curious phenomenon: it is impossible for a bather to sink. The sea water in the lake is rich in more than 40 kinds of mineral substances and trace elements, including sodium, potassium, calcium, bromine, iodine etc. Research has shown that the water in the lake have a positive therapeutic effect on illness related to rheumatism, arthritis, skin, blood vessels or respiratory problems.

(***on the way to Guangde***)

Now we are on the way to Guangde Monastery. It is a Buddhist temple, 1.5km west to Suining city. Originally it was build in the Tang Dynasty in 618, known as Stone Buddha Monastery(石佛寺). After Ke You(克幽), an honorific Buddhist master arrived at the monastery in 765, he began to take charge of the monastery and teach Buddhism there. Since then, Guangde Monastery became known as one of important temples in western Sichuan. In the Ming Dynasty, it was renamed as Guangde Monastery. Every year thousands of pilgrims and local people visit the monastery, especially in February when a temple fair occurs or in September when Guanyin's birthday is celebrated.

(*on the way to Lingquan*)

We are on the way to Lingquan Hill, which lies to the east of Suining city. The highlight of the hill includes Guanyin Highest Peak, Green Dragon Mouth on the Eastern Peak, White Tiger Mouth on the Western Peak, and Wooden Fish Slope along the Southern Peak. Luxuriant forests cover the hill where spring water remains limpid and its pools never dry up. On the hill is an ancient monastery called Lingquan Temple(灵泉寺). Originally it was built in the Sui Dynasty. Lingquan Hill is well known for its quietness, spring water, forests and the temple.

(*on the way to Nanchong*)

Well, travelers, we are now in Nanchong area(南充). Nanchong has a very long history. In 202 B.C., the Han imperial government set up a county-level administration office in Nanchong. After new China was established in 1949, Nanchong city was the location of the provincial administrative offices in charge of North Sichuan. At present, Nanchong is not only the largest commercial centre of Northeastern Sichuan but also the centre of sciences and education. There are five institutions of higher education, including Southwest Petroleum University of China(西南石油学院), Xihua Normal University(西华师范大学), Northern Sichuan Medical College(川北医学院) and Nanchong Technical College(南充技术学院). Nanchong has five counties, three districts and Langzhong city(阆中). under its jurisdiction.

(*on the way to Langzhong*)

Now, we are approaching to Langzhong city. You will visit a number of tourist spots, including Langzhong Fengshui Museum (阆中风水博物馆), fengshui means "geomancy"; Zhang Fei Temple(张飞庙), Langzhong Ancient Imperial Examination Centre(阆中贡院), Langzhong Ancient City(阆中古城) and Tengwang Pavilion(滕王阁).

Now I'd like to offer you some basic information about these places before we arrive at Langzhong city.

Langzhong Fengshui Museum covers an area of nearly 2,000 square meters. It is the first Fengshui museum in China. What is the Feng Shui? In ancient times, the Chinese believed that the movements of the sun and moon did affect spiritual currents which influenced people's daily lives. This "cosmic breath" is known as Feng Shui (wind and water). It is said that it was also affected by the form and size of hills and mountains, the height and shape of buildings, and by the direction of roadways. Ancient people were aware of the importance of geomancy (divination by means of lines and figures) in the location and orientation of buildings and other structures. Geomancy started in the Zhou Dynasty, and a manual of the rules concerned was published around 320 A.D.. In addition to determining the orientation of buildings and doors, Feng Shui masters also counter the influence of negative cosmic breath by the use talismans (dragons and other symbols) on buildings and other structures and charms (power words and other inscriptions) on paper scrolls or tablets.

In front of the museum entrance, some cloth banners are fluttering in the breeze. These banners display the patterns of lucky supernatural beasts. These beasts include Green Dragon(苍

龙，Canglong) that represents the east，Phoenix-Like Beast(朱雀，Zhuque) the south，White Tiger (白虎，Baihu) the west and Tortoise Like Beast(玄武，Xuanwu, with a Snake Winding Round Tortoise Like Beast) the north. These supernatural beasts represent the images of stars，and therefore they are called "Four Images."

As you step into the museum，a narrator will explain Feng Shui in detail and its relation with the construction of an ancient city. By the narration，pictures and photos presentation，visitors can get a general picture of Feng Shui and its affection.

Zhang Fei Temple is located in Langzhong city. The large compound consists of many ancient buildings，Zhang Fei's Tomb and a back yard. According to ancient documents，Zhang Fei garrisoned Langzhong with his army，also in Langzhong he was murdered by his two bad-tempered subordinates when he was in sleep. Local people built up a number of temples across the country to commemorate him. The temple in Langzhong is one of them.

Who was Zhang Fei? He was a black-faced general of the Kingdom of Shu. Toward the end of the Han Dynasty Zhang Fei swore brotherhood with Liu Bei(刘备) and Guan Yu (关羽) at the Peach Garden(桃园). He followed Liu Bei to suppress rebels and defend the Han Empire. It is said that he had large eyes, a pointed and bristling moustache; he spoke in a loud bass voice and looked irresistible. His angry roar feared many brave men. His most spectacular battle was on the Long Slope Bridge (长板坡桥)，where he roared so fiercely that one of Cao Cao's generals dropped from the horse, died suddenly.

Langzhong Ancient Imperial Examination Centre is one of well-preserved places in China, where imperial exams were hold in ancient times. During the Ming and Qing dynasties, Langzhong city served as the provisional capital of Sichuan for 10 years. During this period the imperial examination at provincial level was held several times in the city. Later, the provincial capital was moved away from Langzhong, but the examination Centre in Langzhong continued its service providing exams at prefectural level. The current centre is open to visitors to take a close look at ancient objects, pictures, photos and ancient exam room style.

What is the Imperial Examination System? In the Han Dynasty, ministers, high-ranking officials or local authorities recommended to the imperial court talented persons who excelled in virtue and had an outstanding ability. The court would offered them government posts or promote them from lower positions to higher ones.

Since the Sui Dynasty, the system of imperial examinations was gradually established. All men, virtuous and healthy, could take exams. During the Tang Dynasty, government positions, however, went mainly to aristocrats rather than to people who passed the civil service examination. Only ten percent of government officials were from the imperial examinations.

There were two kinds of examinations during the Tang Dynasty. One kind was influenced by Confucius with the Four Books and Five Classics(四书五经); the other with Daoism. The examination in the Song Dynasty was entirely based on the Confucian Classics, and the Daoist examination was eliminated totally. Over fifty percent of government officials were recruited from the civil service examination. The candidates had to memorize the Five Classics, interpret passages, master their literary style, and use Confucian philosophy to interpret the Classics and construct political advice. By the end of the Song Dynasty, however, the imperial examination became intolerable; it was completely abandoned after the fall of the Qing Dynasty.

Langzhong city is known as one of four major ancient towns in China. The other three include Lijiang in Yunnan Province(云南丽江), Pingyao in Shanxi Province(山西平遥) and Shexian in Anhui Province(安徽歙县).

As you walk along a flagstone laneway in the ancient town of Langzhong, you will be amazed at so many old wooden buildings. Most of the building has just one storey. There are dozens of winding laneways, Red lanterns are hung all sides everywhere. Many wooden buildings and houses could be dated back to Ming or Qing Dynasty, but a few to Tang or Song Dynasty. In the old town there are many courtyard surrounded by four ancient-style buildings. The courtyards connect with each other, forming a deep and quiet passageway. In some courtyards, residents grow flower and plants.

After the tour of this old town, we take a bus to a hill outside the city, where you can have a bird-eye view of the town. You will see that every house is sitting beneath, quite and tranquil. From time to time, you can hear some hustling and bustling coming from the lanes. You will never forget such a beautiful tour in the town.

In China there are several famous towers, Huanghe Tower(黄鹤楼), located in Hubei Wuhan, Yueyang Tower(岳阳楼), a three-storied watchtower at the west gate in Yueyang, Hunan and

Tengwang Tower(藤王阁) on the bank of Gangjiang River(赣江), west to Nanchang City(南昌).

In Langzhong there is a tower also called Tengwang Tower, 3.5km north of the local city. In 662 A.D., Li Yuanying (李元婴) had people build the tower during his official service as a provincial supervisor in Longzhou (隆州) on the present site of Langzhong city. This tower is a Tang-style ancient building with Xieshan Roof (歇山顶). The Xieshan Roof is a nine-ridge roof. It includes one horizontal ridge, four slightly sloping downward ridges and still another four supporting ridges. In front of the tower stands a Sarira pagoda, built in the 4th century.

(***on the way to Bazhong***)

Well, we are approaching to Bazhong area(巴中地区) in northeastern Sichuan. Bazhong abounds with tourist resources. These include the former sites of the General Headquarter of the Fourth Front Army of the Chinese Workers' and Peasants' Red Army(红四方面军总指挥部), and the General Political Department of the same army(红四方面总政治部), the Martyrs' Cemetery Park of the same army(红四方面军烈士陵园), the Museum of Sichuan and Sha'anxi Revolutionary Base(川陕革命根据地博物馆), Nuoshui Scenic Spot(诺水河风景区), Guangwu Mountain Scenic Spot(光雾山风景区) and others. For the trip today, we will visit the sites of the General Headquarter and the General Department, and pay a tribute to the martyrs in the cemetery. Now I'd like to offer you some basic information about these places before we arrive there.

The former site of the General Headquarter of the Fourth Front Army lies in the centre of Tongjiang county (通江县). It faces Tongjiang River (通江河), with Lenin Park (列宁公园)

behind. The former site consists of Dacheng Hall(大成殿), small buildings on the either side of the hall, Lingxing Gate(棂星门), Wanren Site Wall(万仞宫墙)and Panchi Pool(泮池).

Xu Xiangqian(徐向前), commander-in-chief of the Fourth Front Army, and other leaders led the army and established a revolution base in Bazhong area. These leaders and army soldiers underwent hundreds of battles against Kuomingtang reactionary forces and made brilliant victories.

This former site remains well preserved. In 1988, the State Council designated it as a protected treasure of the state. At present, the site has turned into the memorial museum.

The former site of the General Political Department also lies in the centre of Tongjiang county. It is close to the former site of the General Headquarter. All the wooden buildings on the site were built in the Ming Dynasty, and in 1988 the State Council designated it as a protected treasure of the state.

The Martyrs' Cemetery Park is located in Wang Ping Village (王坪村), 40km east of the centre of Tongjiang county. Originally it was called Wangping Martyrs' Mausoleum(王坪烈士墓). Built in 1934, this park occupies an area of one hundred mu, where more than 3,800 officers and men of the Red Army were buried. In 1989, the State Council approved this park as a national martyrs' memorial.

The Museum of Sichuan and Sha'anxi Revolutionary Base is a special museum that focuses on the collection and research of revolutionary historical relics of Sichuan and Sha'anxi revolutionary districts. Located on Nankan(南龛)Slope, south of Bazhong city, this museum has more than 20,000 items of relics, vividly demonstrating the activities of the Fourth Red Army under the leadership of the Communist Party.

In February 1932, the Fourth Red Army arrived at Northern Sichuan and established the revolutionary base that covered 23 counties in Sichuan and Shaanxi with a population of more than 5 million. Their local revolutionary activities lasted until June 1935.

(***on the way to Deng Xiaoping's Former Residence***)

Well, we will soon arrive at Deng Xiaoping's Former Residence. I'd like to give you a brief introduction about the residence.

Deng Xiaoping's Former Residence is 7km away from the centre of Guang'an city. In June 2001, Sichuan Provincial Party Committee and Sichuan People's Government approved the plan to establish a zone for the protection of Deng Xiaoping's Former Residence. Their purpose was to express the immeasurable memory of Comrade Deng Xiaoping.

With the approval of the Central Committee of the Communist Party of China, both Deng Xiaoping Exhibition Hall and Deng Xiaoping Bronze Statue have been set up. The hall consists of several parts, including three exhibition sections, a film projection room and a rare article exhibition section.

The residence is a traditional farming family's courtyard house in North Sichuan. It covers an area of 833.4 square meters, with a group of one-storied buildings, which surround a courtyard on three sides. In this tree-shaded, tile-roofed residence that Deng Xiaoping's forefathers had lived for three generations, and he himself had lived 15 years after his birth on August 22, 1904. In the courtyard compound grow sago cycad trees(铁树)and other plants.

Not far from the residence is Hanlin Courtyard. Hanlin mean "member of Imperial Academy." This courtyard was owned by Deng Shiming(邓时敏), who was a member of the Imperial Academy of the Qing Dynasty. He built it more than 200 years ago after he returned to his native place from the academy. This courtyard appears magnificent, and the structure consists mainly of wooden vertical pillars and crossbeams. In addition, each house is covered with a nine-ridge roof and tiles. After Deng Shiming passed away, his courtyard turned into an old-style private school. In 1909, Deng Xiaoping studied there.

Located in Xiexing town(协兴镇)of Guang'an District, Beishan Primary School (北山小学堂)started in 1009. It was jointly sponsored by Deng Xiaoping's father and some other local gentlemen. It was in this school that Deng Xiaoping studied Chinese language, arithmetic and other courses from 1911 to 1915. In December of 2002, Sichuan People's Government designated the school buildings as a protected treasure of the province.

There is a well in Deng Xiaoping's Residence. It had a history of than 500 years when the Dengs migrated into Guang'an. The head of the well is round in shape, and the surface of water from the well is 60 cm higher than the ground level.

At present, people come and visit Deng Xiaoping's Former Residence across the country. At the same time, this residence works as the base for education in socialism with Chinese characteristics, as well as education in patriotism and in the revolutionary tradition.

Deng Xiaoping was the late leader of the Communist Party of China. He was the core of the "second generation" Communist Party leadership. He established "Socialism with Chinese characteristics," "Chinese economic reform" theory; and opened China to the global market. His goal was a wealthy, modern, powerful China. His method was the open door, establishing ties with the United States and other Western nations, encouraging international investment, private enterprise, family farming and other aspects of a market economy.

Deng Xiaoping Theory(邓小平理论) is the series of political and economic ideologies first developed by Deng Xiaoping. It emphasizes economic construction and stability with Chinese characteristics. Deng Xiaoping Theory has inherited Marxism-Leninism and Mao Zedong Thought and developed on that basis. Deng Xiaoping summed up new experience, put forward new thoughts and created new theories according to China's reality and the latest development of the world.

Well, here we are at the entrance to the residence, Please follow me after we get off the bus. More details will be given to you concerning each part as we arrive at each spot.

KEY WORDS & EXPRESSIONS 关键词汇及表达法

ebb 落潮

upheaval 剧变

salinity 盐度

aquatic 水生的

phenomenon 现象

trace elements 微量元素

sodium 钠
potassium 钾
calcium 钙
bromine 溴
iodine 碘
therapeutic 治疗的
rheumatism 风湿病
arthritis 关节炎
respiratory 呼吸的
honorific 尊敬的
luxuriant 繁茂的
administrative 行政的
petroleum 石油
jurisdiction 管辖权
geomancy 占卜(撒泥于地,观其形推卜吉凶)
divination 占卜
manual 手册
talismans 护身符
supernatural 超自然的
subordinate 部下
commemorate 纪念
bristling 竖立的
spectacular 奇观
prefectural 县的;府的
compound 用围墙(或篱笆等)围起的场地
authority 职权
virtuous 善良的
aristocrat 贵族
candidate 候选人

philosophy 哲学
flagstone 铺石路
passageway 通道
hustling 奔忙的
bustling 熙攘的
supervisor 监督人
sarira 舍利
headquarter 总部
martyr 烈士
cemetery 公墓
commander-in-chief 总司令
residence 住宅
immeasurable 不可计量的
forefather 前辈
cycad 铁树
vertical 立式的
crossbeam 横梁
sponsor 主办者
arithmetic 算术
investment 投资
stability 稳定

Chengdu—Shunan Bamboo Forest
成都—蜀南竹海

Good morning, travellers, we are ready to depart for the trip to Shunan Bamboo Forest (蜀南竹海). Today we will pass Longquan District(龙泉驿区) and counties including Jianyang(简阳) and Ziyang(资阳). On the way we will also visit cities such as Neijiang(内江), Zigong(自贡) and Yibing(宜宾). The purpose of this sightseeing excursion is to explore the local culture and tradition and give you a wonderful picture of Sichuan. I will give you some guide-information whenever it is necessary.

Well, travellers, we are passing Longquan district. It is one of nine districts under the jurisdiction of Chengdu People's Government. Longquan is well known for its production of high-quality fruits, especially juicy peaches. In spring, peach, pear and other fruit trees are all in blossom that is seen everywhere on Longquan hill. During the flower blossoming period, local fruit growers hold a festival, and citizens from the city downtown flow onto the hill where they sit under trees, drinking tea and enjoying the beauty of flowers. In autumn, fruit growers pick up fruits and sell everywhere in and off Chengdu.

Chengdu citizens tend to spend weekends in the countryside, longquan area is their choice. Fruit growers are always ready to host citizens in their courtyards with tasty food and comfortable accommodation, food costs are reasonable. On weekends, they walk into traditional courtyards among the beautiful surroundings on the hill. There they take part in some out-door activities, playing chess and mahjong and enjoying the beauty of natural scenery. The host fruit growers greatly contribute to the charm of the leisure weekend activities.

(***on the way to Ziyang Area***)

We are now in Ziyang area that covers Anyue county(安岳县), Lezhi county(乐至县), and two county-level cities-Ziyang (资阳市) and Jianyang(简阳市). The total population amounts to 4,870,000.

Ziyang possesses a good advantage and traffic convenience for its economical development. Traditionally this area serves as a key grain production base in Sichuan. In recent years, its local agriculture continues its traditional pursuit, and at the same time its diversified economy has made great progress in aquaculture, and processing industry of agricultural and sideline products.

Ziyang area abounds with rich cultural and tourist resources that include Ancient Stone Sculptures in Anyue(安岳石刻) and Sancha Lake in Jianyang(简阳三岔湖).

(***on the way to Sancha Lake***)

Now we are on the way to Sancha Lake (三岔湖), which lies in the southwest of Jianyang, 60km from Chengdu. Actually the lake is a man-made reservoir, but in recent years it serves as a resort for local people. The lake is 18km in length from south to north; 7km in width from east to west, with 113 small islands and islets. Sancha Lake is an ideal place for relaxation where visitors can fish by the lake, row a boat on the lake or stroll on the tranquil islets.

(***on the way to Ancient Sculpture Carvings***)

We are on the way to the Ancient Sculpture carvings in Anyue. The carving started in the Northern and Southern Dynasties and flourished from the Tang Dynasty to Song dynasty. According to recent relic survey across the county, the numbers of stone sculptures total 100,000 pieces, and these are located at some 105 places of which 45 places have been well preserved.

There are several local sculpture sites that are worth attention. The Reclining Buddha Valley(卧佛沟) is located in Bamiaoxiang township(八庙乡), 25km away from the town of Anyue. The 500m long cliffs along the valley present 139 caves with 1,600 carved statues. The highlight of these sculptures is an image of Sakyamuni(释迦牟尼涅) in a reclining position. This 25m long statue is carved on the cliff, which depicts the grand occasion as Sakyamuni enters Nirvana. About twenty busts of Bodhisattvas respectfully stand around in rows.

Yuanjue Cave(圆觉洞), close to the town of Anyue county, is known for its stone sculptures of 12 Pratyeka-Buddhas in various postures(十二圆觉像)and take turns asking questions. Yuan Jue means "total awakening." There are 1,993 statues in and outside the cave.

The carved image of Ziyang Great Buddha(资阳大佛) is located in Dafo township(大佛乡), south of the town of Anyue county. Its carving started in 793 and end in 1131. It is said that this image is considered as the third largest Buddha sculpture in Sichuan.

(***on the way to Neijiang Area***)

We are now in Neijiang area that covers Neijiang city(内江市), and three counties including Zizhong(资中), Longchang(隆昌)and Weiyuan(威远). Neijiang city is one of eight large cities in Sichuan.

Traditionally, Neijiang is a sugarcane-producing area, and its industry is well developed. Neijiang city is honored with the title of "Sugar-Sweet City". In autumn and winter you will see vendors selling sugarcane wherever you are in Neijiang.

Like most other areas in Sichuan, local people in Neijiang enjoy a relaxing lifestyle. In the city parks, people of all ages take part in social dancing, drum dancing or other outdoor physical activities. Teahouses are busy with tea drinkers who chat and drink tea or play chess or mahjiong for fun.

Neijiang abounds with tourist resources. It has 180 cultural and scenic spots, including Zhang Daqian Memorial Hall(张大千纪念馆), Shengshui Monastery(圣水寺)and Guyu Lake(古宇湖) in Longchang.

As we are arriving in Neijiang city, we will go and visit Zhang Daqian Memorial hall, which is worth attention.

Zhang Daqian was one of the most internationally renowned Chinese artists of the 20th century. He was a native of Neijiang and studied painting since childhood. In his 20s, he studied textile-dyeing techniques in Japan. In 1956, Zhang Daqian and Picasso met with each other. Picasso showed him some drawings done in "Chinese" style, but Zhang Daqian remarked that they were not executed with the right tools and gave Picasso a set of Chinese brushes. In 1983, he died in Taibei(台北).

The hall compound is located on the top of Dongyanyuan Hill (东岩园), north of Neijiang city. The compound consists of Datangfeng Hall (大堂风), the Art Gallery, and corridors, pavilians, pools and rockery. Zhang Daqian statue stands inside the main hall, and the art gallery displays paintings and calligraphy by Zhang Daqian and Zhang Shanzi (张善子), the second elder brother of Zhang Daqian.

(***on the way to Zigong City***)

Well, travelers, we are approaching to Zigong city, a prefecture-level city in the south of Sichuan. Zigong has four districts and two counties under its jurisdiction. It is known as the Salt Capital of China, the hometown of dinosaur, and the Lantern City in South China. It boasts Zigong Dinosaur Museum (自贡恐龙博物馆)and Zigong Salt History Museum(自贡盐业历史博物馆). In addition, each year the city holds its traditional lantern festival that attracts visitor home and abroad.

Here we are at the entrance of Zigong Dinosaur Museum, which is located 11km northeast of Zigong city. This museum is also called Zigong National Geological Park, and it is one of the three on-the-site dinosaur museums in the world. The other two museums are the American National Dinosaur Park and the Canadian Dinosaur Park.

About 150 million years ago, a large number of dinosaurs lived in Zigong area. The unearthed dinosaurs include sauropodas, stegosaurs and pterosaurs. The Dinosaur Museum was open in 1987. It was built on the same site where the dinosaur fossils had been unearthed.

Zigong Dinosaur Museum consists of Introduction Hall, Jurassic Fauna and Flora Hall, Specimen Hall and Fossil Cemetery. In the Introduction Hall, there is an electronic map of world that shows the locations of dinosaur fossils on the earth. In addition, a bar chart provides all details about the local dinosaurs unearthed in Zigong. The Jurassic Fauna and Flora Hall displays a collection of animals and plants during the dinosaur age. There are collections of dinosaur specimen like Shunosaurus Lii(李氏蜀龙), Omeisaurus Tianfuensis(天府峨眉龙)and others in Specimen Hall. The Fossil Cemetery covers 17,000 square meters, which displays skeletons of dinosaur species and other vertebrate animals.

(***on the way to Zigong salt History Museum***)

Well, we are approaching to Zigong Salt History Museum. It is located in the downtown area of Zigong city. It consists of Xiqin Guild Hall(西秦会馆) and Wangye Tempe(王爷庙). In the Eastern Han Dynasty, Zigong grew into a largest salt production district, many local people engaged in the salt industrial production. The museum displays the history of well salt(井盐) production technology. Many of the exhibits are over 130 different types of drilling tools dating from the Qing Dynasty to the period of the 1960s. These tools differ in length and weight, and they were used in traditional Chinese well salt drilling industry. In addition, some ancient written contracts, accounting books and Yankou Book(岩口簿)are on show. Yankoubu Book is a minute book that provides information related to drilling preparation, use of different tools in drilling process, daily schedule and information about rock layers.

During the Emperor Qianlong's rein of the Qing Dynasty, merchants from Shaanxi built Xiqin Guild Hall. In the beginning, the merchants planned to use it as a meeting hall so that merchants from Shaanxi could gather together here when they did business in Zigong. Later, the construction continued its expansion, and however, the present architecture still embodies ancient styles dating from the Qing Dynasty due to its meticulous design and wooden structure.

(***Zigong Lantern Festival***)

Here we are at the place where the local Lantern Festival is held. As a traditional cultural activity in China, the Lantern Festival falls on the 15th day of the 1st lunar month. When the Spring Festival comes, Chinese make lanterns and participate in lantern festivals in the evening to view colourful lantern lights that shine under the brightness of the moonlight as tradition.

Zigong Lantern Festival has a long history. It started from the Tang Dynasty. In 1960s, the local lantern festival advanced with the display of poetry, calligraphy, and painting as well as music, dancing, and theatre performance. Since 1987, local people have kept improving quality of the festival, combined with update technology in the fields of machinery, electronics, acoustics, optics, and architecture. Their purpose is to promote Zigong Lantern Festival as an international event, with unique artistic features. In the festival, the highlight is to watch colourful lanterns in varied shapes, which include electric wall lamps, and electric-powered lanterns of life-size animals. In addition, groups of lanterns recount episodes from classic novels.

(***on the way to Yibin City***)

Well, travellers, we are now approaching to Yibin city, which is located at the junction of Minjiang and Jinshajiang rivers. Yibin is a prefecture-level city, with one district and nine counties in its jurisdiction. These counties include Xingwen(兴文) and Changning(长宁).

As you know, Wu Liangye Liquor(五粮液) is produced in Yibin. In 1915, the liquor won a gold medal when Zhang Wanhe (张万和) Distillery exhibited the liquor at the Panama International Exposition. In 1991, it won the title of one of the Ten Top Brands in China.

Yibin abounds with tourist resources, including Shunan Bamboo Forest(蜀南竹海) and Xingwen Stone Forest(兴文石林). According to our schedule, we first of all go and tour Wu Liangye Liquor Distillery and taste the liquor before our trip to the bamboo and stone forests. Now I'd like to give you a brief introduction of Shunan Bamboo Forest and Xingwen Stone Forest.

Shunan Bamboo Forest is located in Changling county, 81km away from Yibin city. This immense forest covers an area of 120 square kilometres with an elevation of 600 - 1,000m. In 1991, this forest was listed as one of the 40 best scenic areas across the country. The forest consists of 27 ridges and 500 hills that are all covered by bamboo groves. There are 58 species of bamboo plants, including Ci bamboo(慈竹), Mian bamboo(绵竹), Xiangfei bamboo(香妃竹), etc. 124 scenic spots spread in the forest such as Tianbao Village(天宝寨), Qinglong Lake(青龙湖), Qicai Waterfall(七彩飞瀑)and Feicui Corridor(翡翠长廊). In summer, trees send forth fragrance and streams murmur. The climate in the forest is comfortably cool. Walking in the tranquil bamboo groves, visitors could hear birds singing and streams murmuring. Their visual senses are overcome by bamboo shoots, which sprout everywhere in the spring season.

Xingwen Stone Forest is located in Xingwen county, and it covers an area of 126.4 square kilometres. The stone forest is well known for its typical shapes of stone and caves due to karst landforms, consisting of stone forest, stone sea and clusters of karst caves beneath ground. Its scenic area mainly consists of Tianquan Cave Scenic Area(天泉洞中心景区), Jiusi Mountain Scenic Area(九丝山景区), Dabazongyuan Scenic Area(大坝综源景区) and Zhoujiagou Karst Cave Scenic Area(周家沟溶洞景区). The rocks and stones stand in great numbers; some of them resemble young dragons with horns, some look like tigers or leopards; no rocks are alike. Each appearance seems imposing, beautiful or strange. Tianquan Cave Scenic Area has 26 caves of which Tianquan cave consists of 5 layers and 12 halls. The cave is 208m deep, 650m at its widest and 490 m at its narrowest. In 2004, the stone forest was added to the list of national geological parks.

KEY WORDS & EXPRESSIONS 关键词汇及表达法

grower 种植者
accommodation 住处
possess 拥有
diversified 各种的
aquaculture 水栽法
sideline 副业
reclining 斜倚的
Nirvana 涅槃
respectful 恭敬的
awakening 觉醒中的
sugarcane 甘蔗
textile-dyeing 纺织染色工艺
execute 制作
dinosaur 恐龙
sauropoda 蜥蜴
stegosaur 剑龙
pterosaurs 翼龙
fauna 动物群
flora 植物群
skeleton 骸骨
vertebrate 脊椎动物
guild 行会
accounting 会计
brightness 明亮
electronics 电子学
acoustics 声学
optics 光学
grove 树丛

murmur 小声说话
visual 视觉的
karst 喀斯特地形
imposing 壮观的

Chengdu—Guangyuan
成都—广元

Good morning, travelers, we are scheduled to leave Chengdu at 8:30 after breakfast at the hotel. We will drive to Guangyuan (广元). On the way we will pass Guanghan(广汉), Deyang(德阳)and Mianyang (绵阳)where we will stop for some sightseeing. I would very much appreciate your understanding in case that we have to make some adjustment to our schedule.

(***On the way***)

Well, travelers, we are on Cheng-Mian Expressway(成绵公路), and usually it takes about 30 minutes to get to Guanghan by private car, or 60 minutes by bus. Guanghan, 23km south of Chengdu, is home to the Civil Aviation Flight University of China (广汉民航飞行学院), where they train most of China's pilots, air traffic controllers and flight attendants. The Duck River(鸭子河) runs through Guanghan and you will discover a 2km stretch of it lined with the usual teahouse and mah-jong set-up. Guanghan has the best Sichuan Pork dish. The pork strips are meatier and thicker than most others.

The main point of visiting Guanghan is to view bronzeware in Sanxindui Museum, which is located about 7km from Guanghan. It happened in spring, 1929 when a farmer and his family were digging an irrigation ditch in Nanxingzhen area (南兴镇). His son found a circular piece of jade when he dug the field with his hoe.

It was on the same spot that 400 valuable relics had been discovered. They included stone jade, jade rings, and other jade articles. Between July and September 1986, archeologists discovered two large-scale covered holes in the ground, where they unearthed more than a thousand priceless treasures. The archeologists believed that the two holes used to be places where ancient people offered sacrifices to their gods or ancestors. In January 1988, the State Council designated Sanxingdui Ruins as a protected treasure of the state. The museum was opened to the public in October 1997. It gives a general profile of Sanxindui Sites, and displays relics unearthed from the No. 1 and No. 2 sacrificial pits. The best part of all the unearthed artifacts include Eyes Protruding Bronze Mask（纵目面具）, Bian Jade Tablet（边璋）, Wheel of the Sun（太阳轮）, Bronze Standing Figure（青铜立人像）, Big Bronze Tree（大型铜神树）, Gold Scepter（金仗）, Gold-Masked Bronze Human Head（金面青铜人头像）and others. The interior in the museum is mood-lit, and it sets the tone for viewing these objects. You need a few hours to see everything.

（***On the way to Deyang***）

Well, we continue our trip towards Deyang city after our tour of Sanxindui Museum. Deyang area is well known for its natural and cultural recourses, including Li Bing Mausoleum（李冰墓）, Deyang Confucius Temple（孔庙）, the numerous former sites dating from the Three Kingdoms Period, the Wall of Stone Sculptures at Deyang（德阳石刻艺术墙）and Mianzhu New-Year Picture（绵竹年画）. Deyang abounds with local dishes like Luojiang Soybean Chickens（罗江豆鸡）, Xiaoquan Fruit-Juicy Beef（孝泉果汁牛肉）, Lianshan Twice-Cooked Pork（连山回锅肉）, Zhongjiang Fine Dried Noodles（中江挂面）and others.

Today we will go and visit Li Bing Mausoleum and Deyang Confucius Temple. I'd like to offer you some basic information about these places.

More than 2,000 years ago, Li Bing served as a local governor of Shu state. He and his son designed a water control system to harness Minjiang River(岷江) that flowed fast down from mountains. As it ran across Chengdu Plain, it frequently flooded Chengdu agricultural area, and local farmers suffered much from the water disaster. When the construction was completed, the dam system automatically diverted Mingjiang River and channeled it into irrigation canals. Afterwards he went to Luoshui area(洛水) where he organized thousands of local people to harness a river nearby. It was said that Li Bing died from fatigue on the construction site and he was buried on Zhangshan Hill(章山).

In 1992, in order to commemorate Li Bing, local people began to rebuild Li Bing Mausoleum, and completed it within three years. The newly reconstructed mausoleum consists of a group of ancient styled buildings that remind visitors of the constructions from the Qin and Han dynasties. The tomb, 10m in diameter, is a round building. It has been decorated with stone carvings, demonstrating Li Bing's life stories. Behind the tomb, stand tablets saying "When the river flows in zigzags, cut a straight channel; when the riverbed is wide and shallow, dig it deeper. (深掏滩,低作堰。)"

Deyang Confucius Temple lies in Deyang city. It is the best-preserved Confuciu Temple in Southwest China, with an area of 29,700 square meters. It includes Lingxing Gate(棂星门), the front portal of the temple; Dacheng Hall(大成殿), the main building in the inner courtyard; Qinsheng Hall(启圣殿), the Shrine of the Great Wise Men.

The temple was established in 1206, and it underwent reconstruction and expansion several times in the Ming and Qing dynasties. The present layout of the temple can date back to 1850, Daoguang period of Qing Dynasty(清道光年间). The temple looks impressive, with red walls and yellow glazed tiles; the main buildings are built on a north-south axis(中柱线), the doors of the main buildings all facing south. Dacheng Hall contains the statues of Confucius, the Four Correlates(四配) and the Twelve Philosophers(十二哲). The wings to the east and west of the hall are devoted to 72 Confucius's disciples.

Temple of Confucius or Confucian Temple is a temple devoted to the memory of Confucius, and the sages and philosophers of Confucianism. The largest and oldest Temple of Confucius is found in Confucius's hometown, Qufu(曲阜) in Shangdong at present. With the spread of Confucian learning throughout East Asia, Confucius temples were also built in Vietnam, Korea, and Japan. In the beginning of 18th century, some were even built in Europe and the Americas.

(***on the way to Mianyang***)

Now we are on the way to Mianyang city after the tour of Deyang Confucius Temple. Mianyang is located in the northwest of Sichuan, with an area of 20,249 square kilometers and a population of 5.29 million.

Mianyang is one of China's major electronic industrial cities. It has well-known research institutions such as China Academy of Engineering Physics(中国工程物理研究院) and China Air Dynamics Research and Development Center(中国空气动力研究

与发展中心). In addition, there are many large-scale enterprises in Mianyang, including Changhong Electronics Group Corporation(四川长虹电器股份有限公司), Jiuzhou Electronics Group(九洲电器集团有限公司), and others. Mianyang is named as a "China Science City" by the State Council. Besides, the city has been conferred the other titles such as "China Excellent Tourism City(中国优秀旅游城市)" and "National Garden City(国家园林城市)."

Mianyang area is well known for its natural and cultural recourses. It is the hometown of Li Bai, a famous poet of the Tang Dynasty. These resourses include Li Bai's Hometown(李白故里), Qinglian Old Town (古镇青莲), Mt. Doutuan(窦团山), Mt. Daitian(戴天山) and many historical relics of the Three Kingdoms Periods. In addition, Mianyang boasts an ethnically rich population. They belong to member of China's minority nationalities, including the Tibetan and the Qiang.

Now we are passing a famous scenic spot called Fule Hill(富乐山), which is 2km south of Mianyang city. It covers an area of 2.1 square kilometers. On the hill stands garden-like architecture among green forests, brooks and gullies. Important sites include Hanhuang Garden (汉皇园), Yizhou Garden(益州园), Mianzhou Stele Forest(绵州碑林), Fule Tower(富乐阁)and Fucheng Guild Hall(涪城会馆).

The hill became a favorite resort even since the Tang and Song dynasties. In ancient China many well-known scholars toured the hill where they wrote poems and calligraphy to express their appreciation of the beauty of the hill. Therefore the hill is called "Treasure-House of Calligraphy in Northwest Sichuan".

At present, local visitors from the city often come and hike the hill to enjoy the natural beauty and appreciate the ancient style architecture.

(***on the way to Li Bai's hometown***)

Now we are on the way to Li Bai's hometown. Li Bai's birthplace is uncertain, however, his family had originally dwelled in present southeastern Gansu, and later moved to Jiangyou in Sichuan, when he was five years old. Li Bai spent his childhood there. He was influenced by Confucian and Taoist thought. He began to travel around China age twenty-five.

Li Bai was a Chinese poet. Along with Du Fu, he is often regarded, as one of the two greatest poets in China's literary history. Approximately 1,100 of his poems remain today. Li Bai is best known for the extravagant imagination and striking Taoist imagery in his poetry.

Li Bai was given a post at the Hanlin Academy(翰林院), which served to provide a source of scholarly expertise and poetry for the Emperor, He remained less than two years as a poet in the Emperor's service. Afterwards, he wandered throughout China for the rest of his life. He met Du Fu in the autumn of 744, and again the following year. These were the only occasions on which they met, but the friendship remained. At the time of the An Kushan Rebellion, Li Bai became involved in a revolt against the emperor, and was exiled the second time to Yelang(夜郎) because of the failure. He was forgiven before the exile journey was complete. Li Bai died in Dangtu(当涂) called Anhui at present.

Li Bai is best known for his yuefu poems(乐府), which are intense and often fantastic. There is a strong element of it in his works, both in the sentiments they express and in their spontaneous tone. His favorite form is jueju（绝句，five- or seven-character quatrain），of which he composed some 160 pieces. Li Bai's language is not erudite but impresses equally through his extravagance of imagination and a direct correlation of his free-spirited persona with the reader.

Well，when we arrive at Li Bai's hometown，we will tour his hometown in Jiangyou county(江油)，40km from Mianyang. The main sights include Longxi Courtyard(陇西院)，Taibai Shrine(太白祠)，the Tomb of Li Bai's Clothes(李白衣冠墓)，Mozhen Stream(磨针溪)，Ximo Pool(洗墨池)，and others. All of them have been classified as the historical relics at provincial level.

Li Bai Memorial Hall was set up in 1962，and it is encircled by water on three sides. The compound consists of Taibai Hall（太白堂），Taibai Study（太白书屋），Xiaoya Room（晓雅斋），Huaixie Hall（怀榭轩），Linjiangxian Hall（临江仙馆）. Li Bai Memorial Hall has a collection of 4，000 historical and cultural relics，which have provided valuable information for research projects related to Li Bai and his poems.

Now I'd like to read a piece of a poem written by Li Bai. It was translated by Witter Bynner.

In the Quiet Night

So bright a gleam on the foot of my bed.

Could there have been a frost already?

Lifting my head to look，I found that it was moonlight.

Sinking back again，I thought suddenly of home.

(床前明月光，疑是地上霜。举头望明月，低头思故乡。)

Now we are scheduled to hike Mt. Doutuan after the tour of Li Bai's Hometown. This mountain，25km south of Jiangyou，is 1，140m in height，and it is nationally known for its tranquility and beauty with three wonders: Feitianzang (飞天藏, Scripture of Flying Apsara), the Double Peaks and the Iron Chain Bridge. Mt Doutuan enjoys a sub-tropic monsoon climate, with early spring, long summer, short autumn and mild winter. It boasts a great variety of plants, fruit trees and plants for pharmaceutical purposes. Li Bai once hiked the mountain, and wrote a couplet in praise of the mountain: Woodcutters and ploughmen enter and exit picturesque veils. (樵夫与耕者,出入画屏中).

On the mountain are some Buddhist and Daoist Temples. In ancient times, Buddhist monks first started building temples on the mountain. Later Daoists followed suit and constructed Daoist temples on the same mountain. There was a period of coexistence between Buddhism and Daoism. Finally Daoism declined on the mountain, leaving Buddhism to continue its development. However, Yunyan Temple(云岩寺), built in the Tang Dynasty, shares both Buddhist and Daoist construction structure. On the same compound, stand Buddhist buildings on the east side and Daoist constructions on the west.

(***on the way to Guangyuan***)

Well, dear travelers, we will soon arrive at Guangyuan(广元), a prefecture-level city, also called Li prefecture (利州). According to our schedule, we will stay overnight there, and tomorrow will go and visit some places of attractions in and outside the city.

Guangyuan, located in North Sichuan, serves as an important intersection, connecting Sha'anxi and Ganshu provinces. It is the birthplace of Wu Zetian(武则天), the only female emperor in ancient China. Guangyuan boasts many former sites dating from the Three Kingdoms Period. At present, Guangyuan's jurisdiction covers 3 districts and 4 counties including Jiange(剑阁)and Qingchuan(青川).

Guangyuan abounds in tourist resources. These include Emperor's Pool Temple(皇泽寺) devoted to Empress Wu Zetian, the Thousand Buddha Stone Sculpture Cliff (千佛崖摩崖造像), Jianmen Gate(剑门蜀道), Cuiyun Corridor(翠云廊)and others.

(***On the way***)

Now we are on the way to Emperor's Pool Temple. It is the place where Empress Wu Zetian offered a sacrificial ceremony to the gods or the spirits of the dead. Located by the bank of Jialing River(嘉陵江), west of Guangyuan, it was constructed in 959. In April 1961, the temple was designated by the State Council as one of the national major historical and cultural sites. The present main buildings in the temple, Dating back to the Qing Dynasty, consist of Heaven Hall(天殿), Great Buddha Tower(大佛楼), Five Buddhas Pavilion(五佛亭), Viewing River Tower(望江楼) and others. Inside the temple there are 50 cave shrines with more than 1200 carved statues that date from the period from the Northern Wei Dynasty (北魏, 386 – 534)to the Qing Dynasty. In the Heaven Hall stands Wu Zetian's status, carved in the Tang Dynasty.

Empress Wu Zetian was the only woman in the history of China to assume the title of Emperor. Wu Zetian entered Emperor Taizong's harem most probably in 639 and was made a cairen(才人), one of the nine concubines of the fifth rank. Emperor Taizong gave her the name Mei(媚), meaning "delicate." By the early 650s, Wu Zetian was a concubine of Emperor Gaozong, and she was titled zhaoyi (昭仪), the highest ranking of the nine concubines of the second rank. In November 655, Wu Zetian was made empress consort. When Emperor Gaozong started to suffer from stroke in November 660, she began to govern ancient China behind the scenes. After she ruled ancient China first through puppet emperors from 665 to 690, Wu Zetian proclaimed herself Emperor Shengshen(圣神皇帝),means Holy in English, the first woman ever to use the title emperor. She ruled personally under the name of Emperor Shengshe from 690 to705.

(***On the way***)

Now we are on the way to the Thousand Buddha Stone Sculpture Cliff. It is located 5km north away of Guangyuan city, and it belongs to one of the national major historical and cultural sites under the state protection. There are 400 caves and niches, with 7,000 stone figure sculptures. These caves are grouped in a layered honeycomb pattern and cover a stretch of over 200m on a 45m cliff. The sculpture carvings started in the Northern Wei Dynasty, and it continued for 1500 years. With Dayun Cave(大云洞)as the centre, the Buddhist carved figures are generally divided between the southern and northern sections. There are inscribed Buddhist texts and explanatory notes that help visitors to understand their stories.

(***On the way to Jian Gate***)

Travelers, we are on the way to Jian Gate, which is located 45km south of Guangyuan. It was established by Zhuge Liang(诸葛亮) during the Three Kingdoms Period, and in the following dynasties it was always considered as the most important gate along the Shu Road(蜀道)due to its strategic position.

On the way to Jian Gate, vistors usually stop at Jianxi Bridge (剑溪桥)in an attempt to view the gate in the distance and walk towards the gate. The gate is named as No. 1 Pass in China(天下

第一关). It is said that Zhuge Liang had his soldiers build the gate and opened up a path, which stretched 30 li in the valley between mountains for the convenience of his northern expedition. Unfortunately, the original gate was destroyed in 1935 when people built up the Sichuan-Shaanxi Road(川陕公路). The current gate was constructed on the same site based on the original layout.

Jianmen Gate scenic area consists of Mt. Dajian(大剑山) and Mt. Xiaojian(小剑山). Liangshan Temple(梁山寺) is on the top of Mt. Dajian, where visitors can view Cuiping Peak(翠屏峰); Xianfeng Temple(仙峰寺) is on the top of Mt. Xiaojian, a Doist monastery where Zhang Daoling(张道陵) practiced Daoism.

(***On the way***)

Now we are on the way to Cuiyun Corridor, south of Jianmen gate. It stretches southeast to Langzhong(阆中), southwest to Zitong(梓潼) and north to Zhaohua(昭化) and Guangyuan. One section of Cuiyun Corridor is under the shade of over 8,000 cypress trees, which line along the corridor. That section is named "Green Great Wall".

In ancient China there were six major tree planting campaigns that took place along the corridor. The first campaign occurred in the Qin Dynasty. At that time Emperor Qinshihuang had his soldiers log down large numbers of trees in Sichuan and transport them for the construction of his palace. So numerous trees were cut down, and complaints were heard everywhere in Sichuan accordingly. In order to appease local people, the emperor issued an order that cypress trees be planted along the post road; the trees planted at that time were called "Imperial Cypresses." The last tree planting campaign took place during the Zhengde period

(正德年间,1506 - 1521)in the Ming Dynasty. Li Bi(李壁), one of the top prefectural officials in Jianzhou prefecture encouraged local people to fill the gaps with cypress seedlings amidst the adult cypresses. Later, these tresses were called "Ming Cypresses" or "Li Gong Cypress".

More than 2,000 years have passed, and the cypresses trees along the roadsides still remain verdantly green as one of tourist attractions in Guangyuan area.

Well, so much for my brief introduction about the local tourist sights. As we arrive at each spot, I will give you more decails.

KEY WORDS & EXPRESSIONS 关键词汇及表达法

civil aviation 民航
attendant 服务员
Confucius 孔子
portal 正门
correlate 相关联的人(或物)
dynamics 动力学
architecture 建筑物
brook 小溪
appreciation 欣赏
extravagant 过度的
imagination 想象力
striking 惹人注目的
scholarly 学者的
expertise 专门知识
fantastic 想象中的
sentiment 感情

spontaneous 无意识的
extravagance 铺张的
correlation 相互关系
persona 小说(或戏剧)中的人物
frost 霜
tranquility 平静
pharmaceutical 药的
coexistence 共存
empress 女皇
concubine 妾
strategic 战略的
convenience 方便
log 伐(林木)
verdantly 青绿地

Xichang—Panzhihua

西昌—攀枝花

Dear travelers, we are ready to depart for a long-distance trip between Xichang and Panzhihua. Now I'd like to let you know the general schedule for the whole trip. We are taking a train tonight and early next morning we arrive in Xichang. After we check in at a hotel, we start our trip. The scenic spots include Lake Qionghai(邛海), Mt. Lushan(泸山), Liangshan Yi Ethnic Nationality Slave Society Museum(彝族奴隶社会博物馆), Xichang Satellite Launch Center(西昌卫星发射中心). We stay overnight in Xichang. On the second day we take a bus to Lugu Lake(泸沽湖). The road snakes around the mountains like a thin ribbon. Here and there, our bus will pass through some small towns and villages, where the inhabitants still dress their ethnic styles. When we arrive there, we will stay overnight in a hotel close to Lugu Lake where we will take a tourist canoe on the water and stroll along the lake. The trip to Lugu Lake also includes a visit to a local village and a monastery. On the third day we take a bus to Panzhihua. It is about 280km between the two places. In Panzhihua area we will visit Ertan Hydropower Project(二滩水利工程)and some other places. Finally we take a train back to Chengdu.

Now we are in Xichang city. Xichang lies almost halfway between Chengdu and Kunming. It is the capital of Liangshan Yi Ethnic Nationality Autonomous prefecture and the major center for the local Yi people. The city's main statue depicts the fraternal brotherhood of the Han and Yi peoples. The statue is depicting the Red Army command Liu Bocheng(刘伯承)downing a toast of blood and wine with a local Yi chieftain, after securing a safe passage for the Long March in 1935. Xichang has been known for centuries as the City of the Moon and so it's suitable that China's major satellite launching operation should take place nearby.

(***on the way to Qionghai Lake***)

We are now on the way to enjoy Qionghai Lake, one of the ten top scenic places in Sichuan. It is several kilometers southeast of the city. The lake is 34m at its deepest. According to scientific research, it was formed due to the earth stratum splitting.

In spring, the bright sun shines and gentle wind breezes; the lake remains unruffled like a mirror; lake willow branches turn green and peach trees are in blossom; people row boats on the lake as if they were entering and exiting a landscape painting.

. In summer, colorful clouds cast shadows on the splashing lake; the water rises and falls; local people actively participate in boating or swimming races. In autumn the sky is clear, and the lake and sky are the same color; as the moon rises, the blue water and bright moonlight enhance each other. In winter sunshine still remains; local maple trees turn red, and pine appears green; water birds frolic across the lake. The natural four seasons of the lake strikes you as vast and infinite, presenting a picture of boundless imagination.

In addition, there are many folk stories about the lake. These include *the Blue and Green Snake and Old Woman*(青蛇与老妪); *the Sea Coral Tree of Qiong hai Lake*(邛海珊瑚树) *and the Woodcutter and an Eel*(樵夫和鳝鱼). The lake boasts some other attractions nearby. These are Qiong Lake Park(邛海公园), Sichuan Water Sports Base(四川省水上运动基地), Fengshen Temple(风神庙), Xinsha Sandy Beach(新沙滩), seafood villages, etc.

Travelers, Mt. Lushan is located on the southern bank of Qionghai Lake. As one of the scenic spots at provincial level, the mountain is 2,317m above sea level. The mountain cover oldest cypress trees dating back the Han Dynasty. In ancient times, scholars highly praised the unique scenery of Mt. Lushan and Qionghai Lake for towering cypress trees from the mountain, blue water from the lake, bright moon from the sky and gentle breeze from Anning River(安宁河).

Amidst cypress trees forest stand many ancient Buddhist and Daoist buildings, including Guangfu Temple(光福寺), Sanjiao

Nunnery(三教庵), Yuhuang Temple(玉皇殿), Wuzu Nunnery (五祖庵), etc. In the past thousand years, Buddhist monks and Daoist priests have co-existed in peace on the same mountain. Guangfu Temple is the largest complex, which consists of the Thousand-Buddha Hall(千佛殿), the Great Buddha Hall(大雄殿), Wenwu Hall(文武宫), Kuixing Tower(魁星阁), etc. There are many exhibition rooms, showing the tablets of earthquake, paintings and calligraphy of ancient dynasties.

A winding path leads up to the summit. The panoramic view of Qiong hai Lake from the top of the mountain is charming, and it has inspired countless Chinese artists because the scenery is best seen as far as visibility extends. The lake is as smooth as a mirror; boats seem no more than tiny dots; the image in the water is closely integrated with the scenery, and it is hard to tell which is the real one or which is a reflection.

(***At Museum***)

Here we are at the entrance of Liangshan Yi Ethnic Nationality Slave Society Museum. It is at the base of Mt. Lushan. The museum was opened on August 4, 1985. In front of the museum entrance stands a sculpture of a soldier of Yi ethnic nationality. Below the sculpture, there are four engraved characters—"Eagle in Liangshan". The strong-built soldier fastens a short sword at the waist and blows a horn.

The museum has been decorated with natural patterns like the sun, the moon, the water, sheep's horns, feathers, fishing nets, etc. Red, yellow and black are main colors, and the whole architectures embody Yi's styles. This museum has a collection of 4,196 historical articles of Yi ethnic nationality, including gold, silver, jewelry, jade, copper, iron, wood, bamboo, leather, bones, animal horns, paper, silk fabrics, etc. The photo and article exhibition is generally categorized into nine parts, each part focusing on a designated topic. These topics include Introduction of the Yi People, Social Productivity, Social Status and Class, Customary Family Branches, Marriage and Family, Religious Belief, Literature and Art, Habits and Customs, and Slaves and Their Struggle against the Slavery System. The tour of the museum will help you obtain some basic information about the history of the Yi people, their life in the old society that expired in 1949.

Yi people mainly live in Liangshan Yi Autonomous prefecture and other counties nearby. Before 1949, Liangshan area was a slave society. The whole society forcibly organized the Yi people into a five-grade hierarchy according to their blood relationship. Hereditary headmen were at the top grade; slaves were at the lowest. Slaves were subject and dependent to slave-owners who could sell or even kill their slaves as they pleased. The savage system expired after new China was established in 1949.

(***on the way to Xichang Satellite Launch Center***)

Now we are on the way to Xichang Satellite Launch Center. As you travel in Xichang, it is a good opportunity to experience high-technology in Xichang Satellite Launch Center.

Xichang Satellite Launch Center is located in Shaba Valley (沙坝峡谷), 65km north of Xichang. It's one of the major satellite rocket launch centers in China, designed mainly to launch powerful thrust rockets and geostationary satellites. The center has two launch pads: one for the launch of geostationary communications satellites and meteorological satellites by Long

March CZ-3 rockets, and the other for the lift-off of Long March CZ-2 strap-on launch vehicle and the Long March CZ-3 series rockets. Tourists usually visit the control center and launch pads, and in the center projection room, videotapes will show the whole process of launches of the Long March rockets from No. 2 Station at the Center.

The facility became operational in 1984. The center now acts as a commercial venture and has launched several countries' satellites on the back of its Long March Rocket. In December 2003, the center launched the first of two Double Star Scientific Satellites(双星计划)due to Sino-European space cooperation. On Thursday, July 5, 2007, "Chinasat 6B(中星 6B)", a French-made communications satellite, rocketed into space from this center.

At present, there are the other two major space launch centers in China: Jiuquan(九泉) and Taiyuan(太原). Jiuquan center was founded in 1958 in Gansu. It was the first center, which is mainly used to send satellites into lower and medium orbits with large orbital inclination angles. Taiyuan center is situated in Shanxi, and it was founded in March 1966. Surrounded by mountains, Taiyuan center stands at an elevation of 1,500 m, and it is an ideal place to launch solar-synchronous satellites.

(***On the way to Lugu Lake***)

Travelers, now we are on the road that leads to pretty Lugu Lake. The distance between Xichang and the lake is about 258km.

Lugu Lake is known for its natural scenery and the unique

culture of Mosuo people(摩梭人). The lake is located between Ninglang county(宁蒗县)in Yunnan and Yanyuan county (盐源县)in Sichuan. The sky is clear and blue, and it is reflected in the lake, which nestles among the green of the mountains nearby like a hidden sapphire. The lake covers an area of 52km. The average depth is 45m, the deepest point being 93m. Among the five islands in the lake, three are in the territory of Yunnan and two in that of Sichuan. There are many cultural sites and scenic spots along the lakeside, including Mosuo villages, plateau hot springs, the Chieftain's Palace(酋长岛), a Lamaism Temple and others.

Mosuo people inherit Lugu Lake area. Tourism has changed the Mosuo community dramatically, with many people developing their homes into small hotels. In addition, local Mosuo people wear their festival costumes to host tourists, leading tourists on horseback or paddling tourist boats across the lake. Young Mosuo girls and boys in festival costumes sing and dance with tourists.

Mosuo people, a branch of the Naxi ethnic nationality(纳西族), still retain some remnants of the matriarchal society with their own customs. Women are the top leaders of the community's extensive families, and all family members are descendants of the same woman. There are no husbands and fathers here. Lovers meet at night but live separately with their own mother's families by day. Men and women are not bound by marriage. They may choose to unite or separate at will. The Mosuos believe that since this so-called "visiting marriage" (走婚) system, it does not need marriage registry.

Children are under the care of and supported by their maternal families. Fathers do not live in the same family with their children and women. Their behavior and custom have been considered as the "living fossil" as a basis for a study of social patterns and matriarchal marriage customs in today's world.

As China has opened up, Mosuo people have had more and more contact with outsiders. They are eager to know about life beyond the mountains, just as the tourists are to know about their own lives. Some of the younger generation has left their traditional homes to try out the life outside, but many have returned after trying it for a few years. They believe that life in Lugu Lake area is much simpler and easier with more happiness in their community, without disputes over property or quarrels over love affairs.

(***In Panzhihua***)

Travelers, we are now in Panzhihua City. It is located at the junction of the two rivers: Jinsha (金沙江) and Yalong(雅龙江). The city is a newly developed steel and iron industrial city in Sichuan. Before the mid-1960s, the present Panzhihua city was just a place inhabited by seven families around a ferry. Since then, the city gradually began to stretch far and wide as the exploitation of iron ore resources in Panzhihua area. In the beginning, the city was named Dukou City(渡口市, the Ferry City), later was then renamed Panzhihua after the name of tall trees, which grow everywhere in the urban area.

Panzhihua area has a great variety of highly concentrated mineral resources, including ferrous, non-ferrous metals and rare earth. It contains 13 per cent of the country's iron, 69per cent of vanadium, 93 per cent of titanium and 82 per cent of cobalt. There are Panzhihua Iron and Steel (Group) Co, largest steel-making center in southwest China, largest titanium and vanadium-producing center of China. Panzhihua abounds with hydraulic water resourses. Ertan Hydropower Project, China's largest

Hydropower Project of the 20th century, is under construction.

The local climate and land is suited to the growth of grains, which are harvested three times a year. Local fruit growers produce tropical fruits like banana, papaya and mango.

The Cycad Forest(苏铁林)is located in the western district of the city. In the forest, there are about 136,000 are adult cycads. Cycads are regarded as "living fossil" because it is a 270-million-year-old rare species. This forest was discovered in 1971 and is designated as "the State-Level Cycad Nature Reserve".

Longtan Karst Stalactite Cave Scenic Area(龙潭溶洞风景区) is 100km away from Panzhihua city. The highlight of the area is Longtan Cave, which is regarded as the first cave in West Panzhihua. The cave inside reveals two unique scenes, one of resembles the Dragon's Palace, and the other Heaven's Palace. The stalagmites in this cave can be imposing, beautiful or strange. In addition, numerous waterfalls produces a tremendous noise in the cave that ethos repeatedly. In the scenic area there are some other places that are worth a visit. These include Longyin Valley(龙吟峡谷), the Natural Potted Landscape Garden (天然盆景园)and the Wild Botanic Garden(野生植物园).

(***on the way to Ertan Hydropower Project***)

Travelers, China has three key hydropower projects. They are the Three Gorges Project(三峡工程)on Changjian River, Longtan Hydropower Station(龙滩水电站)in Guangxi and Ertan Hydropower Project in Panzhihua.

Ertan Hydropower Project is located on Yalong River, an upper tributary of the Changjiang. This tributary flows fast down high mountains and through deep valleys, providing great potential for hydropower production. Scientists and engineers have located several would-be sites for hydropower stations. Ertan is the largest one.

The preparation for Ertan Hydropower Station started in 1950. In 1958, a group of scientists from a designing and survey institute settled down there for the initial process. They built hydrometric stations and collected hydrometric information available to the project. In 1989, the Ministry of Water Recourses and Electric Power approved of the scheme to set up Ertan Hydropower Development Company.

On September 1991, the construction of Ertan Hydropower Station started. The World Bank made a loan of US$930 million to the company. Foreign contractors worked as sponsors in civil construction works; well-known international manufacturers supplied major mechanical and electrical equipment; hundreds of overseas workers and engineers from 47 countries were involved in the construction and consultation. Overseas employees built up their own residences, such as European camp, Pakistani camp and Philippine camp close to the construction site. The European camp consists of beautiful villas and apartments equipped with the latest facilities. The camps also have clubs, bars, swimming pools, and stores.

In 2000, Ertan Hydropower Station was completed. The arched dam is 240m in height, the underground powerhouse complex is 280m in length, 25.5m in width and 65m in height, and each generating unit has an installed capacity of 550. The station produced 3.9 billion KWH in the first year as it started its operation. Since 2000, more efforts have been made to construct more hydropower stations on the same river in order to provide more electricity to Southwest China.

Well, so much for my introduction about all the scenic spots. I will be very happy if my introduction will help you.

KEY WORDS & EXPRESSIONS 关键词汇及表达法

satellite 卫星
launch 发射
hydropower 以水力所发的电力
fraternal 兄弟的
brotherhood 手足之情
stratum 地层
unruffled (水面等)平静的
maple 枫树
frolic 嬉戏
boundless 无限的
woodcutter 樵夫
cypress 柏树
earthquake 地震
distinguished 卓越的
categorize 将……分类
customary 习惯上的
slavery 奴隶制
forcibly 强迫地
hereditary 世袭的
dependent 依靠的
expire 终止
high-technology 高科技
thrust 推力
geostationary (人造卫星)与地球旋转同步的
meteorological 气象的
rocket 火箭

lift-off 吊起
pad 发射台
orbit 运行轨道
orbital 运行轨道的
inclination 倾度
solar 太阳的
synchronous 同步的
remnant 遗风
matriarchal 母系氏族的
descendant 后裔
marriage registry 婚姻登记
behavior 行为
junction 汇合
ferrous 铁的
titanium 钛
vanadium 钒
papaya 番木瓜
mango 芒果
tributary 支流
scheme 计划
villa 别墅
install 安装
capacity 容量

Farewell Speech 欢送词

Ladies and gentlemen, on behalf of my travel agency, my Chinese colleagues and myself, I'd like to take this opportunity to express my thanks for your understanding. I know that your tour of Sichuan would not have been so successful without your excellent co-operation.

I am also glad to see that some of your extra requests have been met in addition to our regularly scheduled scenic spots. During our tour we have been lucky with the fine weather and without transportation problems. Everyone has followed the arrangement, so that the team schedule has been carried out successfully. I'd like to say a few words about our schedule in Sichuan.

For the **first three days** we had inner-city tours. The purpose of these excursions was to help you establish a complete picture of the city and become familiar with the local culture and tradition. Each day we were on a different route. We toured Funan River and walked through the business streets. We also visited Du Fu Thatched Cottage, Wuhou Temple, Chengdu Giant Pandas Breeding and Research Base, and some other spots. We drank tea in the People's Park and enjoyed the magnificent night view of Chengdu.

Between **the fourth day and ninth day** we had a long-distance trip from Chengdu to Jiuzhaigou. On the fourth day we toured the Dujiangyan Irrigation System and hiked Mt. Qingcheng. We got to know Chinese Daoism and viewed the ancient hydraulic dam project. On the fifth and sixth days we drove to Wolong Giant Panda Research and Protection Center, listened to the introduction given by the Giant panda expert, and saw the giant pandas. We also make a long-journey into the forest in the mountain near the center. From the seventh to ninth days we drove to Jiuzhaigou, viewed the villages of the Tibetan and Qiang nationalities, and experienced the natural beauty in Jiuzhaigou and Huanglong.

Between **the tenth and eleventh day** we toured Leshan Giant Buddha and hiked in Mt. Emei. I know the beauty of the mountain and the height of the carved Buddha really overwhelmed all of you.

For **the last three days** we drove to Hailuogou Glacier Park. On the way we toured Bifeng Valley. We stayed in a hotel in Moxi town where the Red Army stayed in 1935. We viewed the glacier that is the lowest glacier in Asia.

During your stay in Chengdu some of you went to the English corner to meet young Chinese students. I know you had a good conversation in English and became more familiar with Chinese culture. In the evening some of you went to the night market near the hotel where we stayed. There you found excellent shopping opportunities and bought traditional Chinese paintings and embroidery silk. You told me that you are going to give them to your friends in your hometown. I believe that they will be valuable gifts from Sichuan, China.

Two weeks ago, we first met; now we are friends. During your tour in Sichuan I did my best to meet your needs and explained to you what I know about Chengdu and other places in Sichuan. I hope you will give me your comments and suggestions so that I can improve my future service.

Today you are leaving Chengdu for Kunming. I really feel sorry and reluctant to say good-bye. Do please revisit Sichuan, and I'd like to provide you with the other four long-distance trips in Sichuan, including the wonderful routes between Chengdu and Shunan Bamboo Forest (蜀南竹海), Chengdu and Guan'an (广

安)，Chengdu and Guangyuan(广元) as well as Xichang(西昌)and Panzhihua(攀枝花). These routes have rich tourist resources like Ancient Stone Sculptures in Anyue(安岳石刻)，Zigong Dinosaur Museum(自贡恐龙博物馆)，Langzhong Ancient City(阆中古城)，Deng Xiaoping's Former Residence(邓小平故居)，Lugu Lake(泸沽湖) and Ertan Hydropower Project(二滩水利工程). Well，I am looking forward to seeing you again. Have a happy and safe journey. Zaijian!

KEY WORDS & EXPRESSIONS 关键词汇及表达法

on behalf of 代表……

tolerance 宽容，忍受

hydraulic 水力的；水压的

valuable gift 贵重赠品

reluctant 不愿的，勉强的

Section Three :

Highlights of Sichuan Province

第三部分：

四川地区面面观

Sichuan Opera 看川剧

When overseas travelers visit Chengdu, arrangements are made for them to drink tea and have Chengdu snacks in Shunxing Ancient Tea-house (顺兴老茶馆). As they sit in the teahouse for tea and snacks, they are offered a variety of entertainment including Sichuan opera, the pouring-tea-into-cup skill and acrobatics. They also will appreciate the on-spot painting or calligraphy show. Of course, Sichuan opera is the highlight of all the entertainments.

The purpose of the arrangement is to help tourists gain some insight into unique art forms, which are almost impossible to see in their own countries. Overseas travelers in Sichuan are curious about Sichuan opera. Each time after the show, most of them say that they enjoyed the exotic-styled performance, colorful costumes and unique skills like spitting fire and changing faces. However, the high-pitched singing and incomprehensive monologues sometimes make them feel at a loss. Therefore, a basic knowledge and understanding about Sichuan opera will enable travelers to become more appreciative of this unique art in Sichuan.

China has an abundance of 1,300 local operas. Sichuan opera is one of China's oldest local operas and is popular in Sichuan Province and some regions of Yunnan and Guizhou provinces. It is the most significant and most interesting opera form from Southwestern China. As a stage entertainment, it conveys the idea of time and space to the audience through performances. The opera is characterized by its unique solo singing, refined acting, rich percussion and irresistibly funny comedians. Sichuan opera also displays its unique skills: the changing faces, spitting fire, and rolling light. Numerous Sichuan opera troupes are active throughout the province, both in the countryside and in the cities. The troupes in Chengdu are rated artistically top level.

KEY WORDS & EXPRESSIONS 关键词汇及表达法

acrobatics 杂技
on-spot painting 现场作画
entertainment 娱乐，娱乐表演
exotic 外来的，奇异的
changing faces 变脸
spitting fire 吐火

The Tunes of Sichuan Opera
川剧的声腔

Some visitors do not appreciate this art, for the opera tunes sometimes sound shrilly. Musically, Sichuan opera combines five different sonic systems. The music is not intended to be melodic, as in the West, but rather used as punctuation to the performance.

In the course of the development of Chinese traditional opera, mutual borrowing has taken place among various types of local opera, and new forms have appeared continually. The classic opera in China consisted of two major schools: Beizaju (北杂剧, the Northern-Style Dramatic Miscellany Opera) and Nanxi (南戏, the South-Style Drama). In the 13th century, Zaju opera was rarely a single dramatic piece. However, it was composed of a number of sequences around set themes.

In ancient times touring troupes usually performed the operas as a popular form of entertainment. However, the troupes were held in low social status, and their performance was considered unworthy of attention from the scholarly class; Nanxi Drama was a local classic. It originated in Wenzhou (温州), Zhejiang province at the beginning of the Southern Song Dynasty (1127 - 1279). Then it spread far and wide in South China. The drama was set to a variety of music tunes popular from 1127 to 1644. Gradually, Zaju and Nanxi process changed into other art forms: Kunqu Opera (昆曲), Yiyang Tune (弋阳腔), Pihuang Opera (皮黄) and Qinqiang Opera (秦腔).

Sichuan opera appeared around the middle of the Qing Dynasty. It has adapted the four major tunes. In addition, percussion instruments are used for a strongly rhythmical accompaniment. However, the adapted tunes still preserve their own individual distinction as a typical style in Sichuan opera.

Kunqiang or Kunshan Tune (昆腔)

Kunshan tune in Sichuan opera is a melodic form. It originated in the southern Changjiang Basin and was later imported to Sichuan. A bamboo flute or a vertical bamboo flute is the dominant melodic instrument. Its tune sounds gentle, clear, and fluent. The traditional repertoire in Sichuan opera has Kunshan tunes. Occasionally some short Kunshan tunes are used as interludes in a high-pitched opera. Some percussion instruments like gongs, drums and cymbals are often used when a Kunshan tune opera is performed. However, in the old days Sichuan Kunshan tune operas were most likely suited to scholars' tastes because they remained refined and elegant.

Huqin Voice（胡琴）

It is a music for voices in Sichuan operas. It is mainly from Xipi（西皮腔）and Erhuang（二黄腔）tune families in Huiju opera（徽剧，Hubei opera），which is an operatic form in Hubei province. Sichuan Huqin tune opera has a large repertoire. The stringed instruments mainly consist of erhu（二胡）and sanxian（三弦）. Erhu is a two-stringed bowed instrument with a lower register，and sanxian a three-stringed plucked instrument. A drumbeat is used to set the music tempo.

Tanxi（弹戏）

Originally Tan opera was one of the oldest kinds of opera in China. During Ming Dynasty it appeared in Shaanxi，Hunan and other areas，where it was popular around the end of Ming Dynasty and the beginning of Qing Dynasty. However，its influence went beyond these areas. As it was introduced into Sichuan，local people called it Chuanbangzi opera（川梆子）. Chuan means Sichuan，bangzi indicates a kind of wooden clapper with bars of unequal length. The clapper is used as an accompaniment instrument to produce a strong rhythm in harmony with loud and clear voices in the Chuanbangzi opera. The main music instrument is gaibanhu（盖板胡），which is a bowed stringed instrument with thin wooden soundboard.

Gaoqiang（高腔）

Gaoqiang is a high-pitched singing style，it is the most highly known style among the multi-tunes of Sichuan opera. It has a distinctive Sichuan local color. Its vocal solo tune is beyond the eight-bar music scale，and its melodic ornamentation sounds both elegant and energetic. The high-pitched tune usually has no accompaniment of stringed instrument. Its solo singing quickly passes up or down the music links and skillfully uses a throbbing effect and artistic addition around the tone. Sparse rhythmical emphasis from wooden clappers usually accompanies the highpitched singing. In addition, a chorus from the orchestra either makes remarks or repeats what the solo voice sings. In the old days, the chorus consisted of percussionists. They were usually in full view on stage, and they had their daily dresses. Nowadays, the chorus works in a fixed place on the stage, which is out of sight of the audience.

Before 1949, the male voice worked as a vocal accompaniment to the high-pitched singing in Sichuan opera. The man beat a drum and conducted the accompaniment band joined by some other percussionists. Since 1949, the female voice or mixed voices have replaced the male voice in vocal accompaniment.

KEY WORDS & EXPRESSIONS 关键词汇及表达法

sonic 声频的
punctuation 标点，标点符号
miscellany 混合物
dramatic 戏剧性的；生动的
sequence 次序，顺序
set theme 固定的主题，主题曲
unworthy of attention 不足道的
rhythmical accompaniment 有节奏的伴奏或伴唱
distinction 特性；声望
originate 引起；发明
vertical bamboo flute 箫；长笛
melodic 有旋律的
repertoire （准备好演出的）节目；保留剧目
operatic 歌剧的，歌剧风格的

tempo 速度，拍子
clapper 拍板
soundboard 共鸣板，响板
vocal solo tune 唱调
ornamentation 装饰
throbbing 颤动的
chorus 合唱，合唱队
percussionist 打击乐器乐手，弹击乐器弹奏者
vocal accompaniment 伴唱

Sichuan Opera Character Roles
川剧的角色

The character roles in Sichuan opera are divided into four main types according to the sex, age, social status, and profession of the character. They are sheng (生), dan (旦), jing (净) and chou (丑).

Sheng refers to male roles. Male roles can be subdivided into different types, including zhengsheng (正生), xiaosheng (小生), wusheng (武生). Zhengsheng refers to a bearded middle-aged or old man who plays the part of a positive character; xiaosheng refers to a young man whose gesture is unrestrained and footwork brisk; wusheng is a military general between 30 and 55 years old.

Dan refers to female roles. The female roles can be sub-divided into the following types: laodan (老旦), qingyi (青衣), huadan (花旦) and wudan (武旦). Laodan refers to an old woman. Qingyi refers to a refined young or middle-aged woman, who is often in a dark pleated skirt and is portrayed as a positive character. Huadan refers to a girl or young woman in a jacket and pants. She appears shrewish or active. During an opera she speaks more and sings less. Wudan refers to woman with martial skills. In her part she mainly shows her martial skills rather than singing or talking.

Jing refers to the roles with painted faces. Jing or hualian (painted faces) refers to male roles that have a frank personality and unrestrained movement. In the operas their facial make-up is multi-colored.

Chou, or clown, is a comic character and can be recognized at first sight for his special make-up (a patch of white paint on his nose). Chou is the main role in a comedy or a satirical opera. Chou can be sub-divided into wenchou (文丑) (male clowns), wuchou (武丑) (clowns with martial skills) and danchou 旦丑 (female clowns). They mainly play the part of positive characters. Sometimes they also act as negative ones.

KEY WORDS & EXPRESSIONS 关键词汇及表达法

beard 胡须
positive character 正面人物
unrestrained 无限制的
footwork brisk 步法轻快
frank personality 坦白的个性
facial make-up 脸部化妆
negative character 反面人物

Facial Makeup and Changes
川剧的脸谱与变脸

When you are watching Sichuan Opera, what impresses you the most is probably the "painted face". Facial patterns date far back in history. Ancient Chinese actors sometimes wore masks known as "dummy faces". Later the painted patterns replaced the mask due to the development of the opera. Facial patterns follow a set mode in composition, sketching and coloring. Facial patterns emphasize multi-color's exaggeration and symbolism in order to suggest a character's personality. The painted faces become what the Chinese call "a mirror of the soul". Judged by painted faces, many Chinese audiences will instantly be able to tell the personality of characters on the stage.

The audiences have long accepted the traditional way of the facial pattern expression. Generally, the Red Face Makeup (红脸) refers to loyal and upright persons, the Black Face Makeup (黑脸) refers to faithful and straightforward persons, the White Face Makeup (白脸) refers to an imperious and treacherous person, the Multi-Colored Face Makeup (五彩脸) refers to ghosts and gods, the White-Colored Face Makeup Between Eyes and Nose (小花脸) refers to a clown's face, which appears funny and humorous.

In Sichuan opera some special characters use stunts by which they can suddenly show their magic power: quick changes of facial patterns without makeup, jumping through burning hoops and hiding swords. Among them the face-changing is the most popular. It is said that in most Sichuan opera characters like a bandit changes his face nine times to escape his pursuers or an evil sorcerer changes faces with his moods.

The face-changing, or "bian lian" in Chinese, is an important intangible cultural heritage in China. Only a few masters have grasped this skill. They know how to change Sichuan opera masks in magically quick succession. As they flourish their arms and twist their heads, their painted masks change again and again and again.

Face changing got its start 300 years ago. At the beginning, opera masters changed the color of their faces during performances by blowing into a bowl of red, black or gold powder. The powder would adhere to their oiled skin quickly. In another method, actors would smear their faces with colored paste concealed in the palms of their hands.

By the 1920's, opera masters began using layers of masks made of oiled paper or dried pig bladders. The masters could peel one after another in the blink of an eye. At present the masters use the full- face, painted silk mask. They can be worn in layers, as much as two-dozen thick, and be pulled off one by one.

KEY WORDS & EXPRESSIONS 关键词汇及表达法

dummy 虚拟的，假的

exaggeration 夸张

symbolism 象征主义

straightforward 正直的，坦率的

imperious 专横的

treacherous 背叛的，背信弃义的

multi-colored face makeup 五彩脸

humorous 幽默的

pursuer 追随者

sorcerer 男巫师

intangible 无形的

flourish 挥动，夸耀

twist 扭弯，扭曲

conceal 隐藏，隐蔽

layer 层，阶层

bladder 膀胱，气泡

in the blink of an eye 眨眼间

Repertoire of Sichuan Opera

川剧的剧目

Sichuan opera has a rich repertoire. Its scripts have a strong literary quality, full of wit, humor, lively dialogue and a pronounced local flavor. It is said that the repertoire included 3,000 items in Tang Dynasty and 800 items in Song Dynasty. The current existing repertoire totals over 2,000 items. Most of them are adapted from traditional historical stories or novels, legends or folk tales. They are related to political and military struggles, ghosts and gods as well as common people's daily life.

In the early days, most scriptwriters were actors in Sichuan opera. After the Opium War (1840 - 1842), some scholars began to write for Sichuan opera. Huang Ji'an (黄吉安) of the late Qing Dynasty, who wrote more than 80 scripts for Sichuan opera. Zhaoxi (赵熙), was a successful candidate in the highest examination taken in the late Qing Dynasty. He revised the script by the name of *the Story About Burning Incense and a Lover's Rendezvous* (焚香记·幽会).

In the 1950s, Sichuan opera had made much progress through its own reform. The opera professionals and artists sorted out the best traditional opera items for performances. At the same time they also created some new items based on historical and modern subjects. At the present time, Sichuan opera has gained a new vitality because of the major reforms associated with scripts and stagecraft.

The following is a list of famous synopses:

Dongxiang Massacre (巴山秀才, Bashan Xiucai)

In Sichuan during the late Qing Dynasty, Dongxiang county

is hit by a serious drought. The victims ask the local government for relief food. But the county magistrate falsely tells his superiors that the local people want to rebel. So the provincial military commander commands his troops to suppress the "rebellion", and 3,000 innocent people are massacred. Meng Dengke, a scholar from Sichuan, voices his sorrow for the 3,000 poor souls. The news reaches Dowager Ci Xi, who orders an investigation into the incident and punishment for those who are responsible for the wrong doing.

Husband-Wife Bridge(夫妻桥, Fuqi Qiao)

The opera is set in Sichuan Guangxian county in Qing Dynasty. At the Fulong Ferry by Minjiang River, many passengers are drowned in summer floods. Zeng Xiwu and Fan Laome are bad and violent men. They control the ferry and extort money from the passengers. He Xiande, a young schoolteacher, is determined to build a bamboo chain bridge. He is supported by the local people but threatened by Zeng and Fan. Due to the actions of corrupt officials and local ruffians, the bamboo chain bridge is destroyed on a stormy night, and the schoolteacher is killed. His wife continues the work left by her husband. With the joint efforts of the people, the bridge is built as last.

Madame Big Feet(大脚夫人, Dajiao Furen)

Madame Yang, known as "Madame Big Feet", is a distinguished lady. She has an honorary title by imperial mandate. Her son is a playboy. He beats an old villager to death and then is accidentally killed by a hero whose name is Wu Xianliang. Madame Big Feet chooses the law over her maternal feelings and orders her son's corpse to be left in the street for three days. Then she adopts Wu as her son, and then they go to join the imperial force to defend the country.

Romantic Confusion (乔太守乱点鸳鸯谱, Qiao Taishou Luan Dian Yuanyang Pu)

Scholar Sun Run meets a young woman whose name is Liu Huiniang; another scholar Pei Zheng falls in love with Xu Wengu. When they exchange keepsakes, the two couples make a careless mistake and receive mismatched mementoes. But the mistake meets their parents' marriage arrangements. Love becomes more confusing at the wedding ceremony, a third "couple" stands in for the two families. Only Commissioner Qiao can unknot these romantic complications and make three "perfect" matches.

Unfaithful Scholar (杜十娘, Du Shiniang)

At Yanjiang, scholar Li Jia falls in love with Du Shiniang, who is a prostitute. Du buys back her freedom with her savings and begins traveling home with Li. But on the way Li meets Sun Fu, a rich salt merchant who warns Li not to bring home a prostitute. In response, the unfaithful scholar promises to sell Du to Sun. Du is burning with anger upon hearing of this deal. Afterwards Du throws herself and a box of jewelry into the river.

Now you can see that Sichuan Opera is similar to popular soap operas seen throughout the world. Watch out! You may become addicted to them.

KEY WORDS & EXPRESSIONS 关键词汇及表达法

scriptwriter 编剧
candidate 候选人, 投考者
vitality 生命力; 生动性
script 手稿, 剧本
stagecraft 编剧才能; 演术

synopses 大意；要略
magistrate 文职官员，地方官员
superior 上级
extort 敲诈，逼取
ruffian 流氓，暴徒
distinguished 著名的，卓越的
mandate 指令，命令
maternal 母亲的，母性的
corpse 尸体
keepsake 纪念品
memento 纪念品
complication 复杂化
prostitute 妓女
unfaithful 不诚实的，不忠实的
jewelry 珠宝，宝石
addicted to 沉溺于某种嗜好中的

Sichuan Restaurant

品尝川菜

Ladies and gentlemen, now we are on the way to a Sichuan restaurant for some Sichuan food. Sichuan cuisine is one of the delights in China. I think that everyone in your group has tried Chinese dishes of some sort at a Chinese restaurant in your country. This is due to the large number of Chinese restaurants in cities big and small throughout the world. However, you are indeed fortunate to visit Sichuan and have an opportunity to try some of the exquisite local dishes. I am sure that you will certainly find a difference in quality, substance, and style in the food prepared in Sichuan, compared with the food you had in your country.

Chinese people value their way of diet very much. There is an old saying that, "Food is the first necessity of the people(民以食为天)". Delicious and nutritious food has been regarded as the basics of ordinary life. There is another popular saying among Chinese people. It is said "Chi zhai Sichuan", which means that people always refer to Sichuan as the place for good food in China. There are quite a number of famous dishes. The cuisine includes Sichuan dishes, snacks and hotpot. Their flavors, and methods of cooking make Sichuan food very special.

Now I'd like to take this opportunity to offer you some basic facts associated with the Chinese way of diet on Sichuan dishes, snacks and hotpot. I hope that this information will help you acquire some understanding about Sichuan food, so that you can better enjoy the food during your stay.

KEY WORDS & EXPRESSIONS 关键词汇及表达法

exquisite 优美的，高雅的

flavor 风味，滋味

texture 肌理

The Chinese Way of Diet
中国饮食习惯

Chinese food is an art, which grew out of a highly developed civilization. Chinese cooking uses almost all of the meat, poultry, fish, and vegetables known to the western palate. It has also embraced other foodstuffs, which may appear rare to western taste.

Since ingredients are not the same everywhere, Chinese food begins to undertake a local character simply by virtue of the ingredients it uses. Generally there are four basic gastronomic areas: Shandong, Cantonese, Sichuan and Yangzhou. These regional cuisines have evolved over centuries. However, their designations have no specific geographical boundaries. Beijing food, for example, falls within the section of Shandong cooking. The cuisine in Changjiang delta area includes Huaiyang, Suzhou, Shanghai and Hangzhou dishes, and falls under the category of Yangzhou cuisine. Chefs from the four regional cuisines influence each other, and their good cooking experience is shared. Despite of that, each regional cuisine has its own history, unique techniques, distinguished dishes and prevailing taste.

One important point is that the Chinese have adopted foreign foodstuffs since the dawn of history. Wheat, sheep and goats were possibly introduced from Western Asia in prehistoric times; many fruits and vegetables came in from Central Asia during the Han and the Tang dynasties; peanuts and sweet potatoes came from coastal traders during Ming Dynasty. These all became integral ingredients of Chinese food.

Chinese food is usually chopped up into thin, bite-size pieces. It aims to make knives unnecessary at the dinner table. The thinness is deliberate for quick cooking and using a minimum of fuel. Chinese food can also appear whole, like fish and pork hocks, but they are deeply cooked so that chopsticks can easily separate them.

In China the ingredients are prepared along tracks of fan (饭) and cai (菜). Fan refers to grains and other starch staple grains; cai refers to vegetable or meat dishes as non-staple-food. Fan is more fundamental and indispensable. The Chinese people have a habit of eating more staple food and less non-staple food. Grains make up most of the caloric intake. Due to tradition an adult may consume two or three bowls of rice or a large bowl of noodles at one sitting. At the daily Chinese dining table, everyone has his or her own bowl of staple food. Banquet menus are quite different in composition, compared with the daily meal at home. Rice or noodles are served last. Even at the end of a banquet meal Chinese habitually eat a small bowl of rice.

For the preparation of dishes, it is a rule to use multiple ingredients and several flavors. Cooked dishes are usually placed in the center of a table to be shared by all the eaters. The way of shared dishes is conducive to family gathering and friendship. In restaurants "public" chopsticks or spoons are used to get food from the dishes or plates in the table center. It aims to prevent the possible spread of disease. No knives are available at the table. However, restaurants and some homes offer knives whenever they are asked for.

When overseas travelers first visit China, they are often surprised to see the size of a typical meal before them. It consists of cold plates, hot dishes, soup and rice. They consider this a lavish spread. However this is a Chinese typical meal. Dinner banquets are social occasions. Upon arrival, the guests are served hot tea or soft drinks. Hosts and guests sit at a table and start their conversation. Traditionally, Chinese hosts ask their guests to help themselves instead of putting food on the guests' plates. They keep saying, "please, help yourselves". If your host serves you some dishes, which you don't desire, you may simply leave it uneaten on your plate. After you are full, you may say you don't want a certain food or that you don't want any more food at all.

When Chinese representatives or Chinese friends offer dinner or banquets, they usually overwhelm guests with food. The host's responsibility is to be hospitable; it is not the guest's job to stuff himself to the point of discomfort. But the fact that the guests eat too little may dismay the host.

During banquets and other formal meals Chinese hosts and guests usually exchange toasts and speeches. Liquor may be served for the purpose of toasting. Beer and soft drinks are also available for toasts. At the beginning of the banquet, the host is likely to make a short speech to welcome the guests and propose a toast in their honor. At this time the guests need only accept these gestures graciously. Towards the end of the meal, the senior guest should give a return speech of gratitude for the hospitality and propose an appropriate toast. Usually the meal ends when the host thanks the guests for coming or offers a final toast.

Chopsticks have been used in China for thousands of years. They are used either to grasp the food or to push it from plate to mouth. They are available for all purposes except eating soup or ice cream. Chopsticks are normally used in China, but you should not hesitate to ask for a knife or fork if you are embarrassed about your ability to eat with Chinese chopsticks. However, if you want to learn how to use chopsticks, your hosts will definitely help you with great patience. As days go by, you will be surprised at how quickly you will progress.

KEY WORDS & EXPRESSIONS 关键词汇及表达法

poultry 家禽
embrace 包含
foodstuff 食品，粮食
by virtue of 凭借于，由于
chef 主厨
prevailing 占优势的，主要的
prehistoric 史前的
deliberate 故意的，预有准备的

minimum 最小的，最低的
fundamental 基础的，基本的
indispensable 不可缺少的
caloric 热量的
banquet 宴会，盛宴
lavish spread 过多的铺张
stuff himself to the point of discomfort 饱食得难受
dismay 沮丧；惊慌
graciously 和蔼地，优雅地
appropriate 适当的
embarrass 使困窘；使局促不安
staple food 主食

General Information about Sichuan Cuisine
川菜概述

Many travelers know Sichuan cuisine for its "hot and spicy" flavors or a few of its most famous dishes, but that is only the beginning. Sichuan cuisine is legendary in China for its sophistication and diversity. The regional cuisine boasts 5,000 different dishes.

The origin of Sichuan cuisine can be traced back to the Qin and Han dynasties. Yang Xiong（杨雄）was a well-known scholar in the Western Han dynasty. He composed an ode to Shudu（《蜀都赋》）. The song described the local food in Sichuan. During the Three Kingdoms Period, the people in the kingdom of the Shu liked sweet food. During the Jin Dynasty, local people enjoyed pungent food. However, pungent food at that time referred to food made with ginger, mustard, chives, or onions. Du Fu（杜甫）, the great Tang Dynasty poet loved Sichuan food during his stay in Chengdu. In one of his poems he said, "The Sichuan wine and dishes are extremely tasty; fish in local rivers is greatly delicious." Down to the Song Dynasty Sichuan food became distinct. The ingredients were delicacies from land and river, edible wild herbs, and the meat of domestic animals and birds.

During the Ming and Qing dynasties many officials and officers came to Sichuan for trips or business. Their cooks came along bringing their different cooking styles that gradually were merged into Sichuan cuisine. The merge and absorption of different cooking styles greatly accelerated the development of local cooking towards a perfect art.

Sichuan cuisine has enjoyed a worldwide reputation. However, most people immediately think of Sichuan food soon after it is mentioned as a hot or spicy food. Actually these flavors were introduced only within the last 200 years. 200 years ago, there were no hot dishes in Sichuan cuisine, and few were cooked with pungent and hot flavorings. Originally, its flavorings were very mild, unlike the present popular dishes with the red or hot pepper.

Based on research documents, the red pepper is native to Mexico, Central America, the West Indies, and parts of South America. It is called Capsicum pepper. The Spanish discovered it in the New World and brought it back to Europe. Before the arrival of Spaniards, Indians in Peru and Guatemala used Capsicum pepper to treat stomach and other ailments.

Before the Ming Dynasty, there were no red peppers in China. The pepper was introduced into China around the end of the 17th century. Local people in Chaozhou area, Guangdong Province call the red pepper as fanjiao (番椒), which means "foreign pepper". At the beginning the red pepper was used for medical or ornamental purposes. Later on it arrived at Southwestern China.

It is unclear how the red pepper was introduced to Sichuan. There are several different sayings about the import of the pepper. One is that Indian missionaries brought the pepper with them during their travels along China's Silk Road. Another saying is that Chinese merchants who traded with Portuguese and Spanish sailors at various seaports brought them in. You may wonder why the red pepper is so popular. Here is a common explanation. Sichuan has a humid climate that encourages people to eat strongly spiced foods. The red pepper may help reduce internal dampness.

Sichuan pepper is another important ingredient in Sichuan cooking. It is known as huajiao (花椒, flower pepper). It is the Chinese pepper, and it looks like a reddish-brown fruit. The peppercorn comes from the prickly ash tree. The pepper flower creates a most sudden numbing effect on one's tongue.

In Sichuan cuisine some dishes are highly spiced and peppery hot. As a result, people often think that numbness, spicing and hotness are the main features of the Sichuan cuisine. Despite this popular belief, Sichuan dishes often contain many other flavors. There is a popular saying that states: "Food is in China, and flavor in Sichuan (食在中国,味在四川)".

Flavors of Sichuan cuisine can be rather complex. Chefs often blend together many spices to create various flavors. For examples, suanla flavor (酸辣味) is the hot and sour sauce, drawing heavily on vinegar; yuxiang flavor (鱼香味) is a tasty fish-flavored sauce, drawing on soy sauce, mashed garlic and ginger; mala flavor (麻辣味) is a numbingly spicy sauce that is often prepared with bean curd; yanxun flavor (烟熏味) is a "smoked flavor" sauce that is used with smoked duck. Besides, Sichuan chefs often use some necessary ingredients such as sesame paste, vinegar, flower pepper, fermented bean paste, fermented black beans, as well as scallions, ginger, garlic, wine and soy sauce.

When cooking, the chefs attach importance to careful selection, meticulous cutting and arrangement, and exquisite cooking. Sichuan cuisine uses quick stir-frying, quick-frying, dry-braising and dry-stewing methods. For example, food is quickly fried over a hot fire and immediately stirred for a short while. There are, however, other dishes that require a more laborious process, like the traditional Sichuan smoked duck that is marinated with more than ten herbs for one day and smoked with tea leaves during the next day before a final 45 minute steaming process.

Sichuan cuisine so carefully balances color, smell, flavor, shape, and nutrition that its dishes not only look pleasant and appealing, but also nutritious. In Sichuan recipes there are several hundred popular dishes. Sichuan cuisine is able to produce 100 different dishes, besides, Sichuan cooks provide dishes that are intentionally toned down for tourists at home and abroad. They have no difficulty in getting Sichuan food that suits their tastes whether it's in a banquet, outstanding lunches, dinners, or snacks.

Here are some well-known Sichuan dishes:

Guoba Roupian (锅巴肉片)

Guoba refers to the crispy bits of rice that get stuck to the bottom of the rice pot. Guoba is put on a hot plate in heap, and then a service person proceeds to sprinkle the rice with hot soup. At the same time the dish steams, erupts in fireworks and makes a hissing sound. The volcanic action doesn't stop until the rice is below the surface of the soup. Soupy additions are meat and vegetables, which soften the rice to a crunchy texture.

Zhangcha Yazi（樟茶鸭子）

Zhangcha Yazi is Sichuan duck smoked with camellia and camphor leaves. Local ducks are soaked in glutinous rice juice mixed with salt, Chinese prickly ash, and peppers. Then the soaked ducks are removed from the juice and are smoked with camellia and camphor leaves. The smoking doesn't stop until the ducks' skin becomes brown. The final step is to steam or deep-fry the brown ducks. Afterwards the ducks smell good. They are dark red in color with a crunchy exterior and tasty tender meat.

Gongbao Jiding（宫保鸡丁）

Gongbao Jiding is the spicy chicken fried with peanuts. Almost all the local restaurants serve this dish. The main ingredients consist of chicken breast meat, dry peppercorns and peanuts. A cook cuts the breast meat into diced size, peppercorns and other necessary ingredients are added, and then it is put into hot oil to fry. When the dish is ready, fried peanuts are added.

According to a legend, a man whose name was Ding Gongbao（丁宫保）from Guizhou province invented this dish. When he served as a governor of Sichuan during the Qing Dynasty, his cook often cooked the fried chicken with dry red pepper. Ding enjoyed this dish, and he himself worked with his cook to further improve its quality. Gradually this recipe became widely spread in Sichuan, and local people named the dish after Ding Gongbao.

Yuxiang Rousi（鱼香肉丝）

Yuxiang Rousi is the fish-fragrant sliced pork. This is a pork dish cooked with bamboo shoots, mushrooms, and Sichuan's special seasonings and spices. The sauce is called "yuxiang", which means the fish fragrance. The dish has no fish, and some eaters may doubt why the dish is named after the fish-fragrance. Some explanations might be helpful. (1) The sauce makes the pork taste like fish. (2) The sauce was originally invented to cook fish. Later it was transferred to pork. Actually the sauce tastes sweet, sour, and hot. It is widely used with pork, fish, chicken, eggplant, and bean curd.

Mapo Doufu（麻婆豆腐）

Mapo Doufu is the Mapo bean curd. Mapo refers to a lady with a pockmarked face. Doufu means bean curd. Mapo Doufu is one of the common dishes in Sichuan. It is characterized by the use of many spices, including chopped scallions, minced garlic, minced fresh ginger, Chinese chilly sauce or crushed dried red chilly peppers and Sichuan flower peppercorn.

Mapo Doufu is a dish of small cubes of bean curd, prepared in a chilli sauce. It is said that a century ago a lady with a pockmarked face set up a shop with her husband near a bridge in Chengdu. The lady served passing peddlers and boatmen her red-hot bean curd stew. Gradually her customers named her bean curd dish after her pockmarked face.

Kugua Rouxian（苦瓜肉馅）

Kugua Rouxian is the bitter squash with meat filling. This food is made with squash and meat. The cook hollows out a squash, and stuffs the hollowed squash with minced pork meat. Afterwards the cook steams the stuffed squash. The meat in the squash tastes mild and the squash tastes bitter. Local people like this dish because they believe that the bitter squash might be helpful to lower body temperature. This dish is very popular in the summertime.

Yutou Doufutang（鱼头豆腐汤）

Yutou Doufutang is the fish head in bean curd soup. The soup is made of fish heads, mushrooms and bean curd. The cook first deep-fries the fish heads and then adds chilli bean sauce, scallion, ginger, minced garlic, salt, pepper and cooking wine. When the fish heads are done, bean curd sheets and water are added and brought to a boil. The soup when done, is sprinkled with garlic shoots. It is tasty.

Fenzheng Niurou（粉蒸牛肉）

Fenzheng Niurou is the steamed beef with ground rice. This dish is made mainly with beef, spiced ground rice and sweet fermented flour sauce. The cook first slices the beef and adds beans, fermented glutinous rice juice, soy sauce, prickly ash powder, hot chilly powder, mashed garlic and ground rice. He stirs the mixture well and then steams it until the beef tastes mild and tender.

Huiguo Rou（回锅肉）

Huiguo Rou is the twice-cooked pork. It is made of pork shoulder with the skin plus garlic bolt, broad beans and sweet fermented flour sauce. The cook usually stews the pork till the meat is tender and the skin is soft. Then he slices the pork when it is cool. Afterwards he stir-fries the pork slices in 6-fold hot oil till the pork is slightly curled. He drops in finely chopped broad beans and continues stir-frying the pork until brown. Then he adds sweet fermented flour sauce and stir-fries until the flavor comes out. This is one of the daily dishes in Sichuan.

Yuxiang Qiezi (鱼香茄子)

Yuxiang Qiezi is the fish flavored eggplant. It is made with eggplant and chilli bean sauce. The cook usually cuts the eggplants into chunks and deep-fries them until soft. Then he removes the fried eggplant. Afterwards the cook fries a chilli bean sauce until the flavor comes out, and then adds the eggplant, finely chopped scallions, ginger, soy sauce, and vinegar. Finally the cook thickens the mixture with a cornstarch solution.

Hongyou Haijiao (红油海椒)

Hongyou Haijiao is Sichuan chilli sauce. It is a traditional chilli sauce used in Sichuan pickles or cold dishes. It is made with vegetable oil, red chilli powder, finely chopped garlic and fresh sliced ginger. The way to produce the sauce is to heat the oil in a wok first and then add the garlic and ginger. Remove the oil from the heat and pour it into a bowl, which contains the chilli powder. Simmer the hot oil and the powder mixture until they cool down.

Sichuan Paocai (四川泡菜)

Sichuan Paocai is the local pickles made in Sichuan. This is a daily dish. Even at a formal banquet the pickles are presented. The way to produce the pickles is first to place the peppercorn and the salt in a clean container and pour in boiling water. Then add wine, ginger, and hot pepper (cut into small pieces) into the container after the water is cool.

Cut the turnip, carrot, and cucumber into small pieces approximately the size of a small finger, and place them in the salt water. Some more vegetables can be added. Afterwards the container is covered with a tightly fitting lid, and the vegetables are allowed to soak for about two or three days.

KEY WORDS & EXPRESSIONS 关键词汇及表达法

sophistication 复杂
diversity 差异，多样性
trace back 追溯
pungent 刺激性的，辛辣
ginger 生姜
accelerate 加速
Capsicum pepper 辣椒
Spaniard 西班牙人
Indian 印第安人
Peru 秘鲁
Guatemala 危地马拉
Ailments 疾病
seaport 海港
numbing 麻木的
vinegar 醋
mash 捣碎
garlic 大蒜
sesame paste 芝麻酱
fermented bean paste 豆瓣酱
meticulous 小心翼翼的
laborious 艰苦的，费力的
marinate 浸泡
sprinkle 洒，喷淋
erupt 爆发
volcanic 火山的
crunchy 易碎的
camellia 山茶
camphor 樟脑

glutinous　黏性的
Chinese prickly ash　花椒粉
seasoning　调味品，调料
eggplant　茄子
pockmarked face　麻子脸
scallion　大葱
peddler　小贩
meat filling　肉馅
bitter squash　苦瓜
curl　(使)卷曲
chunk　短而厚的一块
thicken　(使)变浓
cornstarch　玉米淀粉
boiling water　滚烫的水
turnip　萝卜
leek　韭菜

Famous Snacks
名小吃

Sichuan cuisine includes a number of famous snack dishes. They are called "xiaochi" in Chinese. Sichuan snacks are very popular. They have unique flavors. They are cooked with various seasonings.

Chengdu snacks have a long history. They have a particular style in color, smell, taste and shape. Each restaurant in Chengdu tries to offer a variety of traditional snacks in an attempt to satisfy customers at home and abroad. Such an effort saves travelers much time in searching for snack places marked on the city guide map. A few of the more renowned snack dishes are listed here below：

Lai Tangyuan(赖汤圆)

This snack is Lai Rice-Dumpling. A man called Lai Yuanxin (赖源鑫) invented this dish in 1894. Lai began as a street stall vendor, and his rice dumpling had a delicate visual appeal and tasted sweet. Later, Lai set up his own shop, and local people named the rice dumpling after Lai. Traditionally four dumplings are in a soup with a sesame sauce dish at the side. Each dumpling has a different sweet stuffing inside, and the eater dips a dumpling in the sugar sesame sauce before eating it.

Dandan Mian (担担面)

This snack is a kind of hot-spiced noodles or spicy peanut noodles. It is flavored with a sauce containing dried shrimp, shredded preserved vegetables, crushed roasted peanuts, sesame seeds, chilli oil, soy sauce, vinegar and garlic. Dandan refers to shoulder poles. In the earliest time when a noodle peddler shouldered his pole, he usually carried two baskets on either side as he walked along streets. The baskets contained his noodles and sauce. He sold his noodles to passers-by and residents who lived on the streets. His noodles cost almost nothing, and gradually local people called it Dandan Noodle.

Fuqi Feipian (夫妻肺片)

This snack is made up with slices of beef and assorted entrails of oxen. Fuqi refers to a husband and his wife. It is said that a husband, Guo Chaohua (郭朝华) and his wife invented this snack. People named the snack the Husband and Wife's Slices of Beef and Assorted Entrails of Oxen. Usually, Sichuan chefs slice cooked beef and some oxen entrails, and place them on a plate. Then they add numbingly spicy sauce to the beef and entrails on the plate.

Long Chaoshou（龙抄手）

This snack is a wonton-like dumpling. Chaoshou is Sichuan dialect for soup dumpling. It is made mainly with minced pork, chopped scallions, flour wonton wrappers trimmed into circular shape and Sichuan chilli oil. Chefs mix the pork and scallions, then they fold a bit of the mixture inside each wonton wrapper, pressing the edges together to make flat half-moon shapes. Afterwards they boil the wontons in water until they float (about 5 minutes). Meanwhile, they mix the chilli oil, soy sauce, vinegar, Sichuan pepper, garlic and sugar. When the wontons are ready, they are drained and the oil mixture is poured over them. It tastes sweet and spicy.

There are some other tasty and delicious dishes listed below:

灯影牛肉　Lampshade Beef, cooked sealed in cellophane pouches

叶儿粑　Leaf-Cakes, wrapped in banana of leaves

珍珠圆子　Pearl Dumplings, sweet stuffed dumplings with grains of rice outside

棒棒鸡　Bang-Bang Chicken, a dish of cold chicken shreds topped with a spicy sesame paste sauce

鸡丝凉面　Cold Noodles with Chicken Shreds

玻璃烧卖　Glassy Shaomai, dumplings with meat fillings

KEY WORDS & EXPRESSIONS　关键词汇及表达法

vendor　小贩

visual appeal　视觉吸引力

rice dumpling　汤圆

sesame seed　芝麻

passers-by　过路人

slice 薄片，切片
assorted 多样混合的
entrails 内脏
chopped 切的
chilli oil 红油辣子
cellophane 玻璃纸
pouch 小袋
sesame paste sauce 芝麻酱

Hotpot
火锅

Hotpot is the most famous and favorite dish in Sichuan. It is noted for its peppery and hot taste. Customers gather around a small pot heated with charcoal, electricity, or gas. Each pot is filled with a nutritious soup base. Around the wok are placed a dozen plates of paper-thin slices of raw meat and other ingredients. The customers pick up the raw ingredients and boil them in the soup base. Then they take them out of the wok, dip them in a little bowl of special sauce and eat them.

Hotpot supposedly originated in Chongqing. In the 1920s, there were several oxen slaughterhouses located on the northern side of Changjiang in Chongqing. The slaughterhouses often sold oxen entrails at a cheap price to vendors who owned stalls near the river ferry. The vendors cleaned the entrails and cut them into small pieces before putting them into pots to stew with hot pepper and other sauces. The vendors usually sold the stewed entrails soup to boatmen, laborers and peddlers. It was cheap and tasty.

However, the sliced oxen entrails in soup could only be eaten while it was hot. As weather changed and wind blew from the river, the soup soon became cool, and the cool entrails didn't taste good. So some boatmen set up a big wok full of hot, spiced oil. They skewed sliced entrails and ate them hot. This new way of hotpot eating gradually spread far and wide in Sichuan province. Now it is very popular and can be found at every corner of the city. Many sidewalk hotpot operations and exquisite hotpot restaurants have been set up to meet the demand from the local people.

There are a great variety of hotpots. They include Yuanyang Hotpot (鸳鸯火锅), Four Tastes Hotpot (四味火锅), Yachang Hotpot (鸭肠火锅) and Fish Head Hotpot (鱼头火锅). Restaurant owners offer spicy hotpot at different levels based on customers' tastes so that friends or family with different tastes can huddle around the hotpot. One of the most popular hotpots is Yuanyang Hotpot in Sichuan. Yuanyang hotpot refers to the wok, which has been partitioned into two parts by a thin metal plate. One part is filled with traditional hot-spicy soup and the other with non-hot-spicy broth. This typical hotpot suits many customers at home and abroad. Whatever your tastes are and wherever you travel in Sichuan, you will find something you like to eat.

KEY WORDS & EXPRESSIONS 关键词汇及表达法

wok 锅
slaughterhouse 屠宰场
stew 炖，焖
huddle 挤作一团
partition 分割；划分

Sichuan Wine Store 品尝川酒

General Information

概 述

Wine or liquor means "jiu" in Chinese. Actually the word "wine" gets rather loosely translated. Jiu is used to mean all types of beverages, from beer (pijiu, 啤酒) to liquor of all sorts, including the grape wine (putaojiu, 葡萄酒). Many Chinese "wines" are in fact spirits. Tibetans have an interesting brew called qingkejiu (青稞酒), made from barley.

Wine has been intimately intertwined in almost every aspect of Chinese culture since earliest times. Wine has traditionally been an important part of special celebrations and festivals. Besides, wine is important in cooking, and it is a part of the meal.

It is said that Du Kang (杜康) who lived in the Xia Dynasty invented wine. Today his name is still used to indicate alcohol. There is archaeological evidence of wine production in the agricultural communities along Changjiang 7,000 years ago. As early as in the Shang Dynasty, the use of grain to make wine had become widespread. Inscriptions on bones and tortoise shells as well as bronze inscriptions preserve the records of wine drinking and the worshipping of ancestors with wine in the Shang.

For the most part, grains were used to ferment wine throughout China in ancient times. Ancient governments decided whether to lift their ban on wine making, or how heavy a wine tax to levy based on whether or not the grain harvest was bountiful. In ancient times emperors and kings often held banquets with wine. Every sort of wine vessel also served as an important kind of sacrificial object. Over the ages, wine gradually became directly linked to daily life.

Traditionally, Chinese people drink wine only when eating. It is believed that wine should be consumed slowly to enhance its pleasure. The Chinese play games when they're drinking. The goal of the games is not to get drunk, but to have fun. One of the popular games is finger guessing. Wine aims to heighten the drinking atmosphere. Chinese people do not typically frequent western-style bars. Public drunkenness causes displeased looks from other people.

It is not polite at a formal dinner to drink wine or liquor by oneself. If you want to drink, you may offer a toast to anyone at the table and then enjoy yourself. In the same way, if you happen to be the guest of honor at a meal, or the "object" of numerous toasts, it is perfectly acceptable to raise your glass to your lips and lick the wine lightly. Ganbei (干杯) is a popular toast term in China, which means "empty your glass" or "bottom up". As a rule, toasts are necessary at banquets. If you really can't drink, you can fill your wine glass with tea instead. Usually Chinese women don't drink (except beer) in public.

In China, a host serves three or four different types of beverages during a formal meal. A large glass holds the orange soda pop or beer, or a pleasant mixture of the two sodas; the tiny glasses are for wine.

Beer, though not a native product, has been brewed in China since the 19th century. The best known is Tsingtao beer (青岛啤酒) made with a mineral water. At present, local beer breweries are found in all the major cities. It has become popular, and particularly in summer it is in great demand in many places.

For centuries, China has been producing a wide range of strong clear liquors. The principle ingredient is gaoliang (高粱), a grain belonging to the sorghum family. China was the first country to distill liquor with sorghum. Sorghum and corn have a very similar composition, but sorghum makes better liquor. Famous sorghum liquors include Maotai (茅台) in Guizhou, Fenjiu (汾酒) in Shanxi, and other well-known liquors in Sichuan. The most famous liquor is Maotai. It is used for toasting at banquets. Drinkers are advised to take Maotai in small sips, and not to drink it on an empty stomach.

At present the traditional winemaking techniques and drinking habits continue, and imported wines have also gained acceptance. When dining with friends and relatives, there is now a wide range from which to choose. This has not only enriched the pleasure of drinking, but also it has made the wine-drinking culture of Chinese people more colorful.

KEY WORDS & EXPRESSIONS 关键词汇及表达法

intertwine (使)纠缠,(使)缠绕
alcohol 酒,酒精
ancestor 祖宗,祖先
lift a ban on 取消……禁令
tax 税;税款
levy 征收
bountiful 丰裕的,充足的
consume 消耗,消费
enhance 提高,增强
get drunk 喝醉
beverage 饮料

soda 苏打，碳酸水
composition 成分，合成物成分
drink on an empty stomach 空腹饮酒
winemaking technique 酿酒技术
drinking habit 饮酒习惯

Drinks in Sichuan
四川酒类

Local people started to make and drink wine as early as in the Shang Dynasty according to a recent display on the ancient wine containers and utensils unearthed at Sanxingdui Site in Guanghan county，Sichuan province.

In the Han Dynasty，Sichuan agricultural techniques reached a rather high standard，and grain yield in Chengdu also increased. The whole society appeared prosperous，and the winemaking industry developed.

In the Western Han Dynasty，Sima Xiangru，a well-known scholar and Zhuo Wenjun managed a public wine house as means of livelihood in Chengdu，Sichuan. Sima Xiangru sold wine；Zhuo Wenjun cleaned utensils and cups.

In 1977 and 1978，a large amount of ancient bricks and stones dating back to the Eastern Han Dynasty were unearthed in the suburbs of Chengdu. On the surface of each stone or brick were figures of animals or houses，which portrayed the ancient local people's daily life. Some relief stones display how the people brewed wine，managed public wine houses，or drank wine. However，most of the present well-known liquors didn't come into being until the Tang or Song dynasties. At that time the local liquors were taken as gifts to the imperial court.

Wine drinking is a custom enjoyed by people all over the world. But the culture in wine drinking differs. Ancient Chinese men of letters, after tasting a wine, might write all sorts of wine poems or monographs. I'd like to list some scholars who had those experiences.

Li Bai was one of the greatest poets in Chinese literature. He moved with his family to Sichuan when he was five. He enjoyed drinking wine in Sichuan, and some of his poems described his happiness before or after his wine drinking. His poems on wine drinking have immortalized him.

For the Moment, Dinking Wine（将进酒）

Drink your fill in high delight,

And leave your golden wine-cup empty facing the moonlight.

Heaven born, my talents will find a place,

A thousand gold coins spent, more will come again.

So roast the goats, kill the cattle and let us merry be,

And down three hundred cupfuls,

in a single breath and high glee.

(人生得意须尽欢,莫使金樽空对月。天生我材必有用,千金散尽还复来。烹羊宰牛且为乐,会须一饮三百杯。)

Inquiring of the Moon, Wine cup in Hand（把酒问月）

My only wish is that when wine and song are near

Moonlight will forever linger on this goblet fair.

(唯愿当歌对酒时,月光常照金樽里。)

Du Fu was a well-known poet of the Tang Dynasty. He

frequently used his poetry to expose social injustice and the voices of suffering people. He came to Chengdu in 759. Here he lived in peace, and composed over two hundred poems. These poems expressed his appreciation of the local landscape and good relationships among neighbors. Some of the poems were closely associated with wine drinking. For example:

A Friend Visits (客至)

So far from market, the food is plain.

A needy household can drink is this home brewed wine.

If you like, I'll call across the fence to my old neighbor,

To toast the last cups!

(盘飧市远无兼味,樽酒家贫只旧醅。肯与邻翁相对饮,隔篱呼取尽馀杯。)

Su Shi was also known as Su Dongpo. He was born into a family with a long tradition of government service in Meishan county, Sichuan. He was the leading poet of the Northern Song Dynasty. The following is some lines from his ci-poems, which display that he enjoyed drinking like Li Bai.

***The Beautiful Lady Yu*"** (虞美人)

How fair the lakes and hills of Southern land,

With plains extending as a golden strand!

How oft, wine-cup in hand, have you been here.

To make us linger drunk though we appear?

Written for Chen Xiang at the Scenic Hall.

Prelude to the Melody of Water (水调歌头)

Bright moon, when will you appear?

I ask the sky, holding my wine-cup in hand high...

There are also some legends, which show the power of wine in Sichuan. One story says that a long time ago a kind of pestilence occurred in Luzhou areas. Zhuge Liang happened to station his troops there. He asked his soldiers to collect a hundred medicinal herbs. Then he made a drug with these herbs, and ordered his soldiers and local people to take the drug together with a special liquor wine. The mixed medicine and liquor effectively prevented the pestilence.

Another story says that Zhang Xianzhong, one of the top farmer's rebellion leaders in the Ming Dynasty, occupied Luzhou city with his soldiers. One evening he was patrolling the city when the smell of liquor greeted him. He approached the spot, and saw a big liquor container, which was leaking. Zhang drank a cup of the liquor from the container. Unexpectedly he felt relaxed and happy. With his tongue and teeth full of a sweet scent, he then composed the poem below:

The scent overwhelms the Luzhou city,
And continues flowing ten miles around.
Xianzhong drank one cup only,
And his face radiates with smiles.

(香溢泸州城，芳流十里外；献忠一杯酒，醉颜红可掬。)

In Sichuan there are four special local products. They are liquors, wines, tea and traditional herbal medicine. At the present time the wine production is the main part of the local food industry. Distilleries in Sichuan produce varieties of liquors, which are sold in China and abroad. Government departments concerned with the liquor industry often hold commodity fairs at the national level. During the fairs, experts in the liquor fields judge the quality and value of hundreds of liquor exhibits. Then they nominate the best quality liquors. Traditionally there are ten liquors across China, which are commonly recognized as the top quality liquors. Five of them are from Sichuan. They are Wuliang Ye（五粮液）, Luzhou Laojiao Tequ（泸州老窖特曲）, Jiannan Chun（剑南春）, Quanxing Daqu（全兴大曲）and Gulin Langjiu（古蔺郎酒）.

Jiannanchun Liquor

Jiannanchun Liquor（剑南春）is produced in Mianzhu county, Sichuan province. This county has a 2,000-year history of wine making. In the Tang Dynasty, a wine named Jiannan Zhi Shaochun（剑南之烧春）was produced in this area. Jiannan refers to the geographical location. Shao means "burning". Chun is a refined sounding name for spring. The liquor became famous in the Song Dynasty with the names of Mijiu（蜜酒）and Edan（鹅蛋）. During the Qing Dynasty it was called Mianzhu Daqu（绵竹大曲）. In 1958, it was formally named as Jiannan Chun. In 1979, it joined the list of China's Top Ten Famous Liquors.

The liquor is made from grains and the water from Wangfei Spring（王妃泉）. The grains include sorghum, rice, glutinous rice, wheat and corn. The ready-made liquor looks translucent, has fragrance and tastes mellow. It offers a lasting and agreeable aftertaste.

Wuliang Ye Liquor

Wuliang Ye Liquor（五粮液）is produced in the Yibin area of Sichuan province. Wuliang means five different food grains. Its original name was the Food Grains Liquor. As early as in the Ming Dynasty, the Food Grains Liquor became famous in

Sichuan. The main grains consisted of good-quality rice, glutinous rice, sorghum, wheat and corn. The liquor was made based on the secret recipe preserved by Wen Defeng (温德丰), a well-known distillery. In 1915, the Food Grains Liquor won a gold medal when Zhang Wanhe (张万和) Distillery exhibited the liquor at the Panama International Exposition. In 1929, Wuliang Ye replaced the name of the Food Grains Liquor. In 1952, the local government established a state-owned Wuliang Ye Distillery with better facilities. Later the distillery evolved into Wuliang Ye Group Co., Ltd.

In 1988, the distillery received the quality certificate for its products from the national government and the Quality Control Prize from the National Ministry of Commerce. In 1991, it won the title of One of the Top Ten Brands in China. In 1994, the distillery passed the BVOI International Quality Attestation by the International Quality Inspection Bureau of France. In 1995, the 50th Worldwide Statistics Conference recognized the distillery as the King of Liquor Distillery in China.

Wuliang Ye Liquor is a kind of translucent liquor, which has heavy fragrance. It tastes mellow, sweet and refreshing. The main products of the distillery include 3 types, 18 varieties and 42 specifications of the liquor. They include Wuliang Ye, Wuliang Chun (五粮春), Wuliang Chun (五粮纯) and fruit wines. The products are on sale across China and are exported to more than 130 countries and regions.

Luzhou Laojiao Tequ Liquor

Luzhou Laojiao Tequ Liquor (泸州老窖特曲) is produced in Luzhou area in Sichuan province. The most prestigious product is Tequ Liquor (特曲), followed by Touqu Liquor (头曲) and Erqu

Liquor (二曲). They are made with a kind of ferment called Daqu (大曲). In order to produce high-quality liquor, the experienced wine makers in the distillery set up a 1-to-20 point standard related to the liquor's storage in cellars, taste and rate. During the liquor production the liquor is categorized as Tequ Liquor if its quality is beyond the 16th point. The same case is true if Touqu Liquor's quality is within 10-to-16 point; Erqu Liquor's quality is below 10th point.

Tequ Liquor is a handicraft product with a several hundred-year-old tradition. The liquor distillery started as early as in Ming Dynasty, and now it has lasted over 400 years. The oldest earth cellar is still in existence today. It is said that it is more than three hundred years old. At the end of Qing Dynasty there were more than three hundred households involved in the liquor production. Between 1951 - 1955, two local state-run liquor distilleries were set up in Luzhou: Luzhou's Liquor Distillery and Luzhou City Distillery.

Traditionally, solid-state yeast fermentation and the special Longquan (龙泉) water are used. The water tastes slightly sweet and is a bit acidic. The liquor in each distillery is usually stored in cellars for many years before being blended into Luzhou Laojiao.

Luzhou Laojiao has a heavy fragrance. It tastes mellow and a bit sweet. After drinking, you soon feel refreshed and enjoy a long better aftertaste. In 1915, the liquor won a gold medal at the Panama International Exposition. Since then the liquor has won dozens of other prizes at home and abroad whenever and wherever it has been displayed at expositions or fairs. At present Luzhou Laojiao stands side by side with Maotai liquor made in the town of Maotai in the northwestern part of Renhuai county, Guizhou

Province.

Quanxing Daqu Liquor

Quanxing Daqu Liquor (全兴大曲) literally means prosperity in an all-around way. It is produced in Chengdu, the capital of Sichuan province. During the Daoguang (道光) period of Qing Dynasty, Fushengquan (福升全) Distillery produced the liquor with the water from Xue Tao (薛涛) well. In 1951, Chengdu Distillery was set up on the same spot of the ancient Quanxing Distillery. In 1963, the liquor was put on the list of the top ten famous liquors in China. In 1984, the liquor won a gold medal again conferred by the Chinese authoritative department concerned. Since then, the liquor has won a numbers of prizes at international food expositions or at national wine appraisal meetings.

The liquor is made from sorghum and wheat. It has a heavy fragrance, and it tastes mellow and sweet. Soon after tasting, drinkers feel utterly refreshed.

In 1989, Quanxing Distillery displayed a series of the liquor at the Fifth National Wine Appraisal Meeting. Its alcoholic contents respectively include 38, 52 and 60 proofs. All of its series of the liquor expectedly won gold medals. At present the liquor sells not only in China, but also in other countries and regions.

Gulin Langjiu Liquor

Gulin Langjiu Liquor (古蔺郎酒) is produced in Gulin county, Sichuan province. Gulin Langjiu is unique Sichuan liquor, which enjoys a similar heavy fragrance and taste as Maotai Liquor. By the end of the Qing Dynasty, a local distillery in Erlang (二郎) town, Gulin county, produced a liquor named

Huisha Langjiu Liquor (回沙郎酒), which gained a commendable name both in Sichuan and Guizhou at that time. Erlang town is 70km away from the village, which is the birthplace of Maotai Liquor, and a river called Chishui River (赤水) flows between the two places. because the location near Maotai Liquor Distillery, Gulin Langjiu has similar brewing techniques as used at Maotai. The raw materials are top quality sorghum and wheat.

In 1984, the liquor won a gold medal and was put on the list of the Top Ten Chinese liquors during the Annual National Wine Appraisal Meeting. The distillery has developed its series of products to satisfy the different needs for different consumers. Its alcoholic contents respectively include 53%, 43%, 39%, 28%, and 25%. The other products are Heavy Fragrance-typed Gulin Tequ Liquor (浓香型古蔺特曲), Gulin Touqu Liquor (古蔺头曲) and Gulin Daqu Liquor (古蔺大曲).

KEY WORDS & EXPRESSIONS 关键词汇及表达法

imperial court 宫廷
man of letters 文人
monograph 专论
immortalize 使永恒
merry 欢乐的，愉快的
glee 兴高采烈
inquire 询问
linger on 徘徊，拖延
expose 揭露
injustice 非正义
relationship 关系
strand 线；绳
pestilence 瘟疫

patrol　出巡，巡逻
radiate with　发光；辐射
nominate　提名，推荐
recognize　认可，承认
mellow　芳醇的，酒的芳醇的
aftertaste　余味，回味
Panama　巴拿马
evolve　进化
quality certificate　质量证书
brand　商标
attestation　证明
statistics　统计
heavy fragrance　浓香型
specification　规格；说明书；规范
export　出口
prestigious　有威信的，有声望的
cellar　酒窖
yeast　酵母
acidic　酸的，酸性的
confer　授予，颁给
wine appraisal meeting　酒评会
proof　酒精度
commendable　值得表扬的
consumer　消费者
alcoholic content　含酒精成分
respectively　分别地，各个地

Sichuan Teahouse 品茶

General Tea Facts

概述

When you are in Chengdu, you will see teahouses everywhere on the streets. There is a saying: "China has the best teahouses in the world, and Chengdu has the best teahouses in China." As soon as the guests enter the teahouse, the waiters or waitresses greet them with a smile on their faces, and they hold in their hands teapots and cups. After the guests have been seated, they set the cups on the table and pour the water behind the guests or from above their heads. When the cups are almost full, the waiters or waitresses raise their hands high suddenly, but not a drop of water is spilled.

People who go to the teahouses are not really thirsty. Retired people go to the teahouse and sit there all day long to chat with each other. Sometimes, people bring guests to the teahouses. They chat, drink tea and eat melon or sunflower seeds.

Chinese people like to drink tea. It is the same with Western people who enjoy coffee. Tea was first produced in China, and it has been a part of daily life in China for at least 1,500 years. Teahouses in China have always been the equivalent of the French cafes or the British pubs. Recently coffee shops and pubs have increased in Chinese cities, but there is no danger of them replacing teahouses.

The word "tea" is one of the few words of Chinese origin used frequently in English. It is derived from the plant's name as it is pronounced in South China. In standard Chinese it is pronounced "cha". However, local people in South China have their own dialects, and they pronounce "cha (茶)" as "te" or "tay". The vowel in "te" or "tay" sounds rhyming with the "e".

There are two different sayings concerning the earliest spread of tea outside China.

In the seventeenth century, tea was introduced into Indonesia, where local people in Java picked up the sound of "te" or "tah" from South China. Later Dutchmen arrived there and soon learned how to drink tea. They brought tea back to Europe. Therefore, the "te" pronunciation was transferred into Europe as well as Britain.

The other saying is that the Portuguese opened up the sea routes to China. Some say that the opening-up was as early as 1515. Jesuit priests were on the Portuguese ships, and they took the tea drinking habit back to Portugal. At that time, the sailors from the ships encouraged the Dutch merchants to enter the tea trade. By 1610, tea was shipped regularly to ports in France, Holland and the Baltic coast.

Tea was first used as medicine. Ancient man drank it to relieve poison. *Shen Nong Benchao Classics* (神农本草经) is one of the Chinese medical books. It states that tealeaves tastes bitter, and can make people spirited and think clearly. Hua Tuo (华佗) said in *the Eating Classics* (食经) that a continuous drinking of bitter tea was good for thinking.

It is commonly believed that the habit of drinking tea originated in Sichuan. Three thousand years ago, local people in Sichuan began to drink tea early in the Spring and Autumn Period. During the period of Qin Dynasty the tea drinking habit began to spread into the other areas of China. According to a historic book by the name of *General Sichuan History*(四川志), local people began to plant tea during Western Han Dynasty. Zhang Jingyang(张景阳)of Western Jin Dynasty spoke highly of tea produced on Mt. Qingcheng near Chengdu. In his poem by the name of *Climbing Chengdu Bai Tu Tower* (登成都白菟楼) Zhang said, "The fragrant tea is superior to the Daoist Sixth Quietness, and its pleasant taste spreads to nine districts. (芳茶冠六清,溢味播九区。)"

The custom of drinking tea gradually spread out from Sichuan. Towards the end of the Western Han Dynasty, tea was regarded as the first-class drink in imperial and noble families. From the Jin to the Sui dynasties drinking tea became popular among the common people.

However, tea drinking was more common in the South than in the North. People in the North looked on tea drinking with contempt. They even said, "Though tea is offered at a dinner party, everyone feels distressed to drink it except people from the south".

The fashion of drinking tea was prosperous in the Tang Dynasty. During that period, Sichuan was considered as one of the seven key bases to produce tea. Lu Yu (陆羽) of the Tang Dynasty published his academic book called *the Book of Tea* (茶经). It was the first book about the tea subject in China. In his book he systematically illustrated the Sichuan tea plantation, tealeaves processing through the dry heat of an oven and the tea drinking habits. He also praised highly the "loose tea (散茶)" from Mt. Qingcheng.

There was a history book called *the Supplement to the History of Tang Dynasty* (唐国史补), which mentioned the tea from Mt. Mengding in Sichuan. The book said, "The local people have a custom to entertain their guests with good tea." Even high quality tea falls into many different types. In the Jiannan area both Mengding tea and Shihua tea rank first in terms of their tastes and scent.

Since the Tang Dynasty the local governments started to present the Mengding tea as a sort of the immortal tea to the imperial court in order to show respect for the emperors' leadership.

As tea drinking became more and more popular, the way of drinking tea varied. Before the Tang Dynasty, people were not particular about their tea drinking. They drank tea for thirsty and medical purposes. In the Tang Dynasty, people tended to have more delicate tea tastes. The process seemed complicated. The tea drinker usually had to go through several stages before he/she could perform the preparation process properly. The first stage was to select tea, the second was to choose excellent tea cups and cooking utensils, the third was to prepare charcoal, the fourth was to get water, the fifth was to bake the chosen tea, the sixth was to grind the tea, the seventh was to cook the tea, and the final one was to drink the tea.

People in Tang Dynasty thought the taste might be better through the above procedures. They also took great care in the selection of water. The best water was from mountain springs, and the worst from ground wells.

From Tang to Song dynasties the output of tea production in Sichuan usually ranked first in China. During the Song Dynasty, the tea from Mt. Qingcheng continued to be on the list of tribute articles offered to the imperial court.

In 907, Tang Dynasty finally fell and China split into a number of independent states. The South split into seveval kingdoms, which remained peaceful, and trade and commerce developed rapidly. The tea production in the southern areas at the present sites of Jiangsu and Zhejiang provinces developed so quickly that later these areas gradually became the center of China's tea arts and culture.

People in the Song Dynasty drank tea more delicately than those in the Tang. Tea drinking was very popular among royal families in Tang. During Song Dynasty there were teahouses in some cities. Common people could go and drink tea there. In Chengdu some people set up tea service centers to offer tea for passers-by free of charge. It was called "official tea".

In the Ming and Qing dynasties, tea drinking was different from the previous dynasties. People drank piece-tea instead of solid-tea. Tea-makers split the tea-leaf in an attempt to strengthen the tea-leaf's flavor. People in Ming Dynasty mainly drank green tea. Flower-tea came into being in the Ming Dynasty.

Since Ming Dynasty, the development of Sichuan tea began to slow down. At the same time tea production advanced in Jiangsu and Zhejiang provinces in South China.

Down to the Qing Dynasty, jasmine tea was produced in Suzhou. Oolong tea (乌龙茶) and black tea (红茶) appeared in the Qing Dynasty, also. Incidentally, "black tea" was translated into Chinese as "red tea", and gradually people accepted the translation. Well, what's the main difference between the green tea and the black tea? The green tea is the variety which keeps the original color of the tealeaves without fermentation during processing. The black tea is fermented before baking, then it is developed on the basis of the green tea. There is semi-fermented tea like oolong tea. The jasmine tea（茉莉花茶）falls into the category of semi-fermented tea.

Jasmine buds are intentionally added into the tea, which produce an agreeable scent. Customers usually buy jasmine tea according to its quality grades, which may come in as many as ten or more grades. For example, jasmine tea in grade one is regarded as the best tea.

In the early days, people usually crushed tealeaves to powder or tiny pieces before they were soaked in a liquid. This custom has passed over to the Japanese tea ceremony. Teashops in China sell nearly all tea in leaf form to maintain the natural flavor.

KEY WORDS & EXPRESSIONS 关键词汇及表达法

teapot 茶壶
waitress 女服务生
sunflower seed 向日葵子
equivalent of 相等的，相当的
pub 酒馆
derive 起源
dialect 方言
transfer 转移，调转
Portuguese 葡萄牙的；葡萄牙人的
Portugal 葡萄牙
Jesuit priest 耶稣会士
Baltic coast 波罗的海沿岸
contempt 蔑视
distressed 哀伤的
systematically 系统地
bulk tea 散茶

be particular about　挑剔
preparation process　准备过程
utensil　器具
grind　磨(碎)
green tea　绿茶
flower-tea　花茶
come into being　诞生
Oolong tea　乌龙茶
jasmine tea　茉莉花茶
agreeable scent　好闻的香味
ferment　发酵

Tea Culture in Sichuan
四川茶文化

Traditionally, local people enjoy drinking tea. Usually, local people drink tea at any time they like. A tea drinker commonly brews tea in a cup first by dropping a bit of dry tea leaves into the cup and then fills the cup one-third full with hot boiled water. The drinker refills the cup before starting to drink. People often say that the tea water smells and tastes the best after the third water infusion. Sometimes a heavy tea drinker brews tea twice or even three times.

People usually drink jasmine tea when they sit in teahouses. Jasmine tea is the most enjoyable local tea. In Chengdu teahouses abound in and out of this city. Teahouses sprawl over Chengdu sidewalks, in back-alley sections and suburbs. Teahouses offer hot boiled water and tea snacks, and have a more comfortable setting with bamboo armchairs, low tables and sooty kettles. Local people, especially the elderly usually go to teahouses to sip tea and chat. They enjoy their pastimes and stay in their teahouses all day! Sometimes you will see that in teahouses many of them play games or cards. Some teahouses present performances like singing, local opera and story telling.

At present it is hard to get to know how teahouses were "invented" in Chengdu as well as in Sichuan. However, ever since the ancient times local teahouses remain busy because local people have made it a habit to spend part of their leisure in a teahouse.

In Chengdu, tea drinking utensils are made of bronze or ceramics. They consist of mainly teapots, cups, tea bowls and trays etc. Some first-class teahouses are equipped with high quality tea utensils. The use of tea wares has a long tradition in China. Unglazed earthenware is still used in Sichuan for brewing tea today. It reminds us of the earliest utensils used in ancient China. In the Tang Dynasty tea wares made of metals were used to serve the noblesse; civilians commonly used porcelain ware and earthenware. In the Song Dynasty tea bowls became common. They were glazed in black, dark-brown, gray, gray/white and white colors. Gray/white porcelain tea wares predominated in the Yuan Dynasty, and white glazed tea wares became popular in the Ming Dynasty. Teapots made of porcelain and purple clay were very much in fashion during the middle of the Ming Dynasty. Porcelain wares made in Jingdezhen (景德镇), Jiangxi province and purple clay wares made in Yixing (宜兴), Jiangsu province occupied the top places among various kinds of tea wares.

A servant who offers customers tea in teahouses is respectfully called the Tea Service Master. They provide good service and skillfully brew tea for tea customers. The Tea Service Masters wear a traditional costume and prepare tea water in the traditional way. They have a good knowledge of tea and skillfully mix tealeaves. In fact, the tea servants normally go through years of intensive training before they are able to obtain the title of the Tea Service Master. These experienced masters will not spill even a single drop as they pour the steaming hot water into the tiny teacup in front of tea drinkers.

In Chengdu, some large teahouses are also fixed places for a variety of Sichuan local style entertainment. They include Sichuan Opera, Sichuan dialect storytelling, ballad singing, and puppet shows. They are performed by professionals, amateurs, or retired workers. Such places are difficult to locate, so it's best to find a local tour guide to take you there. Other kinds of entertainment include mahjong and chess playing.

In Chengdu, teahouses also function as places for the exchange of current information. Most Chengdu teahouses cater to tea drinkers, young and old, who come to meet and have a chat about everything ranging from the bride's dowry to a fierce political debate. Sichuan is an inland province in China and transportation is not as convenient as other coast provinces. However, as you sit in teahouses and start to chat with other customers, you will soon know everything under the sun.

Teahouses are places for people from various businesses and organizations to get together. They have some social activities or hold trade talks. Sometimes when people have a quarrel, a mediator will bring them to the teahouse. After their dispute is settled, the person who is wrong will pay for the tea. It is interesting that as soon as the quarrelers enter the teahouse and sit down to drink tea, they almost cool down. Their disputes can be easily settled with the help of the mediator. In the old society before 1949, reactionary gangs were popular in Chengdu as well as in Sichuan. The old teahouses served as their office places to conduct their business. Gradually some more functions came into being. Mass units in all walks of life tended to meet in teahouses for get-togethers. Non-government court was set up in teahouses to settle strikes or disputes among folks. Some local culture and art activities were held in teahouses where artists composed poems, painted pictures and watched performances.

Today all the traditional functions in teahouses are still working except the reactionary gangs' office business. Some more changes have taken place in Chengdu teahouses downtown. They are a sort of pub-type teahouses with a nice balcony view and a pleasant interior decoration. The pub-type teahouses are usually busy in the afternoon and evening. They mainly cater to young people, who come to chat or talk business. However, traditional family-type teahouses are still popular in the suburbs. On weekends, citizens and their families from all walks of life depart from where they stay downtown and walk into teahouses in the beautiful countryside, where they enjoy drinking tea, chatting, playing cards or dozing off in their armchairs. Many pleasant weekends can be spent here over a cup of flower tea at a low cost.

KEY WORDS & EXPRESSIONS 关键词汇及表达法

brew 酿造，酝酿
infusion 浸入，注入
enjoyable 令人愉快的，可享受的
back-alley 后街
sooty 乌黑的
sip tea 品茶
ceramics 制陶术，制陶业

unglazed 未上釉的
earthenware 土器，陶器
noblesse 贵族阶级
predominate 掌握，控制
respectfully 尊敬地，谦恭地
Tea Service Master 茶博士
intensive 强烈的；精深的
painstaking 辛苦的，辛勤的
cater to 对……提供制好的食品或服务
dowry 嫁妆；天资
debate 争论，辩论
mediator 调解人，调停者
quarreler 争吵的人
gang (一)伙，(一)群
get-together 聚会
non-government 非官方的
pub-type 酒吧型的
balcony 阳台；楼座
interior decoration 内装修
family-type 家庭型的
bottomless 无限的

Sichuan Embroidery 蜀绣

Ladies and gentlemen, we are on the way to an embroidery market where many of the embroideries are on display. This unique exhibition appeals to those who are interested in Chinese culture and history because it provides an opportunity to learn something of the mystery and meaning represented in this little-known art form.

Have you ever seen such a lovely fish or a cat on a piece of silk cloth? The fur or scales look quite real. You can see the individual hairs. And the eyes look at you. Just imagine embroidering such a delicate figure with fine silk threads and tiny needles! The exquisite embroidery has been one of China's most famous art forms for many centuries. They're set in a frame, there are no ugly knots and things on the back, and they are usually done by hand.

Sichuan embroidery is a traditional handicraft art. The embroidery products are made with soft satins and colored threads. All of them are stitched by hand, and the varied stitching methods create unique local styles.

Sichuan embroidery is one of the top four famous embroideries in China. The other three embroideries include Suzhou embroidery (苏绣) from Suzhou area, Xiang embroidery (湘绣) from Hunan province and Yue embroidery (粤绣) from Guangdong province. Suzhou embroidery is famous for its extremely delicate stitches. Xiang embroidery for its rich colors. Yue embroidery, by contrast, tends to have rather complicated patterns.

Sichuan embroidery has its patterns chosen mainly from local folk art. The traditional Chinese landscape painting also provides favorite subjects for Sichuan embroidery patterns. Generally, designs on Sichuan embroidery include flowers, birds, landscapes, fish, worms and human figures. The products themselves include quilt covers, pillow covers, cushions, tablecloths, scarves and handkerchiefs.

KEY WORDS & EXPRESSIONS 关键词汇及表达法

mystery 神秘

scale 鳞片(尤指鱼鳞)

knot (绳等的)结;(树的)节

traditional handicraft art 传统手工艺

complicated pattern 复杂式样

quilt cover 被褥套

pillow cover 枕头套

History of Sichuan Embroidery
蜀绣史

Embroidery is one of the ancient handicrafts in China. People started using embroidery in China in early ancient times. Sichuan embroidery came into use on the basis of the skills of the ancient cross-stitch work. Many excellent weaving skills and patterns were first established by the common people and passed to all walks of life. 2,000 years ago, Sichuan embroidery was well-known among the ancient states.

In Han Dynasty, embroidery techniques made tremendous advances. Products were elegantly designed and intricate. Yang Xiong in the Han Dynasty once composed a eulogy on Sichuan embroidery. Towards the end of the third century, Changqu (常璩), a historian of the Jin Dynasty wrote a book by the name of *Huayangguozhi* (华阳国志, *the History of Huayang State*). In his book, Chang spoke highly of Sichuan embroidery and brocade. He considered them valuable treasures in the local areas.

Before the arrival of the modern printing and dyeing process, local people in Sichuan used their own method to dye cotton, silk and linen cloth. However, it wasn't possible to dye more than one color on the same cloth. Therefore, people stitched colorful patterns on the one-colored cloth to make the cloth pleasing to the eye.

Before Tang Dynasty, the chain stitch was the only method used in embroidery. In Tang Dynasty, the satin stitch was invented and quickly replaced the chain stitch. The newly invented method enabled stitching workers to use different stitching styles to create artful patterns.

In the old society, women in Sichuan started to learn how to stitch flowers when they were young. Girls made embroidered incense bags for their lovers as tokens of their love. They often embroidered a pair of mandarin ducks, which are symbols of loving couples. In addition to ducks, other birds, flowers, fish, and animals were the most common subjects for embroidery. The purpose of their ornamental needlework was either for their own use, or to be sold at market. In the past hundred years many women in the countryside near Chengdu were engaged in needlework as a means of maintaining their daily life.

During the Daoguang Period (道光年间) of Qing Dynasty, the Sichuan embroidery business advanced in big strides. Over 80 well-known handcraft workshops were set up in Chengdu's Goutou and Kejia streets to produce embroidery products. Its needlework displayed even stitches, bright threads, closeness and softness in texture. Each local county-level government set up an embroidery management office to take charge of the local embroidery business. Their main products were official clothes, gift, dowries, as well as daily colorful clothes and necessities.

In the old days the embroidery business appeared to be a

traditional occupation of Chinese women. But embroidery was never solely a female activity, and some men also did it. How did the local men obtain such a skill?

A hundred years ago, an official was transferred to work in Chengdu from Jiangsu. A theatrical troupe accompanied him to Chengdu at the same time. There were three experienced male masters, working with the troupe. Their job was to stitch stage clothes for actors and actresses. As they were in Chengdu, they began to recruit their apprentices for the purpose of developing government-sponsored embroidery. However, young women were not allowed to work as embroidery apprentices in public workshops because of a feudal ethical code. Therefore, the three masters had to use local young men instead. Gradually, more and more male workers worked in embroidery workshops.

In 1949, new China was founded. Local workshops began to employ young women. In present workshops or factories, there are more female stitching workers and fewer males.

KEY WORDS & EXPRESSIONS 关键词汇及表达法

come into use 开始被使用
weaving skill 纺织技术
all walks of life 各行各业
speak highly of 赞扬
dyeing process 染色工艺过程
linen cloth 亚麻布
mandarin duck 鸳鸯
ornamental 装饰的
as a means of 以……为手段
advance in big strides 大步前进
necessity 必需品

actress 女演员
recruit 征募(新兵)
apprentice 学徒
feudal ethical code 封建伦理道德

The Embroidery Technology and Its Varieties

蜀绣的工艺特色及其品种

Sichuan embroidery has a strong expression and artistic effect. It focuses on the needlework method relating to minute details and perfect stitched patterns. Stitch lines appear smooth, and embroidery patterns look elegant and delicate. Its materials are colorful satin and silk threads, all produced in the local areas.

Following are some unique stitching skills in Sichuan embroidery. They are often used to achieve sound results.

Xiegunzhen (斜滚针, the slant-ward rolling stitch method)

It is a basic stitch method. Two lines are stitched close to each other so as to form a relatively long and narrow stripe. The stripe is mainly used to resemble flower vines, small flowers' stems, ripples and pine needles.

Qiezhen (切针, the tangent stitch method)

It is an immediate stitch line. It touches a curve or a surface at a point. The line is closer than any other lines going through the point. The tangent stitch method is mainly used to resemble transparent fine gauze, mist and bubbles.

Canzhen (参针, the irregular stitch method)

The method has a strong sense of decoration.

The current embroidery carries forward the good traditions, and furthermore, it also brings forth some innovation relating to stitch methods and modeling arts. The traditional embroidery needlework only displays patterns on one side. At present, workers are able to stitch different patterns on both sides of the same satin cloth. On one side maybe a cat, and the other side a fish. Moreover, three-dimensional stitch embroideries have come into use.

Sichuan embroidery has two main uses. The first use is more practical. It is for daily necessities including quilt covers, bed sheets, pillow covers and cushions. Patterns are neatly concise, and colors bright. The other use lays particular stress on artistic efforts. Many talented needle workers make a meticulous effort to create beautiful embroidery. These embroidered pictures are usually framed in wooden cases or screens to be used as valuable gifts for important visitors. Their efforts also signify the preservation and continuity of traditional Chinese arts.

KEY WORDS & EXPRESSIONS 关键词汇及表达法

stripe 斑纹，条纹
flower vine 花藤
ripple 涟漪，湍流
tangent 接触的，切线的
curve 曲线；曲面
transparent 透明的；明白的
mist 薄雾
bubble 泡
irregular 不规则的，不整齐的
bring forth 使出现；产生
innovation 发明
three-dimensional 三维空间的
concise 简明的，简练的

artistic effort 艺术努力
talented 有才能的
preservation 保存
continuity 连续性，连贯性

Sichuan Brocade 蜀锦

History of Sichuan Brocade
蜀锦史

Ladies and gentlemen, we are on the way to a store where Sichuan brocade is on sale. Sichuan brocade is also known as Shu brocade. It is one of the top four famous brocades in China. The other three styles of brocade are Yun brocade from Nanjing, Song brocade from Suzhou and Zhuang brocade from Guanxi. Shu brocade has a history of over two thousand years.

Sichuan was one of the first areas to start sericulture (养蚕业). The cultivation of the silkworm can be traced back to the third century B. C.. According to archeological discovery, silk and silk fabrics emerged at least 5, 500 years ago. In Zhou Dynasty, a special administration was set up to manage sericulture and silk production. From 138 B. C. to 126 B. C., Zhang Qian (张骞) started his diplomatic mission to the West along the famous Silk Road. Sericulture and silk production techniques gradually spread to other countries.

As early as the fourth century B. C., local people in Sichuan were able to produce a kind of plain silk cloth called bo (帛). The brocade came into use on the basis of the weaving skills of the plain silk cloth, which was first produced in Chengdu.

During Han Dynasty, the brocade made in Sichuan was named Shu brocade. Towards the end of Eastern Han Dynasty a device was invented to weave raised designs on fine silk. The new technique greatly enhanced the quality of silk products, and Shu brocade became important articles of tribute to the imperial court.

In 214, Liu Bei and his troop entered into Sichuan where he replaced Liu Zhang, former governor appointed by the Han emperor. He took bolts of Shu brocade from the local official storage, and he rewarded his assistants and generals, who helped him set up his kingdom with them.

During the Three Kingdoms Period, Zhuge Liang, a renowned statesman of the Shu state placed agriculture and sericulture on the top lists of the state development. Zhuge said in his memorial to the throne, that the brocade was the only financial support to the decisive battle with the enemy state.

Since Sichuan and central China were linked up, the weaving industry boomed. It flourished during the Tang, Song and Yuan dynasties. The varieties, colors and patterns became abundant.

In Tang Dynasty, Sichuan brocade produced a large number of marvelous patterns. Flowers, the red lined lion and phoenix brocade. Animal designs in pairs highlighted the feature. They included pheasant games, playing sheep, flying phoenix and other animals. At that time, only high officials and noble lords could afford to enjoy the use of brocade.

Furthermore, the ancient businessmen traveled along the Silk Road, and brocade was sold in Central Asia, the Mediterranean areas and Europe. Brocade was also sold in Japan, where local Japanese named it as Shujiangfan (蜀江幡, Sichuan River Brocade). At the present time, Japanese temples by the name of

Shyosoin Temple（正仓院）and Houryuji Temple（法隆寺）still store the remnants of Shujiang Xiaofan（蜀江小幡，a Small Flag on the Sichuan River），and Shujiang Taizi Yujuansan（蜀江太子御绢伞，Sichuan Crown Prince's Silk Umbrella）.

In the Northern and Southern Song dynasties the brocade industry advanced into large-scale workshops. The Chengdu Brocade Workshop had 154 looms and 500 workers. The workers were divided into groups. Each group had different jobs. Some groups rolled up silk fabrics，some weaved silk yarns，and others dyed the fabrics.

KEY WORDS & EXPRESSIONS 关键词汇及表达法

sericulture 养蚕业
cultivation 栽培，养殖
diplomatic 外交的
on the basis of 在……基础
articles of tribute 贡品；礼物
storage 储藏库
financial 财政的
phoenix 凤凰；不死鸟
pheasant 雉；野鸡
remnant 残余，剩余

Patterns and Features of the Brocade
样式与特点

Sichuan brocade is a silk product，it is soft and colorful. The brocade developed over twenty centuries，and over several hundred types evolved. Some patterns are so popular that they are taken as pattern models among the other three styles of brocade. At present，handmade brocade has been replaced by modernization of the textile industries. Chengdu Shu Brocade Factory specializes in machine-made Sichuan brocade, its jacquared loom is electronically equipped.

The present Sichuan brocade fabrics include the facing of the quilt, the materials of clothes and other decorative purposes. In Southwest China some ethnic nationalities especially enjoy wearing brocade aprons and headscarves.

Some fashionable patterns are listed below:

Fangfang Brocade（方方锦，the check-patterned brocade）

First of all, the looms weave a single-colored brocade bottom. Secondly on the bottom colorful warp and weft silk threads weave check-shaped patterns. Finally a flower is added into each check by looms.

Yuehua Brocade（月华锦，the moonlight brocade）

Groups of colorful warp and weft silk threads are woven according to designated patterns. The weaving visually transforms from light to dark colors. Then decorative patterns are added to display the high skill of tow-to-thread spinning.

Huanhua Brocade（浣花锦，the fallen flower and flowing river brocade）

Plum, peach and other flowers are woven on brocade fabrics. The pattern shows pleasant scenery with fallen flowers and flowing rivers.

Pudi Brocade（铺地锦）

Pudi Brocade means adding more flowers to the brocade fabrics. First of all, the brocade bottom is woven into geometric figures and small flower patterns. The figures and small flowers are then added to support large flowers in an attempt to make the pattern look more splendid.

Some other patterns deserve comment. They are Sanhua Brocade (散花), which means the brocade is full of hundreds of flowers, Dui Hua Brocade(对花), which means that the brocade flowers have the same numbers exhibiting regular patterns, Min Zu (民族) Brocade which means that the brocade is suitable for ethnic nationalities in the local areas.

Shu Brocade is presently sold at home and abroad.

KEY WORDS & EXPRESSIONS 关键词汇及表达法

specialize 使专用于

visually 在视觉上地；真实地

transform 转换，改变

tow-to-thread spinning 牵经技艺

geometric 几何的，几何学的

Local Bamboo Woven Products

竹编工艺品

Ladies and gentlemen, now we are on the way to purchase bamboo woven porcelains, fans and other bamboo products in a store. I'd like to give you a brief introduction of bamboo and its products.

China is known for rich bamboo resources, and more than 400 species of bamboo grow in China. As early as Shang Dynasty, Chinese people began to use bamboo for making household articles and weapons. Before paper was invented in ancient times, bamboo slips were used for writing.

Bamboo was intimately connected with the daily lives of people in ancient times. People used bamboo as firewood to cook food; they used bamboo to make tiles, paper, rafts, hats, rain capes, and shoes. At present bamboo is widely used for household articles such as mats, beds, pillows, benches, chairs, cabinets, buckets, chopsticks, spoons, baskets, and handheld fans. Bamboo shoots are eatable. Its taste is crisp, fresh and a bit sweet.

KEY WORDS & EXPRESSIONS 关键词汇及表达法

raft 筏子
household 家庭的
cabinet 橱柜
eatable 可以吃的

Bamboo Woven Porcelains

瓷胎竹编

Bamboo woven products are a special handicraft in art form. They include bamboo-woven toy animals, lanterns, flower baskets, trays, tea boxes, screens and curtains. Bamboo-thread woven porcelains are characterized by bamboo splits, which cover the surface of the porcelains. There are various types of local bamboo in Sichuan, but only one kind of bamboo meets the need of this weaving demand. It is called cizhu (慈竹), and grows in the Qionglai mountainous area, one of the birthplaces of the giant pandas.

However, not all the cizhu bamboo is qualified enough to meet the normal standards. Basically cizhu bamboo should be two years old, it is at least 66cm and over between its joints, it has no cutting scars on the surface. Once cizhu bamboo tubes meet the required standards, their skin is cut into splits. Each split is about 60cm long, and looks almost as thin as a hair. 50kg cizhu bamboo tubes produce 400g of splits.

In Chengdu Bamboo Weaving Factory, workers weave bamboo splits on the surface of vases, coffee sets, tea sets and bowls. Many visitors make arrangements to watch this miraculous process. The weavers' work always amazes them.

The porcelain weaving process usually starts at the bottom of a porcelain vase or a teacup. For example, warp and weft splits interlace closely on the surface of the product; splits slowly cover the whole body and usually end on the top of the product, where the ends of splits are tied hard with invisible knots. During the weaving process bamboo splits can't be twisted or placed on the top of one another. The joints between the ends of splits must be hidden from sight.

Bronze was a popular color in the bamboo woven program before the dyeing technique was introduced. Now other colors have been added to bamboo woven products. Handicraft artists have produced varied designs, which resemble geometric figures, city buttresses, flowers and birds. Particularly flower patterns appear jacquarded, indistinct or natural. They appeal to the artistic desires of customers.

At the end of the 19th century, the Qing government sent Chengdu bamboo-woven porcelains to the Panama International Exposition to be exhibited. The products won a silver medal. In 1975, a group of local bamboo handicraft artists went to Japan. There the artists demonstrated on the spot how to weave bamboo splits on porcelains. Their performance was deeply admired by the Japanese audience.

KEY WORDS & EXPRESSIONS 关键词汇及表达法

lantern 灯

scar 伤痕，疤痕
bamboo tube 竹筒
twist 扭曲，绞
indistinct 模糊的，朦胧的
appeal 吸引

Bamboo Curtain Paintings
竹帘画

This special product consists of bamboo, silk thread, and paintings. A handicraft artist skillfully weaves with bamboo splits and silk thread. Warp bamboo splits run along the length curtain, while weft silk threads run horizontally across the width. After the artist completes the bamboo and silk weaving, a painter starts painting pictures or writes Chinese characters on the woven curtain. Chinese painters are most accommodating. If you have a favorite scene you would like to reproduce on a fine curtain, they will make it for you. Usually, painters blend the traditional patterns, landscapes, and creatures with modern concepts. Most of the bamboo curtain paintings are in color and suitable for modern decor in restaurants and meeting halls.

KEY WORDS & EXPRESSIONS 关键词汇及表达法

thread 丝线
horizontally 平行线地
accommodating 善于适应……的

Bamboo Fans
竹扇

Chinese fans are common souvenirs for overseas travelers. The popular fans include folded fans, sandalwood fans, feather fans, palm fans, straw fans and bamboo woven fans. In a Mashan brick mill, Jiangling, Hubei province, archeologists excavated a bamboo fan made in the Warring States Period. Its face surface slightly took the form of stairs. The bamboo splits were in red and black, which made up bright patterns. In 1975, another bamboo fan of Song Dynasty was excavated in Jintan, Jiangsu province. The handle of the fan was made of wood, and the bamboo splits made up its framework. The bamboo splits were thin and smooth. Nowadays bamboo fans are only produced in Zigong, Sichuan province. Zigong fans are woven from fine splits of bamboo. A round fan is no more than 20 centimeters in diameter. It has about 1,000 crossings of the fine bamboo splits, and flower-and-bird patterns or landscapes can be woven into the fan.

KEY WORDS & EXPRESSIONS 关键词汇及表达法

souvenir 纪念品
sandalwood 檀香木
archeologist 考古学者
excavat 挖掘
crossing 交叉点
landscape 风景

Sichuan Medicinal Herbs 四川中药材

Ladies and gentlemen, today we are scheduled to go to a herb store where you can purchase some local herbs. After the visit to the store, we will go for a medicinal meal in a restaurant attached to Chengdu Traditional Chinese Medical University. For a more comprehensive understanding of Chinese culture, I'd like to present to you some basic information concerning traditional Chinese medicine, acupuncture and local Chinese herbs.

KEY WORDS & EXPRESSIONS 关键词汇及表达法

traditional Chinese medicine 中医

acupuncture 针灸

Basic Knowledge of Traditional Chinese Medicine and Acupuncture

传统中医与针灸知识

Chinese traditional medicine is a valuable heritage, and it develops for the promotion of health. Within Chinese cosmology, all of creation is born from the marriage of two polars: yin and yang (阴阳). Harmony of this union produces good health; disharmony leads to disease. The strategy of Chinese medicine is to restore harmony. One of the major assumptions in traditional Chinese medicine is that disease is due to an internal imbalance of yin and yang. So traditional Chinese doctors uses acupuncture, herbs and food to help you correct the yin and yang imbalance until the body returns to a healthy state.

Western medicine assumes that the disease is due to an external force such as a virus or bacteria. Western medicine is based on the Cartesian philosophy that the body represents one functioning system, and the mind another. It accepts that each system may affect the other, but essentially the Western medicine sees disease as either physical or mental. The Chinese assume that each organ has a mental as well as a physical function, and each part of the whole body is intimately connected.

Nature has air, sea, and land. In the same way the Chinese

medicine assumes that the human body possesses Qi（气）, Moisture and Blood. Qi means influence or energy. It is the motivating force behind all movement in our bodies. Moisture is the liquid substance, which protects and nurtures tissue. Blood is the foundation in which bones, nerves, skin, muscles and organs are created.

In the Chinese concept, there are three treasures or san bao（三宝）. They are Jing（精）or essence, Qi or vitality, and Shen（神）or spirit. Shen represents consciousness and our higher mental faculties. The relationship among Jing, Qi, and Shen is that Qi is the forefather of spirit, and essence is the child of Qi, Qi is the root of essence and spirit. When Qi accumulates, it produces essence. When essence accumulates, it makes spirit wholesome.

It is a Chinese concept that Wood, Fire, Earth, Metal and Water make up the nature. Therefore the human body is divided into five functional systems. They are called the Organ Networks, which consists of Liver, Heart, Spleen, Lung and Kidney. These Networks govern particular tissues, mental faculties and physical activities. At the same time they regulate and preserve Qi, Moisture, Blood, Spirit and Essence.

Qi, Moisture and Blood circulate within a web of pathways called channels（经络）that link all parts of the organism. Health exists when adequate Qi, Moisture and Blood flow smoothly. Once their circulation splits, varied symptoms may occur. The common sicknesses include joint pain, headache, anxiety, fatigue, menstrual cramps, high blood pressure, asthma indigestion and others. As Qi, Moisture and Blood are used up, it will lead to weakness, lethargy, frequent illness, poor digestion and inadequate blood flow. If they are too full, it will lead to aches, tension, a distended abdomen, irritability and swelling.

Traditional Chinese doctors treat illness by using acupuncture, herbs and food to help you correct the yin and yang imbalance. As for acupuncture, an acupuncturist usually inserts acupuncture needles at human body critical points for multi-medical purposes.

You may ask me how acupuncture works. The traditional explanation says that in traditional Chinese medicine, there exists a web of pathways called channels that link all parts of the body, and more than 360 acupuncture points are located at these channels. Qi or vitality flows through these channels and passes acupuncture points to support tissue, muscles and organs. When Qi is blocked at a certain critical acupuncture point, the function of tissue, muscles and organs will be weakened. Therefore an acupuncturist usually inserts acupuncture needles into certain points to help Qi flow. At the same time the needlework helps correct Qi imbalances and improves your energy and internal processing.

So you see, many people do not believe that acupuncture can be painless. They may have different sensations. They may feel sore, numb, warm or swelling. People often say that they feel relaxed when the needle is inserted beneath their skin. According to many doctors' experience, most of the time six to eight needles are used during an acupuncture treatment. Ten or more needles may be used if two or more symptoms need acupuncture treatment at the same time. For instance when a patient has back pain and a headache, the acupuncturist treats the patient for the two illnesses at the same time. Some acupuncturists insert as many as thirty or more needles at the same time.

Normally each acupuncture treatment takes 20 - 30 minutes. However it depends on the sensitivity of each individual and the types of diseases and the kind of conditions. Generally speaking, the quality of acupuncture treatment relies on the experience and skill of an acupuncturist. They are a combination of diagnosis of the symptom, accuracy of acupuncture points, timing, and the depth and angle of insertion, etc.

KEY WORDS & EXPRESSIONS 关键词汇及表达法

cosmology 宇宙论
disharmony 不调和
strategy 策略，战略
assumption 假定，设想
internal 内在的
imbalance 不平衡
external 外部的，外表的
virus 病毒
bacteria 细菌
Cartesian philosophy 笛卡尔哲学
mental 精神的
intimately connected 密切地联系
moisture 湿
motivate 激发
substance 物质
nurture 滋养
tissue [生]组织
muscle 肌肉
forefather 祖先，祖宗
wholesome 卫生的，有益的

spleen 脾
channel 经络
organism 生物体，有机体
circulation 循环，流通
symptom 症状，征兆
menstrual cramp 痛经
high blood pressure 高血压
asthma 哮喘
indigestion 消化不良
lethargy 无生气
distended abdomen 腹部肿胀
irritability 易怒
swelling 肿胀，肿大
acupuncturist 针灸师
insert 插入，嵌入
block up 妨碍，阻塞
sensation 感觉,感觉力
sensitivity 敏感，灵敏(度)
diagnosis 诊断
accuracy 精确性，正确度

Traditional Chinese Medicinal Herbs and Main Local Herbs

传统中药与本地主要药材

In China, herbal medicine is made up of roots, bark, flowers, seeds, fruits, leaves and branches. When herbs are combined, they can increase or promote medical effectiveness. Herbal medicine has been a part of the written history of Traditional Chinese Medicine for over 4000 years. According to the legend, the Chinese medicine started with Shennong (神农) who was a legendary miracle doctor. It is said that he had tasted a hundred plants in order to find out useful medicinal herbs. There are over 3,000 different herbs that can be used for medical purposes. Only 300 to 500 of these herbs are commonly used. Moreover, Chinese herbs have low risk of adverse reaction or side effects.

Herbal therapy has three main functions as below:

1. Treat the immediate problem, such as killing bacteria or a virus.
2. Strengthen the body and help it to recover.
3. Maintain the body's health.

Moreover, Chinese herbs have low risk of adverse reaction or side effects.

Herbal medicine is the mainstay of traditional Chinese medicine. The knowledge of Chinese medicinal herbs was handed down from one to another through verbal instruction until the birth of Chinese characters. All the ancient books related to medicines are generally named "bencao" (本草), which means that plants are the basis of medicinal herbs. In ancient dynasties, many books related to medicinal herbs were printed. At present, there are about 300 types of medical books in existence. Some of the best-known books are listed below:

Shennong Bencaojing (神农本草经, Shennong Herbal Medicine Classics)

It was the first known Chinese medical book written during the Eastern Han Dynasty. The book summed up the experience of using herbal drugs, which dated back to the dynasties even earlier than the Eastern Han Dynasty. The account of 365 herbs is included in the book.

Shennong Bencaojing Jizhu (神农本草经集注, the Variorum Edition of Shennong Herbal Medicine Classics)

This book was written by Tao Hongjin (陶宏景) of the Liang Dynasty (490 - 500). It accounted for another 365 herbs collected from the Han to the Wei dynasties. There are 730 herbs in all. The book offers the experience of how to collect and identify medicinal herbs. Furthermore, it also shows how to prepare Chinese medicine by roasting them in a pan.

Xinxiu Bencao (新修本草, Newly Written Herbal Medicine Classics)

This book was also called *the Herbal Medicine Classics of the Tang Dynasty*. The Tang government (657 - 659) arranged to have Su Jing (苏敬) and another 22 scholars compile this book. It accounts for 844 herbs including some man-made drugs of the Tang Dynasty and drugs from other states.

Bencao Gangmu (本草纲目, the Compendium of Materia Medica)

This book was written by Li Shizhen (李时珍) of the Ming Dynasty. It accounted for 1,892 herbs attached with 1,160 pictures and 11,000 drug prescriptions. At the beginning of the 17th century, some foreign scholars began to translate the book into English, Japanese, French and several other languages. The translated versions have made an important contribution to the development of the world science of medicine.

In China, there are eight main herb productive regions. One of them is Yun-Gui-Chuan (云贵川) Herb Production Region. This region includes Sichuan, Guizhou, Tibet and small areas of

Yunnan. It plays the main role in China's herb production. Mountains, hills, forests and plateaus mainly cover the extensive region. There are about 5,000 kinds of Chinese "materia medica", including about 4,500 plants, over 300 animals and about 80 minerals. Many drugs produced in this region are of high quality.

Within the region, Sichuan has rich resources of 3,500 types of herbs. They include about 3,200 plant herbs, 340 animal drugs and 40 minerals. The production of the local staple herbs has made up one-third of the national total output value. Traditionally, Chuan (川), which means Sichuan, is intentionally attached to the names of many local herb products like the Chuan Bulb of Fritillary (川贝母) and the Chuan Rhizome (川芎). Chuan in the names of herbs symbolizes the origin of herbs and their high quality.

Some valuable local herbs are listed below:

Huanglian (黄连, the Rhizome of Chinese Gold-thread)

Chuanxiong (川芎, the Rhizome of Chuanxiong)

Beimu (贝母, the Bulb of Fritillary)

Chongcao (虫草, Chinese Caterpillar Fungus)

Tianma (天麻, the Tuber of Elevated Gastrodia)

Tianma (天麻, the Tuber of Elevated Gastrodia)

This plant has been used for medical treatment for more than 2,000 years. A literal English translation is "heavenly hemp". It looks like a fat, solid, translucent and yellowish white root. The Tianma plant is categorized in traditional Chinese medicine as a sweet and neutral herb. It mainly cures corotraction of armsand legs, hemiplegia, headache or dizziness. The wild Tianma plant grows in mountainous areas around the Sichuan basin, ranging from 700m to 3,000m above sea level.

Traditionally local people gather the plant in spring or winter. However, the winter Tianma plant is better than the spring one. Due to the scientific research efforts, the wild Tianma plant started to grow in farmers' fields, making the production become much higher than before. At present the Tianma plant is found in bulk or in tablets at Chinese pharmacies.

Chuanbeimu (川贝母, the Chuan Bulb of Fritillary)

The fritillary is mentioned in the ancient literature, including a brief statement in *Shennong Herbal Medicine Classics*. But it was not widely used in ancient medicine. This lack of use probably reflects the difficulty in finding adequate quantities of the herb. Chuanbeimu was first introduced formally in *the Compendium of Materia Medica*. It is a larger bulb plant, and the introduction of its cultivation during the Ming Dynasty paved the way for the herb to be utilized regularly thereafter.

The fritillary herb is slightly cold. It affects the lungs by clearing heat and moistening dryness. It is used for hot-type bronchitis with dry cough.

The fritillary herb mainly grows in cold mountainous areas at 3,000m and above. In the past years much effort has been made on the artificial plantation as well as sexual and asexual bulb reproduction. The aim is to grow the fritillary in lower areas. The production out put is expected to increase from 25 to 50 jin per mu.

Today, the fritillary herb is commonly included as a main ingredient in cough syrups such as zhikelu. Zhike means "treating cough", lu means "syrup".

A well-known food therapy for cough is to steam a sliced

pear, in which the fritillary herb powder and sugar fills the emptied core area. The patient who has the cough eats the steamed pear with fritillary powder and consumes the juice that is formed during cooking of one pear per day.

Chongcao (虫草, Chinese Caterpillar Fungus)

This fungus is one of the valuable local herbs in Sichuan. The caterpillar fungus is a traditional medicine that has been widely used as a tonic or medicine by the Chinese for hundreds of years. It mainly grows in mountains and grassland 3,000m above sea level. In the old days, Chinese people thought that the caterpillar fungus (冬虫夏草) were worms. However, after years of study, it was found that it really is a fruiting body produced by the fungus. When the caterpillar dies, the fungus produces a stalked fruiting body that produces spores. The spores are spread in the wind to the next generation of caterpillars. The fungus contains cordyceps sinensis acid, fatty acid, protein and amino acid. The output of the fungus in Sichuan occupies first place in China. In 1981, the artificial fungus plantation became successful. The sale at home and abroad goes on very well.

The use of the caterpillar fungus is believed to have started a thousand years ago. It was either ground into a powder, or mixed with other tonics. Today, the caterpillar fungus is mainly used as a tonic to increase strength or for rejuvenation after a long serious injury. The most common way to prepare the caterpillar fungus is to stuff a duck with the caterpillar fungus and then boil the duck in hot water. Patients drink the liquid. The aroma is pleasant and the broth tastes sweet.

Duzhong (杜仲, the Bark of Eucommia)

The eucommia barks are flakes, 3–7 mm thick and different in size; some are flat in shape; some are slightly rolled up inwardly (two sides). The outer surface is light brown or grayish-brown. The inner surface is smooth, and is dark violet in color. It is crisp in texture and easy to break. It is faint in smell, slightly bitter in taste, and gives a sensation of being gluey when chewed.

For over 2,000 years, the bark has been used for medical purposes:

1. It nourishes the liver and kidney and strengthens the bones and muscles.

2. It produces a desirable result in the treatment of deficiency of the liver-yin and kidney-yin manifested as soreness and weakness of the loins and knees.

3. Miscarriage prevention.

4. Calm and suppress liver-yang.

The eucommia trees grow in Mianyang, Leshan and some other areas. Usually local workers peel the trees to gather the bark for medical uses. However, too much bark peeling will hurt the trees. Therefore, the local agricultural department invited research workers to experiment on how to help the trees renew their bark in a more efficient manner. At the same time, an advanced peeling technique has been widely accepted, and now the local workers try to peel the bark in a circular way that won't hurt the trees.

Huanglian (黄连, the Rhizome of Chinese Gold-thread)

There are two kinds of Huanglian herbs in Sichuan. One is

called Weilian（味连），and the other Yalian（雅连）.

Weilian herb grows in the Shizhu（石柱），Nanchuan（南川），and Wulong（武隆）areas. Many roots are usually connected together，forming a cluster. It resembles a talon. Its surface is rough and grayish-yellow or yellowish-brown in color. In most cases，brown bud leaves remain at the upper part and a short stem remains at the top. The whole root is hard in texture，faint in odor and extremely bitter in taste.

Yalian herb grows in Emei（峨眉），Ebian（峨边）and Hongya（洪雅）areas. It has no branches. Its root is cylinder-shaped and slightly crooked. The herb is usually 4 – 8 cm in length and 0. 5 – 1. 0 cm in diameter. The production output of Yalian herb is low，but the quality remains the best.

Local people have grown the herb for several decades. When seedlings are planted，it takes at least five years for them to grow into the ready-made herbs. Since 1975，a rotation experiment has been carried out for the purpose of increasing the herb output.

The herb is used in the treatment of vomiting，diarrhea，dysentery，hemorrhoid and other symptoms caused by damp-heat in the intestine and stomach. This medicine may be used alone or with others.

Since we are going for a Chinese medicinal meal，I'd like to say something about the medicinal meals. What I say，will be helpful in understanding of the Chinese culture.

The knowledge of Chinese herbal medicine is extensive. It has always been intimately linked with the life extension. Herbs are first and foremost foodstuffs that nourish the body in precise and well-defined ways. When the Chinese discovered farming and agriculture in the early days, they discovered the medicinal properties of food. Since then, food has been studied and analyzed for its medicinal effects on people. This knowledge enables people to use food as the first line of defense to ward off common sicknesses and diseases.

Medicinal meals are unique in the Chinese food culture. It is the preparation of medicinal food dishes with selected food ingredients and superior herbs. It aims to extract the necessary nutrients to treat specific health conditions. It is also considered to be the best tonic for health because it combines fresh and natural foods with superior herbs. There are hundreds of these recipes in circulation, and many households are using them on a regular basis. The recipes can be classified into the following categories: health promotion, sickness prevention, disease control and recuperating. Besides, they are less expensive than drugs and have no adverse side effects.

Making soup is the most common method in preparing medicinal dishes. It is a long and slow simmering process to extract the essential nutrients from the ingredients into the soup. The effects are quick. Soup is suitable for people of all ages, and it is easiest for the body to digest and absorb. Even the weakest person living on a fluid diet can benefit from nutritional soup.

Another popular form of medicinal food is rice soup or rice porridge. It is prepared by cooking rice into a semi-solid form with herbs and adequate water. It is easy to digest as a meal replacement.

Typical dishes include the Stewed Squab with Chinese Caterpillar, the Mandarin Fish Grains with Pine Nuts, the Soft-shelled Turtle with Cordyceps, the Mutton with Candied Dates, the Stewed Pigeon with Ginseng and Cordyceps, the Duck with Chinese Caterpillar Fungus and others.

My basic introduction is over. I sincerely hope that you will enjoy exploring the local culture in the fields of traditional Chinese medicine, herbs and meals. I know that you will find out that your exploration will benefit you and meet your health needs.

KEY WORDS & EXPRESSIONS 关键词汇及表达法

pharmacology 药理学
effectiveness 效用，效果
recover 使恢复正常，使复原
adverse 不利的，敌对的
mainstay 支柱，中流砥柱
variorum 集注本
classic 杰作，名著
identify 鉴定，认出
roast 烘，焙或炒
compile 编辑，汇编
compendium 纲要，摘要
materia medica 药品，药物学
prescription 处方，药方
translucent 半透明的
yellowish 微黄色的
neutral 中性的
contraction 挛缩
hemiplegia 偏瘫，半身麻痹
dizziness 头昏眼花
clear heat 清热
bronchitis 支气管炎
dry cough 干咳

asexual 无性的，无性生殖的
bulb 鳞茎
syrup 糖浆
stalk 茎，柄，梗
spore 孢子
acid 酸
fatty 脂肪的
protein 蛋白质
amino acid 氨基酸
aroma 芳香，香气
broth 肉汤
grayish-brown 浅灰棕色的
gluey 胶的；黏着的
nourish 滋养，使健壮
deficiency 缺乏，不足
soreness 痛
loins 腰部
miscarriage 流产
research worker 研究人员
talon 爪；爪状物
cylinder 圆筒；圆柱体
crooked 弯曲的
seedling 秧苗，树苗
rotation 旋转
vomiting 呕吐
dysentery 痢疾
hemorrhoid 痔
intestine 肠
ward off 防止，挡住

ingredient 成分，因素
prevention 预防，防止
recuperate 使复原，恢复
simmer 煨，炖
extract 汲取
nutrient 营养
fluid 流动的；流体的
nutritional 营养的；滋养的
porridge 麦片粥
replacement 交换；替代者
squab 雏鸟(鸽)
turtle 海龟

Sichuan Ethnic Nationalities

四川少数民族

Sichuan boasts an ethnically rich population. Many of them are members of China's minority nationalities, including the Yi, Tibetan, Miao, Bai, Qiang and nine other groups. Based on recent statistics, the estimated figure of the local minority nationalities is 5.7 million, 7 per cent of the entire population in Sichuan. The minorities are mostly concentrated on the plateau northwest of Sichuan, and the highlands southwest and southeast of Sichuan. Below is a brief introduction of the Yi, Tibetan and Qiang nationalities.

KEY WORDS & EXPRESSIONS 关键词汇及表达法

ethnically 种学上；种族上
concentrate 集中

Yi Nationality

彝族

The population of the Yi nationality is 1. 5 million in Sichuan. The Yi people mainly live in Liangshan Yi Autonomous prefecture and other counties nearby. Traditionally, this area is subdivided into the Greater Liangshan Mountain area (大凉山), which lies east of Anning River and south of Huangmao Dyke, and Lesser Liangshan Mountain area (小凉山), which covers Jinsha River Valley and the south bank of Dadu River. Liangshan Yi Autonomous prefecture is the largest Yi people community in China.

The Yi language has lasted over one thousand years. It is a syllabic language, which belongs to the family of Tibetan-Burmese languages in the Chinese-Tibetan language system. The language has six dialects. Its syllabic script is called the ancient Yi language, formed in the 13th century. It is estimated that the ancient Yi script has about 10,000 words. 1,000 of them are daily words. The ancient Yi script has recorded the Yi history, literature and medicine. After 1949, concerned scholars started to systemize the Yi language. They tried to unify their dialects and writing systems. Since 1974, three major research projects have been carried out in order to standardize the Yi writing systems. They are Sichuan Liangshan Regulated Script Project, Yunnan Alphabetic Script Project, and the Project of Comparison of Scripts in Yunnan, Sichuan, Guizhou and Guangxi. These projects have facilitated the overall progress of the Yi people's writing system in word form and pronunciation. In 1980, the newly standardized Yi language started to be formally used.

The essence of Yi's religion is ancestor worship. It emphasizes that all things on earth have spirits. The concept of the supernatural beings has dominated the Yi people's thoughts and behavior.

Before 1949, the Liangshan area was a slave society. The whole society forcibly organized the Yi people into a five-grade hierarchy according to their blood relationship. Hereditary headmen were at the top grade; slaves were at the lowest. Slaves were subject and dependent to slave-owners who could sell or even kill their slaves as they pleased. The savage system expired in 1949.

The Yi farmers are mainly engaged in cultivation. They grow barley, potato, beans and paddy rice. In addition, farmers manage their animal husbandry. With the gradual introduction of farm machinery into the Yi areas, the Yi farmers have yielded good crops in recent years.

The diet in the Yi areas is based primarily on potatoes, buckwheat, oats and corn. They like eating pork meat, cut into cubes. Their daily eating utensils are made of wood or fur. They are bowls, trays, spoon and cups, which are carved in red, black and yellow colors.

Traditionally, timber structure, soil walls, double-plane roof and wooden tiles characterize the houses in which the Yi people live. Each house inside generally consists of upper, middle and lower rooms. In addition, there is a living room, which faces the house entrance. A fire pan is a symbol of the Yi people's custom, and it is placed in the middle. The Yi people in Southern Yunnan Province live in two-story houses. The kitchen and cattle shed are usually on the first floor, and the living room is on the second.

Traditionally the Yi people's head-turban and clothes have bright and decorative patterns. Everyone enjoys having an unlined blanket-like shawl over his/her shoulders. The Yi people, male or female, all wear a kind of upper outer garment. It is a tight and short jacket, its sleeves are narrow and buttons are slantwise to the right. Male's pants are in different sizes at the bottom. Usually the bottom-sizes are fixed upon different areas where the Yi people reside.

Women of the Yi nationality wear multifold skirts in variegated colors. Unmarried women's clothes look graceful and charming. They are made of multi-color cloth with silk thread; varied patterned silver ornaments are attached to their clothes. Girls enjoy stitching butterflies and flowers on their clothes. It is said that it takes half a year to complete embroidering a delicate suit. Their hats are sewn with big and small silver bubbles, which symbolize brightness and happiness.

The Yi people have their own important festivals. In Liangshan Autonomous prefecture, the Yi Nationality New Year lasts three days starting on October 10 every year. During the festival, local people worship their ancestors and visit their friends. At the same time, traditional sports games are held like horseracing, wrestling and seesaw playing.

The Yi people's Torch Festival is one of the main ethnic traditional festivals in China. The Torch Festival starts on the twenty-fourth of the sixth lunar month. There is a legend about the origin of the Torch Festival. A long time ago, there was an invincible wrestler whose name was Eqilaba. He was so famous that the God in Heaven sent down another good wrestler to have a match with him. Unfortunately the wrestler from Heaven was killed, and the God became angry. He sent down swarms of "Heaven Insects" to destroy crops and damage farmer houses. Eqilaba and his friends went up to the mountains. They cut down bamboo trees and made fire torches with bamboo stems. They lighted the torches and used the burning torches to fight against the "Heaven Insects". Finally, the insects were killed, and the crops and houses remained safe. In order to honor Eqilaba's victory over the insects, the local people repeat the torch ritual every year at the end of the sixth month. During their ritual ceremony, the Yi people hold wrestling, singing and dancing activities. As time went on, the torch ritual ceremony developed into the current torch festival.

Well, early in the morning the Torch Festival starts. People begin to dress up. A man puts on a new embroidered short jacket and a pair of new loose trousers. He has a red or yellow pearl in his right ear and a blue or black turban tied around his head. A woman wears an upper garment embroidered and trimmed with lace, and a multifold skirt in variegated colors. During the daytime, some people participate in wrestling, bullfighting, archery contests, or horseracing. Many others watch the games and drink wine throughout the celebration. At night, people light up torches. They hold fire torches and go around to houses and fields to expel insects. Thousands of torches are seen moving along paths in the fields, and they finally gather together on the village outskirts. Afterwards all the participants gather around a burning fire. They dance in groups, hands in hand. Sometimes boys play bamboo flutes, moon-shaped guitars or big three-stringed instruments; girls do moon dancing. Such a happy occasion may go on until dawn. This is also the occasion for young people to look for a life partner through their antiphonal singing.

KEY WORDS & EXPRESSIONS 关键词汇及表达法

community 团体，社会
syllabic 音节的
systemize 系统化
comparison 比较，对照
dominate 支配，占优势
hierarchy 等级制度
hereditary 世袭的
headmen 头人
dependent 依赖于……
slave-owner 奴隶主
expire 期满；终止
paddy 稻谷
animal husbandry 畜牧业
buckwheat 荞麦；荞麦面
double-plane roof 双平面屋顶；屋面
wooden tile 木瓦片
unlined 无衬里的
slantwise 倾斜的
multifold 多种的；多方面的
variegated 杂色的；斑驳的
wrestling 摔跤
wrestler 摔跤选手
seesaw 秋千
Torch Festival 火把节
invincible 不能征服的；无敌的
bullfighting 斗牛士

archery 射箭

moon-shaped guitar 月琴

antiphonal singing 交互轮唱；对唱

Tibetan Nationality

藏族

The Tibetan people in Sichuan province mostly live in Ganzi Tibetan Autonomous prefecture, Aba Tibetan and Qiang Autonomous prefecture as well as Muli（木里）county of Liangshan（凉山）Yi Nationality Autonomous prefecture. The total population is 1,087,000.

Anduo（安多）and Jiarong（伽戎）Tibetans live in Aba prefecture. Its capital is Ma'erkang（马尔康）. Unlike much of Tibet, the Ma'erkang area is well-watered, and the landscape is breathtaking. Kangba（康巴）and some Jiarong Tibetans live in Ganzi prefecture. Its capital is Kangding（康定）, which is known for a Kangding Love Song（康定情歌）. Fifty years ago, five young Tibetan students sang the song at a world youth party in Vienna（维也纳）. Since then the song has widely spread across the country as well as many parts of the world.

The Tibetan language is an alphabetic writing. It was formulated in the 7th century, which belongs to the family of Tibetan-Burmese languages. There are three major dialects: Weizang（卫藏）, Kangba and Anduo.

By the end of the 14th century, Tibetan Buddhism had had a variety of sects, which had permeated the Tibetan society. One of the sects was called the Red Sect（红教）. It was founded in the 11th century, and is the oldest sect. This sect paid great attention to absorbing the fine points of the Bon religion. The sect called itself Nyingma based on its practice of Buddhism deeply rooted in the Tubo kingdom of the 7th century. The word "Nyingma" in the Tibetan language means "ancient and old". Monks of the Nyingma Sect wore red hats, and therefore it was named the Red Sect.

Another sect is called the White Sect (白教), which was also established in the 11th century. It is also known as the Gagyu Sect. The White sect stresses the study of Tantrism; it advocates that Tantrist tenets be passed down orally from one generation to another. Gagyu, in the Tibetan language, means "passing down orally". The founders of the Gagyu Sect wore white monk robes when practicing Buddhism, and therefore were called the White Sect.

During the 15th century, a sect called the Yellow Sect (黄教) came into being. This sect is the most famous Buddhist sect in Tibetan history. The sect was founded during the reform of Tibetan Buddhism initiated by Zongkapa. At that time, upper-class monks involved in a political and economic power struggle led a decadent life, and rapidly lost popularity with society. Faced with this situation, Zongkapa called for efforts to follow Buddhist tenets. Gelug in the Tibetan language means "commandments". Zongkapa and his followers wore yellow hats, and this is the reason the sect is named the Yellow Sect.

The Tibetan people have their own traditional clothes. They like shirts in white, bright red, azure, pink, and tangerine colors. A man usually appears in a loose woolen garment with the right arm slipped out of the sleeve to show the white undergarment or woolen sweaters inside. His hat is brocade knit, four-flab hat with golden and silvery threads. He wears high boots and has a broad silk sash around his waist. Women's clothes are almost similar to men's, but their dresses are even more colorful. The material used is even better than the men's. The loose garment from the collar down is open on a slant to show the silk blouse inside. Each woman enjoys having a beautiful shawl over her shoulders and a colorful apron around her waist. Both men and women wear earrings.

The diet in the Tibetan areas is based primarily on toasted barley flour, wheat flour as well as mutton and beef. They drink wine made of barley. Tea and salt is their daily necessities.

Zanba（糌粑）is roasted qingke barley flour. It is the staple of Tibetans, similar to fried flour, but its major ingredients are highland barley, peas and oat. Tibetans bring zanba with them when they go to work, herd or travel. They put zanba in the bowl and mix with ghee, the highland barley liquor.

Yacha Tea（雅茶）is made of large leaves of tea shrubs and produced mainly in Ya'an. It is a strong tea. So it is named "Yacha". It was also called Macha in the Ming Dynasty, and Biancha in the Qing Dynasty. Tibetans eat much meat daily, and so they drink Yacha tea to digest food. The ghee tea is butter and milk, mixed up with walnut powder, peanut, sesame, egg and salt. It smells fragrant.

In the Tibetan agricultural areas, a Tibetan family usually lives in a flat-roofed house of timber-earth or stone-timber structure. The house usually has two or three floors. The flat-roof is used as a sunning place to dry their crops. The top floor is a meditation hall where the whole family prays to Buddha and recites Buddhist scriptures. Rooms on the second floor are used as a living room and bedrooms. The family always has their house windows and doors painted.

Tangka（唐卡）is Tibetan painting with a history of over 1,000 years. The paintings have strong ethnic and religious sense. Before painters start to work, painters usually spend several days on preparation. Their work is a religious act so that they seldom write their names on their Tangka paintings when they are completed. Usually painters use local natural minerals as pigments with gold, silver, agate, vermilion and others. Painting processes are complicated. The minerals are ground several times and mixed up with a bit of ox gallbladder to antisepticise paintings. All the gold powder is made as pure as possible. To increase the luster of gold, they repeatedly polish the Tangka painting with "lezi" (opal) until it becomes splendid.

The Tibetan New Year is one of the most important holidays. The day is calculated according to the Tibetan lunar calendar, and it happens at about the same time as the Chinese New Year. It is said that the Tibetan calendar was introduced to Tibet by Princess Wencheng（文成公主）, and remains in use today.

As a cock crows early on the first day of the Tibetan lunar January, housewives get up and carry "new water". The fuller the bucket with the "new water" is, the more prosperous the family will become in the coming year. It is said that Heaven offers the "new water" to Tibetan people. Anyone who drinks the "new water" will be free from illness and enjoy a healthy and long life.

In the morning of the first day, all the village men will ride to the Village Holy Hill for prayers. In daytime of the first day, all the villages will hold a horseracing event. On the second day, people go out to visit other families and exchange greetings. Hosts offer wine. In the evening people hold recreational activities, which last for at least three to five days. In some places, a grand meeting is held, in which a sorcerers' dancing is performed. People in colorful dresses wear weird masks when they sing and dance. Tibetans are good singers and excellent dancers. Songs are melodious and words are in rhyme. During the holiday people also exchange greetings with hada (哈达). Hada is a specially made long silk scarf in different colors. Mostly it is white in color, semi-transparent and extremely light. To offer someone a hada means offering him a pure, friendly heart.

KEY WORDS & EXPRESSIONS 关键词汇及表达法

breathtaking 惊人的
permeate 弥漫；渗透
absorb 吸收
tenet 原则
initiate 开始；发动
decadent 颓废的
popularity 普及，声望
bright red 大红
azure 蔚蓝
tangerine 橘子色
garment 外衣
undergarment 内衣
sweater 厚运动衫
shawl 披肩，围巾
earring 耳环，耳饰
toast 烤暖，烤火
barley 大麦

oat 燕麦
ghee 酥油
flat-roofed house 平顶屋
meditation hall 念经屋
pigment 颜料，色素
agate 玛瑙
vermilion 朱红色的
gallbladder 胆囊
antisepticise 防腐，消毒
luster 光彩，光泽
polish 磨光，光泽
opal 蛋白石，猫眼石
the Tibetan lunar calendar 藏历
exchange greeting 互致问候
recreational activity 娱乐
melodious 音调优美的

Qiang Nationality
羌族

The Qiang nationality has a population of 200，000. They mostly reside in Wenchuan，Lixian，Maoxian，Songpan in Aba Tibetan and Qiang Autonomous prefecture，and Beichuan in the Mianyang region. They dwell in hilly areas and locations by rivers and streams. A small number live with Tibetan，Han and Hui groups in places，including Wenchuan，Heishui（黑水）and Songpan.

The Qiang nationality has a long history. The Qiang has established a splendid civilization in the Northwest and Southwest of the country and be counted as one of the important founders of civilization in China. Some 3,000 years ago, ancient Chinese characters were carved on tortoise shells and animal bones. These characters supply information about this nationality.

The Qiang people call themselves Erma (尔玛). "Qiang" was a name given by ancient Hans to the nomadic people in West China. The word "Qiang" indicates herdsmen who grazed sheep in West China.

As legend has it, when the ancestors of the Qiang moved to the upper reaches of Minjiang River in Sichuan province, they came upon a strong enemy. The leader of the Qiang was instructed in a dream to overcome the enemy with white stones. The leader and his people followed the instructions, and the Qiang people finally defeated their strong enemy. The Qiang nationality therefore began to worship the white stone as a way of expressing their gratitude to the god who had appeared in the dream. This tradition has been passed on from generation to generation ever since. After the Qiang nationality settled along Mingjiang River, they put white stones on the top of their houses, on shrines for idols, as well as on the sides of roads and fields.

The Qiang people are mainly engaged in cultivation. The chief farm products include corn, wheat, highland barley, and a variety of beans. The white beans called snow mountain beans are the local specialty. The Qiang people also raise sheep. The mountain areas where the Qiang people live have rare animals, such as pandas, flying foxes, and golden monkeys. It also grows the main raw materials of valuable Chinese traditional herbs.

From a linguistic point of view, all modern Qiang people speak the Qiang language, which is a member of the Tibetan-

Burmese linguistic family. However, the local dialects are extremely varied. Qiang scholars created their own writing system and compiled a dictionary of the Qiang language. They started in the middle 1980's after receiving approval from the State Council. They used a Romanized alphabet based on the standardized Qugu (曲谷) dialect. Since 1994, teachers have been trained to learn the standard Qiang language and the new writing system. After training, they are sent to Qiang villages to teach local villagers. The Qiang people believe that they are speaking the same language.

The Qiang and Han peoples have had time-honored close ties in political, economic and cultural fields. In ancient China the imperial courts in different dynasties had political units in the Qiang-occupied areas. In the early Qing Dynasty the central authority set up a system to appoint local hereditary headmen to rule over the Qiang. The central administrative system helped enhance the ties between the Qiang and Han ethnic groups.

The Qiang people lived in primitive conditions, marked by slash and burn farming. The primitive life ended in 1949. Nowadays, the life of the Qiang people has been changed considerably. The industry and agriculture in the Qiang inhabited areas has undergone remarkable progress. Many small and medium sized hydropower stations have been built. Electricity has replaced pine torches for lighting. Besides, TV sets and electric cookers are commonly used.

Traditionally, Qiang village buildings are built with stones, and the roofs are flat. The houses are connected to form a village. In some villages all houses face inwards, the back walls are connected, forming the outer rampart. The structure is solid. In ancient times wars frequently broke out. The Qiang people were forced to build houses with strong defensive capabilities. The houses usually have three stories. The first floor is used to house domestic animals. The second provides a living area and the third floor is used to store grain and other odds and ends. A long corridor links all the houses in the village.

The symbol of a fortress village is its defense towers. These towers were built of stone. Each is about 15 to 20 feet across at the base, and becomes gradually narrower up to the top. Many exceed 100 feet in height. According to the natives, all these defense towers were built at least 80 years ago.

Like other ethnic nationalities in China, the Qiang nationality is fond of dancing and singing. The Qiang flute is a popular musical instrument. It produces a clear and pleasant sound in accompaniment to dancing and singing. Guozhuang (锅庄) is a kind group dancing that is commonly believed to be shared between the Tibetans and the Qiang in Aba prefecture. Since 1989, both the standardized Guozhuang dancing of the Qiang and that of the Jiarong Tibetans were gradually introduced to all the people. Guozhuang dancing is widely practiced in every official or private celebration, it is not only a symbol of the Qiang culture but also a symbol of unification of the Jiarong Tibetans and the Qiang in Aba prefecture. One cannot think of the Chinese culture without including this fascinating proud ethnic group.

KEY WORDS & EXPRESSIONS 关键词汇及表达法

reside 居住

idol 偶像，崇拜物

barley 大麦

local specialty 特产

raw material　原材料
time-honored　由来已久的
primitive　原始的，远古的
slash and burn farming　刀耕火种
considerably　相当地
defensive capability　防御能力
domestic animal　家禽
corridor　走廊，回廊
be fond of　喜爱的

Section Four :

Descriptions of Some Scenic Spots

第四部分：

部分景点讲解词

Du Fu Thatched Cottage 杜甫草堂

Life Story of Du Fu

杜甫生平

Ladies and gentlemen, here is the entrance to Du Fu Thatched Cottage. I'd like to give you some biographical information about Du Fu before we enter the cottage grounds.

Have you had an opportunity of reading some classic Chinese poems before your visit to China? Maybe some of you did, and some didn't. Classical Chinese poetry has been in existence for a thousand years. The epitome of the poetry was in the Tang Dynasty. Its most famous poets were Du Fu and Li Bai. Based on the judgment of some Western critics, Du Fu is the most representative figure. The nature, content and sound of his poems have made him very appealing to the world.

Du Fu was born in Gongxian county, Henan province in 712. He was also known as Du Zimei. He spent the greater part of his boyhood in Luoyang. In 746, he went to Chang'an, the Tang capital, in an attempt to obtain an official post. However, he had only reached a minor post as he entered the age of fifty.

Du Fu lived at the turning point of the Tang Dynasty when its prosperity began to decline. In 755, An Lushan Rebellion broke out. It permanently weakened the dynasty. The rebellion lasted from 756 to 763 and forced the Tang court into exile. Du Fu fled the capital, but was captured by the rebels. Du Fu escaped in 757 and offered his services to the new emperor. In 759, he resigned and came to Chengdu. He died in 770.

Chinese critics from the Song Dynasty referred to Du Fu as the poet-historian. He lived through the disasters of the period alongside the common people. Du Fu witnessed a typical political and social situation, the common people lived in poverty, the emperor and his top officials enjoyed a foolishly luxurious life. Du Fu frequently used his poetry to expose social injustice and voice the suffering of the people. His poems include *the Song of the War Chariots* (兵车行), *Three Officials* (三吏) and *Three Departures* (三别). His poems expressed his dissatisfaction with the government and his great pity for the common people. Throughout his life, Du Fu was deeply concerned with politics, and many of his poems were on current events.

Du Fu's poetry came to be recognized even during the Tang Dynasty. Readers of many different periods have considered Du Fu as the greatest poet of the Chinese tradition. Besides, his landscape and pastoral poems sound beautiful. In 759, he arrived in Chengdu where he set up a modest cottage. He had a simple and peaceful life for three years, writing about 240 poems. Most of his poems were inspired by the cottage, the stream nearby and the scenery in Chengdu. They sound like he had enjoyed his stay in Chengdu.

Well, ladies and gentlemen, the immense variety of Du Fu's work holds up quite well to different tastes from readers both at home and abroad. Like Shakespeare in the English tradition, Du Fu's poetry became deeply bound up with the literary culture of China. The poets and critics in his following generations always rediscover their interests and values in some aspect of the poet's work.

KEY WORDS & EXPRESSIONS 关键词汇及表达法

epitome 缩影
boyhood 少年时代
turning point 转折点
An Lushan Rebellion 安史之乱
permanently 永存地，不变地
exile 放逐，充军，流放
rebel 造反者，叛逆者
resign 辞去(职务)
a typical political and social situation 特殊的政治社会形势
foolishly luxurious life 荒淫奢侈的生活
dissatisfaction 不满，不平
pastoral poem 田园诗
immense 极广大的，无边的
Shakespeare 莎士比亚
be bound up with 同……密切联系

Front Gate

正门

Ladies and gentlemen, here we are at the parking lot near the Front Gate. Please get off the bus and walk towards the entrance.

Du Fu Thatched Cottage is located in the western suburbs of Chengdu. It used to be Du Fu's former home. The present cottage consists of six important parts: Front Gate (正门), Lobby (大廨), Hall of Historical Poetry (诗史堂), Water Pavilion (水槛), Gongbu Shrine (工部祠) and Thatched Pavilion (茅屋). These ancient style architectures, pavilions, pagodas stand among age-old trees and green bamboos.

Here is the Front Gate. Some people call it the Main Entrance. A stream flows nearby, and its name is Huanhuaxi (浣花溪). "Huan" means "washing", "hua" means "flowers". Why did people named the stream Huanhuaxi or the Flower Washing Stream? There is a folk story related to the origin of its name.

A long time ago, a pretty young lady lived near the stream. It is said that she had a kind heart and often did something good for her friends and local people. One day a monk arrived when a group of ladies were washing their clothes by the stream. The monk had serious skin disease. He scratched his skin as he walked towards the ladies. At the first sight of the monk, all the ladies ran away as quickly as possible. However, the pretty young lady stayed and continued her washing.

The monk had some clothes in his hand. Those clothes looked very dirty. It seemed that they had not been washed for several months.

The monk kept scratching. He said to the lady, "Would you like to wash my clothes?"

"Yes, I will." said the lady. She took the dirty clothes from the monk and then put them into the stream.

The young lady dipped the clothes into the water, and immediately lotus flowers appeared and blossomed. Lotus flowers were everywhere in the stream.

"It's amazing." said the lady to herself. She turned to the monk, but there was no sign of the man. Upon hearing the wonder, local people came and saw the flowers. Since then, they have called the stream huanhuaxi or the Flower Washing Stream.

Well, isn't it a beautiful story? Following is another story from local legend, and it is also associated with the Flower Washing Stream name. A long time ago, the local people near the stream made their living by making paper. People used water from the stream to produce a kind of multi-colored writing paper. The stream was therefore named huanhuaxi after the colorful paper.

It is said that during the Tang Dynasty the stream was much wider and deeper than the current one, and large boats could anchor near the place where Du Fu lived. In a poem by Du Fu, two lines say:

"And the ships that will sail east for Dong Wu
They lie at anchor in the sun-filled doorway."
(门泊东吴万里船。)

Now please look up at the horizontal board on the top of the entrance gate. Two big Chinese characters written on the board say: "Caotang(草堂)." It means the Thatched Cottage. It was written by a prince of the Qing Dynasty. A couplet hangs on either side of the entrance says"The cottage is near the West side of Wan Li Bridge, and to the North of Baihuatan (万里桥西宅,百花潭北庄)." The couplet indicates the original location of the cottage.

Let's walk into the cottage. I know that you will find ancient buildings hidden among trees, bamboos and clear streams.

KEY WORDS & EXPRESSIONS 关键词汇及表达法

anchor 抛锚,锚定

Lobby
大廨

This is Daxie building. Daxie is the name of a type of administration buildings where ancient officials worked in the feudal society. Daxie means the lobby in English. Du Fu served in the Tang government. One of his official titles was Zuoshiyi (左拾遗). This official job was mainly responsible to give a mild warning to the Tang emperor. Du Fu also advanced reasons for important cases. However, Du Fu was not a skilled survivor in government politics. His straightforward warnings or suggestions often made the emperor unhappy. At last, Du Fu gave up this post and set off with his family to Qinzhou in Northwestern China. After a short stay, he moved on again and came to Chengdu. As the building was completed, it was named daxie to remind visitors of Du Fu's short, but excellent service in the Tang government, and it also indicated the respect local people had for Du Fu.

Please get close to the bronze sculpture of Du Fu in the center of the lobby. It was made by Qian Shaouwu (钱绍武), a well-known sculpture artist from the Central Academy of Arts in Beijing. Du Fu remains in a kneeling position. He holds a poetry book in his hand and looks slightly upwards. What does his poseture suggest? Du Fu himself experienced disasters during the Tang chaotic period. He was anxious to do something for his people who lived in poverty. However, his capacity to serve society was limited. Besides, he was far away from home and family. He could do nothing but use his poems to express his unbearable loneliness and failure in officialdom.

Now please come here and view the cottage compound picture. In 765, Du Fu left Chengdu. He continued wandering in the southern provinces and eventually died of illness in 770. Shortly after his death, the cottage was destroyed completely. During the Northern Dynasty (11th century), a Chengdu governor sponsored the rebuilding of the cottage on the original site to honor the great poet. However, the cottage, through the following dynasties, was destroyed and rebuilt at least more than ten times. I have to say that the reconstructions, which took place in 1500 and 1811, are worth mentioning. These two major constructions enlarged the compound, and more architecture was built. When Du Fu came to Chengdu in 759, he borrowed money from his friend to build a simple cottage. At that time, the whole garden covered a space of no more than a couple of mu. One Chinese mu is 0.0667 hectares. Now the present compound covers over 200 mu.

Please come and view the couplet hung on the walls. It was

written by Gu Fuchu（顾复初），a well-known scholar of the Qing Dynasty. Literally the couplet means：Du Fu and I came from different dynasties. Like both of us，many scholars since ancient times have failed to realize their lofty aspirations. We all could do nothing but be like a dragon curling and a tiger crouching.

KEY WORDS & EXPRESSIONS 关键词汇及表达法

lobby 大厅
straightforward 正直的，坦率的
give up 放弃
academy 学院
be anxious to do sth 渴望做某事
unbearable loneliness 不堪忍受的孤独
officialdom 官场政治
sponsor 发起
aspiration 愿望
curling 蜷曲；蜷缩；藏（龙）
crouch 蹲伏；弯腰；卧（虎）

Hall of Historical Poetry
诗史堂

Now let's go to the third memorial building—the Hall of Historical Poetry. It was named in the 19th century. Please follow me into the hall.

Here in the middle of the hall is another Du Fu sculpture. It is a half-length bust. A couplet hangs on the either side. It says："The thatched cottage lasts many generations；the poetry sage remains well-known for a thousand centuries（草堂留后人，诗圣著千秋）."

The Water Pavilion and the Thatched Gate

水槛和柴门

Ladies and gentlemen, as you walk out of the Hall of Historical Poetry, you will cross a stream before arriving at the Thatched Gate.

This is a water pavilion, and it spans over the stream. Both the thatched gate and water pavilion has its own Chinese name. The first one is called shuikan (水槛) and the latter chaimen (柴门).

A historical doctrine says that Du Fu had a kind of shuikan and chaimen in his small cottage garden during his stay in Chengdu. At that time chaimen was a simple bamboo gate, and shuikan was no more than several pieces of wood fixed together near the stream for the purpose of fishing. The current shuikan and chaimen are called the Water Pavilion and the Thatched Gate in English. They look completely different in shape because these constructions were built in later dynasties in honor of Du Fu.

One couplet on the gate pillars is well worth attention. The couplet was written in the Ming Dynasty. Literally the couplet means that Du Fu's poetry shines boundlessly, and his poetry amazes readers at home and abroad. In the past thousand years, many people far and wide traveled over great distances on horse back or carriages only for a visit to Du Fu cottage.

Today many visitors keep coming to the cottage. They experience the tradition and culture deeply bound up with the literary value of Du Fu's poetry.

KEY WORDS & EXPRESSIONS 关键词汇及表达法

boundlessly 无穷地,无限地

amaze 使吃惊

carriage 马车

The Gongbu Shrine and the Thatched Pavilion
工部祠和茅屋

Now we arrive at Gongbu Shrine. Probably, Gongbu was the title given to an official in charge of the local industry. The Gongbu Shrine here is the last memorial building on the compound.

Du Fu left Chengdu after 762 and wandered in the southern provinces. After his death, the people of Chengdu built a shrine on the site of his cottage to honor him. Since then, many visitors come for their visits to the shrine.

Here is another couplet, which hangs on the top of the front door. The couplet reads that Du Fu owned Jinjiang River and the spring breeze, on the seventh day for human beings did I come and visit his cottage(锦水春风公占却,草堂人日我归来。).

I wonder what's the meaning of the seventh day for human beings? A scholar of the Qing Dynasty wrote this ancient couplet. His name was He Shaoji (何绍基). He composed the couplet when he visited the cottage on the seventh day for human beings. In ancient times this seventh day was around the middle of February, and it was named Renri (人日).

In ancient Sichuan, local people thought the first seven days in the first lunar month were devoted to different animals and human beings. Accordingly, the first day was for chicken, the second day for dogs, the third day for pigs, the fourth day for sheep, the fifth day for cows, the sixth day for horses, and the seventh day for human beings. We don't know why Scholar He chose Renri for his visit, but many other scholars followed suit and went to the cottage on the seventh day each year. Gradually, common people joined the visit as a local custom.

Please look at the statues inside the hall. As you know, the Gongbu Shrine is a small hall, dedicated to the memory of Du Fu. Therefore, it is at the center of the six important sites on the cottage compound. The hall contains a statue of Du Fu in the middle. There are two other statues flanking him. Who are these figures? The one on the right is Huang Tingjian (黄庭坚, 1045 - 1105), and the one on the left is Lu You (陆游, 1125 - 1210). These two figures were well-known poets from the Song Dynasty and occupied an important place in traditional Chinese literary history.

Huang Tingjian was from Xiushui in Jiangxi. Because he worked in the Song government, Huang was involved in political party struggles. Later when his opposition party was in power, he was dismissed from his major official post and banished to Yizhou. He studied Du Fu's poetry seriously and intentionally carried out the poetry innovations made during the early Song Dynasty.

Lu You was from Shaoxing in Zhejiang. Lu You was a prolific poet and more than nine thousands of his poems have survived. Although he worked as an official in the Song government, he was unable to affect any of the political reforms he advocated. Both Huang Tingjian and Lu You are noted for their ardent patriotism.

Visitors may ask why Huang Tingjian and Lu You were chosen to accompany Du Fu at this memorial cottage out of the thousands of poets in traditional Chinese literary history. Some critics have tried to figure out reasons for the choice. The following facts may sound reasonable.

1. Huang Tingjian and Lu You both made great achievements in studying Du Fu's poetry.

2. They enjoyed their stay in Sichuan, although they were not born here. During their short stay, they composed many local

landscape poems. As they departed, they took away good memories.

3. Du Fu's statue might feel lonely in the Gongbu Shrine if there were not any companions. So people placed the statues of these poets in the same hall, thinking that the three poets might have time to talk about their poetry. People also call the hall the Shrine of the Three Sages.

Well, ladies and gentlemen, besides the three statues, there are two valuable stone tablets from Qing Dynasty. The tablets show us the design and development of the cottage dating from Qing Dynasty. Also there are another two stone tablets in the hall. These tell us the history about the refurbishment of the cottage and the reasons of co-existence of the three statues in the same hall.

Here we are at a straw-roofed pavilion. It is on the left side of Gongbu Shrine. I think that the purpose of the construction is designated to remind visitors of the simple life Du Fu had in his cottage. Inside is placed a huge tablet with the two engraved Chinese characters. It is called caotang (the thatched cottage). They were written by Prince Guo of Qing Dynasty when he visited the cottage. It is also an ideal place to have a picture taken for a good memoir.

Ladies and gentlemen, our tour to Du Fu Thatched Cottage is approaching the end. At present, Du Fu Thatched cottage serves as a museum. It has a rich collection of over 30,000 bound volumes and 2,000 cultural relics besides Du Fu's poems, which have been translated into many languages.

Now you are free to walk around the cottage grounds, and I will meet you at the entrance in an hour. At some of the shops, sometimes there are poets who will compose a personalized poem for you for a slight fee. Now have a pleasant walk and experience the tradition characterized by Du Fu's poems. I know that the cool greenery will rest your eyes, running water will sooth your ears, and the utter quietness will refresh your hearts.

KEY WORDS & EXPRESSIONS 关键词汇及表达法

in charge of 主管,掌管
memorial 纪念的
dismiss 开除,解职
banish 流放,放逐
innovation 革新,创新
prolific 多产的,丰富的
ardent patriotism 强烈的爱国主义
companion 同伴,共事者
refurbishment 整修

Chengdu Wuhou Temple 成都武侯祠

Development of the Temple
武侯祠沿革

Ladies and gentlemen, here we are at the entrance to Wuhou Temple. It was constructed in memory of Zhuge Liang, who was a well-known strategist and statesman during the Three Kingdoms Period. I think it's necessary to provide you with some historical background to help you better understand what the displays in the temple are.

China has a recorded history of some 3, 600 years. It began with the Shang Dynasty (商朝, 16th - 11th century B. C.). The whole ancient history is divided into three stages. The first stage is the primitive society. The history was much associated with the presumed pre-Xia Dynasty (夏朝, 21st- 16th century B. C.). The second major stage lasted from about 2, 000 to 200 B. C.. The history dated the beginning of the slave society from the Xia Dynasty. The third stage extended all the way from 221B. C. to the Opium War (鸦片战争) of 1840. Historical documents name the third stage as the Feudal Imperial Society. At the end of the Eastern Han (东汉, 25 - 22), the feudal society in China came into a period of disunity. Traditionally it is called the Three Kingdoms Period.

Now let me focus on what happened in this particular period. Towards the end of the Eastern Han, a great peasant rebellion broke out. Many local officials became autonomous regional warlords. They suppressed the rebellion, and at the same time they took the opportunity to build up their own political and military strength. Finally the warlords carved the Han Empire into three kingdoms of Wei, Shu and Wu.

I don't know if you have read a classic Chinese novel. Its name is *the Romance of the Three Kingdoms*. The novel is so popular that most Chinese families each have a copy. The novel basically traces the rise and fall of the three kingdoms and vividly depicts the turbulent social conditions at that time. Cao Cao(曹操) and his son established the Kingdom of Wei at Luoyang. Actually, Cao Cao controlled the North China homeland. The other two rivals soon proclaimed themselves emperors elsewhere. The Kingdom of Wu with its capital at Nanjing occupied Changjiang Valley. The Kingdom of Shu controlled Sichuan and parts of the Southwestern China highland. Its capital was in Chengdu.

Wuhou Temple is much associated with the Kingdom of Shu. It is a memorial to Zhuge Liang, Prime Minister of the kingdom. Wuxianghou (武乡侯) was a top official title conferred upon Zhuge Liang when he seried the kingdom. After his death, another title was given to him. It was zhongwuhou (忠武侯). People respectfully called him wuhou.

There are some different opinions of when it was built. Some think that the temple was built at the end of the Western Jin Dynasty. Unfortunately, historical documents have no records to confirm the construction date. Du Fu, a top Tang Dynasty poet composed a poem called *Prime Minister of Shu Kingdom* (蜀相). Two lines in the poem say:

"Where would I find the Prime Minister's shrine?
Somewhere outside Jinguan, in dense cypress trees."
(丞相祠堂何处寻,锦官城外柏森森。)

We are able to conclude from the meaning of the poem that Wuhou Temple had existed even before the Tang Dynasty.

Between the Tang and Song dynasties, Zhuge Liang and

Emperor Liu Bei had their independent temples. At the beginning of the Ming Dynasty, the two separate temples merged into one. Towards the end of the Ming Dynasty the merged temple was destroyed during war chaos. The present constructions date from the Qing Dynasty in 1672.

Ladies and gentlemen, please look at the horizontal inscribed board on the top of the main entrance gate. It says "Han Zhaolie Temple (汉昭烈庙)". Han refers to the Kingdom of Shu, Zhaolie was Liu Bei's posthumous title. The board indicates that the whole temple was built in honor of Liu Bei. Why do all the people call it Zhuge Liang Temple or Wuhou Temple? It is said that in the Ming Dynasty, a member of the royal family saw that there were many more visitors to Wuhou Temple than to Liu Bei's. He felt that was improper because Liu Bei was the emperor. So he demolished Wuhou Temple and moved the statue of Zhuge Liang into Liu Bei's Termple. However, the people did not like this arrangement. Instead of building a special hall for Zhuge Liang, they kept calling the combined temple Wuhou Temple instead of Liu Bei's Temple. Gradually through common practice more and more people accepted the new name. It also testifies to the people's love for Zhuge Liang. In the people's view, Zhuge Liang has been immortalized in *the Romance of the Three Kingdoms*. His contribution is historically invaluable, and his management of state-affairs and military strategies have influenced following centuries.

Now let's walk into the temple and pick up a guide-map on the left side of the entrance. The map offers a picture of the temple and its illustration is in English. Generally speaking, the temple compound occupies a space of 37,000 square meters. The compound consists of five main buildings: the Front Gate, the Second Gate, Liu Bei's Hall, Zhuge Liang's Hall and Liu Bei's Tomb. The compounds have a series of inner courtyards, the main buildings are built on a north-south axis (中轴线), the doors of the main buildings face south.

Making houses face south is a traditional practice in Chinese domestic architecture. Archeologists have found that many Neolithicperiod houses were rectangular with a south-facing door. Settlements in the Zhou Dynasty were also organized on a north-south axis. These early dwellings no longer exist, but houses from the Ming Dynasty in China also show a tendency to face south. This practice is related to sunlight, and the direction of prevailing winds, especially cold winds.

The temple has 47 clay figures, 40 tablets, as well as 30 inscribed boards and couplets. It also stores over ten valuable ancient drums, stoves, bells and cooking vessels. Frankly speaking, the temple functions as a memorial hall in honor of Liu Bei and his subordinates.

Here are the six huge stone tablets. They flank the yard between the front and the second gates. Four of them were from the Qing Dynasty. The other two came either from the Ming or the Tang dynasties. The Qing tablets state the stories about the reestablishment of the temple, the Ming tablet illustrates its development.

Please get close to the Ming tablet and view a stone animal that is supporting the huge tablet on his back. What does the animal look alike? Visitors always say the animal is a tortoise. A tortoise is called "wugui" (乌龟) in Chinese. This animal is called "bixi" in Chinese. It is a legendary animal and looks like a tortoise. As an old saying goes, the dragon has nine sons. Bixi is one of them. Each son has his own skill. Because of its great strength and endurance, Bixi always carries a tablet on his back.

Please come to the Tang tablet. It is better known than the other tablets. It is called the Three Perfection Tablet (三绝碑). Why do we highly praise the Tang tablet? The main reason is that several top scholars and well-known artists were involved in making the tablet.

The essay began in 809 during the Tang Dynasty when Wu Yuanheng (武元衡), a local top military commander in Western Sichuan and his 27 assistants arrived at the temple to worship Zhuge Liang. Soon after the visit, the tablet was created to mark the special worship occasion. The first scholar involved was Pei Du (裴度) who used to work as a prime minister for three Tang emperors in different times. He composed the tablet essay. In the essay, Pei Du eulogized Zhuge Liang for his great contribution to the process of unifying the whole China. He also commented on Zhuge Liang's state-affairs management and military strategies, and encouraged the Tang officials to learn from Zhuge Liang. The second scholar was Liu Gongchuo (柳公绰) who was a well-known Tang calligraphist. He copied the essay in a beautiful Chinese calligraphy style. As you know, Chinese calligraphy is a kind of art, drawing characters with a Chinese brush. The Chinese word for calligraphy is shufa (书法), which means the writing method. There are several popular scripts. They include kaishu (楷书, the regular script), xingshu (行书, the running script), and caoshu (草书, the grass script). The grass scripts' styled characters have a swift appearance and the strokes flow together in a cursive manner. These characters are so freely made that ordinary people have difficulty in reading them. You may ask me what kind of scripts the tablet has. I think it's a regular script. Chinese artists call it the Liu-styled calligraphy. Well, the third person involved was an artist. He was Lu Jian (鲁建), a famous Tang stone mason. He engraved the essay on the tablet according to the pattern of LiuBei's calligraphy. You see. The three important figures joined hands to perfect the tablet. That is why people called it the Three Perfection Tablet.

KEY WORDS & EXPRESSIONS 关键词汇及表达法

associated with 与……有关联的
the feudal society 封建社会
warlord 军阀
rise and fall 兴衰
proclaim 宣布
cypress 柏树
horizontal inscribed board 横匾
demolish 拆除；毁坏
be superior to 较高于
the north-south axis 中轴线
rectangular 长方形的
tendency 趋向，倾向
vessel 容器，器皿
subordinate 下属
endurance 忍耐(力)
eulogize 称赞，颂扬
spare-no-efforts 不遗余力
calligraphist 书法家
cursive 草书体的

stone mason 石工

Liu Bei Hall
刘备殿

Ladies and gentlemen, please come into the Second Gate courtyard where Liu Bei Hall is located. First of all, let's go straight to view Liu Bei's statue.

The statue stands behind the front altar, and his son and grandson flank him. Liu Bei was commonly called Liu Xuande (刘玄德). It was said that he looked larger than a life figure. His ears were long, the lobes touched his shoulders, and his hands hang down below his knees. His eyes were very prominent, so that he could see backward past his ears. Liu Bei remained solemn and displayed little emotion.

Liu Bei started his life as a shoemaker and a weaver of mats. He made his name against the Yellow Turban rebels (黄巾起义). Liu Bei, Guan Yu (关羽) and Zhang Fei (张飞) swore brotherhood at the Peach Garden to destroy the rebels and defend the Han Empire. Liu Bei was a kind and sincere man. He won the hearts of thousands of his followers through his virtuous ways and fought in wars all around China. Before the age of fifty, Liu Bei was constantly in the service of others, including Gongsun Zan (公孙瓒), Yuan Shao (袁绍) and Liu Biao (刘表).

In 208, all of this changed when Liu Bei obtained the help of Zhuge Liang as his advisor. Together, Liu Bei and Sun Quan's (孙权) united forces defeated Cao Cao (曹操) at the Battle of the Red Wall.

In 221, Liu Bei become the first emperor of the Kingdom of Shu. Afterwards, he started a series of military expeditions against Wu, in revenge for the death of Guan Yu and Zhang Fei. Frustration and repeated defeats broke him down completely. Liu Bei knew that he was going to die very soon. He immediately summoned Zhuge Liang to Baidi (白帝) town from Chengdu and entrusted his only son to him. He said to Zhuge Liang, "If my son is good, you are to help him succeed to the throne. If he does not have the necessary qualities to be an emperor, you mustn't make him the emperor of Shu in Chengdu." Zhuge Liang was moved to tears upon hearing this. He said, "How does your humble subject dare not to assist your son with every effort and not to be utterly loyal to him until the day your humble subject dies!" Liu Bei died of illness in Baidi town soon after his meeting with Zhuge Liang.

On the walls of Liu Bei Hall hang wooden carved essays. They were written by Zhuge Liang. One is named *Longzhong Plan* (隆中对) and the other is *The Letter to the Throne before a Military Expedition* (出师表).

Please come to view the Longzhong Plan, and I will let you know the background of the plan.

Since against the Yellow Turban rebels, Liu Bei had led his troops for almost twenty years. He fought here and there and couldn't find a fixed base of operations. In 207, Liu Bei garrisoned at Xinye (新野) on the current side of Hanyang city in Hunan). He realized that he would not be able to reunify China until he found a truly learned advisor. Xu Shu (徐庶) was Zhuge Liang's good friend, and he recommended Zhuge Liang to Liu Bei.

Xu Shu said to Liu Bei, "Zhuge Kongming is a dragon lying in wait, but ready to fly. Would you like to meet him?"

"Bring him with you to see me!" Liu Bei replied.

"This man has noble aspirations," Xu Shu responded. "You

cannot simply summon him. He would only come if you personally went to call him. He can't be forced to come to see you. You'd better go to his house to ask him."

Thereupon Liu Bei took Guan Yu and Zhang Fei to went to Longzhong to pay a formal visit to Zhuge Liang. They had to go three times before they could see him. It is said that the first time, Zhuge Liang had gone traveling, so they didn't meet him. The second time, he was also out, and they were only able to meet his younger brother. It was only on the third time that they received Zhuge Liang's warm hospitality.

On the third visit when Liu Bei finally met Zhuge Liang, they discussed great matters concerning China. Zhuge Liang knew many strategies. He analyzed the contemporary situation for Liu and suggested plans for the future. Liu Bei listened to him and asked questions. *Longzhong Plan* was actually a dialogue between Liu Bei and Zhuge Liang when they had their discussion. Afterwards Liu Bei came to completely respect Zhuge Liang. Since that time Liu Bei relied on him for advice in all matters. In order to repay the favor Liu Bei had shown him, Zhuge Liang gave his utmost to help Liu Bei establish political power for the Kingdom of Shu. Even after Liu Bei died, he continued to support loyally the slow-witted successor, Liu Chan (刘禅).

Ladies and gentlemen, here is the other wooden carved essay: *The Letter to the Throne before a Military Expedition*. It was a petition written by Zhuge Liang to the young emperor, Liu Chan in 227. He wrote this petition to ask the emperor for permission to start his northern expeditions. In his letter he said to the emperor, "Rewards and punishments should be meted out equitably. There should be no place for favoritism or inequality under the law." In his letter Zhuge Liang also recommended some able and learned generals and scholars. Finally Zhuge Liang showed his loyalty to the late emperor and his determination to realize the dreams of his master and himself. "His Late Majesty knew that your humble subject was prudent, so he entrusted your humble subject with the Great Task before his death. Since accepting this responsibility, your humble subject has toiled days and nights lest the job be wanting or fallen short of His Late Majesty's expectations."

Well, now let's view the other statues. On the east side of the Liu Bei statue is a figure whose name was Liu Chen (刘谌). He was one of Liu Bei's grandsons. Liu Chan was Liu Bei's son. His statue used to be placed on the west side of the Liu Bei statue. During the Song Dynasty his figure statue was moved away. Since then Liu Bei had no son to accompany him. As I told you earlier, after Liu Bei's death, Zhuge Liang wholeheartedly supported the young emperor until the day he died. Unfortunately, Liu Chan was one of the weakest and stupid emperors in Chinese history and finally lost the kingdom to the Wei. He was taken away from Chengdu to Luoyang, the capital of Wei. During his stay in Luoyang, the Wei emperor offered him a comfortable life. He was so happy that he soon forgot the disgrace of having his kingdom conquered by the Wei.

To the right of the main hall is a red-faced figure called Guan Yu. He has a huge frame, long beard and deep red lips. His whole appearance looks dignified. Guan Yu was the sworn brother of Liu Bei and Zhang Fei. Five years before the Yellow Turban Rebelion, he murdered a wealthy bully and was a fugitive until he met Liu Bei. His unswerving loyalty and strength were crucial to Liu Bei's efforts. He was killed with his son Guan Ping (关平) when they were captured at Maicheng (麦城). Well, now I'd like to tell you a story about Guan Yu. This story is taken from *the Romance of the Three Kingdoms*. It tells that Guan Yu is playing Weiqi (围棋) while undergoing an arm surgery.

The episode began with Guan Yu and his soldiers' attack on Fancheng. During his attack a poisonous arrow wounded him. The poison reached the bone, and his right arm was badly swollen. He was unable to move. At this moment, Hua Tuo (华佗), the famous physician, arrived on a boat. Hua examined Guan Yu, and concluded that Guan Yu needed an operation immediately. Guan Yu did not want Hua to put him to sleep during the operation, for he worried that the enemy might attack them. Hua suggested that Guan should tie his arm to a pillar and have his eyes covered. Hua was afraid that Guan Yu couldn't stand the pain and would move during his operation.

When Guan Yu heard Hua's suggestion, he laughed, saying "This is such a simple procedure. There is no need to worry." Guan Yu asked for some wine, took off his shirt, and stuck his arm out for Hua. Guan Yu started to play Weiqi against Ma Liang (马良), his assistant.

Hua took out a surgical knife and proceeded to cut open Guan Yu's arm, removing the infected area. The poison had reached the bone, and it turned blue. Hua had to scrape the bone to get the poison out. Everyone couldn't bear to see the blood and hear the scraping sound, except Guan Yu. He was talking, drinking and playing Weiqi. After Hua had finished his operation, Guan Yu said to Hua, "My arm is good as new and there is no pain at all. You are really the best of all doctors!" Hua replied, "In my whole life, I have never seen anyone as brave as you. You are the best of all heroes!" It seemed that Guan Yu used Weiqi to divert his attention during his surgery, but his bravery was still unmatched throughout history.

To the left of the main hall is a black-faced figure called General Zhang Fei. Zhang Fei was the sworn brother of Liu Bei and Guan Yu, the youngest one of the three. He had large eyes, and a pointed and bristling moustache. It is said that he spoke in a loud bass voice and looked irresistible. His angry roar brought fear into the hearts of many brave men. His most spectacular battle was on the Long Slope Bridge (长板坡桥), where he roared so fiercely that one of Cao Cao's generals dropped from the horse died suddenly. Zhang Fei was hot-tempered. He usually got drunk and flogged his officers. At about age 54 he was murdered by his two bad-tempered subordinates when he was in his sleep.

Ladies and gentlemen, there are two galleries in the same yard. They contain 28 terracotta figures dating from the Qing Dynasty. General figures are on the right, and ministers on the left. Pang Tong (庞统) heads the civil officials' gallery. Zhao Yun (赵云) heads the military officials' galleries. Let's view the figures in the galleries, who are well-loved by many Chinese people generation by generation.

This is the figure by the name of Zhao Yun. He was one of the most famous warriors in the Three Kingdoms Period. Zhao Yun used to be under the wing of Gongsun Zan. Later Zhao Yun left him. He found out that Gongsun was a selfish man who cared little about the suffering of the people. Zhao then came under the wings of Liu Bei. Zhao Yun was known for his loyalty and courage. During the battle of Changban Slope, Zhao Yun came to rescue LiuBei's wife and the newly born baby. LiuBei's wife was injured and she couldn't move. The Cao forces heavily encircled them. Under this atypical situation LiuBei's wife gave the baby to Zhao Yun and asked Zhao Yun to leave immediately. Zhao Yun couldn't go without her. So she committed suicide for she knew that she would only be an obstacle to Zhao Yun. Zhao Yun thus placed the infant inside his chest armor and fought through the heavy encirclement of the Cao troops. He fought through, killing generals and soldiers, without getting himself injured and dropping the baby. Finally Zhao Yun escaped safely from the heavy encirclements with the baby. This was the battle that made Zhao Yun famous.

During the Three Kingdoms Period, the rulers of the independent states fought each other for political power. The figures in the corridors are just holy to thousands of Three Kingdoms enthusiasts. The well-loved figures are the historical sources from which later novels and drama have captured the imaginations of generations of Chinese readers and audience.

KEY WORDS & EXPRESSIONS 关键词汇及表达法

prominent 杰出的,著名的
virtuous 善良的,有道德的
expedition 远征
in revenge for 报复,报仇
frustration 挫败,挫折
move to tears 感动得流泪
humble subject 卑下

garrison 派……驻防
recommend 推荐
summon 召集,召唤
utmost 最大可能的
slow-witted 迟钝的,笨的
petition 请愿,请愿书
mete out 给予
favoritism 偏爱,得宠
inequality 不平等,不同
prudent 谨慎的
fall short of 缺乏,达不到
expectation 期待,预想
wholeheartedly 全心全意地
disgrace 耻辱,失宠
bully 恶霸,暴徒
fugitive 逃跑者,逃亡者
unswerving 坚定的,始终不渝的
surgery 外科手术
poisonous 含毒的
physician 医生
procedure 程序,手续
surgical knife 手术刀
infected 被感染的
unmatched 无比的,无匹敌的
moustache 胡子
irresistible 不可抵抗的
hot-tempered 脾气暴躁
flog 鞭打,鞭策
under the wings of 在……保护下

commit suicide 自杀，自毁
infant 婴儿
encirclement 包围圈
enthusiast 热心家，狂热者

Zhuge Liang Hall

诸葛亮殿

Ladies and gentlemen, please come into Zhuge Liang Hall.

The hall is behind the second yard. Zhuge Liang Hall is obviously lower than Liu Bei's. Visitors have to walk down several steps before they can get into the third yard. As you see, Zhuge Liang Hall in the temple sits on a lower ground than Liu Bei Hall. It is a deliberate arrangement to reflect the different status between Liu Bei and Zhuge Liang. In ancient China, the emperor was the son of Heaven, he was superior; and all other people were his subordinates.

Please look at the horizontal wooden board that hangs on the top of the entrance gate of Zhuge Liang Hall. It says, "Eternal Glory Remains All over the World (名垂宇宙)." Inside the hall, horizontal inscribed boards and couplets fill up the walls. They carry words of praise for Zhuge Liang. Among them is the most famous couplet in the middle of the hall. Literally, it means that try to persuade an enemy to stop his attack during a war, and the war will then disappear. No soldier wants to fight since ancient times. Try not to forget the conditions and situation, otherwise leniency and strict punishment will all fail. Those who come to manage Sichuan should think it over.

This couplet contains two stories. One story says that once Zhuge Liang served as the general commander of the Kingdom of

Shu, and he was scheduled to attack the Kingdom of Wei in North China. He was worried that the troops of the minorities might take this opportunity to harass the Shu in southwestern China, so he went to the southwestern areas with his troops. Zhuge Liang wished to establish a good relationship with the minorities. Meng Huo (孟获) was the top leader of the minorities, and he didn't accept Zhuge Liang's good-wish. He sent his soldiers to fight against the troops from the Shu. However, Zhuge Liang successfully defeated his attack and caught Meng Huo. Instead of punishing Meng Huo, Zhuge Liang set him free. Then Meng Huo launched another attack, and he met with the same defeat. Zhuge Liang set him a free again. On the seventh time when Meng Huo was caught again, Meng Huo prostrated himself before Zhuge Liang. He said that he and his soldiers had given up on attacking him, and he would like sincerely to have a good relationship with the Shu. From then on, the minority people and people of the Shu lived in peace.

The other story tells how Zhuge Liang made his discipline strong. The story happened during a military campaign against the Kingdom of Wei. Zhuge Liang ordered Ma Su (马谡) to garrison the Shu army troops in Jieting (街亭). Ma Su was his close assistant. Zhuge Liang trusted him with this important job because Jieting was a vital strategic place. However, Ma Su thought of himself highly and placed his troops on the top of a hill near Jieting. As result, the Wei army soldiers occupied the strategic place. Ma Su and his soldiers were defeated. Zhuge Liang had to withdraw his troops back to the Shu. His carefully arranged campaign failed only because of the loss of Jieting. Ma Su had a close relationship with Zhuge Liang. He was a hard worker and made major contributions to the development of the Shu's army. In spite of that, Zhuge Liang had Ma Su executed for his error. It is said that tears ran down Zhuge Liang's face when he made that order.

These two stories describe Zhuge Liang as a military official who was able to convince his opponents with his wisdom and earned his soldiers' respect and loyalty with his discipline.

Well, here is a bell tower on the right and a drum tower on the left. An iron incense burner looks most unusual. It is placed in the middle of the path, which leads to the hall. Zhuge Liang's statue stands in the middle. It is 2m high. His son is on the right, and his grandson on the left, and they accompany Zhuge Liang in the hall. Zhuge Liang is dressed in a golden overcoat with a feather fan in his hand. He looks as if he is still concerned about his state and his local people. On the left side of Zhuge Liang's statue is a bronze drum. It's said it's a relic dated back to the 5th century. Ancient ethnic groups in Southwest China often used it as a cooker. Later it became a sort of music instrument for some special occasions. It was said that during Zhuge Liang's southwest military expedition, his soldiers used it as a cooker during the day and struck it at night as a warning sound.

Zhuge Liang was considered by historians to be the most accomplished strategist in the early Three Kingdoms Period. He was a native of the Shandong areas. Historically, Zhuge Liang was also known as Zhuge Kong Ming (诸葛孔明). He was nicknamed the Hidden Dragon. People around him underestimated his capacity to achieve great things. Other translations of his nickname were the Crouching Dragon and the Sleeping Dragon.

For a while, Zhuge Liang lived in a thatched cottage in Longzhong, Hubei area. He quietly chose to farm his land and make friends extensively with the refugee-scholars from North China. Zhuge Liang seemed to live alone away from the current politics. Actually he analyzed the situation and integrated his knowledge with the practical struggle for power. He studied carefully the books of every school, pursuing a life of study concerning the classics of ancient literature, history, and military affairs. It is said that Zhuge Liang particularly admired the career and achievements of Guan Zhong (管仲-645 B. C.). Guan was a famous statesman of Qi, and he used his wise consul to help his state to prosper. On an invitation by Liu Bei, Zhuge Liang left his home to join him. At that time, Zhuge Liang was 26 and Liu Bei 47 years old. This became a major turning point for Liu Bei. Together they later established the Kingdom of Shu in Sichuan.

Throughout his life, Zhuge Liang was dedicated to resisting the Wei and maintaining the independence of the Shu. He later served as prime minister of the Shu for Emperor Liu Bei and his son Liu Chan. During his administration Zhuge Liang brought peace to the state due to his northern and southern military expeditions. Besides his military and engineering achievements, Zhuge Liang pushed for law enforcement and adopted strict disciplinary measures, as well as carefully giving impartial rewards and punishments. These measures effectively promoted the development of the kingdom.

Well, ladies and gentlemen, there is one more spot to go to. It is Liu Bei's tomb surrounded by a circular wall. It is 12m high and 80m in circumference. For 1700 years the tomb has remained untouched, and what is inside is unknown.

The tour of Zhuge Liang's Temple will soon come to an end. I hope that all of you have enjoyed my introduction. Now you are free until 11:30, and I'll meet you at the entrance of the temple. If any of you have further questions, do not hesitate to ask me at any time. If you see Zhuge Liang's ghost do not be afraid, He still thinks that he must protect Liu Bei. He will not harm you.

KEY WORDS & EXPRESSIONS 关键词汇及表达法

the son of Heaven 天子
leniency 宽大,宽厚
give up 让步
withdraw 收回,撤销
execute 处决,处死
opponent 对手,反对者
accomplished 熟练的,多才多艺的
nickname 诨号,绰号
underestimate 看轻,过低估计
law enforcement 法治
liege 君主,王侯
circumference 圆周,周围

Tomb of Wang Jian 王建墓

How Was the Tomb Discovered
王建墓发现始末

Ladies and gentlemen, here we are at the entrance of the Tomb of Wang Jian. It is located in the northwestern suburbs of Chengdu city. When you were in Beijing, you visited the Ming Tomb. The tomb of Wang Jian is much smaller, compared with the ones in Beijing. However, this tomb is much older and was built during the Five Dynasties and Ten States Period (907-960). Historically it was named Yongling Mausoleum. I think it is worth visiting this atypical tomb in Chengdu.

Wang Jian (王建, 847 - 918) was the first emperor of the Former Shu Kingdom during the Five Dynasties and Ten States Period. At the beginning of the 10th century, the Tang Dynasty collapsed, and China once again split into a number of short-lived independent dynasties and states. During this period, five dynasties came into being. They occupied the areas covering the middle and lower sections of the Yellow River. The other areas split into the ten states. Most of them were located in the South. So this period is often referred to as the Five Dynasties and Ten States Period.

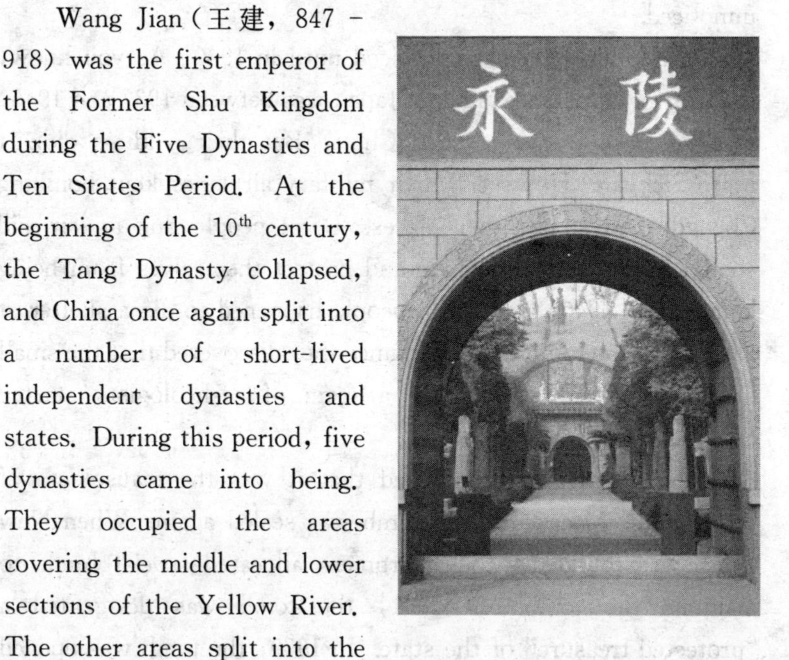

The Former Shu was one of the ten states. Wang Jian served as the first emperor for 12 years. He was buried in this tomb. Originally his mausoleum was spectacular. It included a hundred grand frescoes. During the Northern Song Dynasty (960 - 1127) many of the mausoleum constructions were destroyed.

The remaining buildings were used as a Buddhist temple by

the name of Yongqingyuan (永庆院). Later, a terrible fire broke out and burned down the temple. Nothing was left but the tomb. As years went by, trees and grass covered the whole surface of the tomb, and it looked like a small and desolated hill and went unnoticed.

The tomb remained unnoticed until in 1940. As you know, the War of Resistance Against Japan was between 1937 and 1945. The Japanese troops invaded China. But their soldiers didn't reach Sichuan. However, their military airplanes kept bombing Chengdu and some other places. Local people dug an air-raid shelter in an attempt to hide and protect themselves from being bombed. In 1940, a group of people happened to dig a shelter at the foot of the tomb hill. By chance they discovered that the small hill was a tomb. In 1942, a team of archeologists started excavating the tomb.

Their excavation confirmed that it was the mausoleum of Wang Jian. Afterwards the tomb was sealed again. When New China was founded, the government allocated special funds to maintain the tomb. In 1961, the tomb was designated a "protected treasure" of the state. In 1979, the tomb was opened to visitors. The current mausoleum covers an area of 50 mu.

KEY WORDS & EXPRESSIONS 关键词汇及表达法

mausoleum 陵墓

typical 典型的

short-lived 短命的

fresco 壁画

desolate 荒凉的，无人烟的

unnoticed 不引人注意的，被忽视的

an air-raid shelter 防空掩蔽处

designate 任命，指定

Inner Tomb Structure and Sculpture

墓内结构与石雕

Ladies and gentlemen, we are in the tomb compound. Please look at the mausoleum. It is built above ground. The tomb is 15m high and 80m in diameter. Fourteen huge double vaults and red-colored sandstone walls support the burial chambers. Gray bricks are laid against the sandstone walls. The bricks are placed upon bricks to form a thick wall to further protect the tomb. On the surface of the brick protectors are piles of soil rammed down in shape of the tomb.

In North China, most of the mausoleums are built underground, including the Ming Tomb. You may ask me why the Tomb of Wang Jian is built above ground. You know. Chengdu is located in the Sichuan Basin surrounded by hills and mountains. Its terrain is very low. People often say, "You will get water if you dig a hole three feet deep beneath the ground in Chengdu." The ancient builders were afraid that the tomb might have been flooded if they had placed it underground.

Well, the tomb contains three chambers: the fore-chamber, the center-chamber and the innermost-chamber. The fore-chamber serves as a path or a corridor. It leads to the center-chamber where an ornamental coffin platform reposes. Twelve carved men of unusual strength and a relief of 24 musicians and dancers are on the east, west and south sides. The innermost-chamber contains a life-sized statue of Wang Jian in a relaxed sitting position. Originally, each chamber had its own individual doors to separate chambers. Now only the fore-chamber has a wooden door. It's a copy to display the shape of the original huge doors. Look, some incomplete paintings still remain on the top of the third vault. They are decorative patterns made with red and blue mineral pigments. These patterns are over 1,000 years old based on a historical document.

Ladies and gentlemen, please come here and view the four carved Chinese characters on the ground of the fore-chamber. They are called Dongchuan (东川) and Jingshui (金水). These Chinese characters are the names of places in the Chengdu areas. They tell us that most of the stone materials for the tomb construction were moved from these places.

When the first group of archaeologists came into the tomb, they discovered that the tomb had been robbed. It might have happened soon after the Former Shu State was defeated. The ancient robbers came into the tomb through the upper-left of the tomb gate. The archaeologists found the coffin platform in a state of disorder and the inside was in ruins.

The archaeologists guessed that the ancient robbers were responsible for the mess. On the platform was a large amount of mercury. In ancient times mercury was used as a preservative for corpses, but the archaeologists didn't find any remains of the dead. They deduced that the dead emperor had considerable valuable jewelry on his person and in his burial costume as he reposed on the platform; the robbers probably pulled the corpse out of the chamber in order to obtain them. However, the archaeologists still found silver and jade wares left inside the chamber. The robbery must have happened only once, otherwise nothing would have been left.

In terms of historical culture, the most valuable relics inside the tomb are the chambers and the carved stones. They remain intact. Now please get close to the coffin platform in the center chamber. It's made of red sandstone and placed a bit back of the center. A jade plate is on the platform. On the plate was a three-tiered wooden terrace. The coffin was placed on the top. The coffin and terrace deteriorated into soil long ago. There were still some remaining iron hoops and nails that were used as the coffin's ornaments.

Please come and view the carved stones on the top of the platform. Dragons are carved in forceful gestures, playing a pearl among musicians with lotus flowers and my thical birds. Originally, the musicians were painted red in coats and apricot yellow in skirts; the dragons were gilded with a thin layer of gold; the whole inner chambers were also painted.

Ladies and gentlemen, have you noticed a series of relief sculpture around the platform? It's the most valuable relic in the tomb, I think. It consists of two dancers and another 22 musicians, who make up a court band. The feature attraction here is the relief of 24 musicians for their classical instruments. The dancers dance rhythmically with light steps, the musicians play their music instruments together. The music establishment looks very similar to the authentic portrait of a Tang court music band with northern Hebei style（唐代宫廷燕乐）. The fine relief carvings depict Tang musicians or musicians of the Former Shu state in this tomb. It was popular in the court of the Tang Dynasty as well as the Former Shu State.

These reliefs of musicians have provided valuable research

evidence of the imperial music of the Tang Dynasty. Some musicians have faded through ages, and some are still vivid. The archeologists also find out the carved Tang styled clothing. This carved band has its own distinctive features as following:

1. There are 23 musical instruments. 20 of them are in different shapes.

2. Each musician is beautifully shaped and are dynamically dancing or playing their instruments. They all have a full moon shaped face and delicate features.

The carved figures help us gain some insight in the aspects of the use of ancient musical instrument and social status.

Follow me, please. I'd like to show you some carved instruments.

Pipa（琵琶）

Pipa is a plucked instrument. It's in a pear-shape with four strings and fretted fingerboard. Pipa was introduced from west Asia and became one of the main music instruments during the Tang Dynasty and the Five Dynasties. The musician played music on Pipa strings with a wooden stick. Pipa and clapper musicians look a little taller and slightly different in their dress and hairstyles, compared with the other musicians. This difference indicates that Pipa is the leading instrument, and the clapper is to keep the music beat.

Zheng Drum（正鼓）**and He Drum**（和鼓）

Zheng and He drums are a pair of waist drums. A musician beats Zheng drum with sticks held in both hands. The carved relief band has nine drums. Eight of them are different in shape. Besides the drums, there are clappers, bronze cymbals and a conch. The band consists of percussion and wind instruments. It is easy to imagine that when the band played the music would have surely sounded rapid and excited. Traditionally, the Chinese music band consists of stringed and wind instruments. The carved band has percussion instruments. This evidence shows that foreign music influenced traditional Chinese bands during the Tang Dynasty. If you have studied Chinese history, you would know that the Tang Dynasty was a period of great economic prosperity and cultural growth and had frequent contacts with foreign cultures.

Bili (荜篥)

Bili is a vertical bamboo flute. It is about 40 cm long. A thin piece of wood or metal is inserted inside the top of the flute. A big flute has nine holes, a small one has six holes.

Jie Drum (羯鼓)

Jie drum is a two-stick drum. It's one of the main percussion instruments in the Tang Dynasty. The drum is usually placed on a small ivory-inlaid bed.

Tao Drum and Jilou Drum (鼗，鸡娄鼓)

These two drums are played by one musician at the same time. Tao drum is a drum-shaped rattle. It makes quick and little sounds as the sticks hit the drum. Jilou drum is usually pressed inside the armpit on the left, the right hand beats the drum with a stick.

Dala Drum (答腊鼓)

Dala drum is in a flattened shape. It is beat by hands and looks similar to a tambourine, used by the Uygur and other nationalities.

Chuiye (吹叶)

Chuiye means blowing a tree leaf. A musician extends her

right forefinger and middle fingers first. She blows the tree leave with her fingertips pressing the leaf between her lips. Chuiye is a kind of folk musical instrument. It is interesting to see that the simple instrument has joined in the court band. This evidence shows that ancient folk music also influenced the court music. Because leaves are easily broken, the musician has some leaves in her left hand in case she needs them.

Shu Konghou (竖箜篌)

Shu konghou is a vertical instrument with 22 - 23 strings. Non-Han nationalities in the North and West often used this instrument during the Tang Dynasty. It looks like the current harp.

Xiao (箫)

Xiao is a vertical bamboo flute. The carved flute has eight pipes in a row. Usually this kind of the instrument consists of 17 or 21 pipes. The musician squeezes a rolled paper into each pipe or seals it with wax to assure that it has the right music notes.

On either side of the coffin platform stand 12 carved stone busts. They are called 12 men of great strength in suits of armor. Their hands stretch under the platform as if they were ready to lift up the platform and move it away. They have a ferocious profile looking towards the entrance gate. It is said that they work as tomb guards to drive out evil spirits.

KEY WORDS & EXPRESSIONS 关键词汇及表达法

vault 拱顶

coffin 棺材

repose 建立于,坐落

incomplete 不完全的,未完成的

decorative pattern 修饰模式

robber 强盗,盗贼
disorder 杂乱,混乱
mercury 水银,汞
preservative 防腐剂,保存剂
deduce 推论,演绎出
deteriorate (使)恶化
hoop 箍,铁环
apricot yellow 杏黄色
relief 浮雕
rhythmically 有节奏地
music establishment 音乐组合
authentic 真正的,确实的
distinctive feature 不同的特色
dynamically 充满活力的
pluck 弹(乐器)
fret 按压琴弦
fingerboard 指板
musician 音乐家
cymbal 铙钹
conch 贝壳,海螺壳
stringed and wind instruments 管弦乐器
percussion instrument 打击乐器
insert 插入
inlaid 镶嵌的
rattle-drum 拨浪鼓
flatten 把……弄平,平整
tambourine 小手鼓
forefinger 食指
middle finger 中指

harp 竖琴
squeeze 压榨,挤
wax 蜡
ferocious 残忍的,凶猛的

Life Story of Wang Jian
王建生平

Ladies and gentlemen, we are at the innermost chamber. It contains a statue of Wang Jian in a sitting position. He is 86cm tall, wearing a head-kerchief and an informal dress. He has a high nose bridge and sunken eye sockets. Earlobes hang down to his shoulders.

Wang Jian was born in Henan Province. It was said that he was a rascal when he was young. He slaughtered cows, robbed donkeys and smuggled salt. Later he joined the army. He was promoted to a troop officer because of his bravery and cleverness. Towards the end of the Tang Dynasty, he took charge of the emperor's palace guards. Later he served as a prefecture governor of Li Zhou (利州) at the present site of Guangyuan (广元). Gradually, he occupied the vast area in western Sichuan. In 903, he became the king of the Shu State. In 907, Zhu Quanzhong(朱全忠) established the Later Liang Dynasty (907 - 923) after he defeated the Tang. Wang Jian took the opportunity to claim himself to be the emperor of the Former Shu and began to exercise his local power.

According to historical records, Wang Jian didn't have much education, but he enjoyed talking with well-learned scholars. Wang Jian treated them very well and offered them good jobs in his government. At that time, the war occurred frequently in central China, constantly creating chaos. So many well-known scholars arrived in Sichuan and worked for Wang Jian in his state.

During the early time of the Former Shu State, Wang Jian issued a series of policies, which benefited the state and local people. His policies lightened the heavy tax burden on local farmers and encouraged local farmers to develop agriculture and sericulture. The state remained prosperous for a number of years. However, as he grew old, Wang Jian believed the rumors from his eunuch and his concubines, and appointed one of his sons, Wang Yan (王衍) to be his heir to the throne. After Wang Jian died, Wang Yan became the emperor, and then the Former Shu State began to decline. In 925, the troop from the Later Tang Dynasty (923 – 936) attacked the Former Shu State. Within a couple of months the state was completely defeated.

Well, ladies and gentemen, our tour of the tomb is approaching to the end. The tomb has survived for centuries. The inner tomb structure and carved stone figures have highly artistic and cultural value. Particularly, the carved music band is the most striking. It provides valuable information to those who study music history and culture. Since 1950, all the Chinese historical books related to music have contained the pictures of the carved stone musicians and their explanations. So now you know that your trip to the Tomb of Wang Jian has been worthwhile. Aren't you glad that you are not an emperor who has to worry about his tomb being robbed?

KEY WORDS & EXPRESSIONS 关键词汇及表达法

earlobe 耳垂

smuggle 私运,走私

claim oneself 自称

chaos 混乱
lighten the heavy tax burden 减轻繁重赋税
concubine 妾，小老婆
heir 继承人，后嗣

River-Viewing Tower Park 望江楼

Main Entrance
正门

Ladies and gentlemen, here we are at the entrance gate of the River-Viewing Tower Park. It is called Wangjianglou Park in Chinese. Its ancient name is Yunüjin (玉女津, the Fair-Lady Ferry). The park was built in memory of Xue Tao (薛涛), a female Tang Dynasty poetess. At the beginning of the Ming Dynasty, a workshop was set up on the spot to produce Xue Tao style writing paper. During the Qing Dynasty Li Yaodong (李尧东), Chengdu governor arranged for construction workers to refurbish a well. It is said that the well was used by XueTao during her stay here. Later, local people named it XueTao Well. The workers also built several pavilions such as Yinshilou (吟诗楼, the Poem-Composing Pavilion), Zhuojinlou (濯锦楼, the Brocade-Washing Pavilion), Huanjianlou (浣笺楼, the Writing-Paper-Washing Pavilion). In 1886, Chongli Tower (崇丽阁) was built. Since the buildings were set up along Jinjiang River, it attracted visitors to ascend to the top of the buildings to view the river. Gradually, this group of buildings has become a symbol of the ancient culture and history of Chengdu.

In China, there are nine famous towers. The most famous

two are Huanghe Tower (黄鹤楼), which is located at Wuhan, Hubei province; it is called the First Tower on the Earth. Another one is Yueyang Tower (岳阳楼), which is a three-storied watchtower at the west gate in Yueyang, Hunan province. There's an old saying, "Dongting Lake surpasses all the water scenes in the world, Yueyang Tower deserves to be the most famous tower all over the world(洞庭天下水,岳阳天下楼)." Wangjiang Tower, also called Chongli Tower, is also one of the nine towers. It is a splendid and exquisite building featured with South China characteristics.

Ladies and gentlemen, here is the main entrance gate building. It is modeled after the northern style imperial palace. The building gives the structure an imposing manner. The pillars are painted and the beams are carved; the tiles are glazed and the wall is red.

A horizontal inscribed board hangs on the top of the gate. It says, "Wangjianglou Park (the River-Viewing Pavilion Park)."

Now please follow me and walk into the park. The main entrance opens into the passageway. You will way is covered with a canopy of green bamboo. In summer, passers feel cool under the shady green canopy. The passageway leads to the One-humped Camel Rockery in a small pool. Green bamboo, clean water, and pines add beauty to the rockery. Qilixiang Corridor (七里香长廊) spans twists and turns, which offers a clear view of a busy road across the river. Qilixiang is a type of small white-colored flower, and its fragrance is said to spread as far as seven li (3.5km) away, so local people have named the flower the Seven-li Fragrance.

KEY WORDS & EXPRESSIONS 关键词汇及表达法

watchtower 瞭望塔
surpass 超越，胜过
canopy 天篷，遮篷
the One-Humped Camel Rockery 单峰骆驼假山

Brocade-Washing Pavilion
濯锦楼

Here we are at Zhuojinlou Pavilion (the Brocade-Washing Pavilion). It is a two-floor building made entirely of wood supported by three principle pillars. The pillars are painted, and the beams carved; the lattice doors and windows are decorated with well-carved wooden figures, birds and animals. The pavilion is uniquely shaped much like a colorful boat sailing towards the city. In Han Dynasty the brocade weaving industry had been successfully established in Chengdu. The brocade trade brought so much prosperity that the city became known as Jincheng (Brocade City). It was said that brocade workers used to wash their brocade products in the river before they were sold. So the river earned the nickname "Zhuojinjiang (濯锦江)", which means the Brocade Washing River. The building was therefore named Zhuojinlou due to its location close to the river.

Ancient Chinese architecture features unique timber framework. The top load of a structure will be transferred to its groundwork through its posts, beams and joints. Because of the timber framework, paint is the main ornament used on ancient Chinese architecture. At the beginning, paint was used on wood for antisepsis. Later, painting became an architectural ornament. Painting gives the structure a clear-cut and magnificent image.

Sharp color can achieve artistic effects.

KEY WORDS & EXPRESSIONS　关键词汇及表达法

principle　主要的

pillar　柱子，栋梁

lattice　格子

antisepsis　防腐；消毒

architectural ornament　建筑装饰

clear-cut　清晰的

magnificent　高尚的；宏伟的

image　偶像；形象化的比喻

Chongli Tower

崇丽阁

Here we are at Chongli Tower. It was built in 1889. Chongli means loftiness and prettiness.

Chongli Tower is a four-storied building. It is made entirely of wood, and it is 26m high. Its exquisite design presents the most gorgeous tower, which rises lofty by the river. The top two stories have eight sides with a painted golden roof. The following two stories have equal square sides and gently upturned eaves. The bottom base of the tower has four sides, which symbolize that the universe is round in the sky and square on earth. The ceilings inside are all decorated with paintings about phoenix among peony flowers and other scenes. They were drawn by a local artist called Luosonglin (罗松林). The glazed golden roof shines in the sunlight among green trees and bamboos. Chongli Tower is one of the focal points of the park. Situated near Jinjiang River, the tower is also named Wangjianglou (River-Viewing Tower). Several years ago, the tower was opened to visitors who

could climb to the top floor. The panoramic view of the river and the city from the top floor has great charm, and has inspired countless Chinese artists. At present it is closed. The tower keepers are afraid that the ancient structure may not be able to support many visitors inside the tower.

Well, please come here and view a long couplet. It hangs on the wall of the lowest floor. The couplet has 212 Chinese characters, written by Zhong Yunfang (钟云舫), who was a scholar of the late Qing Dynasty. Once Zhong Yunfang accused some officials of their corruption, and those officials sent him to prison. Therefore, Zhong Yunfang composed the couplet to express his indignation over the case.

There is a folk story explaining why the local people built the tower. It was said that during the Ming Dynasty a local scholar by the name of Yang Sheng'an (杨升庵) (1488 - 1559) obtained the Number One Scholar Title when he was 24 years old. The title was usually conferred on the one who was first in the highest imperial examination. Since then, no one in the Shu area had obtained such an important title. This situation lasted 300 years. Some local gentry thought that the superb spirit of literary talent in the Shu area might have flowed away down the river, and too much flowing had weakened the earth vein. They all thought that literary talent couldn't develop successfully without the nourishment of the earth vein. So they donated to build Chongli Tower for the purpose of keeping the river under control so that the earth vein could grow healthily. After the tower was built, when the setting sun bathed the tower, it cast its shadow right on the surface of the river. It seemed that the shadow crosscut the river. The gentry thought the shadow had kept the superb spirit in the Shu area. Unexpectedly, the next year after the tower was built, another scholar in a county near Chengdu successfully obtained the Number One Title.

KEY WORDS & EXPRESSIONS 关键词汇及表达法

loftiness 崇高
upturned eave 飞檐
phoenix 凤凰,不死鸟
corruption 腐败,贪污
earth vein 地脉
nourishment 营养,滋养
crosscut 横切
gentry 贵族们

Poem-Composing Pavilion
吟诗楼

Yinshilou Pavilion is a spacious and bright pavilion. It is entirely made of wood with gently up-turned eaves and ends. The pavilion is bordered by miniaturized rock-fill hills. Some of the rocks are shaped as the pavilion stairs. The pavilion stands by the river, and shows its refined design much like a pleasant garden in the south of the lower reaches of Changjiang.

KEY WORDS & EXPRESSIONS 关键词汇及表达法

miniaturize 使小型化

the lower reaches of the Changjiang 长江下游

Xue Tao Well and Her Life Story

薛涛井与薛涛生平

Here we are at a well. It is called Xue Tao Well. Legend says that Xue Tao drew water from the well to dye a special kind of paper. Xue Tao enjoyed composing her poems on her home-made paper that looked simple and elegant. This type of writing paper soon came into vogue by the name of Huanhuajian (浣花笺).

At the beginning of the Ming Dynasty, a workshop was set up on the spot to produce the Xue-Tao style writing paper. Since then the well has remained as a historical relic. A stone memorial tablet stands near the well. The three Chinese characters (薛涛井) written in 1664 are carved on the tablet to remind visitors to stop. The well has a sand layer at the bottom, which functions as a natural filter. The water in the well is therefore clean and tasty. Local people like drinking tea made with the water here in the park.

Ladies and gentlemen, please follow me to view the white-marble statue of Xue Tao. We have to retrace our steps into the bamboo forest towards a central isle around a pond.

Here is the statue of Xue Tao. It stands on a carpet of green grass. Xue Tao has a graceful posture in her female robe, and her high hairdo symbolizes a hat. The set of her serene eyes, the turn of her head, and her hands emerging from the heavy sleeves, all indicate that she is walking slowly in the bamboo forest, thinking deeply how to compose her new poem.

Xue Tao was born in 770, and died in 832. Her hometown was in Chang'an, Xi'an, at present. When she was young, Xue Tao moved to Chengdu with her father who obtained a job in the local government during the Tang Dynasty.

Xue Tao had shown exceptional intelligence even as a child. She began to compose poems at the age of eight. One day her father decided to test her to see if she had made any progress in her poetry composition. They stood in a yard where her father pointed at a Chinese parasol tree and orally composed the first two lines of a four-line poem. Right after her father had finished the lines, Xue Tao spoke out the other lines impromptu. Her father was very happy to hear what his daughter had responded. Here is the poem:

In the yard an old parasol tree stands,
High up into clouds.
The tree branches welcome birds from the south or north,
The leaves deliver the passing breeze.
(庭除一古桐,耸干入云中。枝迎南北鸟,叶送往来风。)

Wei Gao (韦皋), the top military commander in Sichuan sent a memorandum to the throne. In his memorandum he recommended Xue Tao for the position of official in charge of proofreading. The memorandum sincerely showed deep respect for Xue Tao. At the same time, they thought that it would be a great pity if Xue Tao were to be neglected. She was acknowledged and admired by her contemporaries for her poetic work.

By the time she was in her mid-teens, her father had died. The frustration in her lifetime began. It is reported that once she was banished to Songzhou on the site of present Songpan (松潘). She went there to serve a prison sentence for her guilt. It was a long distance trip along snowcovered mountains and deep valleys. It was in winter, and there was a cold nip in the air. Xue Tao composed a number of her poems to express the circumstance.

Xue Tao finally came back to Chengdu from the Tibetan area. Afterwards she secluded herself in the west suburb of Chengdu. She continued to write poetry and remained a respected literary figure. When she died, she was buried near the park.

Xue Tao was of the scholar-gentry class and used to work as an assistant in Wei Gao's headquarters. However, she is remembered chiefly as a female poet. Her poems appealed to others far beyond her close friends and people she knew. It is commonly said that Xue Tao composed about 500 poems, but at present, only 91 poems are in existence.

It is commonly believed that Xue Tao loved bamboo. The River-Viewing Pavilion Park has more than 150 kinds of bamboo, and the lush bamboo forests provide plenty of shade in the summer.

In 1953, the park workers started to use bamboo to create multiple perspectives and sceneries. At present, the park is well known through the country mainly because of the particular use of bamboo spaning the whole park. The workers also introduced rare species from other provinces and countries in Southeast Asia into the park. One of the most interesting is a square bamboo. The bamboo is basically square but with rounded edges. Among the forest, various rocks and stones are beautifully shaped like watermelons, peaches, flowers, leaves and other unique shapes. All this has added a lively and charming atmosphere to the serene bamboo forest.

Because of the close location to the city, local people enjoy spending their weekend holidays in the park where they drink tea in the teahouses or expose themselves to nature by walking among the bamboo forest. Now I will allow you some time to take leisurely wander around the park and possibly be inspired to compose some lines of poetry. I know this would please Xue Tao. The bus will leave in one hour.

KEY WORDS & EXPRESSIONS 关键词汇及表达法

come into vogue 成为时尚，流行
filter 滤波器，过滤器
retrace 折回
isle 小岛，岛
hairdo 发型，发式
poetry composition 诗歌写作
impromptu 即席的，即席演出
parasol 阳伞
memorandum 备忘录，便笺
proofread 校正，校对
acknowledge 承认，答谢
contemporary 同时代的人
frustration 挫败，挫折
serve a prison sentence 服刑
a cold nip in the air 寒气逼人
multiple 多样的，多重的
illusion 幻想
watermelon 西瓜
atmosphere 环境

Precious Light Monastery 宝光寺

Chinese Buddhist Monasteries
佛教寺庙简介

Ladies and gentlemen, here we are at the entrance of the Precious Light Monastery. Before we walk into the monastery, I'd like to tell you some basics facts about Chinese Buddhist architecture. Generally speaking, Chinese Buddhist architecture consists of a temple, pagoda and grotto. Buddhism was introduced into China in Han Dynasty. At the same time the Chinese styled Buddhist architecture came into being. The architecture displays Chinese architectural aesthetics and culture.

Monasteries and temples are the main Chinese Buddhist buildings. In ancient times, many kings or emperors in different dynasties believed in Buddhism. Due to their imperial influence, the construction of Buddhist buildings was greatly advanced. In Northern Wei Dynasty (386 - 534), there were more than 30,000 temples across the country. Later, glazed tiles, exquisite engravings and delicate paintings joined in the Buddhist structure, making buildings look more splendid.

Chinese Buddhist architecture follows a symmetric north-south axis. Main buildings are built on the invisible line named zhongzhouxian axis（中轴线）, facing the south. Usually the monastery buildings are fashioned after the imperial palaces and bear very little resemblance to the temples in India or other Buddhist countries. Generally each monastery or temple has three groups of buildings, separated by courtyards or walls.

In the monastery or temple the front hall has four huge images. They are usually made of wood or earth. Two are on each side. The four are called the Four Heavenly Kings. In this hall, the statue of Maitreya Buddha, known to the Chinese as the "Laughing Buddha," is in the middle of the four kings. He has a happy face and seems to greet visitors at the entrance. Behind the happy Buddha is Wei Tuo（韦驮）, the protector of Buddhist temples and the Faith. A wall separates them, too. Wei Tuo is fully armored, holding either a gnarled staff or a scepter-shaped weapon. He always faces the Great Buddha Hall（大雄宝殿）across a courtyard.

The Great Buddha Hall is devoted to the statue of Sakyamuni Buddha and other Buddhas of the Past Yala. It has a main altar for daily Buddhist ceremony or practice. The arrangement and choice of Buddhist images in the altar varies from temple to temple. Usually the altar houses is Sakyamuni Buddha, and his disciples stand on both sides. On the right and left of the main altar, sometimes stand the statue of Manjusri and Samantabhadra. The Great Hall also has the statues of the Eighteen Arhats（罗汉）. They stand against the east and west walls in the hall. It is said that all of them possess various kinds of supernatural powers.

The Back Hall is usually partitioned into several small rooms. The central room is the altar of a Buddha or a Bodhisattva; the right room houses the funerary tablet of the temple founder; the left room may function as a teaching or meditation hall. Living quarters, kitchens, dinning halls and storehouses usually have their particular locations on the right side of the main buildings; the buildings on the left side are offered for the visitors.

KEY WORDS & EXPRESSIONS 关键词汇及表达法

engraving 雕刻
symmetric 对称的
resemblance 类同之处
armored 披甲的，装甲的
gnarled 多瘤的，粗糙的
grotto 洞穴，岩穴
scepter 笏，节杖
altar 祭坛，圣坛
Arhat 罗汉
supernatural power 神力
funerary 葬礼的，埋葬的

Main Buildings in the Monastery
宝光寺主要建筑

Ladies and gentlemen, I know that you have a general idea of the structure of a Chinese monastery or temple through my brief introduction. I hope that it will be of much help to you in your tour of the Precious Light Monastery today. Now let's walk to the monastery.

The Precious Light Monastery is an active Buddhist temple at Xindu (新都). It was founded during the Eastern Han Dynasty, and now it is about 1900 years old. In 881 A. D. , the monastery provided refuge for one of the Tang emperors. He fled from the Tang capital when it was occupied by the rebellion. Through centuries the monastery suffered from war or fire destruction. In 1671, it was reconstructed on its original foundation. The construction workers followed the pattern of the Buddhist Chan-Sect(禅宗) monasteries. At present the monastery consists of five halls and 16 courtyards. They are surrounded by bamboo.

Ladies and gentlemen, this is the entrance gate. It is named the Three-Gate-Hall (三门或山门). The three gates stand side by side. The middle gate is large, and the other two are smaller. Inside the hall stand two Vajras. They are Buddha's warrior attendants, holding golden pestles in their hands. The two attendants look like guardians at gates, and their duty is to defend the power of Buddha. Next to the attendants are statues of the figures of the Ming Dynasty. Do you know why the local people placed them in the hall with Buddhist images? These persons donated much money to refurbish the monastery. One of them was Yang Sheng'an. At age of 24 Yang obtained the Number-One-Scholar Title as he ranked first in the highest examination.

We are now in the hall, which is called the Hall of the Heavenly Kings (天王殿). It contains a statue of Maitreya (弥勒佛) in the middle and the Four Heavenly Kings on either side. Traditionally, the four-armed kings have their own title. Each stands on the body of a monster. The first king is the South King. He has a magic sword in his hand and takes charge of wind. The second one is the East King. He carries a Chinese 4-string lute (Pipa) and takes charge of music. The third one is the West King. He has a huge umbrella in his hands and takes charge of rain. The fourth one is the North King. He has a pagoda sitting on his hand and is always ready to bring all the ghosts and evils under his control. The four kings guard Buddhism and also assure favorable conditions for growth of crops each year.

Please look at Maitreya who is the future Buddha. People call him Laughing Buddha. He sits with his legs crossed, holding his Buddhist beads, and his belly is exposed. He seems to greet visitors. Buddhist scriptures say that Buddhism will exist for 10,000 years. Afterwards Sakyamuni's doctrine will perish of itself because the morality of all sentient beings is gradually enlightened. Maitreya will descend to the world to replace Sakyamuni and continue preaching Buddhism for the next eight million years. Buddhism has it that the statue of Maitreya acts as a symbol to remind all sentient beings that everyone has a great possibility for Buddhist enlightenment in his/her own heart because Maitreya, on his way to Buddha-hood, keeps emitting rays of love to them.

Maitreya has many reincarnations. However, people fail to discover him no matter how he uses his reincarnations to indirectly suggest his existence. There is a story about Maitreya. It says that during the Five Dynasties a monk by the name of Qici (契此) lived in Yuelin Monastery (岳林) in Fenghua (奉化), Zhejiang area. The monk often carried a cloth bag, begging alms along streets. He behaved himself very strangely as if he suffered from an illness of the mind. He slept wherever he was, no one could understand what he spoke. The local people failed to realize that he was the reincarnation of Maitreya. Instead they called him the Cloth-Bag Monk（布袋和尚）. He died as he sat cross-legged on a huge stone in Yuelin Monastery.

Ladies and gentlemen, please look at Sarira Pagoda（舍利塔）. It is also called the Buddhist Relics Pagoda. Look. It inclines gently to the west. The pagoda is 30 m high, Contains 13 stories with a glazed gold top. The pagoda was built to guarantee good harvests in Sichuan Basin areas. However, in the Zhenguan period（贞观年间）of the Tang Dynasty an earthquake occurred. It kept shaking the pagoda. In spite of risk the local people immediately started to set up a high protective framework around the pagoda. Their action deeply touched the god in Heaven who sent his four deities to join in protecting the pagoda. Each deity stood at each side of the pagoda, propping it with his shoulders or back. The deity on the east side propped it higher than the one on the west side, and the pagoda thus slanted gently to the west.

Of course, this is a legendary story. In fact, the pagoda fell down when the earthquake occurred. The current pagoda was rebuilt in the late Tang Dynasty. In 881, as Huang-Chao Rebellion（黄巢起义）soldiers occupied Chang'an, the capital of the Tang Empire, Emperor Xizong（僖宗）fled to Chengdu. One night the emperor stayed in the monastery. During the night, he walked around, and he saw colorful rays emitting from the ruins of the fallen pagoda. He was frightened. A monk, who accompanied him, said that the rays came from the Buddhist relics underground. The emperor ordered some people to unearth the relics. As expected, they found a small stone box buried in the ruins, and there were 13 Buddhist Sarira（舍利）pearls in the box. The emperor was so delighted that he ordered the monk to build a 13-storied pagoda on the site of the ruins, and he named it the Precious Light Monastery.

Ladies and gentlemen, a pagoda is part of the Buddhist architecture. It has varied styles and strong local favors. The Pagoda followed Buddhism into China during the Han Dynasty. Soon after that, it developed into a pavilion-like pagoda and immediately became combined with traditional Chinese architecture. In China, one will see timber pagodas, brick pagodas, stone pagodas or pagodas made with bronze or iron. Most Chinese pagodas are multi-storied ones but early pagodas were usually made with wood. Some had four sides; some had six sides, some others had twelve sides. During the Sui and Tang dynasties, pagodas tended to be stone and brick ones. In the Song, Liao and Jin dynasties, flower pagodas came into being. They were decorated with assorted carved flowers, honeycombed shrines, animals and Buddha figures and other sculptures. Generally speaking, pagodas became more and more gorgeous.

Please look at a bell tower and drum tower on the either side of the pagoda. Beyond the drum tower is the residence for monks.

Here we are at the Seven Buddhas' Hall (七佛殿). It contains seven Buddhas of the Past Yala, and each Buddha has his own title. Please view the image of Buddhas. They look serene and quiet. Usually, the harmony of his physical proportions is the expression of great beauty. The Buddhist doctrines have recorded the standard patterns of ideal physical proportions. Every detail indicates harmonious proportions. For example, the spot between the eyebrows marks the eye of wisdom. The tip of the nose has its own special place and length, the ears are exaggerated. The Diamond-Seat or lotus flower seat supports the statue of Buddhas. Buddhas may stand or sit with legs crossed. They are usually viewed in Buddhist meditation.

Well, please come and view a statue of Wei Tuo at the back of the Seven Buddhas. He is one of the eight generals under the leadership of the Heaven Kings. According to Buddhism, Buddha has ordered Wei Tuo to guard Buddhism and protect those who have become monks or nuns. Wei Tuo has his India origin, but he appears as an ancient Chinese military general in a suit of armor. He holds in his hand a Monster-Surrender Stick. It is said that he uses the weapon to conquer ghosts or devils. Wei Tuo stands behind the Seven Buddhas and faces the Great Buddha Hall (大雄宝殿) as a monastery guardian.

Now we are at the Great Buddha Hall. It is the main hall in the monastery, and it was built in 1859. Inside the hall a number of huge stone pillars support the vault of the roof, and each pillar is carved with well-known couplets. On the top of the entrance hangs a board, which says Daxiong Baodian. Daxiong means the Great Buddha or the Great Hero. It is an honorable title conferred on Sakyamuni for his morality and his Buddhist power. The hall contains a main altar, on which Sakyamuni sits cross-legged on the lotus throne. His two closest disciples, Kasyapa (迦叶) and Ananda (阿南) flank him. In Chinese Buddhist monasteries and temples, you may see that the statue of Sakyamuni may be in different positions. As he sits, he is in meditation, his left hand is on his left foot, and his right hand points downward to the earth. It suggests that Sakyamuni had sacrificed much before he founded the Buddhist religion. As he stands, he points his left hand downward and raises his right arm upward. The left hand shows that he is able to satisfy the wishes of all sentient beings, the right hand suggests that he is able to save them from sufferings. As he lies on his side, he stretches his legs, his left hand is placed on the legs, and his head is supported with his right hand. Legend has it that Sakyamuni is talking to his disciples about his final arrangements right before his death.

Below the alter, there are many cotton cushions placed in rows on the ground, accompanied with a bell, a drum, and a muyu (wooden fish). Do you know the purpose of these cushions? Monks mainly use the hall to chant Buddhist scriptures in the morning and later in the afternoon, or to hold some important Buddhist ceremonies. Sometimes they sit on the cushions in meditation.

Now please follow me to the back of the hall. A statue of Amitabha (阿弥陀佛) stands there. He is the founder of the Western Paradise and holds a lotus flower in a niche. According to Buddhist scriptures, if the sentient beings worship Amitabha and recite his name everyday, Amitabha will be aware of it, and he will come down and usher them up to the Western Paradise after they pass away.

Look to the left outside of the Great Buddha Hall. It is the monks' dining room, and on the right side is the dormitory for those who come here in the hope of attaining the full status of a monk.

Here we are at the Buddhist Scripture Library Hall (藏经

楼). The building has a two-tiered roof and two floors. The top floor contains Dazangjing (大藏经). It is a valuable Buddhist scripture printed during Yongzheng (雍正) and Qianlong (乾隆) periods of the Qing Dynasty, and it has 6,361 volumes. The former monastery abbots usually use the ground floor to teach their Buddhist doctrines. Besides, the ground floor has some paintings and calligraphy on display. Two of them are the Picture of Presenting the Buddha with a Handful of Sand (捧沙献佛图) and Jiufen Buddhist Calligraphy (九分禅字). They were created by a monk whose name was Zhushan (竹禅) of the Qing Dynasty. The Picture presenting the Buddha with a handful of Sand was painted based on a Buddhist story. It says that one day Sakyamuni and his followers passed by a village where a group of children were playing a game. As Sakyamuni passed by, a child scooped some sand from the ground and presented it to the Buddha with his hands. One of the followers said that the sand didn't make sense, but Sakyamuni thought that the sand was invaluable because it came from the child's heart.

As for Jiufen Buddhist Calligraphy, it is reported that the monk had practiced for over 50 years before he was able to produce such amazing calligraphy. The calligraphy is 6m high and 5m wide. The monk calligraphist wrote down on huge paper the preface to the Buddhist Huayan Scripture (华严经).

Ladies and gentlemen, the monastery abbot's resident yards are on the either side of the Buddhist Scripture Library Hall. The West Abbot Resident Yard is named Longtan (龙潭, the Dragon Pool) and is provided for retired abbots. The East Abbot Resident Yard is named Shiku (狮窟, the Lion Cave) and is provided for the current abbot. These beautiful yards have several houses. During the daytime the yard gates are usually closed. Without special permission, visitors won't be allowed to enter, but this time our group is welcomed to visit the East Abbot Resident Yard. One of the monks will be our yard tour guide. So before our entay, I'd like to let you know what you will view inside. The yard stores some famous calligraphy or paintings. Some of them hang on the walls of the reception rooms. They include Shuiyue Guanyin (水月观音, Guanyin Between the Water and the Moon) by Zhang Daqian (张大千), the Horse by Xu Beihong (徐悲鸿), the Silk-Stitched Calligraphy by Yuefei (岳飞) as well as the Bamboo and Stone (竹石), and the Black Lion (墨狮) by Monk Zhushan. We will stay in the abbot yard for half an hour before we go to the reception room and view these artistic arts. Please speak quietly. After our visit to the East Abbot Resident Yard, we will go to another garden-like yard. It consecrates the memorial tablets of the founders and the important leaders of the Chan-Sect Buddhism.

Ladies and gentlemen, here we are at a small temple inside the Precious Light Monastery. It is called Jingtu-Sect (净土宗) Buddhist Temple. What is Jingtu-sect? It means the Pure Land Sect in English. Perhaps it is the oldest of the Chinese Buddhist sects. It based its theology upon a number of Indian texts describing a Pure Land in the West and developed a method of practice to be reborn there. It was designed for the layperson that found traditional Buddhist moral rules and meditation discipline too restrictive.

A huge Screen Wall (照壁) faces the entrance gate. The temple mainly consists of the Longevity Buddha Hall (寿佛殿),

the Western Paradise Hall（极乐堂）and the Buddhist Scripture-Chanting Hall（念佛堂）.

In the Longevity Buddha Hall, the statue of the Boundless Longevity Buddha four Vajras flanking. They represent the Earth, the Water, the Fire and the Wind. Legend has it that during the Tang Dynasty there was a monk who practiced his Buddhism in Mt. Heng（恒山）. Then he set up a Jingtu-Sect temple. He died at the age of 132. Afterwards his disciples painted his dead body with raw lacquer and laid it on the altar as a deity. For many years local people continued to worship him. The body remained in good shape and didn't deteriorate. Emperor Xizong（僖宗）granted him the title of the Boundless Longevity Buddha.

The West Paradise Hall contains a white jade Buddha. It was delivered to the monastery from Burma by monk Zhengxiu（真修）during the Guangxu period（光绪年间）of the Qing Dynasty. In the White Lotus Hall stands granite carved stupa. It is 6m high, and it was said that towards the end of the Qing Dynasty an artist and his disciples spent three years finishing this granite carving.

KEY WORDS & EXPRESSIONS 关键词汇及表达法

pestle 杵
refurbish 整修
monster 怪物，妖怪
bring all the ghosts and evils under his control 降伏妖魔鬼怪
perish of oneself 毁灭，死亡
emit rays 发出光线
in spite of risk 不顾危险
protective framework 保护支架
prop 支撑，维持

slant (使)倾斜，歪向
Sarira pearl 舍利
assorted 多样混合的
honeycomb 使……成蜂窝状
residence 住宅
Buddhas of the Past Yala 过去佛
physical proportion 身体的均衡
standard pattern 标准模式
harmonious 和谐的，协调的
the diamond-Seat 菱形座
the lotus flower seat 莲花座
origin 起源，起始
monster-surrender stick 金钢杵
guardian 护卫者
honorable title 荣誉头衔
sacrifice 牺牲，献出
cushion 垫子，软垫
usher 引，领
pass away 去世
two-tiered roof 双层房顶
scoop 舀，铲
theology 神学
layperson 居士
discipline 宗教戒律
restrictive 限制性的
chant 咏唱
disciple 门徒，信徒
Boundless Longevity Buddha 无量寿佛
granite 花岗岩

stupa 佛塔
layperson 外行

Arhat Hall
罗汉堂

Ladies and gentlemen, we are now at Arhat Hall (罗汉堂). It was built in the 19th century. The hall contains 500 clay figurines, and they represent Buddhist saints and disciples. Most of them are two meters in height. There are some different stories about the powerful Arhats. Some Buddhist scriptures say that these 500 Arhats are Sakyamuni's disciples. They gather together to listen to Sakyamuni's sermon. Some other scriptures say that Kasyapa gathered these 500 Arhats together after Sakyamuni's Nirvana. Generally, Arhats are people who have achieved Nirvana. They are usually depicted in grouping of 16, 18, or 500. They are based on real Indian holy men, and they are frequently seen in paintings, or as statues in temples.

During the Five Dynasties the worship of those 500 Arhats became increasingly prevalent, and halls of their statues spread up in great numbers. In the Southern Song Dynasty there was a man by the name of Kao Taosu. He did every means possible to give names to the Arhats and placed a name tablet in front of each Arhat statue accordingly. At present the famous Arhat halls in China are located in the Temple of the Azure Clouds (碧云寺) in Beijing, the Precious Light Monastery in Chengdu, Guiyuan Monastery (归元寺) in Wuhan and Jiezhuanglü Monastery (戒幢律寺) in Suizhou. The 500 Arhats are enormously powerful and numerous in number. Monks and ordinary people worship them in some renowned Buddhist temples and monasteries.

Ladies and gentlemen, I'd like to tell you about a traditional game before you step into the hall. Please use the game when you walk in. Well, listen. Please count the Arhat figures one by one clockwise as soon as you step into the hall. Keep counting the figures until you reach the number of your age. Then you stop and look at that Arhat figure, the last one you counted. He will reveal your personality type. The game is interesting, and of course you may forget which one is typical of yours when you are out of the hall.

Of the 577 clay figurines in the hall no two are alike. They have been molded, painted and gilded into detailed features. Each appearance is refined and detailed in exquisite proportions. The molding technique creates scenes of great complexity. The elaborate figures appear in varied postures. Some sit cross-legged, some close their eyes in meditation with the palms put together, some over-stretch their arms or hug their knees. Their facial expressions vary. They look philosophical, cheerful, comical, stern, sad, serious, or non-committal. Some figures are highlighted with three heads, or five eyes, some figures are outfitted in dresses that remind us of the ancient Chinese people. Emperors Kangxi and Qianlong stay among the Arhats. They are dressed in their royal costumes, beards, boots and capes.

Well, my introduction is over. Now you are free till 12:00, and I will meet you at the entrance of the monastery. Have a good time in Arhat Hall, and don't forget to look for the Arhat with your personality.

KEY WORDS & EXPRESSIONS 关键词汇及表达法

figurine 小雕像

clockwise 顺时针方向的

complexity 复杂(性)
over-stretch 伸长
philosophical 贤明的
comical 滑稽的，喜剧的
non-committal 含糊的
cape 披肩；斗篷

Sanxingdui Museum 广汉三星堆

Ladies and gentlemen, here we are at the entrance of Sanxingdui Museum. Before we start our tour, I'd like to give you some general information so that you will have a better understanding of what the museum displays.

The Process of Discovery
发掘过程

Sanxingdui Museum is located in the Northeast of Sanxingdui Site. It is 40km south of Chengdu. The whole site cover an area of 12 square km, which used to be the town of the state of the ancient Shu.

You may wonder how and when the site were discovered. It happened in spring, 1929 when a farmer and his family were digging an irrigation ditch in Nanxing Zhen area (南兴镇). His son found a circular piece of jade when he dug the field with his hoe. It was on the same spot that 400 valuable relics had been discovered, including stone jade, jade rings and other jade articles.

The discovery of the valuable jade was brought to the

attention of a circle of archeologists in China. In 1933, a team from the West China University Museum (华西大学) arrived, and started excavating Sanxingdui ruins. The archeologists realized that the ruins used to be the town of the ancient Shu. Gradually they identified the location of the town walls in the east, west and south, and unearthed the ruins of huge palaces and over ten thousand relics.

All the city walls were packed tightly with clay. The eastern city wall was over 1,700m long. The remaining part is about 1,100m in length. It is over 20m wide on the top, and it is over 40m across at the base. The wall was composed of three parts: the main city wall, outside city wall and inner city wall. The south city wall is 200m long. The remaining part of the west city wall is 600m long, and 6 to 10m in height. The north side of the ancient city had no wall because the Duck River (鸭子河) flows by providing a natural protection.

In spring, 1934, Ge Weihan, an American professor, and Ling Mingjun, a clerk in West China University, arrived here with an archaeological team for another excavation in Sanxingdui Site. Their excavation lasted ten days. About 400 pieces of jade wares and other objects were unearthed.

Between July and September 1986, archeologists discovered two large-scale covered holes in the ground, where they unearthed more than a thousand priceless treasures. The archeologists believed that the two holes used to be places where ancient people offered sacrifices to their gods or ancestors, and they named the holes as No. 1 and No. 2 sacrificial pits.

The work started on March 1st, 1986. The excavation covered an area of 1,325 square meters. On July 18, the workers discovered the No. 1 pit. It was on the site of Lanxing Second Brick Factory located south of Sanxingdui area. Here the workers uncovered over ten jade dagger-axes and jade tablets. Soon after hearing the news, the archaeologists immediately arrived at the spot and worked out a large-scale schedule, and the excavation continued. Gradually a pit was exposed. On the 25th and 26th, the workers unearthed some bronze dagger-axes. A gentle bronze image with long hair, a helmet and facemasks followed these bronze relics. At 3 : 00 am on the 27th of July, something golden attracted the workers. They cried, "Look! It's gold!" The archaeologists quickly used the earth to recover this spot, and armed policemen arrived to heavily guard this place. During the following two weeks the archaeologists unearthed as many as over 400 pieces of cultural relics. Each one was invaluable. They included gold vessels, scepters, masks, tigers, blocks, bronze vessels, figures, bronze dragon-shaped ornaments, jade tablets, dagger-axes, swords; pottery cups, basins and utensils.

The No. 2 pit was discovered on the evening of August 14th 1986. It was about 20 to 30m away from No. 1 pit. Workers in the brick factory saw a bronze image when they were moving away the earth. The bronze image had decorated eye sockets, eyebrows and lips. The archaeologists quickly arrived at the site and started another excavation on August 20th. It lasted ten days before they found a large lower jaw of an animal-faced sculpture. Then they found over ten ivory pieces. The other objects seemed to be put in the pit in the following order.

At the base of the pit were clamshells, jade ware, bronze animal-face sculptures, cockatoos, small bronze objects, and bronze tree branches and trunks etc. Above the base were large bronze wares, standing male sculptures, images, sculptured male heads, and tree bases, etc. Elephant tusks were put on the top. Almost all the containers were painted bright red. The containers stored clamshells and jade wares. The archaeologists concluded that most of remaining things might have been intentionally destroyed before they were put into the pits. The total relics were over 800 pieces. Most of them were bronze wares.

The excavations at Sanxingdui Site have unveiled the history of Ancient Shu from a period 5,000 years ago. Archaeologists have confirmed that the remains of Sanxingdui Ruins display an ancient culture, a city and a country. In January 1988, the State Council designated Sanxingdui Ruins as a protected treasure of the state.

Later, a museum was set up on the ruins and opened to the public in October 1997. It gives a general profile of Sanxingdui Site, and displays relics unearthed from the No. 1 and No. 2 sacrificial pits.

Ladies and gentlemen, please look at the museum in front of us. The design of the museum seems simple but solemn in style. The main feature of this building is a deformed spiral, and a curved line rises step by step. The building illustrates poetic charm, historical feature and cultural art. It seems to let each visitor know that Sanxingdui culture was broad and profound, and it needs to be investigated.

On top of the building is a triangular tower. It symbolizes the connection between Heaven and Earth, as well as gods and human beings. Three large bronze masks hang high on the top as a symbol of Sanxingdui Museum. They express a warm welcome to guests and visitors who come from every part of the world.

Now, let us walk into the museum to have a close look at the relics.

KEY WORDS & EXPRESSIONS 关键词汇及表达法

irrigation ditch 灌渠沟
bring sth to the attention 注意
clerk 牧师，僧侣
offer sacrifice 献祭，供奉
dagger 短剑，匕首
helmet 头盔，钢盔
facemask 面具
eye socket 眼窝
jaw 颚，颌
clamshell 蛤壳
cockatoo 美冠鹦鹉
bright red 大红
unveil 显露，露出
deformed 不成形的
spiral 螺旋形
profound 深刻的，意义深远的

Entrance Hall
序展厅

This is the entrance hall. It mainly contains a bronze sculpture that has a human head and bird body, and a huge photo behind it. Both the statue and photo reveal the themes"land and people","people and culture". It indicates the people of the ancient Shu wanted to fly up into Heaven like the large bird. The bird expresses that everything on earth has a soul. Human beings and deities are interrelated; Heaven and human beings are combined into one.

The main point of the display in the museum is to picture what had happened at that time. The relics unearthed from Sanxingdui Site are of important values relating to history, culture and arts. They should be classified as one of the top-class cultural heritages in the world. The discovery of the ruins and their relics undoubtedly confirm the existence of the state of ancient Shu as well as the advanced economic development that occurred 3,000 years ago.

The museum consists of four units, including the Splendor of Ancient Culture, Mystery of Primitive Faith, Exquisite Relics, and Sanxingdui Excavation and Cultural Studies.

KEY WORDS & EXPRESSIONS 关键词汇及表达法

interrelate 使相互联系

heritage 遗产

The First Hall
第一展厅

Please come into the first hall. It consists of five parts. The cultural relics in this hall show the excellent achievements in every field in ancient times.

Part One outlines the history of the ancient Shu. This is a model that panoramically illustrates Sanxingdui Ruins. It includes the ancient walls and the town proper. No. 1 and No. 2 sacrificial pits have been unearthed right in the town. Besides, numbers of unearthed pottery wares, photos, and information materials convince visitors that Sanxingdui Ruins used to be a big town in Southwest China during the early days of the ancient society. Possibly it was a kingdom that dominated the whole area, and the site or the ruins served as the center of the ancient kingdom.

Part Two displays the development in agriculture and business in ancient Shu. It contains big pottery basins, jars and pots. The pottery wares are in various shapes. Some of them were used to preserve grains or wine. The pottery wares show that agriculture had advanced, and that local people had extra grains to make wine.

Look. Here are numbers of domestic animals' bones and well-shaped animal objects. They tell us that the animal husbandry had developed to a certain sophisticated level.

Look at the seashells, elephant ivory, lacquer wares and bronze statue. They were for cloth ornaments. These relics indicate that an elaborate labor division occurred in society of ancient Shu. Commerce and trade came into being. Archaeologists think that the elephant ivory might have been brought to the state of the Shu from Yunnan as a tribute to the king or for trade.

Part Three mainly contains a variety of jade wares. All the jade wares here are made of these stone materials. It includes the Jade Hill, which is made up of three huge jade stones. On the hill are some marks of rough cuts. Archaeologists conclude that the marks were made 3,000 years ago.

Here is a unique jade tablet by the name of bianzhang (边璋). It is 22cm wide and 1. 6m long. On the tablet are some engraved lines.

Look at this spectacular jade object. It is huge, round and flat. There is a hole in its center. It is 70cm in diameter and 7cm in length. Do you know how much it weighs? It is over 50 kilos, and even two or three persons have to make great efforts to move it.

Generally speaking, over a hundred jade wares have been unearthed from the ruins. They were used for various purposes. Most of them were used as weapons or sacrificial utensils during rites or ceremonies.

Part Four displays the achievements in the pottery technology from the ruins. It contains a superb collection of pottery wares in various shapes. Look at the small-sized animal objects, utensils with lids, pottery statue in large-size and pottery pots. It shows the imagination and high skills of the people of the Shu.

According to studies on archeology and typology, pottery is an important staff to determine dates and ascertain cultural levels of a system. The unearthed pottery wares consist of a stemmed cup or bowl with a high handle, a flat-bottom pot and a bird-head spoon. Accordingly archeologists can use these objects to determine the Shu cultural connotations and relations concerning inheritance.

Here is Part Five. It contains a golden leaf, bronze tiger, a dragon-shaped article for ornaments, a bronze rock, and numerous bronze bells. Pure gold accounts for 85 per cent of the precious wares, and silver for the other 15 per cent.

As for bronze wares from the ruins, the alloy composites fall into five categories. The unearthed bronze wares contain much lead. Why did the ancient craftsmen use so much lead? The main reason is that lead is fluid and soft, so the craftsmen were able to shape bronze wares more delicately. The bronze wares from the ruins have been considered the most representative of the bronze-age cultural development in Southwest China.

This part also contains a group of bronze eyes in various shapes. Some of the eyes open widely, others are shut in deep thought. The expressions of the eyes indicate that the ancient people never stopped asking questions about Human, nature, and space.

KEY WORDS & EXPRESSIONS 关键词汇及表达法

cultural relic 文化遗迹，文物
sacrificial 牺牲的，献祭的
utensil 器具
stemmed cup 有把的杯子
flat-bottom 平面底
connotation 内涵
inheritance 遗传，遗产
representative 典型的，典型
the bronze-age 青铜时代

The Second Hall
第二展厅

The second hall consists of four parts. The cultural relics in this hall show the political structure and social relations of the ancient Shu, as well as the spiritual world of the ancient people.

Part One contains models of the No. 1 and No. 2 sacrificial pits. Here is No. 1 Pit. It appears rectangular and has three passageways. The pit contains 400 wares, made of bronze, gold, jade, stone, bones or ivory. It also contains hundreds of seashells. The gold scepter was also unearthed from the pit.

Here is No. 2 Pit. It looks larger and deeper than No. 1 Pit. There are over a thousand seashells. It also contains 800 wares, including some uncommon treasures like a bronze holy tree, a bronze standing figure, grotesque bronze masks, a jade tablet and a gold-masked bronze human head.

Part Two contains groups of carved bronze statues. It shows that the ancient political system and social patterns were characterized by the integration of politics with religion.

There are about 50 bronze human heads, 20 bronze masks and 10 full-size bronze figures, which have been unearthed from the pits. These statues symbolize ancestors, heavenly and earthly gods, worshiped by the ancient people at that time. At the same time the statues reflect the social estate system. Generally speaking, the huge bronze standing statue symbolizes their supreme ruler, other human heads symbolize high-ranking members in their ruling clique. The bronze masks represent deities. Sorcerers at that time enjoyed the same status as the kings, and common people also worshiped them as deities. It is difficult to make a distinction between a king and a sorcerer, or people and deities because human beings and gods are interrelated; kings and sorcerers combine into one.

Part Three designates to reveal the spiritual world in the ancient Shu. It contains a three-tiered terrace that offers a simulated grand ceremony for sacrificial rites.

Please get a close view of the terrace. This is a copy of the unearthed one from the ruins. There are crowds of carved figures around the terrace. They form a grand procession for sacrificial purpose. A bronze spiritual altar is laid in the center. The altar is a three-tiered terrace, six times as large as the original one. The first terrace is round in shape with two monsters. The second terrace also appears round, figures stand and face outwards with sticks in their hands. The third terrace is shaped like a hill, and a spiritual temple is placed on it. On the top of the temple birds stand at four sides, and figures have human heads and bird bodies.

What does the ceremony mean? In the ancient Shu state, the sacrificial rite was of prime importance in their state affairs. At that time people believed that everything had a spirit. People came to the alter to offer sacrificial goods to deities from Heaven and Earth. They wished to gain blessings and good harvests. During the grand ceremony sorcerers played the part of mediums between human beings and deities. The people sincerely believed in supernatural beings, and sorcerers accordingly made full use of their belief to exert their magic arts. At the same time sorcerers were high-ranking members in their ruling clique. Therefore, the early state regime had been deeply combined with the power exerted by sorcerers.

Part Four contains a bronze holy tree which is considered a superb object unearthed from the ruins. Please come and view the tree. It is a copy, 3. 5 times as big as the original one. A dragon pattern forms the tree and the vaulted base. Look, The tree consists of three parts. Each part has three branches: the left, the right and the middle ones. The left and right branches each have a fruit bud; one fruit bud faces upward, and the other downward. A bird stands on each fruit bud and faces upwards. The tree stem is inlaid with a dragon that has a horse head and a rope-patterned body; he has two horns on his head, and knife-patterned wings; his front paws support the base, and his body twists along the stem.

The holy tree expresses the concept of the universe and reflects the sincere worship of the deity of the sun from the people in the ancient Shu. In the sense of traditional mythology the sun has been portrayed as the nine birds, and the nine-bird holy tree can interrelate with spirits, deities and Heaven. Therefore, sorcerers used the tree to interrelate between Heaven Earth, and human beings and deities.

KEY WORDS & EXPRESSIONS 关键词汇及表达法

political structure 政治结构
social relation 社会关系
spiritual world 精神世界
No. 1 and No. 2 sacrificial pits 一号、二号祭祀坑
seashell 海贝壳
gold scepter 金杖
human beings and gods are interrelated 人神一体
sorcerer 男巫
kings and sorcerers combine into one 王巫合一
simulate 模拟
procession 行进；队伍
spiritual temple 神庙
medium 媒介
high-ranking 高等的；高官的

ruling clique　统治集团
exert　尽(力)；施加(压力等)
mythology　神话

The Third Hall

第三展厅

This unit contains the best part of all the unearthed artifacts from the ruins. They are commonly believed to be of rich historical value and artistic quality. These high-quality artifacts symbolize "the soul" from the people in the ancient Shu. Please follow me to view them.

Eyes Protruding Bronze Mask（纵目面具）

The mask has its own unique design. It has a prominent forehead, which has a towering crest ornament, its spectacular eyes protrude 10cm outward. The mask looks awe-inspiring and prestigious as if a deity descended into the world from Heaven. It is believed that due to the limited knowledge of nature, the people in the ancient Shu imagined that their ancestor, Cancong（蚕丛）might have spectacular eyes, crest ornament and prominent forehead. It shows that the ancient people longed to understand the world and the universe.

The mask is a representative piece of the bronze culture in Sanxingdui Ruins. Similar masks have been found in the Chengdu Plain.

Bian Jade Tablet（边璋）

This jade tablet is unique among unearthed jade wares. It is named bianzhang, and 54. 5cm in length. The tablet has engraved patterns. Each pattern has four mountains. On the side of the mountains is placed a tablet, which is used to worship mountains.

The engraved figures have put themselves in a worship position. All these factors contribute to the possible conclusion that the tablet was a utensil used to offer a sacrifice to hills and mountains.

Wheel of the Sun（太阳轮）

The wheel appeared smashed and burnt when it was unearthed. The archeologists found six wheels among the smashed pieces. It is the first time in China to have unearthed bronze wheels of the sun from ruins. Sun worship was a practice dominating the daily life of the ancient people in the state of the Shu.

Bronze Standing Figure（青铜立人像）

This statue consists of the figure and the base. The total length of the figure and base is 2. 62m. The figure has a crown on his head, and is dressed in three clothes; he stands bare-foot and has bracelets on his feet; his hand looks as if he were holding something.

Archeologists speculate that the figure might concurrently represent a king or a top sorcerer. Generally the statue symbolizes the deity, the top ruler of the ancient Shu society.

Big Bronze Tree（大型铜神树）

Eight bronze trees appeared smashed and burned when they were unearthed from the ruins. All of them are incomplete. Only this four-meter-high-tree appears almost perfect after its renovation.

Bronze Birds（青铜鸟）

Numerous bronze wares have been unearthed from the ruins. The groups of the bronze figures rank first for its value. However, numbers of the bronze birds remain the focus of attention. The image of the bronze birds is the symbol of the sun, which indicates the worship of the sun in the ancient Shu.

In the Chengdu Plain similar birds have been unearthed. They are around the sun. The image of birds around the sun suggests that the ancient state practised some forms of totem worship. The sun was carried up to the sky in the morning and pulled back to earth at dusk by four giant birds.

Dragons and Snakes (龙与蛇)

This pattern is designated to make visitors understand the relations between a dragon and a snake. Look at the shape of a snake. It is 55cm in length, and it is portrayed true to life. The dragons on display are featured with more abstractive colors.

In ancient times people never saw what the dragon looked like, but they used their imagination to full play, and created a dragon to meet their spiritual need. The people's imagination enabled the snake or other animals to evolve into a supernatural being, and gradually the image of the dragon came into being. As time went by, the dragon's position kept enhancing. As China entered into the feudal society, the dragon became the symbol of the supreme authority.

Bronze Spiritual Alter (青铜神坛)

The Alter is a three-tiered terrace. It is of great cultural value as described previously. Archeologists have figured out that it is one of the important sacrificial instruments for a grand ceremony used during the period of a certain kingdom in the ancient Shu. In the ancient Shu state, the sacrificial rite was of prime importance in their state affairs. The Alter might have been used for the purpose of gaining blessings and good harvests. The Alter is related to the knowledge of Heaven, Earth, deities and human beings, and it reflects the concept of the universe that the ancient people had.

Three Exquisite Bronze Figures（三件人物精品）

The first figure sits in a kneeling position. Below the figure is a base in the shape of a hill. He is naked to the waist, wearing a shirt, and having a ribbon around his waist. He has a statue on his head and another one held up in his hand.

The second figure only has the upper part of his body. His crown resembles the head of an elephant. He appears dignified and imperious. The people from the ancient Shu may have worshiped him as one of the deities.

His bird-paw feet characterize the third figure. The incomplete figure is 31.2cm tall, and the bird 50cm. As the figure was unearthed, archeologists found out the figure had some paint on the body. It was cinnabar and black color. He is the most unusual object unearthed from the ruins.

Bronze Head（青铜大鸟头）

This bronze bird is regarded as the king of birds among all other bronze birds from the ruins. It looks rather like a majestic eagle that shuts its beak and widely opens its eyes.

Gold Scepter（金杖）**and Gold-Masked Bronze Human Head**（金面青铜人头像）

The gold scepter and the gold-masked bronze human head are placed in the gold ware showroom. The gold-masked Bronze human head has the same features as described in the Eyes Protruding Bronze Mask. The glittering head looks dignified as if he were a deity descending from Heaven. But gold masks like this have never been found elsewhere in China, probably because artisans elsewhere had not developed sufficiently sophisticated techniques to smelt gold during the Shang and Zhou dynasties.

The gold scepter is 1. 42m in length, and 2. 3m in diameter. As it was unearthed from the No. 1 Pit, archeologists found out there were some carbonized wooden sediments in the gold scepter. They deduced that the ancient craftsmen first hammered a gold bar into a thin sheath and then used the hammered gold sheathe to enclose the wooden scepter as we view it today. Towards the end of the scepter is a pattern that is 46cm in length and consists of three units. The first unit, closest to the end, has two human heads that have exact likenesses. The two men look radiant with smiles, wearing the same five prong crowns, and having earlobes in triangle shape. The other two units consist of two birds whose heads face each other, and the two fish whose backs stand opposite each other. An arrow like object presses the necks of the birds and the heads of the fish.

The gold scepter is a symbol of absolute power. However, there are different explanations to the pattern at the present time, but none of them are convincing. The pattern remains a mystery to this day.

KEY WORDS & EXPRESSIONS 关键词汇及表达法

artifact 史前古器物
forehead 前额
crest 鸟冠
awe-inspiring 使人敬畏的
prestigious 有威信的
dominate 占据
bracelet 镯
speculate 推测，思索
concurrently 共存地

totem 图腾，标志
supreme authority 至高权威
spiritual alter 神坛
imperious 专横的
cinnabar 朱红
majestic 宏伟的，庄严的
glittering 闪光的
carbonize 炭化
sheath 外壳
enclose 把……放入封套，把……装入
likeness 相像
prong 尖头
convincing 令人信服的，有说服力的

The Fourth Hall

第四展厅

This unit consists of four parts. It is designated to offer current information about the ruins in different fields, its influence at home and abroad, and its significant position in academic studies.

Between July and September 1986, the archeologists discovered the No. 1 and No. 2 sacrificial pits in Sanxingdui Sites. They unearthed more than a thousand priceless treasures. Such a discovery greatly excited the whole country. The academic circles in China have considered the discovery unprecedented. Many of the unearthed objects have amazed archeologists both at home and abroad.

As the treasures of the national relics, some of the objects from the ruins have been on display in Beijing, and in some other countries. The purpose of the display is not only to introduce Sanxingdui discovery, but also to help viewers appreciate their artistic value and gain insight into their cultural significance. The influence of Sanxingdui Ruins will be far-reaching as the relics exhibitions and excavations continue.

On August 23rd 1986, Xinhua News Agency reported, "So far, the excavated Sanxingdui Ruins remains the largest among all of the early Ba Shu cultural remains. This excavation pushes the Ba Shu history back 1,000 years to the time from 1,000 B.C. to 2,000 B.C.. The exquisite arrangements and the house remains show that agriculture, animal husbandry, handicrafts and architecture had developed, creating the foundations for a highly civilized society".

On August 13th 1987, the British newspaper *The Independent* carried the comments by David Kince. He said, "The discovery in Guanghan maybe is the richest discovery. From the metallic cultural relics, we may change our views on the craftsmanship of the East. Chinese bronze craftsmanship has always been regarded as the most remarkable. But this discovery will elevate the view of the Chinese technique for creating metal to a higher level, not only in terms of quantity, but also quality".

Below are some major events, which happened recently:

In April 1988, preparations began for the establishment of Sanxingdui Museum.

In June 1992, an academic discussion meeting was held to discuss the 60 year-excavation of the Sanxingdui Ruins.

In August 1992, a foundation stone laying ceremony was held for Sanxingdui Museum.

In May 1993, some relics from Sanxingdui Ruins were put on

show in Lausanne Olympic Museum.

In December 1995, some relics from Sanxingdui ruins were on show in Munich Hybary Foundation Arts Museum in Germany.

In April 1996, some relics from Sanxingdui Ruins were on show in Zurich Art Museum in Switzerland.

In September 1996, some relics from Sanxingdui Ruins were on show in British Museum.

In February 1997, some relics from Sanxingdui Ruins were on show in Denmark.

In October 1997, Sanxingdui Museum in Guanghan city was opened.

In February 1998, some relics from Sanxingdui Ruins were on show in Guggenheim Museum in New York.

In June 1998, some relics from Sanxingdui Ruins were on show in Japanese cities of Tokyo, Kyoto, Fukuoka and Hiroshima.

In July 2000, Sanxingdui and Yinshang Civilization International Academic Discussion was held in Guanghan, Sichuan.

As Sanxingdui Sites and the unearthed objects are on display, many archeologists and historians consider that the studies on the ruins and objects are a challenge to them, and it is a new academic research field to explore.

Historians re-examine the ancient Shu society in an all-around way based on the materials from the ruins. They explore the political system and social formations in the early evolution of human beings according to the typical model of the state of the ancient Shu in Sanxingdui area. A new category in archeology has been set up. It is called Sanxingdui Culture. Apart from its historical and archeological values, the studies continue in other fields in politics, religion, mythology and arts.

Dating back 3,000 years, the site of Sanxingdui Sites is believed to have served as the capital for several kings of the state of the ancient Shu. The discovery of Sanxingdui Ruins proves for the first time that Chinese civilization has diverse origins. Historians believe that the Cradles of Chinese Civilization include Sichuan Basin apart from the Yellow River Valley and Changjiang Valley. However, many major academic issues still remain a mystery to this day. Following are some of the issues for the current scholars to answer:

1. What happened to the ancient people of Sanxingdui site after the disappearance of their city? One of the answers is that the king of the ancient Shu probably moved to Chengdu following the sudden collapse of Sanxingdui settlement. There is clear evidence linking Jinsha and Sanxingdui ruins. However, there used to be a city wall at Sanxingdui Ruins. So far no trace of a city wall has been found at Jinsha Ruins. Historians wonder whether Jinsha Ruins served as the Shu's capital city.

2. What is the source of Sanxingdui culture? Is it either from the New Stone Age culture in the upper reaches of Su River, or is it from a certain kind of ancient regional culture? Is there any relationship between Sanxingdui culture and Longshan culture in Shandong?

3. What was the ancient Shu Kingdom really like? What were the nature of politics and religion? Was it a loose tribal military league? Or was it a regional kingdom ruled by a dynasty in the central plains?

4. Some scholars think that the religious worship in Sanxingdui was totems; some others think it is the worship of nature. But most scholars believe that the religious worship is a complex system, which involves a mixture of many types. They include the nature, ancestor and god worship.

5. How did Sanxingdui bronze smelting technique come into being? Did the Shu people independently develop it? Did they obtain the technique from the states nearby? Many scholars confirm that the bronze wares have displayed a combination of the ancient Shu culture and foreign culture.

6. How long did the ancient Kingdom last? Why did it disappear suddenly? Maybe it had disappeared by the end of the Shang Dynasty. The reason of its disappearance might have been the change of the regime.

7. What was the date of the two pits? Were they in the period of the Shang Dynasty? Scholars tend to accept the date of the Shang Dynasty.

There are some more issues concerned. What is the nature of the two sacrificial pits? When were the groups of the bronze figures and gold scepter produced? What is the relation between the state of the ancient Shu and the Zhou Dynasty? How many more treasures are still buried underground?

Well, so much for my introduction in the museum. Do you have any question to ask? Do you want an hour to walk around before we take the bus back to Chengdu? Maybe as you walk around, you can come up with some answers to the unsolved mysteries I just mentioned.

KEY WORDS & EXPRESSIONS 关键词汇及表达法

priceless treasure 无价的财宝

unprecedented 无前例的，空前的
appreciate 赏识，鉴赏
far-reaching 影响远的
metallic 金属(性)的
quantity 量，数量
foundation stone laying ceremony 奠基仪式
an all-around way 全方位地
diverse 不同的
the cradle of Chinese Civilization 中国文明的摇篮
combination 结合，联合
unsolved 未解答的，未解决的

Dujiangyan Irrigation System 都江堰

General Information
景点概况

Ladies and gentlemen, here we are at the entrance of Erwang Temple (the Two King's Temple). This is the first stop of our Dujiangyan tour. The temple is near the mountaintop, and it is a popular place for sightseers. Please come with me to the viewing stand for a unique view of most parts of the water project.

(***At the viewing stand***)

Please look at Dujiangyan Irrigation System below. It is an ancient technological wonder of the country. More than 2,000 years ago, Li Bing (B. C. 250 - 200 B. C.) served as a local governor of Shu State. At that time, Minjiang River flowed fast down from mountains. As it ran across Chengdu Plain, it frequently flooded Chengdu agricultural area, and local farmers suffered much from the water disaster. Li Bing and his son designed this water control system and organized thousands of local people to construct the project. The headwork is a large hydraulic water project. It consists of three main parts: Fish Mouth Water-Dividing Dam, Flying Sand Fence and Bottle-Neck Channel. More details will be given to you as we arrive at each spot.

When the construction was completed, the dam system automatically diverted Minjiang River and channeled it into irrigation canals. Gradually, Chengdu Plain turned into one of the most fertile places in China. Since 1949, expansion has been undertaken, and at present, the system works very effectively. It irrigates farming land across 33 counties in West Sichuan Province. The system benefits local people, and they are proud of the system.

On the 29th of November 2000, Dujiangyan Irrigation System and Mt. Qingcheng were placed on the World Cultural Heritage list.

Well, please follow me into Erwang Temple (二王庙).

KEY WORDS & EXPRESSIONS 关键词汇及表达法

sightseer 观光客
technological 科技的
fertile 肥沃的，富饶的
expansion 扩充，扩展

Two Kings' Temple
二王庙

Erwang Temple was built to commemorate Li Bing and his son. "Erwang" means "two kings". Originally, the temple was called Wangdi Temple (望帝祠) in memory of Duyu (杜宇), the king of the ancient Shu. Later Wangdi Temple was relocated in Pixian area during the Southern and Northern Dynasties. So local people renamed the temple as Chongdemiao（崇德庙）in order to express the respect of Li Bing and his son. Chongde means the

worship of virtue or reverence. During the Song Dynasty the temple was called Wangmiao（王庙）, which means the king's temple. Down to the Qing Dynasty it was called Erwang Temple. People offered Li Bing and his son the posthumous title of Wang (king).

The temple complex occupies an area of 10,072 square. The ancient timber buildings remain similar in design and style to the ones you saw in other places. The broad roof, perfect decoration, strict size and traditional use of color meet in harmony with the mountaintop environment. However, the temple buildings are not placed based on the concept of the north-south axis.

Here we are at the rear hall. It is devoted to Li Bing's son. His son's statue is newly molded. The figure stands firmly with a tool in his hands as if he was ready to level down mountains and build the weir. Behind is Minjiang River, which serves as the background. Li Bing's son had a name called Erlang（二郎）. Erlang is a popular legendary figure in Chinese folk literature. In the folk stories, he has a close relationship with Li Bing. It should be pointed out that no recorded historical evidence could be found to show Erlang was Li Bing's son. In Chinese feudal society, it would be a great problem if a family had no offspring. So in ancient times, local people regarded Erlang as Li Bing's son. They sincerely wished that Li Bing would have a son so that Li's family tree would continue.

Here we are at the main hall. It is devoted to Li Bing himself. The statue is newly molded. The old statue was a larger-than-life painted statue, and the figure looked like a wise scholar looking at the rushing river below. The newly molded figure has a silk map in his hand, and his eyes are bright with wisdom. It appears as if he is thinking about the blueprint of the project.

According to the folk tale, July 24 of the Chinese Lunar Calendar is Li Ping's birthday. On that day many local people visit the temple where they prostrate themselves before the image of Li Ping and his son and burn incense to honor them. At the same time the beatings of drums and gongs resound to the sky as incense smoke curls upwards.

Li Bing's hall is a compound. The hall faces an opera stage across the courtyard below, surrounded by other buildings. On July 24 of the Chinese Lunar Calendar during the Ming and Qing Dynasties local operas would be performed on the stage. Many people would gather in the courtyard and watch the performance. It is said that the actors offered the performance mainly for Li Bing as a tribute for his great contribution to local people.

Here we are at a delicate pavilion called Guanlanting（观澜亭）. Carved characters are on both sides of stonewalls. These are quotations of how to manage Dujiangyan Irrigation System. One of the famous inscriptions engraved on the wall is an eight-character quotation from Li Ping. It says: "*When the river flows in zigzags, cut a straight channel; when the riverbed is wide and shallow, dig it deeper.（深掏滩，低作堰。）*"

KEY WORDS & EXPRESSIONS　关键词汇及表达法

reverence　尊敬，敬重；敬畏感
weir　鱼梁
offspring　子孙，后代
rushing　急流的
prostrate　使俯卧
burn incense　烧香
Chinese Lunar Calendar　农历
quotation　引用语

Suspension Bridge
安澜吊桥

Our second stop is Anlan Suspension Bridge. It is one of the five ancient bridges in China. The total length is 320m. Its ancient name was called the Rope Suspension Bridge or the Bamboo and Cane Suspension Bridge. Unfortunately, a war fire by the end of the Ming Dynasty destroyed the original bridge. In 1803, a new bridge was built. It was made with local bamboo rope chains, and the bridge bottom floor was replaced with wooden plates. The old bridge lasted until the 1970s when it was replaced by a steel chains bridge.

Well, now let's cross over the river on Anlan Suspension

Bridge. Maybe you will see that some visitors, as they cross the bridge, catch hold of the steel chains, and start swinging back and forth on the bridge for fun.

KEY WORDS & EXPRESSIONS 关键词汇及表达法

suspension 吊桥
steel chain 钢链(索)
swing 摇摆，摆动

Three Main Projects
三大主体工程

Fish Mouth Water-Dividing Dam(鱼嘴分水堤)

The Fish Mouth Water-Dividing Dam is built in the middle of the river. It is the main part of Dujiangyan Irrigation System. The Fish mouth functions to divide the river into an inner canal and an outer canal. Long ago, when Li Ping worked as the local governor of the Shu State, he found the old river canal was too narrow to hold much water, which often overflowed the banks and caused disastrous floods. Based on natural geographic conditions, Li Bing organized the people to build a man-made dam. The whole dam looks like a fish, and the front dam has a circular cone shaped like a fish mouth. It is the dam that diverts water into the outer canal and the inner canal. The inner water canal functions as the main stream for irrigation purposes; the outer river is mainly used to drain excessive water and sand. During flood seasons the inner canal holds 60% of the water in the river, and 40 percent of the water flows into the outer river. It is vice versa in dry seasons. About 80 percent of the silt is carried away along the outer river.

Flying Sand Fence(飞沙堰溢洪道)

The water flows along the inner canal towards the Bottle-Neck Channel. On the way it passes the Flying Sand Fence, which has a 200m wide opening from south to north. The fence joins the inner and outer canals. The fence functions to control the flow of water and discharge excess into the outer canal from the inner canal. During the dry seasons the fence doesn't work much, but when floods occur, the river rushes forward along the inner canal. As it approaches the fence, the river begins to turn round fast, and soon many whirlpools are formed. The whirlpools change quickly, sweeping away sand and pebbles, and throwing them into the outer canal. During the flood seasons, this spillway transports 80% of the sediments into the outer river, and at the same time excessive water flows over the Flying Sands Fence into the outer river. In ancient times, there was no cement in use. Instead, huge bamboo cages were used as the fence. They were filled with stones and pebbles. However, at present, a reinforced concrete weir has replaced the ancient fence.

Bottle-Neck Channel(宝瓶口进水口)

The inner canal leads to the Bottleneck Channel, which is the entrance of the extensive irrigation system. A trunk canal cuts the mountain into two parts. The small part was later called Li Dui (离堆), which means an isolated hill. Chengdu looks like a large bottle, and the trunk canal between the mountain and the hill takes the shape of a bottleneck. During the flood seasons, the water will not overflow into the trunk canal. Instead, it flows in whirlpools into the outer canal. The trunk canal works as a check gate to safeguard Chengdu Plain.

The trunk canal technically has two functions.

1. It distributes the water to irrigate the farming land in western Sichuan.

2. The trunk canal works together with the Flying-Sand Fence to keep the flow below a certain point in the inner canal during the flood seasons.

Some stone tablets stand on the isolated hill. They are engraved in Buddhist Sanskrit. The local people hope that the Buddhist tablets can influence the Buddhist superpower to harness flood disasters. Actually, the three main projects have worked in harmony with one another for centuries. They form a complete and scientific irrigation and drainage network, which successfully ensures that there will be water in Minjiang River for irrigation.

(***On the way to Fulongguan*** (The Dragon-Taming Temple))

The Dragon-Taming Temple is our final stop at Dujiangyan Irrigation System. Then we will take the bus back to Dujiangyan city for lunch. The temple is located in the beautiful Lidui Park, which is close to the city.

The temple was built in the 3rd century. Originally, it was devoted to Fan Changsheng (范长生, the founder of Tianshi Dao 天师道, one Daoist sect) in the Jin Dynasty (265 - 420). During the Five Dynasties and Ten States, Li Bing was conferred the posthumous title called Da'anwang (大安王), and his hall was set up here in honor of him. A popular legend during the Song Dynasty was that Erwang, Li Bing's son, had subdued an evil dragon here. So the temple was renamed as the Dragon-Taming Temple accordingly. In 1974, a stone statue of Li Bing was unearthed from the river base. The carved figure looks graceful. Now it is placed in the middle of the main hall. It is 2. 9m in height and 4. 5 tons in weight. Based on archeological studies, the statue was carved in 168 during the East Han Dynasty.

Well, as we arrive at the temple, please follow me and go up to the temple to have a bird's eye-view of the Bottle-Neck Channel. Besides, there are some gift shops in the temple, which is your chance to purchase some gifts for your families and friends.

KEY WORDS & EXPRESSIONS 关键词汇及表达法

function 起作用，功能
overflow 使泛滥
circular 圆形的
excessive 过多的，过度的
inner canal 内江
outer river 外江
discharge 使放出，排出
whirlpool 旋涡
spillway 泄洪道
sediment 沉淀物，沉积
pebble 小圆石，小鹅卵石
reinforce 加强，增援
Sanskrit 梵语
harness 控制
subdue 征服
a bird's eye-view 鸟瞰

Mt. Qingcheng 青城山

General Introduction of Daoism
道教简介

Good Morning. Let's get on our bus now. Today we are

going to visit Mt. Qingcheng. It is situated about 68km west of Chengdu. It takes an hour and half to get there. While we are on the bus, I'd like to tell you about Daoism. As you may have known, Mt. Qingcheng is one of the birthplaces of Daoism and is still a Daoist center.

Daoism or Taoism is a Chinese native religion. It came into being among the Han nationality, and took shape during the reign of Emperor Shun Di (顺帝, 125 - 144) of the East Han Dynasty (25 - 220). It greatly influenced economy, culture and political thinking in feudal China for more than 1,700 years. Its doctrine was built on the ancient witchcraft, recipes for immortality and the concepts of Huang Di (Yellow Emperor) and Lao Zi.

First of all, I'd like to say something about the ancient witchcraft. It started a long time ago between the 21st and 11th centuries B. C.. The ancient people worshiped ghosts and gods. There were many ghosts and gods in the form of supernatural beings. There were human ghosts as well as heavenly and earthly gods. The heavenly gods were blue, yellow, white and black kings; there were gods of the sun, the moon, stars, wind, rain, thunder and lightening. The earthly gods were town gods and the gods of the land and grain; gods of the rivers, as well as the gods of the five mountains [Taishan Mountain (泰山) in Shandong province, Hengshan Mountain (衡山) in Hunan province, Huashan Mountain (华山) in Shaanxi province, the other Hengshan (恒山) Mountain in Shanxi province and Songshan Mountain (嵩山) in Henan province] are also included. The human ghosts were ancestry, sages and personages of virtue, loyalty, filial piety, justice and chastity.

From the Spring and Autumn Period (770 - 475 B. C.),

many people wanted to live forever. Some ancient books clearly described how supernatural beings lived. One process was to increase one's Qi (气). Qi literally means "vitality". Vitality exercises suggested absorbing Qi from outside the body. At the same time, another process to make people live forever was being developed. It was called alchemy. Alchemists attempted to produce Dan (丹), a pill made through the refining cinnabar. People expected to have a long life after they ingested Dan. Daoism allowed the recipes for immortality to become the part of its key content.

Do you know anything about Huang Di and Lao Zi? Maybe someone in our group knows that we Chinese people often refer to ourselves as the descendents of Huang Di, the Yellow Emperor. Ancients believed that he was a part-real and part-legendary important person. In the early time of the Western Han Dynasty (206 B. C. - 24 A. D.), the ruling class believed and taught Huang Di's and Lao Zi's way of seeking peace and quiet. They wanted this belief to dominate the whole country. At the beginning, Daoism worshiped both Huang Di and Lao Zi. Later the Daoists shifted the emphasis of the worship to Lao Zi who was generally admitted to be the founder of Daoism.

It is said that Lao Zi (Lao Tzu) lived about the same time as Confucius. However, few people know about his life. Lao Zi cultivated Dao (道, the way) and virtue. He lived in the Zhou State for a long time. When he saw the state decline, he departed. According to an old story, Lao Zi rode a purple buffalo to the fabled land of the west. As he passed through the Hangu Gate, a guard said to him: "As you are about to leave the world behind, could you write a book for my sake?" Lao Zi did it. He wrote a book in two parts, setting out the meaning of Dao(道,the way) and virtue. The whole book has some five thousand characters. Afterwards Lao Zi departed. No one knew where he went.

Dao De Jing (道德经) is a prose poem full of philosophy. It has had an influence on Chinese thought. It is often referred to as the book of five thousand characters. It has been translated into European languages. In English alone there are at least over thirty translations. I have a suggestion. If you are interested in Dao De Jing, please go and buy the book in English translation after your visit to the Daoist mountain. For your better understanding of Daoism, I'd like to tell you something about the book to pass the time on the bus.

Dao literally means the way. The way is considered the central idea in the book. It begins by saying:

The way is that can be spoken of
Is not the constant way;
The name that can be named
Is not the constant name.
(道可道,非常道;名可名,非常名。)

In chapter 32 it says:

The way is forever nameless.(道常无名朴。)

The Dao can be described, but there is no name that is applicable to the Dao. Language is totally good enough for such a purpose. The Dao is thought to be responsible for the creation as well as the support of the universe. In chapter 42 it says:

The Dao begets one;
One begets two;
Two begets three;

Three begets the myriad creatures.

(道生一,一生二;二生三,三生万物。)

From these passages we can see that the Dao existed before the universe came into being. Beyond this there is nothing we can say about Dao. Someone may think the book is misleading to say that the Dao produced the universe. Listen, the book says that it did not produce the universe in the same way that a father produces a son. The Dao produced the universe only in an imaginary sense.

As you read the book, you will find out there is no clear and full support to be found. The idea of opposite terms plays an important role in the thought of Lao Zi. All things have their opposites. Each of the two contradictory aspects transforms itself into its opposite. We describe one thing as strong, but also describe another thing as weak. The same goes for the long and short, the high and low, female and male, and dark and light. The Dao may be compared with the Yin component in the ancient yin-yang dualism. It's a pair of opposites in harmony. Thus Non-being as well as Being has a positive value. Both members of the duality are needed. Yang has been overemphasized, and yin must be restored to its right place. The Dao is like the yin or humble because it is passive, yielding, not active and dominating.

Well, I can see some of you have been carried away by what I have been saying. As you know, the Dao is like the yin or humble, Daoism is fully interested in a man's place in the natural world. The nature of the mysticism is simply to advise a man to abandon self-effort and ease himself into the rhythm of the universe and life and death. In the chapter 66 it says:

Desiring to rule over the people,

One must, in one's words, humble oneself before them;
And, desiring to lead the people,
One must, in one's person, follow behind them.
(是以圣人欲上民,必以言下之;欲先民,必以身后之。)

This behavior reminds me of the Chinese term Wu Wei(无为). It literally means "action by non-action" out of harmony with the flow of things. It seems he is like water in his movement, in his stillness he is like a mirror, in his response he is like an echo... He never leads but always follows behind others. A man can achieve his own happiness by following closely the happiness of others, or he becomes happy only by forgetting about his own happiness.

Well, so much for the Dao or Daoism. I can tell that some of you have been carried away by what I have said. Maybe someone will ask what is the relationship between Daoism and Confucianism? To be perfectly honest, it is hard to say in one word. Generally, both Daoism and Confucianism have similar values. What sets them apart is their approach. Daoism rejects all formalities. Daoists think formalities are pointless and repressive. Confucianism seeks to arrange life within the framework of moral conduct. Daoism believes there is no absolute distinction between good and bad. Confucianism focuses on man while Daoism focuses on Dao, and Dao runs through everything.

Excuse me, one gentleman sitting over there asks me to give a brief introduction of the ancient development of Daoism. Well, Daoism took shape during the Eastern Han Dynasty as I said just now. During the reign of Emperor Shun Di, Zhang Daoling (张道陵) founded the Five-Piculs-of-Rice Sect (五斗米教). This sect was a form of Daoism in its early stage. The followers worshiped

Lao Zi as their great teacher. Of course, Dao De Jing became their accepted standard of thought. They believed that a man could obtain immortality through cultivation.

Towards the end of the Eastern Han Dynasty, a peasant rebel leader named Zhang Jiao (张角) established another Daoist sect called Taiping Dao (太平道, Peace Sect). He managed to gather ten thousand followers, and organized an uprising by the name of sect. His uprising heavily weakened the feudal ruling class.

During the Southern and Northern Dynasties, Daoism was divided into two major sects. They were the Northern Sect and the Southern Sect. Up to the Tang and Song dynasties, Daoism became populous. Its monasteries and temples grew rapidly and spread across the country. But since the Ming Dynasty, the religion began to decline. However, it still exerted some influence among the Chinese people.

KEY WORDS & EXPRESSIONS 关键词汇及表达法

birthplace 诞生地
Daoism 道教
Han nationality 汉族
take shape 成型，发展
doctrine 教义
witchcraft 巫术
recipe for immortality 长寿方法，长寿秘方
concept 观念
remote ages 远古
supernatural beings 神仙
sage 圣人
personage of virtue 有德之人

filial piety 忠孝
chastity 贞节
preserve or enrich one's Qi 养气
alchemy 炼金术
alchemist 炼金术士
refining cinnabar 精炼的朱砂
have a long life 长寿
descendents of Huang Di 炎黄子孙
dominate the whole country 统治全国
worship 崇拜
cultivate the way and virtue 修道
purple 紫色的
philosophy 哲学
constant 持续的
be applicable to 可适用的
beget 产生
misleading 易误解的
produce the universe 创造天地万物
figurative sense 比喻的含义
opposite term 对立的条件
contradictory aspects transform itself into its opposite 矛盾的对立面向自己相反的方向转变
be compared with 与……对比
overemphasize 过分强调
mysticism 神秘主义
abandon self-effort 摒弃自身努力
the rhythm of the universe 宇宙的韵律
remind sb of sth 使人想起
in harmony with 与……和谐

been carried away by 被……着迷
Confucianism 儒教
formality 形式
pointless 无意义的
repressive 压抑的
within the framework of moral conduct 在道德规范下
obtain immortality through cultivation 修炼成仙
uprising 起义
popular 流行的

Brief Introduction of the Mountain Qingcheng
青城山简介

May I have your attentions, please. In 20 minutes we will arrive at the foot of the mountain. Before our arrival, I'd like to offer you some more information concerning the mountain itself.

The doctrine of Daoism believes that all things in the universe have their own spirits (gods). The Daoist gods are said to live far away in their ten celestial caverns and seventy-two happy lands. Mt. Qingcheng is known as the Daoist fifth cavern.

The mountain has 36 green peaks, 8 huge caverns, 72 small caverns and 108 scenic spots. In 1982, it was listed as one the best scenic areas across the country. Recently the mountain and Dujiangyan Irrigotion System have been admitted into the World Cultural Heritage List. Seeing is believing. Soon you all will experience how beautiful the mountain is.

Qingcheng literally means Green City. It is named because some of its green cliffs are shaped like city walls. This multi-peaked mountain rises up to 1,600m and has thick green vegetation. Mt. Qingcheng is commonly known for its *you* (幽)

in China. Frankly speaking, I have no appropriate words or names in English that are applicable to the *you*. The *you* aims to describe varied objects. In this mountain the *you* conveys such implicationsas: secluded woods, faintly fragrant flowers, peaceful zigzag paths, delightful sounds of birds and leisurely flowing streams.

Mt. Qingcheng is the Daoist mountain. As early as in the Eastern Han Dynasty, Zhang Daoling came to the mountain where he founded the Five-Piculs-of-Rice Sect. Zhang was born in Anhui. In his early years, Zhang studied Confucianism. Later he became dissatisfied with some of the Confucian principles because these principles failed to offer methods of immortality. So he began to study the way to immortality. Zhang soon mastered the process of producing dan (丹), a sort of helper to living forever. Do you know why he came to Sichuan? In his hometown, Zhang couldn't afford to buy herb materials for his dan production. Zhang and his followers therefore came to Sichuan and settled down in Mt. Heming (鹤鸣山), Dayi county (大邑县), where he could get enough herb materials. Zhang continued his Daoist studies, and at the same time, he used Daoist methods to offer medical treatment to local people. Zhang gathered ten thousand followers. The Five-Piculs-of-Rice means that each follower in his sect should pay to the sect some rice or firewood. The Five-Piculs-of-Rice sect was officially formed in Sichuan. The sect followers worshiped Lao Zi as their great teacher, and Mt. Qingcheng was the regular place for Zhang to practice his Daoism.

The Daoist followers are supposed to stay away from the human world, and cultivate themselves in the Daoist celestial caverns and seventy-two happy lands. In the following dynasties, Daoism gained in popularity in the mountain, its monasteries and temples developed rapidly. It is said there used to be about 70 temples across the mountain. The temples blended into the natural picture. They stood either among thick trees, or near waterfalls, or over misty valleys, or below peaks.

Do you know why Mt. Qingcheng was chosen as a Daoist celestial cavern? It is probably because of its *you* in nature that the Daoists followers practice their belief in this mountain. They keep experiencing various moods of sunshine and mist, the changing seasons, the balance of peaks and low water courses. They think it is a most satisfying way to feel a sense of exchange with Nature and know oneself to be part of the whole universe.

KEY WORDS & EXPRESSIONS 关键词汇及表达法

ten celestial caverns 十大洞天
seventy-two happy lands 七十二福地
the World Cultural Heritage List 世界文化遗产名录
Seeing is believing. 眼见为实
green cliff 绿崖
luxuriant vegetation 林木葱茏
appropriate word 恰当的词语
zigzag path 弯曲的小径
leisurely flowing stream 潺潺小溪
be dissatisfied with 不满意的
afford to 买得起；供应得起
herb material 草药
offer medical treatment to local people 为当地人治病
stay away from the human world 隐居
gain in popularity 声望鹊起

imperceptibly 微妙的

feel a sense of exchange with Nature 感受与自然交流

Jianfu Temple

建福宫

Attention please. Here we are at the foot of the mountain. The majestic entrance gate and green trees seem to welcome us. I know you are all eager to start your hiking. Please follow me for a visit to Jianfu Temple.

The temple is at the mountain entrance. It could date back to Kaiyuan period (开元年间) of Tang Dynasty. It was first named Zhangren Temple (丈人祠), and renamed as Huiqing Jianfugong (会庆建福宫) during the Song Dynasty. The current temple was built in 1888 during the Qing Dynasty. The whole temple mainly consists of three halls in honor of some Daoist gods and founders.

Here is the first hall. It is called Changsheng Hall (长生殿). The hall contains a statue of Fan Changsheng (范长生), the founder of Tianshi Dao in the Jin Dynasty (265－420).

Here we are at the second hall. It is called Zhangren Hall (丈人殿). In the middle of the hall sits Ning Feng (宁封) in statue. I will tell you a legend about Ning Feng. A long time ago, Ning Feng obtained his Daoism through practice in Mt. Qingcheng. He could even fly up and down with clouds or go through fire and water. Once the Yellow Emperor came to the mountain. He visited Ning Feng for advice of how to fight against Chiyou (蚩尤), his opponent, and to unify the whole China. Ning Feng taught the emperor how to fly in the sky. Afterwards the emperor used the magic skill to defeat his opponent. Besides, Ning Feng also helped the Yellow Emperor unify the whole country. Due to Ning Feng's distinguished contribution, the emperor offered him a grand title, Wuyue Zhengren (五岳丈人), which means the top leader in charge of the five Chinese famous mountains.

This is the third hall. It contains the statues of Lao Zi (太上老君), Donghua Dijun (东华帝君) and Wang Chongyang (王重阳). Lao Zi was the founder of Daoism as you know. Donghua Dijun was a highly privileged title. It was given to one of Daoist gods who was regarded as a person in a much earlier time. This dignified god was commonly said to live in a building with purple clouds as the roof and green clouds as his city moat. Wang Chongyang was the founder of Quanzhen Sect of Daoism (全真教), which originated in 1163. Quanzhen Sect began to decline at the end of the Yuan Dynasty (1271 - 1368). Later on, the sect split into two parts: the Quanzhen Northern Sub-Sect and Quanzhen Southern Sub-Sect.

OK, ladies and gentlemen, we will start our hiking. On the way up to Tianshi and Shangqing temples, we will fully experience the scenes of the *you* in Mt. Qingcheng. Besides, there are some tiny pavilions which stand along the path. The barked roof and wooden structure make the pavilions look primitive. Each pavilion has its own poetic name. Visitors can't help walking into the pavilions where they relax themselves and enjoy the beauty around.

Now, let's get moving.

KEY WORDS & EXPRESSIONS 关键词汇及表达法

majestic 雄伟的

hiking 徒步旅行

in honor of 向……表示敬意

distinguished contribution 卓越的贡献
highly privileged title 德高望重的头衔
city moat 护城河
relax oneself 放松自己

Tianshi Temple
天师洞

Here we are at Tianshi Temple. The temple is devoted to Zhang Daoling, who founded the Five-Piculs-of-Rice Sect or we call Tianshi Dao Sect. It is the place where Zhang preached his Doaism.

The temple dated back to the Sui Dynasty (581 - 618). In the late Qing Dynasty, the current temple was reconstructed. As you can see, the temple stands on a hill. The foreground mountain separates a valley, which runs directly away from our view back into the distant bottom. The foreground is dropped in here by dark trees, but mountain outlines are intentionally dissolved in wet washes, giving an exhilarating sense of vast space.

There is a legendary story about the valley. It says that when Zhang stayed in the mountain, he decided to punish the local mountain ghosts. These ghosts often made troubles. One day, Zhang and the ghost head signed an agreement after a formal talk. Afterwards Zhang dipped his writing brush into red ink, took it out and wrote something on the mountain. Immediately the mountain split along his handwriting mark into this deep valley. Zhang displayed his supernatural power and scared all the ghosts on the spot. They soon moved away from the mountain.

Here is Daoist Trinity Hall (三清殿). Dao develops into

three different eras: Hong Yuan (洪元世纪, Flooding Era), Hun Yuan (混元世纪, Chaotic Era) and Tai Chu (太初世纪, Remotest Era). Look at the three Daoist Emperors in the hall. They symbolize the three eras respectively. The Hong Yuan Emperor has a pearl in his hands, the Hun Yuan Emperor holds the universe, and the Tai Chu Emperor has a feather fan. The Daoist followers worship the three emperors as the Buddhists worship Sakyamuni.

This hall is worth viewing. A majestic double-roof covers the Daoist Trinity Hall, where Daoist ceremonies are performed. The hall appears imposing. A flight of stone steps leads to the hall portico supported by six huge stone pillars in a row. Each pillar stands on 1.2m high stone base. They are decorated with a motif of lions, and other mythical animals. There are twenty-eight inner stone pillars supporting the hall. It is amazing to see that each pillar is made of a single huge stone block. Sixteen of them are inscribed with couplets. Figures, birds, animals and flower patterns are carved on the supporting arches and curves on the top of the pillars. They appear in harmony with the Daoist hall.

Well, I'd like to mention a couplet engraved on a stone pillar in the Trinity Hall. Please come and have a look. It embraces the Daoist basic concept and creed. It says, "Dao creates vitality. Vitality splits into *Yin* and *Yang*. (*Yin* and *Yang* are the two opposing principles in nature. The former is feminine and negative, and the later masculine and positive.) *Yin* and *Yang* merge into one and then gasify the whole universe. The gasification makes all things on earth come into being. Man follows the way of earth. The earth follows the way of Heaven. Heaven follows Dao, and Dao follows nature."

Do you know what the couplet means? It displays that Dao is omnipresent and all embracing. Without Dao there would be no vitality. Dao is the driving force in nature. Dao can't be exhausted. Man should arrange his life in line with the natural order of the universe.

Above the hall is Wuji Hall (无极殿). It means the omnipotent hall. Some valuable relics are stored in the hall. They include the carved eight-leaf wooden screen of the Ming Dynasty, and a horizontal board inscribed with the words"Dantai Bidong(丹台碧洞)". It was written by Kangxi (康熙), an emperor of the Qing Dynasty. The words means the red table and the green cave. It was a Daoist priest who brought the emperor's handwriting to the mountain from another Daoist mountain by the name of Mt. Wudang (武当). That mountain stretches for 400km across northwestern Hubei province.

Look at an old ginkgo tree near the hall. As a folk story says, the tree is 1,800 years old, and was planted by Zhang Daoling. Do you know how big it is? It is 30m tall and 6m around the trunk.

Please come and view some carvings on the stone railings in front of the hall. There are laughing and cheerful figures. They have no hair, and the top of their skull is slightly sunken. Besides, they all wear open-seat pants like infants. Many visitors, when they arrive here, try hard to guess what the patterns mean. The carved figures display the people in a childlike state. They have no knowledge and so no desire beyond the immediate objects of the senses. According to the Daoist doctrine, these patterns display the ideal state of the Daoist. In the Daoist state, people are innocent of knowledge and free from desire. The "desire" here doesn't mean the desire for basic necessities like food and clothing. More likely, they resemble the "uncarved block" as a symbol for the original state of man before desire is produced in him by artificial means.

Well, after our visit to Tianshi Temple, we will continue our hiking up to Shangqing Temple. We will pass through the Gateway. Its name is longqiao Xianzong (龙跷仙踪) which opens into a path leading to a cave. It is commonly said that Zhang used to stay in the cave for his Doaist practice. The cave is dedicated to the statue of Zhang in his shrine. You may go for a quick look at the dignified statue. Zhang has three eyes with a sword in one hand and the other hand facing outside. A seal in his hand is said to be a priceless treasure. Zhang used the seal to guard the whole mountain.

KEY WORDS & EXPRESSIONS 关键词汇及表达法

foreground 前景
give an exhilarating sense of vast space 给人以辽阔空间愉快的感受
imposing 雄伟的
hall portico 殿前门廊
a motif of lions 石狮浮雕
embrace 包括
embracing 无所不包的
concept and creed 概念与信条
gasify (使)气(汽)化
gasification 气(汽)化
omnipresent 无所不在的
valuable relics 有价值的文物
horizontal board 匾

ginkgo 银杏
skull 头盖骨
wear open-seat pants 穿着开裆裤
be innocent of knowledge 无知
be free from desire 无欲
basic necessities 基本需要
uncarved block 未雕之木
original state 原始状态
artificial mean 人为手段
priceless treasure 无价之宝

Shangqing Temple
上清宫

Ladies and gentlemen, we now arrive at Shangqing Temple. Shangqing Temple is devoted to Lao Zi, the founder of Daoism. Mt. Qingcheng consists of two parts: the Front Mountain and the Back Mountain. The Shangqing Temple is located at the summit of the Front Mountain. It was originally built in the Jin Dynasty, but the current temple was actually constructed in the Qing Dynasty.

Please look at the couplets hanging on both sides of the entrance. One of them was written by Yu Youren (于右任), a well-known calligraphist. The couplets means that even the grass and plants across the mountain have been bathed in the rays of Daoist immortals; this mountain always welcomes visitors far and near since ancient times.

Behind the entrance gate are two halls. One is on the right side, and the other on the left side. The right-side hall contains a dragon and the left-side hall has a tiger. They function as temple guardians. Well, please come with me to view two wells in the temple.

Here we are. Look, one well is square and the other is round. The two wells stay together and the water in the wells is from the same source. Can you tell me what is different between the two wells? You see. The water in one well appears muddy, and in the other well clean. People have named the two wells the Mandarin Duck Well (鸳鸯井). Maybe someone will ask why people use mandarin ducks for the name of this well. Well, mandarin ducks in China symbolize a couple in deep love. No matter what happens, the male and female ducks always stay together.

Near the well is a stone tablet carved with three characters: Yuanyang Jing. Written by Zhang Daqian, who was one of the top masters of Chinese painting. In 1938, Zhang toured the mountain. Later he moved his family up to the mountain, and he stayed in the Shangqing Temple for a while. In 1941, when he came back from Dunhuang (Mogao Caves), he continued his stay in the mountain for two years. During his stay he produced many paintings. He also offered his inscriptions to the temples and other spots. In his late years, Zhang moved to the United States. There he wrote" Shangqing Temple in Mt. Qingcheng" in a Chinese style calligraphy and asked his daughter to bring it to the mountain. His calligraphy has expressed his sincere love for Mt. Qingcheng.

Here is an inscribed horizontal board with four carved Chinese characters. It says, "Dao Bu Wai Qiu(道不外求)", which means that Daoism doesn't have to look for other help. What does it mean? Daoism advocates self-reliance and self-support. Often we come across Buddhist monks who are out of their monasteries to beg alms from other people. However, Daoist priests seldom do that.

There are three pavilions in the Shangqing temple area. They are guanriting (观日亭, Sun-Viewing Pavilion), shengdengting (神灯亭, Magical Lamp Pavilion) and huyingting (呼应亭, Echo Pavilion). This area offers three natural wonders. Visitors are able to see the sun rise in the Sun-Viewing Pavilion in the morning, in the misty evening, glowworms usually fly in swarms, and they give a faint and unsteady light near the Magical Lamp Pavilion. The Echo Pavilion stands on the top of the summit, where a visitor shouts at distant lower hills and can hear echo back from them. Some visitors stay overnight at the Shangqing Temple if they want to watch glowworms flying at night and hike up to the summit for the sunrise the next morning.

Fellow hikers, the sightseeing trip in the mountain must eventually come to an end, and we will go down to the foot of the mountain to catch our bus at 4:30. I hope that all of you have enjoyed the brief glimpses of the beauty of the mountain and the Daoist culture. Don't forget to look in the bookstore for the book I mentioned earlier. I have enjoyed being your tour guide today. If any of you have further questions, do not hesitate to ask he on our bus ride back.

KEY WORDS & EXPRESSIONS 关键词汇及表达法

temple guardian 护法神
symbolize 象征
inscription 题词(字)
express one's sincere love 表达真诚的爱
self-reliance 自力更生
self-supporting 自食其力
beg alms 化缘
glowworm 萤火虫

The Giant Buddha of Leshan 乐山大佛

General Information of the Giant Buddha
大佛概况

Travelers, here we are at the head of the Leshan Giant Buddha. I'd like to give you general introduction of the Giant Buddha and some other information concerned. I hope that my introduction will be informative and interesting.

Leshan Grand Buddha is also known as Lingyun(凌云)Grand Buddha or Jiazhou(嘉州)Grand Buddha. The cliff-carving project was begun in the year of 713 A. D. The huge stone Buddha has been chiseled on the face of the cliff between Jifeng(集凤峰)and Xiluan Peaks(栖鸾峰)of Mt. Lingyun, standing at the place below the convergence of the three rivers. The Buddha, as high as the hill, sits bordering on the confluence of the three rivers. It is not only the largest cliff-carving of Maitrya in sitting position (the Happy Buddha) in China, but also the largest religious stone-carving art treasure in the world. Wei Gao(韦皋), the top commander in charge of Jiannan West Sichuan during the Tang Dynasty, composed a memorial note by the name of *the Events of Maitrya Stone-carving Figure in Lingyun Monastery, Jiazhou* (嘉州凌云寺大弥勒石像记), saying that the project lasted 90 years, and it was completed in 803. Monk Hai Tong (海通) in Lingyun Monastery started the initial project design and funds collection for the construction. Hai Tong, who was from Guizhou, traveled round until he arrived at Mt. Lingyun. During his stay in Lingyun Monastery, he saw that the three rivers rushed rapidly together producing dangerous spots. Hai Tong was therefore determined to cut down stones and rocks off a cliff at height of 10,000 *ren*(ren is an ancient measure of length, equals to seven or eight *chi*), hoping that the stones and rocks might level up on the river bases and slow down the swift currents. Hai Tong started collecting funds for this Buddha carving, and as a result, the donation he collected amounted for a billion *liang* of gold (*liang* is a unit of weight equal to 50g). Unfortunately, Hai Tong died before the completion of the Buddha carving, and the funds run out of shortage. Later Zhangchou Jianqiong(章仇兼琼), top military commander in Jiannan areas(剑南), offered 200,000 *guans*, which enabled the construction continue (One *guan* is a string of 1,000 coin in cash). During the Kaiyuan period of Tang Dynasty(唐开元年间), the Tang imperial government issued a special decree, saying that the fund from hemp and salt tax could be used to support the construction. However, the construction stopped again only because of shortage of more fund. In 789 the Tang imperial government issued another decree to refurbish old or ruined Buddhist monasteries. Accordingly, Wei Gao donated 500,000 *guans* to support the ongoing construction, and in 803 it was ultimately completed. At that time the Grand Buddha statue shone brightly with gilded gold and colored pattern. In addition, a seven-stories-and-thirteen-eaves pavilion was terraced on the same ground, sheltering the Buddha. It was named both Dafoge Pavilion(大佛阁 Giant Buddha Pavilion) and Daxiangge Pavilion(大像阁 Grand Image Pavilion). As Dafoge Pavilion sheltered the Grand Buddha, the whole construction looked breath-takingly magnificent and splendid. Later, disastrous wars destroyed the pavilion. At present only the ruins of some holes for the pavilion columns on the west side of the Grand Buddha cliff are left to remind us of the former gloriousness.

"The hill is the Buddha, the Buddha, the hill." Leshan Buddha is imposingly huge. It towers 58.7m in height, and its figure can be seen even several *li* (0.5km) away. The grand Buddha is thrice as high as the tallest Buddha figure in Yungang Grotto, Shanxi; 18m taller than the demolished Bamiyan Buddha in Afghanistan. By this token, Leshan Grand Buddha is considered as the largest stone-carving Buddha figure in the world. It is also the largest stone-carving of Maitrya Buddha in a sitting position in the world. Only by standing on the other side of the river can one view the panorama of the Buddha in distance.

The Grand Buddha's head is 14.7m in height, and 10m in diameter. In addition, the Buddha has 1,021 hair buns on the head. Over ten persons can sit around, or a big round table can stand on each bob. Its ear is 7m long, and each ear cavity can hold two persons. Its eye is 3. 3m long, nose 3. 5m long, eyebrow 3. 7m long, shoulder 24m wide and middle finger 8. 3m long. The distance between his feet is ten *zhang* (each *zhang* is equal to 3. 33m); its instep, 8. 5m wide and 11m long, is large enough to seat over 100 people. Each toes is longer than the total length of two adult. As an adult standing next to his foot, he is not as tall as the Buddha's instep.

You may find out many interesting details if carefully observes the Buddha's body. For example, the Buddha has 1,021 hair buns on the head. In 1962, maintenance men used chalks counting these curls up to these numbers. However, one can't see these curls but the head when viewing from distance. Actually many stones are inlaid one by one beneath the surface of each curl. One of the hair curls remains exposed at its base between the curl and the head scale. The exposed part discloses a visible crack of how stones were put together without cement sticking up inlaid stones. Two layers of mortar have been plastered on the surface of each curl, and the inner layer is lime white. Each layer is between 5 to 15mm in length. In 1991 when the Buddha was under refurbishment, maintenance men picked up three pieces of old stones for the curls. They were left behind in the sunken spot of the right foot, and two of them remained relatively intact.

During the refurbishment period, they found out that there was a 25cm-in-depth-hollow cavity, located in each of the Buddha's ears. Maintenance men picked out of the many cavities broken pieces, which turned out to be rotten wood and lime mortar. Thus it shows that what *the Accounts of Wu Boats*(吴船

录)say is true. The accounts were written by Fan Dacheng(范大成)of Southern Song Dynasty, they said, "*The Buddha is the greatest Buddha figure statue under the sun, and his ears are specially made with wood*.(极天下佛像之大,两耳犹以木为之。)" each 7m-in-length ear was not carved out of the cliff. Instead of the ancient construction, workers built the ears with wooden pillars, and then spread lime mortar to cover the structure for decoration. The maintenance men also found out that right below the nostrils was a hollow which disclosed logs cut off in three sections and shaped like a Chinese character 品. It shows that the built-up nose had been structured with wood and added with lime mortar for external decoration. However, no research is able to prove whether this technological process was implemented in 803 or it was used later when maintenance men refurbished the Buddha.

The Buddha's water drainage system covers its whole body. The Giant Buddha has lasted over a thousand years, and still survives in good shape. It is mainly due to this scientific drainage system. On the head of the Buddha are 18 layers of the buns, of which the 4th, 9th and 18th layers each have a crosswise drainage ditch. It was built by piling up lime mortar, and it is invisible when viewing it from distance. The Buddha's robe collar and pleats have ditches, too. In front of the Buddha's chest is another ditch, which goes towards the left until it joins with another ditch at the back side of the Buddha's right arm. There are two cavities, which open to each other. Each cavity at the back of the Buddha's ear, closed to the cliff. In addition, there are two holes at the back of the chest. One hole is at the right side, and the other at the left. These ingeniously-made ditches, holes and caves form a scientific drainage and ventilation system, which have played an effective role for over a thousand years in protecting the Buddha from being eroded and weathered. As a result, the inner wall of the cavities is moist and the bottom of the cavities has stored some water, moreover, water still keeps dripping from the mouth of the cavities, moistening a two-meter-in-circumference spot on the chest. Evidently, it is because of the cavities that are not linked up with other ditches. No one knows why the construction workers didn't open up the drainage system along this way.

The Giant Buddha in Leshan is the largest ancient carving of Maitrya in China, and it is also the largest stone-carving art treasure in the world. The carving is therefore honored as the classic-work of religion, hydraulics and carving art. Over a thousand years ago, the ancient craftsmen and artists used simple tools to create the huge and majestic carved statue, which fully indicates their great talent and boldness of vision.

KEY WORDS & EXPRESSIONS 关键词汇及表达法

informative 见闻广博的
chisel 凿,雕
confluence 汇合
discontinue 中断
ongoing 前进的
panorama 全景画
instep 脚背
maintenance 维修
sunken 凹陷的
cavity 凹处
external 外面的

drainage 排水系统
collar 衣领
pleat 褶裥
ingeniously 有才能地
ventilation 流通空气
circumference 圆周

Jiuqu and Lingyun Cliff Paths
九曲栈道和凌云栈道

When you descend along the left side of the Giant Buddha, and you can directly stop at the end of Lingyun Cliff Path. In 1983 this path started to be constructed and was completed in 1984. This path is 500m long, zigzagging from the northern end near the Giant Buddha and stops at the southern end of Bijin Tower(碧津楼). In addition, this path links up Jiuqu Cliff Path on the right side of the Giant Buddha, forming a winding and circuitous route for tourists.

You can detour around the feet of the Giant Buddha, walk through Dongtian Cavern(洞天)and arrive at the northern end of Lingyun Cliff Path. Legend says that this is path where Ao Guang(敖广), prince of the Dragon king in the North Sea used to walk upwards to pursue his studies from Su Dongpo(苏东坡). Therefore, this path is also named as "location where the prince returned to the sea" One section, further forward away from the starting point, is a hundreds-step hanging cliff path built on posts. You're able to see that the torrential river down beneath your feet as walking along this path. You start climbing precarious sloping steps where the space is narrow, and your head almost touches the cliff on the top. Then you ascend "the Heaven

Steps" before arriving at Songyun Pavilion(松韵亭)for a rest. 10m away from the pavilion is a huge stone, unattached and 30m in height. It is called Xiangmozuo (降魔杵 Monster-Surrender Stick). After a rest in Songyun Pavilion, you can continue your walking along the path, and then arrive at another pavilion in a square shape. It is named Duiyue (兑悦亭 Adding Happiness Pavilion), which is close to the southern end of the cliff path.

On the cliff, right side of the Giant Buddha, is a steep cliff path zigzagging from top to bottom. This is the well-known Qiuqu Cliff Path, which means in English "the Nine-Bend Cliff Path." Chiseled during Tang Dynasty when Giant Buddha was under construction, the path is extremely steep with 173 steps. At the end of the path on the topside is a corridor-patterned pavilion by the name of Jinheting Pavilion (近河亭 Close-to-the River Pavilion). As you stand in Jinheting pavilion, you're able to view Mt. Emei that looks dark green, and the river that seems to come from the sky. As far as one can see, mist covers the river, and greenness expands endless." On the first bend of the path are numbers of elegantly carved sutra-illustrations on which figures possess a natural grace, and carved lines remain exquisite. In addition, some towers, pavilions and pagodas have been carved onto the stone illustrations. All of these are considered as valuable resources for the studies of architecture and stone carving arts dating back to Tang Dynasty.

On the cliff face along the path are thousands of small-sized Buddha niches. More than 90 niches still remain intact, including the one by the name of the Buddhist Western Pure-Land. Poet Si Kongshu(司空曙)who participated in the statue carving at that time said "The gold gilded Buddha expands to a height of over a *hundred zhang* on the green cliff; Buddhist lights blazing in thousands of niches, disperse the surrounding thick mist(百丈金身开翠壁,方龛佛焰隔烟箩。)" Obviously the saying shows the spectacular occasion when the carving project was completed.

KEY WORDS & EXPRESSIONS 关键词汇及表达法

zigzag "之"字形的
circuitous 绕行的
torrential 奔流的
illustration 说明

Haishi Cavern

海师洞

Haishi cavern means "Master Hai's Cavern". It is located at the foot of the Xiluan Peak, 20m away from the Giant Buddha's head on Lingyun Hill. It was the place where Hai Tong sat cross-legged for his Buddhist meditation during the period of the carving project. Inside the cave is the Hai Tong statue in sitting position, and the inscription for the entrance board was offered by Gu Guangxu(顾光旭), a Sichuan top official of the Qing Dynasty. Gu Guangxu also composed an essay that later had been carved on the rock outside the cave. The name of the essay is *the Record of Haishi Cavern on Lingyun Hill*.

Hai Tong's sitting statue is 2m in height. He supports a tray on which there is an eyeball. The carving image is derived from a story from *the Record of the Stone Figure*. It says, "At that time an official saw that Hai Tong had collected so much money, so he attempted to obtain it by force. Hai Tong refused him in strong terms and said, "I'd rather gouge out my eyes than give the Buddhist funds to you." The official spitefully pressed Hai Tong to do so. Then Hai Tong remained calm, resolutely digging out his one eye and putting it onto a tray. Hai Tong surprised the official who felt ashamed and went away. In later generations, visitors from different places are visibly moved upon hearing the story and filled with deep esteem for Hai Tong.

KEY WORDS & EXPRESSIONS 关键词汇及表达法

meditation 冥想
gouge 挖出
resolutely 毅然地

Lingyun Hill
凌云山

Lingyun Hill is 423m high, and well known for its nine peaks whose names are Jifeng, Xiluan and others. The hill is 1km away from the east of Leshan city, and both the city and the hill face each other across the river. At the beginning of Tang Dynasty, Lingyun Monastery was built on the hill, so people in the following dynasties called the hill Lingyunshan (Lingyun Hill). It is known for its beautiful landscape and rich culture since ancient times, and always enjoys the following saying, "The most beautiful landscapes in China are at Sichuan. Jiazhou owns the prime scenes in Sichuan. Lingyun Hill is the jewel in Jiazhou's crown. (天下山水之冠在蜀,蜀之胜曰嘉州,嘉州之胜曰凌云。)"

Departing from Leshan city, you can take a vehicle down to Leshan dockside Gate where you may take a ferryboat to other docksides at the foot of either Lingyu or Wuyou hills(乌尤山). You can take a vehicle across Minjiang River Bridge, stop at the Stone Gate of Lingyun Hill. On the top of the gate is a horizontal inscription board carved "Lingyun Hill" in Chinese. Right inside the gate is a 13m-in-length cave where Maitreya Buddha statue sits. Maitreya smiles and his belly is exposed. The Buddha statue has remained for over a thousand years as the relics since Five Dynasties. In addition, the Buddha statue is also named as "Everyone-Is-Happy", reminds all the visitors that it is auspicious as they hike the hill. The vermilion stone stairway leads upwards. On the right side of the stairway is a stone cliff that drops downwards over a hundred *zhangs* in length. Beyond the cliff, the river flows east. You can see that mighty waves surge over and over, boats look so small like floating leaves and their masts like tiny spots. The left side of the cliff stone-way has been filled with carved inscriptions and poems composed by celebrities since the Tang and Song dynasties. In addition, there are numbers of carved Buddha figures on the cliff. After passing Fangsheng Pool (放生池), you can view another two pools embedded inside the cliff. One is called Longqiu(龙湫 Dragon Pool)and the other Huxue(虎穴 Tiger Cave). The names of the two pools are derived from the two lines "The returning wind stirs the Tiger Cave. The occasional drizzle rattles the Dragon Pool(回风吹虎穴,片雨当龙湫。)". The Dragon Pool covers a space of about 5 square meters. Beyond the pool is a cliff on which a huge Chinese character has been carved. It is called Long (龙 dragon), about 3m in height. It is said that the calligraphist had completed the character writing without a break, and his running-styled calligraphy makes the character look like a real dragon swimming in the sea. Halfway up the stair-steps, you will come across another stone carved inscription of the Ming Dynasty. It says, "here is the place where Su Dongpo carried his wine and passed by during his tour of the hill." Near the cliff side is a pavilion called Zaijiuting (载酒亭 Wine-Delivery Pavilion). The name is derived from a poem by the name of "To Jiazhou Governor Zhang," composed by Shu Dongpo. It says,

"A young man like me doesn't like to be an official in charge of ten thousand households,

Nor do I wish to get acquainted with Governor Han of Jingzhou prefecture.

Instead, I'd rather like to serve as the governor of Jiazhou,

Often carrying wine and touring Lingyun Hill."

(生不愿封万户侯,亦不愿识韩荆州,但愿身为汉嘉守,载酒时作凌云游。)

On the pavilion, you gaze at the distance, the scenery of the city and river are all right under his eyes. Outside the pavilion is a stream hanging on the cliff. As a gentle wind strokes the stream, it turns into a drizzle or sweet dews moistening visitors' clothes and refreshing their hearts. Nearby is a carved inscription by the name of Yuhuatai (雨花台 Raining Flower Terrace). Before the arrival at this pavilion, you are able to view the sight of Lingyun Monastery on the way up.

KEY WORDS & EXPRESSIONS 关键词汇及表达法

derive 衍生出
calligraphist 书法家
gaze 凝视
drizzle 毛毛雨
moisten 使湿润

Lingyun Monastery
凌云寺

The monastery was built between 618 and 620 A. D., and

people in later dynasties called the hill after the name of the monastery. Because of the location of the carved Giant Buddha, it is also called the Giant Buddha Monastery. Originally each of the nine peaks on the hill had its own monastery. However, in 841, the emperor issued an imperial edict ordering that all monasteries in China be demolished, only the Lingyun Monastery survived on the hill. In despite of its existence, this monastery still suffered frequent destruction or ruins during the periods of the Five Dynasties and Song Dynasty as well as the transitional period between Song and Yuan dynasties. In Ming Dynasty, the monastery expanded two times on a large scale, and as a result, Lingyun Monastery at that time became one of the largest monasteries in Southwest China. There was a popular saying, "Visitors usually ascend Mt. Emei for the pilgrimage, and descend to the Lingyun Monastery for worship." Toward the end of the Ming Dynasty, the monastery was destroyed again by war disasters. In 1667 the monastery was reconstructed. In addition, construction workers renovated the Grand Buddha Hall and Maitrya Hall. In 1930 a scripture library hall was built. Between 1949 and 1972 the monastery and the library hall had been used for other purposes. In 1972 the Leshan County Cultural Center took over the control of the monastery. Due to the importance of protection of historical relics, Lingyun Monastery remains under the management by the local official departments related to culture and historical relics. Therefore, the monastery remains a "monkless monastery".

On the entrance of the monastery hangs a short couplet says, "The river flows east; Buddha power comes west (大江东去，佛法西来。)". The two lines in Chinese are well matched in sound and words; the sense is profound and lasting. This couplet can be rated as a double perfection in writing and word usage.

The monastery has four halls. As you walk into the entrance gate, you are able to view the Heaven King Hall, behind Maitrya Buddha Hall is the Grand Buddha Hall and the Library Hall. The temple complex consists of a compound with four-sides enclosed with courtyards. Each main hall contains side-halls on both sides. The central open space is a garden-typed Sichuan courtyard that features high-rise ancient trees, and each courtyard is in elegant and quiet natures. The Grand Buddha Hall was built in the Ming Dynasty with a system of wooden brackets inserted between the top of a column and a crossbeam. Zhao Puchu(赵扑初), a well-known scholar in Buddhism, wrote the inscription of the hall horizontal board. The hall building falls into the fore-hall and the innermost-hall. All the figure statues in the two halls were made in the Ming Dynasty. The former houses the Three Image Buddhas, while in the latter hall stand the statues of Wenshu, Puxian, Dizang (Kistigarbha) and Guanyin. Several units or departments used the Library Hall for many years, and therefore the hall structure has become quite different from what it used to be. Now the hall doesn't serve as a place to store Buddhist scriptures. Instead there are three figure statues made in recent years. One is Hai Tong who was the initiator for the Giant Buddha carving, the second is Zhangchou Jianqiong who was Jiannan's local top military commander, and the third is Wei Gao who was Jiannan Western Sichuan top military commander.

In front of the monastery grows dense trees by the name of Chinese ŋanmu(楠木). In addition, there are a number of ancient tablets, which record the events related to the monastery restoration in the past dynasties. On the side of the cliff is a pavilion called Jinhe (Pavilion Close to the River). It is said that the pavilion was built in Song Dynasty, and it is an ideal place to view the scenery of the river and the city. Right below the pavilion is an ancient stone path. It zigzags with 173 steps, starting at the foot of the Giant Buddha and linking up Lingyun Cliff Path. You walk to the left outside the Monastery, pass the head of the Giant Buddha and then arrive at another pavilion by the name of Jingxiu Pavilion(竞秀亭, Scenery Beauty Competitive Pavilion), which faces Jinhe Pavilion in a distance. Behind Haishi cavern is a path. Along this path upwards, you are able to hike Xiluan Peak and climb to Su Dongpo Reading Tower Compound.

Lingyun Monastery has been considered as one of the famous monasteries in China ever since ancient times. In addition, it is also one of places of attraction in Sichuan. In the past dynasties celebrities and scholars composed numerous inscriptions, poems and essays to praise the monastery. Censhen (岑参), a well-known poet of the Tang Dynasty, once served as the governor of Jiazhou prefecture. He printed out a collection of his poems by the name of *the Collection of Poems Written by Jiaozhou Governor Cen*(岑嘉州诗集). His collection highly expresses his appreciation of Jiazhou scenery. Today as we read his poems, all the scenery expressed by the poet comes clearly to our eyes as if we had seen them yesterday.

KEY WORDS & EXPRESSIONS 关键词汇及表达法

edict 布告
demolish 拆除
pilgrimage 朝觐
profound 渊博的

initiator 创始者
tablet 碑

Wuyou Hill
乌尤山

Wuyou Hill is located 1. 5 km away from the south of Leshan city, where the three rivers converge (Minjiang, Dadu, and Qingyi rivers) on the eastern bank along Minjiang River. The hill is 434m above sea level, bordered by Minjian River in the West where the bank is cliffy and steep. Wu you Hill faces Lingyun Hill across Mahao River(麻浩河) in the North. Wuyou Hill is also named Leshan Lidui(离堆), which means isolated hill.

Censhen highly praised the hill in his poem, "Qingyi Hill stands towering and majestic; its cliff, vigorous and cragged. The water surrounding the hill expands for seven miles; the long-length waves tightly circle the hill(青衣之山,在大江之中,屹然迥绝,崖壁苍峭,周广七里,长波四匝)." During the Song Dynasty the hill was called Wuniu Hill(乌牛山). Wuniu means "the black cow", because the hill looks like the shape of a black cow lying on the river. A famous poet named Huang Tingjian (黄庭坚) in Northern Dynasty once toured the hill. He thought that Wuniu didn't sound tasteful, and he renamed it to be Wuyou. Wuyou is an alphabetical translation from Sanskrit, which means "Mianran (面然)," one of 12 fine images presented by Guanyin Buddha. Actually hill is dedicated to Guanyin's ritual site where Guanyin is thought to preach Buddhism. The site also includes a statue of "Great Master Miran(乌尤大士)," which has remained on the hill since ancient times.

The cliff on Wuyou Hill, which borders on the river, has

been carved with an inscription "The Pillar Rock in the River(中流砥柱)" in Ming Dynasty. This is one of the hugest carved inscriptions in China for each character is 4m long, and 3m wide. The places of attraction on the hill include Erya Platform(尔雅台) where Guo Sheren(郭舍人) of the Han Dynasty annotated a book named *Eryan*; Wuyou Hill looks like a firm huge pillar in the river with a dense forest of Chinese nanmu tree covering the whole hill and casts green shadows on the river.. Celebrities of the past dynasties, whenever opportunities available, gave unstinted praise to the beauty of the hill. Zhang Chuanshan(张船山) of Qing Dynasty composed a poem by the name of "Wuyou Hill" which says "Layers of green shadow never disperse, and three sides of Wuyou Hill can be viewed from the boat. (绿影一堆漂不去,推船三面看乌尤。)" This writing is rated as the peak of poetic perfection for it sounds like the finishing touch to the beautiful hill.

KEY WORDS & EXPRESSIONS 关键词汇及表达法

alphabetical 照字母次序的

annotate 注解

unstinted 吝惜的

Wuyou Monastery
乌尤寺

The monastery is called by the name of Wuyou Hill, it was originally built in Tang Dynasty, and it was named Zhengjue Monastery(正觉寺). Censhen once toured the hill, and he composed a poem said, "*The monastery is open to the West, and it faces Mt. Emei the in distance. (兰若向西开,峨眉正相当。)*" This saying infers that the monastery had become well known at that time. The buildings in the monastery encountered frequent destructions since Song Dynasty, and the present buildings were reconstructed after the Tongzhi period of Qing Dynasty(清同治年间). Its layout reveals craftiness for the monastery was terraced up in conformity to the physical features of the hill. The Heavenly Kings Hall is set up behind the entrance gate; opposite to it is Maitreya Hall leaning against the cliff. The principal buildings are generally named as Zhengjue Monastery, consisting of Maitreya Hall behind the entrance gate, the main Hall as the Grand Buddha Hall, Guanyin Hall at the left back and the Back Hall as the Buddhist Scripture Library or called Sakyamuni Buddha Hall. The monastery attracts visitors as a place of unique scenery; the compound remains quiet and refined; the buildings stand high and low. All these are well matched and harmoniously scattered on the hill in accordance with its physical features. In 1980, the monastery was designated a protected treasure of the province.

You can reach Wuyou Hill by a bus or vie ferry. Departure from Leshan city, a bus driver takes visitors to the foot of the Giant Buddha Monastery. First of all, you may tour Giant Buddha Monastery, then walk by Mahao Cliff Tomb Museum(麻浩崖墓博物馆), cross Haoshang Bridge(濠上大桥) and finally hike along a quiet and meandering path, which leads to the peak of Wuyou hill. Another option is taking a ferryboat at Leshan dockside. While the boat moves downwards, you are able to view the majestic appearance of the Giant Buddha and Wuyou picturesque scenery before arriving at the foot of Wuyou Hill. As getting off the boat, you can start hiking the hill along a path that contains hundreds of stone steps leading up to the main entrance of the monastery. The entrance gate is located at the side of the hanging cliff with two inscribed boards; one board is lengthwise and the other crosswise. The former says, "Qingyi Unique Island (青衣别岛)" while the latter "Wuyou Monastery". There is a carved couplet, a medley of poetry lines by Su Dongpo of Song Dynasty and Dufu of Tang Dynasty. It hangs at either side of the gate, which says, "*High above, the monastery gate opens on to wild and expansive fields. Half of the vast, stark cliff is shrouded by billions of clouds piled up on each other,(寺门高开洞庭野,苍崖半入云涛堆。)*" Behind the entrance, gate is the Heavenly Kings Hall with a horizontal inscribed board hung at the top of the hall gate. Behind the Heavenly Kings Hall is a niche in which Maitreya leans against the cliff. This image looks extraordinary, with a gold gilded body and its right hand hanging down in the shape of the Good Luck Seal. As you enter the second entrance gate, you will view an ancient cypress that flourishes like a huge canopy. Right below the canopy is the entrance gate to the inner monastery called "Zhengjue Monastery." From the gate, an imaginative north-south axis expands, and along the axis stand Maitreya Hall, the Grand Hall and Sakyamuni Buddha Hall.

As you enter the monastery, you are able to view two stone-laid towers that stand in front of Grand Buddha Hall. One is a bell tower and the other a drum one. They are each 7m in height with octagonal sides, a pointed roof and upturned double eaves. The surface of the two towers is carved with a Buddhist scripture. Since Buddhism was introduced to China, the bell and drum has become regular Buddhist instruments and each instrument has its own historical story. The drum used in monasteries is named

"Buddhist drum" in an attempt to differentiate the traditional Chinese drums. The Buddhist drum is an absolutely necessary instrument in the Buddhist lecture hall where Buddhism is preached and the Buddhist conversion is conducted. Apart from Buddha figures, Buddhist seats and Buddhist screen, the Buddhist bell and drum are absolutely necessary instruments. Usually, the bell is placed on left and the drum on the right. There are two kinds of the drums in the same hall. The one at the northeastern corner is called "Buddhist Drum", and the other at the northwestern "the Cha Drum." A wooden fish shaped percussion instrument is also a necessary Buddhist instrument. It is used to caution people not to be drowsy and inert. Accordingly in monasteries monks usually beat the wooden fish-shaped instrument while chanting assigned Buddhist scriptures.

Based on the monastic system, the bell tower usually stands in the east, and the drum tower in the west. In many cases, they stand at the either side of the entrance hall or between the entrance gate and the Heavenly Kings Hall or between the entrance gate and Grand Buddha Hall. Those two towers are same in appearance. Besides, they face with one another, which indicate one of the features of the Chinese traditional architecture. The drum tower grew out of "Buddhist Text Storage Tower" used to store the whole collection of Buddhist texts. As the amount of the text versions in Chinese translation increased, the storage tower had no enough space to keep them. Accordingly the Buddhist Scripture Library Hall was set up to provide more space for the storage purpose, and the former storage tower therefore turned into the drum tower that is in use from generation to generation up to present time.

Behind the bell and drum towers is Grand Buddha Hall in which Sakyamuni statue stands with his two close attendants: Wenshu and Puxian. Delicately carved out of the camphor wood, the three statue are of exquisite workmanship with vivid expression and lifelike lines and folds of their clothes. Behind is a niche in which stand the statues of Amitabha(阿弥陀佛), Mahasthamaprapta(大势至菩萨) and Guanyin(观音). All of them are made of cast iron. The innermost hall is Sakyamuni Buddha Hall, and it is also called Buddhist Scripture Library Hall, which was rebuilt during the Tongzhi period of the Qing Dynasty. The Buddhist Scripture Library is on the top floor while in the hall downstairs stand "Five Buddha Images", 18 Arhats and wooden carved 24 Heavenly Deities. As for "Five Buddha Images", it is unique to see them in the same hall of Chinese monasteries. At the left back of Sakyamuni Buddha Hall is Guanyin Hall, built in 1918. The hall is devoted to Guanyin Buddha, and people usually come to the hall and pray for male children. Legend has it that it comes true on many occasions.

Before I end my introduction, I'd like to let you know the new discovery of the sleeping Buddha nearby. We will board a tourist ferry to view the Buddha on the boat. As we approach the Buddha, the boat guide will highlight the sleeping Buddha, which was discovered a few years ago. Under the direction of the boat guide you will see that the sleeping Buddha is formed by three mountains (Wuyou, Linyun and Guicheng Mountains). It floats on Qinyi River, with arms and legs proportionally built. The Giant Buddha happens to be the heart of it. The head of the sleeping Buddha is Mt. Wuyou. The stones, bamboos, shades, mountain paths, pavilions and temples appear to be its hair coils, eyelashes, bridge of nose, lips and lower jaw. The body is Mt. Linyun. Nine peaks connect to each other, as if these were the broad chest, perfectly round waist, vigorous and graceful legs. The feet of the sleeping Buddha is a part of Mt. Guicheng. The Sleeping Buddha looks true to life, and is in harmony with the surrounding nature.

KEY WORDS & EXPRESSIONS 关键词汇及表达法

principal 主要的
meandering 曲折的
ferryboat 渡船
picturesque 图画般的
medley 集锦
octagonal 八边形的
lifelike 栩栩如生的
proportionally 相称地
eyelash 睫毛

Mt Emei 峨眉山

Travelers, we are on the way to Mt. Emei after our visit to Giant Buddha in Leshan. It will take 40 minutes to get to the foot of the mountain. While we are on the bus, I'd like to give you some Buddhism information on Mt. Emei and other subjects.

Origin of Puxian's Buddhist Rites on Mt. Emei
普贤道场的由来

Puxian is one of numerous Bodhisattvas (pusa) in Indian Buddhism. When did Buddhism come to Mt. Emei?

It is said that an old man called Pu(蒲)hiked Mt. Emei to

collect medicinal herbs. On the ground he saw a trail of a sika deer's footprints, resembling lotus flowers. Curious, Pu followed the track all the way up to the top of the mountain where the trail of footprints disappeared unexpectedly, and were replaced by shining golden rays in a swirl of purple air around the mountaintop. The myriad rays and colors inter-twined miraculously to form a huge braided ring of light. This phenomenon astounded the old man who later searched out an eminent monk on Mt. Emei and questioned him. This monk was over a thousand years old and had come from the Western Regions. He told the old man that the Fa Image Halo of Bodhisattva Puxian appears for the purpose of protecting Buddha; Puxian revealed himself on Mt. Emei because of his desire to protect all Buddhas and all living creatures. This is the earliest recorded documents about the arrival of Buddhism on Mt. Emei. However, most knowledgeable personages and scholars in religious circles believe that the aforementioned legend of the Song dynasty drew the wrong conclusion. Zhao Kuangyin(赵匡胤), the first emperor of the Song Dynasty believed in Buddhism and Daoism. His courtiers and local officials tried to cater to the emperor's whims by making up numerous reports, saying that more and more people had seen the Buddhist or Daoist Halos. In 960, according to the relevant historical document, officials in Jiazhou prefecture (Jiazhou is the ancient name of Leshan) kept presenting testimonials to the emperor, saying that Puxian had revealed himself. The emperor therefore sent Zhang Zhong(张重), one of his eunuchs to Jiazhou where he had local people engrave Buddhist scriptures and refurbish Buddhist figures. Zhang Zhong also managed to build Dage'an Hall(大阁) in the Puxian Monastery on the current site of Wannian Monastery. It is generally considered that Buddhism might have come to Mt. Emei during the period of the Jin dynasty (265 - 420).

According to *Huayan Scripture*(华严经), the meaning of Puxian infers that his moral conduct is boundless and immeasurable. So his name indicates universal benevolence. In short, Puxian is an abbreviation for all the above meanings, as he works throughout the Buddhist world from his lofty and exalted position. Puxian has many images and transformations, which generally fall into three categories. One is his "Fa Image(法身)", which people often see in monasteries. The second one is his "Bao Image(报身)" revealed in the Buddhist Western Paradise. The last one is "Suilei Image(随类身)", the reincarnation of Puxian, which is able to reincarnate at will into the body of any dead person whose soul has been released from purgatory. He uses the body forms to advise others with his own experience. The seventy-two changes attributed to the Monkey King in *Pilgrim to the West*(西游记) originated from Puxian's third change. It is said that Puxian, with an image deeply loved by the broad masses of people, enters the world on his six-tusk white elephant and appears on Mt. Emei. Therefore, Buddhist followers who piously worship Puxian will certainly visit Mt. Emei to pay Buddhist homage. Puxian ride on his six-tusk white elephant symbolizes the six super-powers displayed by the Buddha, which include the foot super-power, the eye super-power, among others.

During Song Dynasty in 980, the Song emperor offered to Baishui Monastery 3,000 *liang* of gold, which was cast into Puxian statue on the elephant. Consequently the fame of Mt. Emei and Baishui Monastery rapidly increased. The other monasteries followed suit, placing Puxian statues for worship.

Some monasteries even built halls for Puxian. His hall usually stands behind the Grand Buddha Hall because Puxian is considered to be one of Sakyamuni's close assistants. In some monasteries Sakyamuni, Wenshu and Puxian statues are placed in the Grand Buddha Hall for worship. However, there is one exception. In Fuhu Monastery on Mt. Emei Puxian Hall stands behind the Hall of the Heavenly Kings but in front of the Grand Buddha Hall.

KEY WORDS & EXPRESSIONS 关键词汇及表达法

Bodhisattva 菩萨
sika 梅花鹿
trail 踪迹
myriad 无数的
miraculously 神奇地
astound 使震惊
personage 要人
aforementioned 前面提及的
courtier 朝臣
whim 奇想
halo 光环
testimonial 推荐
eunuch 太监
boundless 无限的
benevolence 善心
abbreviation 缩写
transformation 转变
reincarnation 转世
consequently 结果

Literary Notes on the Buddhism History of Mt. Emei

峨眉山佛教历史漫话

Today, it is difficult to trace the origins of the history of Buddhism, and the lack of historical evidence about Mt. Emei is not unique. Dating back to Jin Dynasty and further, the whole Buddhist history is short on authentic written records, at least in Sichuan. However, before Buddhism entered China, Daoism was well established in Sichuan and first sprang up on Mt. Emei towards the end of Eastern Han Dynasty. There is a folk story, which is still popular on Mt. Emei. It recounts that during the Western Jin Dynasty, Qian Ming(乾明), a Daoist priest built Qianming Temple at the base of Zhongfeng Peak(中峰). The temple accommodated more than a hundred Daoist monks. Later, because of a dispute caused by personality clashes, monks were going to split into different circles. As the story goes, an eminent Buddhist monk exposed the witchcraft of a priest who was attempting to deceive people. Ming Guo(明果), an eminent Buddhist monk, came to the temple and held a discourse with the Daoist priests about Buddhism. For his noble-minded moral conduct, MingGuo was honored by most of the Daoist priests who expressed the wish to be converted to Buddhism. They eventually persuaded Ming Guo to take charge of the temple. Ming Guo turned the Daoist temple into Zhongfeng Monastery. What is more extraordinary is that many Daoist temples turned into Buddhist monasteries on Mt. Emei with their original names unchanged. It seems that this collective conversion happened only on Mt. Emei. By reading some names of temples on Mt. Emei, you can gain some insight into the historical origins of these temples with Daoism. Such temples include Chunyang Hall(纯阳殿), Xianfeng Temple, Yuxian Temple (遇仙殿 Meeting-Immortal Temple), Leishen T[illegible]ple (雷神祠 Thunder-Deity Temple) and others.

Hui Chi (惠持) came to Sichuan in 399 based on the information from a book by the name of *The Biography of Eminent Monks* (高僧传) written by Hui Jiao(惠皎) of the Liang state during the Southern Dynasties (420-589). Admired by Mao Qu(毛璩), Yizhou Prefectural Governor, he stayed in Longyuan Monastery(龙渊) in Chengdu to preach Buddhism. Before long, he went to Mt. Emei where he built Puxian Monastery. It is said that this was the first monastery on the mountain, according to the recorded historical documents. The current Wannian Monastery grew out of the earliest temple.

During Northern Dynasty and Southern Dynasty (420-589), Buddhism flourished and monasteries sprang up all across the country. This was mainly because the rulers of the dynasties during this period were practicing Buddhists. Between 502 and 549, some eminent monks came to China from the Western Regions to preach and spread their Buddhism. They also traveled around the interior of the country. At this time there was a legendary monk whose name was Bao Zhang(宝掌). It is said that Bao Zhang lived to be 1,072 years old, and died in 657. Because of his longevity he was given another name, "Thousand-Year-Old Monk." Bao Zhang came to Sichuan during the period of the Liang state (502 - 557). He first resided in the Daci Monastery (大慈寺) in Chengdu and then went up to Mt. Emei, where he built a hut as his residence. His residence area is now called Baozhang Peak (宝掌峰). According to *The Annals of Emei*

County(峨眉县志) written during the Qing Dynasty, Bao Zhang built Lingyan Monastery(灵岩寺). The monastery lasted through the Tang, Song, Yuan and [illegible] nasties, and it finally became the largest monastery in Western Sichuan. It was said that the monastery consisted of 48 halls, extending ten *li* amid dark pine trees. There was a popular saying that the monastery was so extensive that the monks who did not work in the same hall in Lingyan Monastery might not get to know each other, and that visitors had to ride horses to travel from one hall to another for purpose of burning incense. Later, Bao Zhang traveled beyond Lingyan Monastery until he arrived at Baoyan Monastery(宝岩寺) in Zhejiang. During his stay there, Bao Zhang was on good terms with Lang Chan(朗禅), the monastery abbot. While residing in the same monastery they corresponded daily by letter. Whenever their letters were ready, a white dog in the monastery was responsible to deliver letters between the two monks; a blue monkey was responsible to wash bowls whenever the two monks had their vegetarian food together. There is a couplet by the name of *The Two-Hundred-Long Couplet*, which hangs in Hongchun Monastery on Mt. Emei. The literary quotation from the couplet says, "*The white dog fetches letters; the blue monkey washes bowls (白犬衔书,青猿洗钵。).*"

According to *Chanzhenyishi*(禅真逸事 Anecdotes of Eminent Monks) written in the Ming Dynasty, Dan Ran (淡然), an eminent monk, came to Mt. Emei between 534 and 549 A. D.. He built a hut to practice his Buddhism in Zhongfeng Ridge area. Later, he was appointed abbot of Zhongfeng Monastery. Due to his noble-minded moral conduct, many sinful persons who had been reincarnated as pigs, dogs, tigers and other animals, came to Dan Ran and begged him to release their souls from purgatory, which he did. The main hall in Zhongfeng Monastery still stores a wooden screen with a colorful painting on it, displaying a martial-looking monk who holds a sword in his hand and glares at a tiger, a pig and a dog. These animals hide themselves behind the eminent monk. The painting was produced based on the above story.

During the Sui and Tang dynasties, the unified and centralized power of the state was established and then strengthened. The imperial governments supported religions in an attempt to stabilize society and meet the demand for spiritual life. Therefore, Daoism and Buddhism competed with each other for patronage and favor from government. Meanwhile, in order to cater to their followers, the two schools learned from each other's strength, and with each passing day co-existed more harmoniously. During this period, quite a number of folk stories, reflecting the peaceful co-existence between Buddhism and Daoism, were already circulating around Mt. Emei.

According to *the Annals of Mt. Emei* of the Qing Dynasty, during the Kaihuang period of the Sui Dynasty(隋文帝开皇年间 581－604), Master Zhi Kai(智凯), the founder of the Buddhist Tiantai-Sect arrived at Mt. Emei and resided in Zhongfeng Monastery. At the same time Sun Simiao(孙思邈)lived in a stone cavern in Niuxin Monastery, and every day he collected medicinal herbs or made bills of immortality. Daoism respectfully honored Sun Simiao as the Chinese Medicinal Herb King. Sun Simiao and Zhi Kai lived at the foot of different peaks, and every fourth day two persons would hike up their respective mountains, stand on the top and greet each other from a great distance. People in the following generations named the two hills the Echoing Peaks. There was a huge stone in the forest in front of Zhongfeng Monastery. Under the stone was an ever-flowing spring. Those who drank the spring water were cured of their ailments. Therefore monks considered the water from the spring to be supernatural. One day, after Master Zhi Kai had returned to Yuquan Monastery(玉泉寺) in Jiangling, he felt a little ill. He walked out of the monastery and saw a spring of water gushing out. Immediately Zhi Kai thought of the supernatural water on Mt. Emei. It was at this moment that the dragon's daughter, who was in the form of a village girl, suddenly appeared before Zhi Kai and expressed the wish to go and fetch the supernatural water for him. They agreed to meet again in front of Yuquan Cavern the next morning. The next day as scheduled, Zhi Kai arrived at the cavern. There he saw his Buddhist Chan-cane and alms bowl in the cavern stream. The bowl was full of pure spring water, which tasted different from the water of Yuquan stream flowing in the cavern. It is indeed the Emei supernatural spring water, the monk thought. Since then people say that Yuquan stream is connected to the supernatural spring water on Mt. Emei. In 1626, a monk on Mt. Emei engraved an inscription on a stone by the stream, saying, "The Supernatural Water Flows to Chu Regions(神水通楚)". (Chu covers the regions in Hunan and Hubei.) Once, Yang Shengan(杨升庵), a Sichuan's scholar of the Ming Dynasty stopped at the stream as he toured Mt. Emei. He composed a poem called *the Supernatural Water*; his reaction to the stream and the stone. Literally it says

"*This stream flows to Jianaling, so mountain monks say,*

To preach Buddhism, Master Zhikai came, and to pray.

The dragon's fair daughter flew high in the air.
And the water is constant throughout the whole year;
Cool in the summer and in winter quite warm.
No ordinary water can with it compare.
The Creator has reasons for the gifts of creation.
Who fathoms the scope of the Spirit's vast nature?"
(山神言此泉,下与江陵通。智师昔说法,龙女为飞空。夏冽冬复暖,凡水焉可同。造物有此理,灵源谁能通?)

Xuan Zang(玄奘), an eminent monk of the Tang Dynasty became a monk in Chengdu. He once went to Mt. Emei to visit Puxian. According to *The Annals of Mt. Emei*, as he approached to Jiulao Cavern(九老洞 Nine-Immortal Cavern), Xuan Zang came across an old monk who offered him a Buddhist scripture. The old monk spoke the following divine words loudly:

Send your Banruo Boat,
And with kindness guide all sentient creatures.
Puxian, from your boundless good will,
Bestow you infinite mercy on all.
(付汝般若舟,慈悲度一切。普贤行愿深,广利无边众。)

Xuan Zang was immediately enlightened upon hearing these words. The old monk disappeared soon after Xuan Zang offered thanks to him. Puxian put himself into the bodily form of the old monk in legend. People in later generations said that Yuexian Cavern(月仙窟 Moon-Celestial Being Cavern), close to Jiulao Cavern, was the spot where the old monk received the Buddhist scripture.

Daoism had no temples, images or statues when it came into being. At that time Daoist ascetic practitioners usually resided in caverns in remote mountains for their Daoist practices. The names of *the Nine Immortals and the Moon Celestial Being* from the above stories are believed to be closely related to the origin of Daoism.

According to *the Annals of Mt. Emei* of the Qing Dynasty, during the Xizong period of the Tang Dynasty(唐僖宗年间 874 - 888), Hui Tong(惠通), an eminent monk, came to Mt. Emei for a Buddhist visit, and he resided in Puxian Monastery. Later, all the monks recommended that Hui Tong become the monastery abbot. To more widely disseminate Buddhism, Hui Tong had the noble aspiration to re-establish Puxian Monastery. Later, he also had people refurbish and expand other monasteries, including Zhongfeng Monastery, Huayan Monastery, Niuxin Monastery and Huazang Monastery. In addition, he had people build a new place of worship, Qingyin Pavilion. However, in subsequent dynasties, fire disasters frequently ravaged the monasteries on Mt. Emei. The mountain was born in the year of the fire, and therefore, Hui Tong used the Five Element Saying (metal, wood, water, fire and earth) to rename each monastery; Huayan Monastery as Guiyun Pavilion (归云阁 Returning Clouds Pavilion), Zhongfeng Monastery as Jiyun Monastery (集云寺 Gathering Clouds Monastery), Niuxin Monastery as Woyunsi Monastery (卧云寺 Crouching Clouds Monastery), Puxian Monastery as Baishui Monastery (白水寺 White Water Monastery) and Huazang Monastery as Heshui Monastery(黑水寺 Black Water Monastery). Hui Tong intentionally worked out the pattern of "Three Clouds and the Black and White Uncertainty," hoping that the clouds would create water, and then the water would subdue the fires. As a reward for Hui Tong's grand moral conduct, Emperor Xi Zong granted him a Buddhist cassock and music instruments used in a Buddhist mass. After Hui Tong passed away, his body remained intact and did not decay. In addition, it produced a rare scent. His body was laid on the altar in the Zudian Hall of Heshui Monastery for the worship of people from following dynasties. The body even existed during the Ming Dynasty, but later the whereabouts of the body became unknown.

According to *The Annals of Mt. Emei*, there was a nun by the name of Hui Xu(慧续) who was Hui Tong's younger sister. She came to Mt. Emei and resided in Huazang Monastery and was considered the first nun to live on Mt. Emei. Hui Xu had extraordinary powers. It is said that when she resided in Huazang Monastery, a black tiger patrolled the corridor in the evening, and crows announced the break of day in the morning. There was a pool outside the monastery where over a hundred eagles often swam in groups. Whenever monks in the monastery chanted scriptures, frogs in the same pool sang as an accompaniment with the bells and drums played by the monks. The frogs sounded like the music from a zither, full of eight-tone music scale melodies, So the pool was named as the Eight-Tone Scale Pool.

Zhu Yuanzhang(朱元璋), the first Ming emperor used to be a monk when he was young. When he ascended the throne, the emperor continued to be especially fond of Buddhism. Other emperors through out the Ming Dynasty also frequently granted imperial favors to Mt. Emei. These gifts sustained the prosperity of Buddhism on Mt. Emei. It is said that Master Guang Ji and Zhu Yuanzhang used to work together as monks in Huangjue Monastery(皇觉寺). Toward the end of the Yuan, Guang Ji traveled round until he arrived at Longxin Monastery(龙心寺).

When Zhu Yuanzhang became an emperor, Guang Ji secluded himself in Niuxin Monastery on Mt. Emei. On several occasions, the emperor summoned him to the Ming capital, but Guang Ji kindly refused his invitation. Consequently Guang Ji's reputation kept increasing. As his fame increased, he attracted many more pupils. Consequently, Niuxin Monastery attracted more and more visitors and pilgrims.

During the Hongwu period of the Ming Dynasty(明洪武年间), Monk Bao Tan(宝昙)arrived at Mt. Emei by the imperial order. He resided on Xijin Peak(锡金顶 the Tin and Gold Peak) and had the Iron-Tile Monastery reconstructed. He also had the Puxian statue cast in gold. Monk Bao Tan spent 10 years in Sichuan where he perfected Buddhist disciplines. His influence kept increasing. Later, he returned to the capital upon the imperial summons, and then he passed away as he sat crossed-legged in Tianjie Monastery(天界寺).

In 1534 a wandering monk named Bie Zhuan(别传) from Hubei arrived at Shengji Monastery on Mt. Emei. He resided on the mountain for 40 years and greatly contributed to Buddhism on the mountain. Ming Emperor Shenzong(明神宗)gave Bie Zhuan another name, "Hong Ji 洪济" which means "Grand Aid." During his life Bie Zhuan supervised the casting of three bells. The largest one weighs 125,000km and is more than 2m in height. It is the largest bell on Mt. Emei, and is considered to be the second largest in the country. The largest bell is now in Dazhong Monastery(大钟寺)in Beijing. On the day when the Mt. Emei bell was scheduled to be hung, Bie Zhuan suddenly remembered that he had forgotten to cast an iron chain to hang the bell. At that very moment, a golden dragon unexpectedly jumped out of the pool outside the monastery. Bie Zhuan quickly appointed his men to catch the dragon and to pull it through the huge handle attached to the bell. The dragon body was used as the chain to hang the bell.

In 1567, Bie Zhuan built the Golden Dragon Temple in Qingyin Pavilion area and set up a Golden-Dragon Column for worship from the people. In 1579, Bie Zhuan passed away on Mt. Wutai, and was buried in Sihui Pavilion(四会亭) in front of Wannian Monastery. The big bell in Shengji Monastery was well cast, and its sound resonates for many miles around. Commonly known as "Shengji Evening Bell", it is one of the ten traditional Emei Best Attractions. In 1958, when the Grand Iron and Steel Smelting Movement occurred, the bell came within an inch of being destroyed. It was moved away to a foundry. Fortunately, the staff from the Relics Management and Protection Administration recovered the bell in time. At present "Shengji Evening Bell" is placed in Shengji Pavilion on the Phoenix Fortress outside Baoguo Monastery.

In 1568, Master Tong Tian(通天) arrived at Mt. Emei and built a hut on Qianfu Peak(千佛顶 the Thousand Buddha Peak). Later he renovated Dacheng Monastery and built Zushi Hall. In English, Zushi means, "founder of a sect of Buddhism". His reputation spread far and wide. While working as the abbot in the Tianmen Monastery(天门), he toured Guangxiang Monastery(光相寺) one evening. As he walked, Tong Tian saw rays of light radiating from the foot of a cliff. So Tong Tian, using his hands, climbed down to the base of the cliff. When he arrived, he sat and began his meditation, which lasted for three consecutive days. Upon his departure, Tong Tian placed his cassock in the cave at the foot of the cliff. A fortnight later, a peal of thunder roared around the foot of the cliff and Tong Tian's cassock flew back to Tianmen Monastery. This miracle surprised all the monks in the monastery who now considered Tong Tian to be a celestial being. Tong Tian had some pupils who worked as officials in the imperial government. These pupils reported this miracle to Emperor Wanli who then presented Tong Tian with another cassock and *the Longzang Scripture*(龙藏经). The emperor also had his eunuch safeguard the transfer of valuable gold all the way to the monastery and had him build an iron-tile monastery. From that time on, the monasteries on Mt. Emei often received imperial gifts, and more and more monks and laymen attended Buddhist Services by eminent monks. The attendance was often as many as a thousand persons for each service.

In 1599, a fire destroyed Puxian Hall in Baishui Monastery. In the following year the emperor dowager favored the monastery with gold and had the hall rebuilt. A monk by the name of Taiquan(台泉) painted and decorated the new hall's appearance based on Rena Monastery in India. The hall was built with bricks and then named the Beamless Hall because no ridgepoles were used in its construction. This beamless hall is the only one of its kind on Mt. Emei. Its appearance is that of an Indian Buddhist monastery. On the occasion of his mother's 70-year-old birthday, Emperor Shenzong endowed the monastery with his inscription for the monastery's horizontal board. It said, "the Imperial Longevity Wannian Monastery". From then on Baishui Monastery was renamed Wannian Monastery.

In 1601, by order of the emperor, Monk Miao Feng(妙峰) convoyed Dazang Scripture(大藏经) to Mt. Jizu(鸡足山) in

Yunnan. On his way back from Mt. Jizu, Miaofeng came to Mt. Emei for his Buddhist visit where he made a vow to cast Buddha figures to be placed in a copper hall. After he returned to the capital, Miao Feng collected tens of thousands of *liang* of gold from King Jin, and he himself went to Jingzhou(荆州)in Hubei to supervise the casting project. Later the cast figures were transported to the summit of Mt. Emei for worship. These figures stayed on the summit of the towering mountain and shone so gloriously that it became known as the "golden summit" among the people. Later, Miao Feng cast three copper halls in Chang' an, and he delivered Buddha figures to Mt. Wutai, Mt. Jiuhua and other places. When the copper hall for Mt. Emei was completed, Emperor Shenzong granted the hall his inscription for its horizontal board, read " Light Everlasting Huazang Monastery". The emperor dowager donated 41 sets of Buddhist scriptures and one eaglewood tower.

Toward the end of the Ming and the beginning of the Qing dynasties, chaos occurred everywhere in Sichuan because of wars. Many monasteries on Mt. Emei could not escapc the disasters of war and became dilapidated. At the beginning of the Qing Dynasty, a number of eminent monks arrived at different times at Mt. Emei. They started to remold and repair Buddha statues among the brambles and wild grass. Gradually, Buddhism on Mt. Emei returned to its former prosperity.

Duing the Shunzhi period of the Qing Dynasty(清顺治年间), a monk arrived at Mt. Emei for a Buddhist visit. His name was Guan Yi and, he came after a disastrous war and during the year of food shortage. It was a poverty-stricken situation in which monks in monasteries had not enough food to eat and not enough clothes to wear. Guan Yi generously supported them. In addition, everywhere he went, he collected alms to provide the monks with food. More than that, Guan Yi led his pupils to reconstruct Fuhu Monastery. It was 20 years before it was completed with its 13 key halls. Fuhu Monastery therefore became the largest monastery on Mt. Emei. Over the years, Ke Wen(可闻), Guan Yi's pupil, reconstructed Woyun Nunnery, the Boundless Hall and the Cool Breeze Bridge. In addition, Ke Wen moved and then reconstructed the Huizong Hall(汇宗堂), which grew into the current Baoguo Monastery. Monk Sun Ji(孙寂), a discipleof Guan Yin planted altogether as many as 100,000 trees around Fuhu Monastery. Each time he planted one tree, he chanted out loud one character of the Mahayana Scripture. Ten years later, those trees grew into the towering, thick forest, which is now known as "Bujing Forest." Bujing means that here is the Buddhist world, and its land is covered with gold.

Today, there are over 30 temples at the mountain, and the total building space is over 100,000 square meters. Many temples were built against hillside or hidden in a dark forest. Both Baoguo and Fuhu monasteries now are the largest ones on the mountain.

Here is a poem, written by May Holdsworth from Odyssey Illustrated Guide to Sichuan:

Emei Shan is more than a mountain;

It is a frame of mind.

That is not just because looking up at monumental heights

Induces in the beholder a sense of his own frailty and insignificance.

It is also because for centuries Chinese belief has endowed Nature

With a mystical influence on man's character,
And Nature is supremely exemplified by mountains.
Mixed up with this tradition was the ancient folk belief
That mountains were the magical habitations of immortals.
Although Daoist in origin, these ideas have been gathered
Into the Chinese Buddhist's view of the universe
Like much else of the indigenous cult.

KEY WORDS & EXPRESSIONS 关键词汇及表达法

authentic 可信的
recount 重新计算
eminent 出众的
discourse 交谈
convert 皈依
conversion 转变
biography 传记
annal 记录
corroborate 确证
harmoniously 和谐地
Creator 造物主
infinite 无边的
ascetic 苦行者
practitioner 实践者
aspiration 志向
refurbish 刷新
subsequent 后来的
cassock 法衣,袈裟
seclude 使隐退
resonate 起回声
renovate 修理

beamless 无梁的
horizontal 横的
everlasting 不朽的
dilapidated 快要倒塌的
nunnery 尼姑庵
beholder 观看者
frailty 脆弱
insignificance 无足轻重
habitation 居住
indigenous 本地的
cult 膜拜
zithe 筝

Main Scenic Sections
重点景区

Mt. Emei is characterized by its unique geological relief, biological soil and climate. The ecological environment nurtures numerous kinds of plant and animal species. The mountain is known as Kingdom of Plants and Paradise of Animals. The forest coverage on Mt. Emei is 87%. Five vegetation belts are defined according to vertical zones. 1,500m below it, is a subtropical evergreen broad-leaved forest; 2,800m above it is an evergreen and deciduous broad-leaved mixed forest, a coniferous and broad-leaved mixed forest, a sub alpine coniferous forest and sub alpine shrubs. There are 3,200 verified species on Mt. Emei, which is one tenth of our nation.

Mt. Emei is inhabited by over 2,300 species of animals, of which 29 species are listed under the state protection. The animal species comprises 51 mammals, 256 birds, 34 reptiles, 33 amphibians, 60 fishes, 42 oligochaetes and over 1,000 insect species. Above all, Mt. Emei is famous for its miraculous power and wondrous beauty.

The mountain is shrouded in an ever-hanging cloud of fog. Fir trees, pines and cedars clothe the slopes; lofty crags, cloud-kissing precipices, butterflies and azaleas together form a nature reserve of sorts. As travelers hike the mountain, passing the main monasteries and temples, they usually come across a diversity of landscape, which includes the Buddhist Temples in Clouds, the Seas of Azaleas, Chinese Orchids at Stalagmite Valley, and a beautiful view at the Golden Summit. The peaks or ridges rise one higher than another; the footpaths snake through and are difficult to follow. In spring, the forests look green; in summer, the azaleas are in full bloom; in autumn, colorful leaves cover the mountain; in winter, snow covers the mountain like a silvery world.

Tourists usually start their ascent of the mountain at Baoguo Monastery(报国寺). There are two paths to Jinding (Golden Summit). The northern path (44km) is wide and easy to follow. The southern path (63.5km) is more rugged and winding. Because it is easier to go up than to come down, most people ascend by the southern rout and return on the northern one. Usually, they take 3 days up and 2 days downhill. Of course, many others do it even more quickly. They take the cable cars and mini-bus that could make the ancient site accessible to masses of tourists.

The hiking is spectacular and tiring. No matter whether you ascend or descend, you have to keep a cautious eye on the next step. You should stop occasionally to get a longer view and enjoy the beautiful scenes. The scene is also a place for rest and slowing down the pounding hearts . Whenever you come across a lovely waterfall and spectacular gorge, you should sit down, and become content with the stately beauty and blessings of that spot.

There is a popular saying: "No place under the heaven is as beautiful as Mt. Emei." I will introduce the four main scenic spots in the mountain.

Baoguo Monastery(报国寺)

Baoguo Monastery was built in 1615, located below the Phoenix Terrace(凤凰坪). The founder was a Daoist priest called Ming Guang(明光道人) who vowed to build a monastery that would contain the figures of Confucians, Buddhism and Daoism. His purpose was to collect sufficient donations for the construction of monasteries.

One day, while walking along a road, Ming Guang came across Xu Liangyan(徐良彦), a top Sichuan official in charge of the army, government and criminal affairs. Xu made a substantial donation, and even made Emei county governor supervise the monastery construction. The monastery was completed next year, and memorial tablets were placed in the hall for worship. These included Bodhisattva Puxian(普贤), Daoist Guang Chengzi (广成子)and Confucian scholar Lu Tong(陆通). The name of the monastery was Hui Zong Hall(会宗堂), with Hui Zong Memorial Archway set up in front the monastery.

Later Ming Guang converted to Buddhism. During his lifetime he wrote and annotated over 200 scriptures. In 1702 Qing Emperor Kang Xi(康熙)gave the monastery a new name "Baoguo Monastery", Bao guo means "dedicating oneself to the service of one's country". During the Anti-Japanese War (1937 - 1945)

Feng Yuxiang（冯玉祥），a well-known general wrote on a horizontal board an inscription beside the name of the Gateway to Mt. Emei. Below the Bell Tower in the monastery is a tablet dedicated to Honored Shang who obtained the title of Ganlin Minister（甘陵相）in the Han dynasty. This tablet is regarded as a rare piece of exquisite workmanship among the tablets of the Han dynasty. The original tablet is no longer in existence，but the present tablet has been engraved in accordance with the rubbing from the inscription. However，it still remains as a unique example of tablet engraving in the country.

The Ancestor's Hall is on the left and Buddhist Doctrine Hall on the right of the Great Buddha Hall. Wing rooms include rooms facing west or north and Wuguan Hall（五观堂）. Zhiyuan Hall（祇园）is on the left at the back of the Great Buddha Hall，which is the largest Buddhist Lecture Room among the monasteries，covering a floor space of about 1,000 square meters. Behind the great Buddha Hall stands the Seven Buddhas' Hall，containing seven Buddhas. Buddhist doctrines say that Sakyamuni had six Buddhist images before he entered Nirvana. The Buddhist figures have been molded based on the traditional "sand deprivation（脱沙）" technique. Craftsmen intertwined the sand mold patterns with ramie and other lightweight materials. Then，after the figure designs had been finished，they removed the sand，and the hollowed figures remained，light and durable. Even though each gilded figure is six zhang（丈）in length（a unit of zhang is 3 1/4 m），one is able，by hand，to raise each figure above the head. Inside the hall，there is a set of eight carved wooden scrolls hanging on the wall，which has been considered as a treasure of the monastery.

On the Phoenix Fortress(凤凰堡), outside the monastery is "Shengji Evening Bell(圣积晚钟)" Pavilion, there is a bronze bell in it. The bell is regarded as the King of Bells in the Sichuan area. It is called the Eight Diagrams Bronze Bell. Originally, it was located in Shengji Monastery, 2. 5km south of Emei county center. Shengji Monastery was also regarded as the largest monastery at the entrance to the mountain. The bell ringing ritual occurred 24 times in the lunar Chinese calendar year, taking place on the first and the fifteenth evening of each lunar month. In the evening, after 9 o'clock, the monks walked up to the tower with their lanterns, and then chanted Buddhist scriptures commonly called "the Bell Sentences". Each sentence consists of four Chinese characters. At the beginning of the scripture chanting the monks rang the bell once for each four-character sentence. This was called the slow ringing. Then the bells were rung for each sentence consisting of only one Chinese character. Then the bell ringing accelerated even more as the monks chanted each one-character sentence faster and faster. This was called the quick ringing. The slow and quick ringing were each repeated three times, to a total ringing of 108 times. Each bell ringing series lasted one minute and 50 seconds. Its sound was loud and deafening nearby, but clear and melodious at a greater distance. The sound of the bell traveled even up to the Golden Summit in the late and quiet evenings. In 1958, the Shengji Monastery was destroyed, and the bell was moved to the current pavilion outside the Baoguo Monastery.

Fuhu Monastery(伏虎寺)

Located below Fuhu Mountain, the monastery had become well known even in the Tang Dynasty. During the Ming Dynasty its name was Hu Xi Chan Ling(虎溪禅林), which means the Tiger Stream and Buddhist Forest. Towards the end of the Ming, the monastery was destroyed by the disasters of a war. In 1651 Guan Zhi(贯之), a Buddhist monk, reconstructed the monastery on the same site. It took 20 years to complete, and it remains as the largest monastery in the mountain, but called by another name, Hu Xi Jing She(虎溪精舍). Literally, it means "the Tiger Stream and House of Essence". Fuhu Monastery stands about 1km to the right of the Phoenix Pavilion outside the Baoguo Monastery. On the way one passes a wooden signboard tower built in Qing Dynasty and called "Fuhu Monastery". You may cross three bridges before entering Bu Jing Forest(布金林)

In the mid 16 century, one of Guanyi's disciples by the name of Sun Ji(孙寂). You must cross three bridges before entering Bu Jing Forest(布金林) had the grand aspiration of chanting the entire Mahayana Scripture. He made it a practice to plant one tree for each character of scripture sung. Consequently, he planted as many as 195, 048 *nan mu*(楠木) and pine trees around the monastery. By the good care of other monks, they all grew into the surrounding forest. There is a memorial archway in the forest, with a horizontal inscription board, reading "Bujing Forest". Based on Buddhist documents, Bujing means that this is Buddhist soil and its land is golden.

Behind the entrance gate stand the Heavenly Kings' Hall, Puxian Hall, and then the Great Buddha Hall. The Grand Buddha Hall is commonly called Nanmu Hall. It is made of nanmu trees and covers a construction space of about 1, 000 square meters. The hall is regarded as the largest on the mountain. All the buildings of the monastery are integrated and intertwined with the live trees of the forest, but it is incredible that fallen branches and withered leaves disintegrate and never remain on the roofs of the buildings the year round. Upon hearing of this, Qing Emperor Kangxi gasped in admiration at the wonder of it. He wrote an inscription, Li Gou Yuan(离垢园), which means literally, "No-dust Yard". Today, the inscribed board still hangs on the entrance of Puxian Hall. In the Grand Buddha Hall, Sakyamuni's three Buddhist images are worshiped. To the left of the hall are Arhats Hall and Huayan Copper Pagoda. The latter was set up here in 1982. The pagoda was cast in copper in 1342 and was originally set up in Shengji Monastery. The pagoda is 5.8m high and has 7 sides and 14 stories. Its surface is covered with Huayan Scripture (华严经) and 4,700 Buddhist figure images. Flowing down to the pavilion is Huquan Stream(虎泉). Beside the stream grow spinulose tree ferns, which are a living fossils dating back to even before the prehistoric age, during the dinosaur period.

Outside the entrance gate of Fuhu Monastery is Shanjue Monastery(善觉寺), which was built in 1571. In 1702, Yuan Xiang(元享), a monk from Shanjue Monastery received an imperial order, and he went to the imperial court to preach Buddhism. Qing Emperor Kangxi, bestowed an inscription on the monastery, which reads, "Dragon-House Shanjue Monastery." Close to the monastery is the Phoenix Terrace, the ruins of Daoist culture. It is said that on this terrace Xuan Yuan Emperor (轩辕帝)learned Daoism from an immortal. There once were 305 rooms on the terrace, including the Daoism Instruction Platform, Daoist Discipline Hall, and many secluded rooms.

Leaving Fuhu Monastery, you can pass over Yushu(御书)

and Jietuo(解脱) Bridges, and then climbs up the Jietuo Slope before arriving at Leiyin Monastery(雷音寺). In the monastery, Guanyin Hall is dedicated to the Thousand-Hand-and-Eye Guanyin (Avalokitesvara Bodhisattva). On the entire mountain this is the one and only wooden Buddha figure statue in existence, exquisitely engraved on poplar. Countless visitors stream to this site to worship, because it is said that this wooden statue of Guanyin will respond to every plea. From Leiyin Monastery one hikes up to Huayan Monastery(华严寺), one of the six largest monasteries in the mountain.

Half a kilometer to the right of Fuhu Monastery is Luofeng Peak Nunnery(萝峰庵). Behind it is the pagoda forest where a number of eminent monks were buried. The top of Luofeng Peak is flat, like the floor of a stage, where aged pines have twisted roots and gnarled branches and white cranes fly about among trees. Down below the peak is a deep and quiet valley, blanketed by dark nan mu trees. From the top of Luofeng Peak is an ideal site to view Emei plains. It also offers Sunny Clouds over the Peak, perennially one of Emei Best attractions.

Zhongfeng Monastery(中峰寺)

Zhongzheng Monastery has an old name, Qianming Temple (乾明观). Qian Ming, a Daoist abbot, built the temple in 4th century. Between 420 - 534 A. D., according to the relevant historical documents, a Buddhist monk by the name of Ming Guo (明果) stayed under the foot of Baozhang Peak(宝掌峰) of Mt. Emei. Every March 3 of the Chinese Lunar Calendar, Monk Ming Guo saw Qian Ming practice witchcraft to deceive people by spreading the story in which Qu Wu (瞿武) of the Eastern Han dynasty ascends to Heaven as an immortal. Monk Ming Guo knew that it was the mischief done by the evildoer. So he gathered some local people to subdue the witchcraft with arrows and bows. Everyone agreed to obey Ming Guo because of his persuasive power. Even Daoist priests in Qianming Temple were all converted to Buddhism, and Daoist temple became a Buddhist Monastery named Zhongfeng Monastery, which means "Central Peak".

The monastery gradually became one of the six largest ancient monasteries on the mountain. During the Tang and Song dynasties many eminent monks and celebrities gathered in Zhongfeng Monastery, which was magnificent in scale and layout. White peonies grew around the monastery, and the whole peak was crowned with flowers, plants and gardens. The present monastery retains a horizontal board inscribed Zhongfeng Ancient Monastery. It is said that it is a relic of the Song dynasty. A huge stone remains in front of the monastery. In legend, this was the site where Lu Tong(陆通), a well-known scholar of the Chu state, built his house for his studies and for farming during the Spring and Autumn Periods. Huang Tingjian(黄庭坚)of the Song named the stone as Gefeng Platform (歌风台, Singing Phoenix Platform). Behind the monastery is a strange stone, yellow in color, commonly called Realgar Stone(雄黄石). In legend, Sun Simiao(孙思邈) used to stay here making bills of immortality. It is said that Li Longji(李隆基), one of Tang emperors took refuge in Sichuan from a war disaster area. One evening the emperor dreamt that Sun Simiao was staying at the foot of Mt. Emei, and Sun asked the emperor to offer him the realgar bills of immortality. The emperor had someone send the bills up to the mountain where clouds and mist filled the air, and the there was no sign of Sun Simiao but written words of gratitude for the emperor left on Realgar Stone.

Qingyin Pavilion(清音阁)

Qingyin Pavilion is considered as an extraordinary monastery on the mountain. It falls into the foreyard and the backyard. The two yards are separated by 2.5km in distance. The foreyard is called Qingyin Pavilion, and the back yard Yanfu Temple(延福寺). Because Niuxin (牛心, Or-heart) Ridge separates the two yards, they are commonly called the Fore and Back Niuxin Temples. During the Tang Dynasty the Fore Niuxin Temple was also called Woyun temple(卧云寺). At the beginning of Ming Dynasty Monk Guang Ji(广济) re-built the temple, which was then renamed Qingyin Pavilion. The name of Qingyin, which means "pure sound" in English, was originally drawn from a line in *Zhaoyin*(招隐), composed by Zuosi(左思) of the Jin Dynasty. The line says, "No need to play stringed instruments or bamboo flutes; nature herself creates pure sound(何必丝与竹,山水有清音。)."

The pavilion's layout looks extraordinary. The mountain is the backdrop to the pavilion and streams flow nearby; the buildings are terraced up from the low to the high ground and all are artistically spaced. At the lowest level is Xixin Terrace(洗心台) by Baoxian Stream(宝现溪). On each side of the terrace is a bridge, and on the terrace stands a small pavilion called the Glass and Water Pavilion (Niuxin Pavilion) where the Black and White Dragons' Streams merge. A couplet hangs on the pavilion, written by Liu Guangdi(刘光弟). Liu Guangdi was a well-known scholar of Qing Dynasty and also one of the six noble men involved in the Reform Movement of 1898. A black basalt boulder, rising like a huge column, dominates the middle of the stream. The turbulent waters rushing against the stone play it like an instrument and create pure sound. The bridges on the either side of the pavilion are traditionally called Sanhuang Bridges(三皇桥). Legend says that here Xuanyuan Emperor met an immortal called Sanhuang. During the Song dynasty a great poet and monk by the name of Wei Zheng(为政) from the Jingtu Monastery in Hangzhou arrived here. He produced his fast running calligraphy, which said "Double Flying Dragons Bridge". An example of his calligraphy can still be seen on the stone near the bridge. Behind the pavilion is a hundred-step stairway leading to Back-Niuxin Yard, which is now named Guangfu Temple. There is a sacred 1. 8m-tall Buddha statue and a jade Buddha from Burma, presented by monks from Jizushan area (鸡足山) in Yunnan. Starting from the temple, you have to climb 2. 5km upward before arriving at Yanfu Temple. Behind the temple is Yaowang Cavern(药王洞) in which Sun Simiao is said to have stayed making bills of immortality.

Qingyin Pavilion and the Dragon-Gate Cavern are traditionally considered as the two wonders along the stream scenery. A poem written by Tan Zhongyue (潭钟岳) of the Qing Dynasty says, "*The main pavilion produces pure sound; like an immortal descending, playing the zither. I stand on the double bridge straining to hear; the sound, the Ox-heart boulder being washed by the two streams (杰然高阁出清音,仿佛神仙下抚琴。试立双桥一侧耳,分明两水漱牛心。).*"

Hongchun Monastery(洪椿坪)

Leaving Qingyin Pavilion, you pass the Black-Dragon Plank Road along the Face of the Cliff and then walk through a deep cliff where the sky is seen as only a thin piece of thread. Afterwards, you have to cross three bridges, climb a thousand steps and then arrive at a memorial archway. Finally, you get to the Thousand-Buddha Image Monastery in Hongchun Terrace. The terrace is named after the three age-old Chinese toon trees outside the monastery. The origin of the monastery can be traced back to the eighth century. It is said that there was no spring water in the monastery at that time. The water shortage lasted until the Ming dynasty when Monk De Xing(德心)dug for spring water using his tin can, and the water gushed out instantly in front of Guanyin Hall in the monastery.

The monastery is nestled among green hills, and surrounded by tall, age-old, well-spaced trees. The area remains evergreen like spring all year round. Emperor Kangxi offered an inscription called Wang Chen Lu (忘尘虑, Carefree from Mortality and Worry), which remains as an engraved calligraphy on the stone inside. A horizontal inscribed board hangs on the top of the monastery entrance gate. The inscription was provided by Lin Sen (林森), one of the late Chairmen of the Kuomintang government. To the left side of Guanyin Hall there is Lin Sen's Small Garden where Lin Sen stayed temporarily during the Anti-Japanese War. In June 1938, it was in this garden where the ambassador of the former Soviet Union presented to Lin Sen the letter of credence. In July, Lin Sen gathered 32 eminent monks in the garden to hold a seven-day Buddhist Ullambana Festival(盂兰盆会) to release from purgatory the souls of generals and soldiers killed in the battles, as well as the masses of slaughtered civilians.

In Guanyin Hall there is a Buddha Tower with Wenshu, Puxian and Guanyin figures statues placed inside for worship.

Right in front of the three figures hangs a seven-sided lotus lantern, 2.25m in height. In addition, the lantern has 231 exquisitely carved Buddha figures and lively carved dragons and other spiritual beasts lying among the lantern sides. The lantern displays a series of folk and Daoist stories related to supernatural beings. These legends and artifacts show how the diverse cultural features of Chinese Buddhism and Buddhism on Mt. Emei have merged and become intertwined over centuries of development.

Outside the monastery there is a Chinese toon, 28m in height; its central section is 3.14m in diameter and the tree crown is 19m in diameter. Its branches and leaves flourish so splendidly that the tree provides a perennial, vast, green canopy. It is said that the tree is more than a thousand years old. Hongchun terrace is well known for its solitude and beauty. The phenomena of "Morning Raining" can be experienced most frequently in early spring and summer mornings, shortly after a rain shower. It appears to be raining but it isn't; it looks like fog but it isn't. The sound of the wind in the trees and of birds chirping cheerily can be heard, but nothing is visible. An intangible mist masks scenery and sight. The essence is there without substance. As Wang Wei(王维)said in his poem *A Trip to the Mountain*(山行), "*No rain at all, along the mountain path; but misty leaves moisten my clothes (山路元无雨,空翠湿人衣).*"

Leaving Hongchun Monastery, one continues walking 15km upwards before arriving at Xianfeng Monastery (仙峰寺). Opposite to Xianfeng Monastery is Daping(大坪) where Jingtu Monastery, one of the six largest monasteries on the mountain, is located.

Xianfeng Monastery(仙峰寺)

Walking out of Hongchun Monastery, one crosses a bridge and climbs along the Path of 99 Bends. Soon after one passes Lingxiao Pavilion(凌霄亭), he arrives at Xianfeng Monastery.

The monastery was built originally in 1281. In the following dynasties it was destroyed by fire disasters and rebuilt many times. The current main buildings date back to the Qing Dynasty, and they include Xianhuang Stage, Maitreya Hall, the Great Buddha Hall, Sarira Pagoda and beautiful mountain villas. All the buildings are now roofed with tin tiles for the purpose of fire protection. As one views the roofline of the monastery, the tin tiles glowing among luxuriously green trees look much like silvery or white jade. Therefore, the monastery is described as "Elongated Jade Tablet Among the Dark Green Sea".

Sarira Pagoda, the third key hall, is also called Pali Hall(贝叶殿). In the hall there is a gold gilded copper Sarira pagoda with seven-story, which stores three Sarira pearls and two volumes of Pali sutra. They are all regarded as the treasures guarding the monastery. The pearls were brought into China from Sri Lanka by Monk Qing Fu(清福) and stored in Shanghai Longhua Monastery(龙华寺) during the period of the Republic of China (1921－1949). In the monastery guest hall hangs the paintings produced by Japanese monks in 1863. The brush strokes of these paintings possess a natural grace and elegance. One of the paintings is named *the Nine Immortal Drawing*(九老图), and the other *A Bell Among Innumerable Valleys*(万壑一钟图). To the left of the monastery is the Nine-Lotus Pool, one of the famous pools in the mountain. Several miles further beyond the pool is the Nine-immortal Cavern. Legend has it that the cavern used to be a place where some Daoist immortals secluded. Behind the Xianfeng Monastery is an age-old tree, whose height is 26m and central section 5. 1m in diameter. The tree is at least 500 years old. The stone pavilion in front of the monastery is Xianhuang Stage. This is the place where Xuanyuan emperor, while traveling, encountered Immortal Tianhuang(天皇真人)in legend. Several miles beyond the pavilion is Xiangui Stone(仙圭石). Around the stone are dove trees, covering a space of hundreds of mu. In April and May of each year, the countless flowers in full bloom look breath-takingly magnificent. These blossoms, bursting with light, seem to dye the undulating forest with splashes of white, as if numberless pigeons were hovering in flocks.

Walking out of the monastery, one passes a bridge, climbs Changshou Slope(长寿坡)and steps into Yuxian Monastery(遇仙寺). Yuxian means "coming across an immortal". In Yuxian Monastery there was a well-known celebrity of the Han Dynasty whose name was Douyi(窦谊)once came across an immortal that rode a dragon flying up into the sky. Behind the monastery stand two upright stones; and the mountain path goes through the monastery, leading to an exceptionally unique cavern. Miraculously, fresh vegetables and fruits do not rot, even when stored for a long time in the cavern. Even dry or decayed vegetables and fruits turn green after one day of storage inside. Outside the monastery there is a platform where one is able to view the surrounding scenery and have fun with wild monkeys.

There are four Emei monkey communities, large or small, along the route between Qingyin Pavilion and Hongchun Monastery. Monkeys usually stand along the path, begging tourists for food. One of the main attractions on Mt. Emei is to have fun with monkeys as one tours the mountain. In Xixiang Pool section there are other groups of monkeys who are on intimate terms with human beings. Monkeys often enter houses where they sit down with human beings, eating or drinking together. Their behavior seems refined and polite.

Huazang Monastery(华藏寺)

The full name of the Monastery is the Light Everlasting Huazang Monastery(永明华藏寺). In legend, it is said that Pugong(蒲公)of the Eastern Han Dynasty originally built it as Puguang Hall(普光殿) or the Zudian Hall(祖殿). Between the Tang and Song dynasties both Puguang and Guangxiang halls had a shared name called Guangxiang Monastery (光相寺), which was considered as one of the six largest monasteries on Mt. Emei. At the beginning of Ming Dynasty, Bao Tan(宝昙), the national Buddhist master refurbished the hall, and its roof was covered with iron tiles. It became known as the Iron-tile Hall. During Wanli period of Ming Dynasty(明万历间)a copper hall was constructed behind the Iron-tile Hall. The copper hall had a double-eaves roof, an engraved ridge, and delicately latticed tiny windows. Inside the hall sat Puxian in the center, surrounded by thousands of other Buddha figures. Right outside each corner of the hall was a copper pagoda, alloyed all with gold. Therefore, the pagodas shone so gloriously on the top of the mountain that the name of "golden summit" had circulated among the people. Zhu Yijun(朱翊钧), one of the Ming emperors (1573 - 1620) named the hall as the Light Everlasting Huazang Monastery. In 1854, Puxian on the elephant statue was placed in the hall for worship. It was copper cast and presented by Dalai Lama from

Tibet. However, disastrous fires destroyed Huazang Monastery several times. Reconstruction of the current monastery began in 1986. In 1990, it was completed and opened to the public.

Standing side by side with Huazang Monastery, Woyun Nunnery(卧云庵) was built during the Jiajing period of Ming Dynasty(嘉靖, 1522－1560) and is located on the Viewing Terrace at 3,054m above sea level. It is also called "the Silvery Summit" because of the tin-tiled roof of the nunnery. In the Jade Buddha Hall of the nunnery there is a jade Buddha statue, presented by a Buddhist visiting delegation from Burma. Behind the nunnery is a small viewing platform. The first and final appearances of the Buddhist Halo are seen here, on this platform. Therefore, the platform is considered as the ideal place from which to view the scenery. In addition, there is a spring well to the east of the nunnery. The well is able to supply over a thousand people with water.

The Cliff of Self-Sacrifice, the Viewing Terrace and others are the ideal places on the Golden summit from which to view the four wonders: the Sunrise, the Buddhist Halo, the Sacred Lamp and the Sea Clouds. You are able to see the sun rise over the summit in every year about 200 days. Most sunrise days occur in summer and autumn. The Buddhist Halo is bestowed with the most legendary flavor, compared with the other three wonders. The circle of Buddhism believes that the Buddhist Halo is "Baihao Image(白毫相)", one of the 32 images that the Buddha has. You can view the halo in any season, but it occurs on about 80 days throughout the year. The Sacred Lamp is also called the Buddhist Lamp. Generally, it is called the "Innumerable Bright Lamps Toward Puxian". There are four natural conditions that enable the Sacred Lamp to appear. It happens at midnight after the rain has just stopped; when there is no moon in the sky; when there are no clouds below the peaks; and when there is no breeze on the mountaintop. Compared with the halo, it is even less probable to view the Sacred Lamp. The Sea of Clouds is most likely to appear in summer and autumn on Mt. Emei. As it appears, clouds often remain around the mid-mountain area. The peaks, being higher than the clouds, appear to gallop over the sea of clouds. Buddhists describe the phenomenon as "the graceful guidance of all sentient beings."

Wannian Monastery(万年寺)

From Baoguo Monastery the path leads to the right, up to Wuxian Ridge(五显岗). Then the hike goes upwards along Baoxian Stream(宝现溪), climbs the Sunny Slope, passes the White-dragon Temple and ascends the Elephant-tusk Slope. Eventually, you can enter the Da'e Tower(大峨楼) and then arrive at Wannian Monastery. The building of the monastery was begun in 400, sponsored by Huichi(惠持), an eminent monk of the Eastern Jin Dynasty. The monastery was named "Puxian Monastery in honor of Puxian Buddha statue placed inside for worship. The monastery was reconstructed during the Tang Dynasty. It was renamed as White-water Monastery mainly because the surrounding mountains looked like they were on fire, and it was hoped that the white water might protect the monastery from any fire disaster. During the Song Dynasty the monastery had further reconstruction. The Song imperial court offered 3,000 liang (One liang equals 50 grams.) of gold, to the monastery, which gold was cast into Puxian statue riding on the elephant. It was again renamed the White-water Puxian Monastery.

During Wanli period of the Ming Dynasty a fire destroyed the monastery. The emperor had people reconstruct the monastery and renamed it as Shengshou Wannian Monastery(圣寿万年寺). Shengshou means "imperial longevity", and Wannian "10,000 Years". This accounts for the origin of the current name of the monastery. At present, the monastery has seven halls and is considered as one of the six largest monasteries on Mt. Emei. Since 1952, much repair work has taken place. To the left of Maitreya Hall in the monastery is Zhiyuan Garden(致园). In this garden Li Bai and Monk Guang Jun(广浚)played a zither while composing poems in legend. Behind the hall is a beamless brick hall. To the left of the hall is the Xingyuan Tower(行愿楼)in which three treasures are stored. The first is a Buddhist scripture, presented to the royal family from Burma; the second is Kasyapa's teeth Sarira, taken back from Sri Lanka; the third is the Seal of Wish King Puxian, presented by the emperor of the Ming Dynasty. The last hall is the Grand Buddha Hall. Huang Yunhu (黄云鹄), a well-known Sichuan calligraphist, wrote an inscription for its entrance horizontal board. His strokes are vigorous and elegant. Most entrance board inscriptions to Grand Buddha Halls in monasteries across Sichuan area come from the rubbings on this inscription. In the center of the hall is the "Three-image" Copper Buddha Statue, 5.35m in height. Cast in 1534, the figure has a body of gold and is 6 zhang in height. Close to the monastery is Shengci Nunnery(圣慈庵). At the beginning, it offered sacrifices to Shengci Empress Dowager of an emperor of the Ming Dynasty; later, it was named after the title of the dowager.

The way uphill from the monastery, leads to the Heart-resting Home; the way downhill leads to the White-dragon Cavern. Master Ming Guo of Jin Dynasty who subdued the dragon was in the cavern. Guanyin Figure also stands in the cavern, which was cast during the Jiading period of the Southern Song Dynasty(宋嘉定年间). In the same cavern there is a jade Buddha figure presented by the monks from the Zuoshan Monastery(坐禅寺)in Burma. Leaving the White-dragon Cavern, one enters Yusun Forest(玉笋峰林)where you can view a spectacular geologic phenomenon - a stalactite forest. This is the only place on the mountain from which you can get a full view of the stalactite growing high and low; green and luxurious like innumerous trees towering up to the sky. In addition, mountain orchids grow primarily in Yusun Forest, which also provides the most of valuable and unique orchids.

Well, so much for my talk. The bus is approaching to the foot of the mountain. I know that you are looking forward to the tour of Mt. Emei. It will be spectacular and joyful.

KEY WORDS & EXPRESSIONS 关键词汇及表达法

nurture 养育
subtropical 亚热带的
evergreen 常青的
deciduous 每年落叶的,非永久性的
coniferous 结球果的
alpine 高山的
shrub 灌木
reptile 爬行动物
amphibian 两栖动物
oligochaete 贫毛类蠕虫
miraculous 神奇的

wondrous 令人惊奇的
crag 险崖
precipice 绝壁
azaleas 杜鹃花
orchid 兰花
stalagmite 石笋
rugged 高低不平的
cautious 谨慎的
occasionally 偶尔
phoenix 凤凰
terrace 台地
sufficient 足够的
donation 捐献
workmanship 手艺
rubbing 拓印
deprivation 脱沙
intertwine 纠缠
diagram 示图
melodious 旋律优美的
integrate 使成一体
incredible 难以置信的
spinulose 多小刺的
gnarled 多节的
perennially 永驻地
mischief 伤害
realgar stone 雄黄石
artistically 艺术地
basalt 玄武岩
boulder 大圆石

turbulent 汹涌的
immortality 不朽
archway 拱道
shortage 缺少
gush 使直流
nestle 安卧
Ullambana Festival 盂兰盆会
purgatory 涤罪
canopy 顶篷
chirp （小鸟）发啁啾声
sarira pagoda 舍利塔
elongate 拉长
innumerable 无数的
encounter 偶然相遇
exceptionally 特殊地
decayed 腐败的
lattice 用格子装饰
circulate 循环
legendary 传说的
sentient 有感觉力的

Jiuzhaigou National Park 九寨沟国家公园

General Information and Legendary Story

九寨沟概况与传说

Ladies and gentlemen, welcome to Jiuzhaigou National Park. I think I am very lucky to be your tour guide. It is a full day tour, exploring the beautiful forests, pools, lakes and waterfalls in this

National Park. During this time, I will put my heart, my mind, and my whole effort into my service, hoping that my service will please the whole group, and make your visit here a pleasant one that you will forever remember.

Now we are at the entrance gate of the Park. It was built shortly after Jiuzhaigou was added to the World Natural Heritage List in 1992. The gate reflects the features of Tibetan areas. The log bark wraps around the gate, and it appears primitive. It seems to tell us that you will find yourselves in the world's most exciting and unspoiled natural reserve. In 1982, Jiuzhaigou Park was admitted into the first group of scenic areas under special state protection. In 1990, Jiuzhaigou was listed as one of the 40 best scenic areas across the country. Jiuzhaigou has been also crowned with several other titles: the World Bio-Sphere Reserve, the Green Globe 21 and the State 4A-Level Scenery.

Jiuzhaigou scenery is located in Jiuzhaigou county, Aba Tibetan and Qiang Nationality Autonomous prefecture in Sichuan province. Jiuzhaigou literally means nine Tibetan village valleys. They are all located in the scenic area. The names of the villages are Heye (荷叶), Shuzheng (树正), Zechawa (则查洼), Heijiao (黑角), Panya (盘亚), Yala (牙拉), Jianpan (尖盘), Rexi (热西) and Guodu (郭都).

Jiuzhaigou National Park belongs to a carbonate barrier lake landform. The scenic area covers a space of 80 square km. The scenery was formed due to the geographic movement in glaciations, earthquakes and calcification. Jiuzhaigou scenic area is in the shape of "Y." It consists of 108 lakes, 47 springs, 17 splashing waterfalls, 12 turbulent streams, 5-karat shoals and three Tibetan villages. All these scenic sites create a unique landscape, and attract tourists in China and the rest of the world.

There is a popular saying that no other water will interest you after you visit Jiuzhaigou. Local people believe that water is the soul of the beauty in Jiuzhaigou. It is so clean that you can see to the bottom of lakes and streams even at 30m in depth. Besides, each site and each image illustrates something special—the true essence, the spirit, the magic of Jiuzhaigou. Jiuzhaigou's wonders inspire the country's top photographers and artists to do their best creative work here. Others express their feelings through words, and there are numerous quotes from writers or visitors.

However, many others declare that this land is indescribable. As one saying goes, it is better to see once than hear a hundred times. I think Jiuzhaigou's reputation has attracted all of you to come here for a visit. I believe that our tour of Jiuzhaigou will be a perfect way to remember its unique site and beauty in days to come.

Now here is a folk tale that vividly describes the formation of Jiuzhaigou. A long time ago, a male and female hill deities fell in love with each other. The man was called Dage and the woman Wonuo Semo. They decided to reside in Jiuzhaigou because they both deeply loved Jiuzhaigou's birds, animals, forests and mountains. Unexpectedly a devil called Shemozha fell in love with the female deity. He didn't want the male deity to live here in Jiuzhaigou. So he waged a war in an attempt to drive Dage out so that he could marry Wonuo Semo. A fierce battle occurred between Dage and the devil. During the battle, the devil snatched away Wonuo Semo. She was so scared that she dropped to the ground her precious mirror given to her by Dage. The mirror was broken into over a hundred pieces, which at once turned into over a hundred high mountains and beautiful lakes.

The battle continued, as Dage and the devil fought all the way from inner Jiuzhaigou to the entrance with no sign indicating who would win the battle. At this critical moment, Zhayizhaga (扎依扎嘎), the king of multi-mountains arrived, and he joined the fight on the side of Dage. The king put a huge screen-shaped cliff behind the devil. Afterwards the king crushed and buried the devil beneath the cliff. Only his head remained visible on the rock cliff. Later local people called it the Devil Cliff. Since then, Jiuzhaigou has been peaceful and more beautiful due to the newly added colorful lakes and mountains, and Dage and Wonuo Semo still live together here to safeguard Jiuzhaigou.

Ladies and gentlemen, please get closer to view the cliff that is over a thousand-ren (仞) cliff [an ancient measure of length equal to seven or eight chi (尺)]. There is a bizarre image on the cliff. What does it look alike? It is a devil's face, isn't it? It is now called the Precious Mirror Cliff. Down the cliff is a valley called Zharugou (扎如沟), where Zharu Monastery (扎如寺) stands. The local Tibetan people believe in Lamaism. The monks in Zharu Monastery belong to the Black-Sect of Buddhism that is also called Benbon. Benbons worship nature gods that dominate all the natural phenomena like wind, rain, thunder, mountain, forest and animals. This sect is influenced by an indigenous religion that is centered on the principle that everything has spirit. Benbon followers pray to gain happiness and drive out disasters.

Ladies and gentlemen, be aware of the dense forest growing

along the sides of the road. Evergreen plants, red-leaf plants, and yellow-leaf plants are the main trees in Jiuzhaigou. The evergreen plants are Chinese pine, hemlock, fir and dragon spruce. The red-leaf plants are maple, little tiller, smoke tree and others, the yellow-leaf plants are birch, golden-rain tree, elm, larch, poplar and walnut trees. These three-color plants are mixed in harmony, creating a rainbow of natural scenes that are pleasing to our eyes.

It is commonly believed that this colorful vegetation is one of the main features manifested in Jiuzhaigou. As spring arrives and snow begins to melt, mountain flowers blossom, and the water in streams begins to rise. In summer, Jiuzhaigou becomes a lush verdant green. Chinese pines and dragon spruces present greenness layer upon layer. In autumn, the plants keep changing their colors, and the remote sky is clear and bright. Colorful leaves and forests are mirrored on surrounding lakes, the stunning colorful scenery seems to allure viewers into a dreamlike world. In winter, snow covers the mountains and woods. The ice on the lakes keeps changing its colors with temperature changes. Look at the distant forests and the mountains nearby. It is pity that we cannot absorb all of the lovely natural scenes during a time-limited tour.

KEY WORDS & EXPRESSIONS 关键词汇及表达法

pleasurable 快乐的，愉快的
the World Bio-Sphere Reserve 国际生物圈保护区
the Green Globe 21 绿色环球 21
the State 4A-Level Scenery 中国 AAAA 级景区
carbonate 碳酸盐
landform 地形
glaciation 冰河作用

earthquake 地震
splash 溅，飞溅
shoal 浅滩，沙洲
indescribable 难以形容的
wage a war 发动战争
visible 看得见的
bizarre 奇异的
hemlock 铁杉
fir 冷杉
spruce 云杉
little tiller 小蘖
smoke tree 黄栌
birch 桦树
elm 榆树
larch 落叶松
poplar 杨树
walnut tree 胡桃树
lush 翠绿茂盛的
stunning 极好的

Shuzheng Valley Scenic Spots
树正沟景区

Here we are at Shuzheng Valley. It occupies a major position in Jiuzhaigou. The main paths and roads are flat and have been newly paved with asphalt. In this valley there are at least 20 scenic sites, including Potted-Patterned Landscape Lake (盆景滩) Reed Lake (芦苇海), Sleeping Dragon Lake (卧龙海), Shuzheng Lakes (树正群海), Shuzheng Waterfall (树正瀑布) and Rhinoceros Lake (犀牛海).

Now let's walk to the Garden-Patterned Landscape Lake. It will inspire your passion to appreciate the poetic scenery of Jiuzhaigou.

Here we are at the Reed Lake. If you close your eyes, you may feel as if you were in the region of rivers and lakes in South China. Actually, the sea is a type of swampland that suits the growth of varied water plants. Some fish swim in the shallow lake, and they have a strange name, called the naked carp. They have no scales and belong to the carp family. Wild ducks and egrets arrive when the reeds blossom. They fly over reed flowers swaying from side to side.

Here is Shuanglong Lake (双龙海). In English it is called the Double Dragon Lake. Sometimes, swans and mandarin ducks arrive and swim in groups here. Today we are not lucky enough to see swimming ducks and swans. However, you can dimly see two calcified lower reefs in the shape of ribbons. When the waves in the lake surge, the banks seem to wriggle like two dragons. A local legend says that there are four dragons in Jiuzhaigou. Two of them are under this lake. The two dragons take charge of local rain and hail. However, they are not responsible. They often fail to provide rain when it should rain, and they fail to provide hail when it should hail. Later Gesa'er (格萨尔), the Tibetan hero subdued the two evil dragons and imprisoned them at the bottom of the lake.

The water here is a form of calcification. The water from Rizegou Valley (日则沟) has rich content in the ion of calcium and magnesium. Due to the suitable temperature in the water here, the flowing ion easily turns into particulate matters, which stick to plankton or tiny sediments, and deposit on the lower earth bank, narrow mounds, trunks and tree branches at the bottom. Gradually the calcified segments have fully covered the objects, forming a unique natural phenomenon.

Speak softly because we are now at the Sleeping Dragon Lake and do not want to awaken him. The lake covers a space of about 61,838 square meters, and it is 22m in depth. Please look at the bottom of the lake. It is a bank of calcified calcium. What does it look alike? Many observers think it looks like a dragon lying across the bottom of the lake. When the wind breezes, and waves sway, the dragon seems to twist its body and blink its scales. According to local legend, a long time ago there was an evil black dragon living in Heishui River (黑水, the Black River). Once the black dragon saw that the water in Jiuzhaigou was pure and clean, he sucked up all the water and poured it out into his Black River. Seven days later, Jiuzhaigou became dry, and trees and grass withered. There was a white dragon living in Bailong River (白龙河, the White Dragon River). Every day the white dragon used Bailong River to water Jiuzhaigou. Day by day, Jiuzhaigou gradually revived and returned to normal. The black dragon was very angry about the white dragon's behavior. He started a fight with the white dragon. During their fight the black dragon poured out his black fog, which poisoned the white dragon. As the sun set in the late afternoon, the white dragon fell down into this lake. Zhayizhaga, remember him? He was Dage and Wonuo Semo's savior, arrived on time. He subdued the black dragon and took the dragon back to Heishui River. Since then the white dragon stayed in the lake as his home.

Ladies and gentlemen, here is Shuzheng Waterfall, one of the main scenic sites in Jiuzhaigou. The waterfall is 11m in height and 62m in width. An unseen stream comes from a high terrace, and meanders among the forests until it reaches the edge of the cliff. There trees, bushes and rocks divert the unseen stream into many waterways, and they drop downwards creating a splendid huge waterfall. Down below the cliff, rich trees and bushes grow among protruding rocks. The falling water keeps noisily splashing off these objects and turns into a myriad of cascading waterfalls in varied shapes. Look at the trees on the rocks. They seem to grow unexpectedly out of the middle of the waterfall.

Beyond Shuzheng Waterfall is a flat terrain. Near the road is Xiniu Lake (the Rhinoceros Lake). It is 2km in length and 18m in depth. The lake is broad and dark blue. Toward the southern end of the lake is a forest where a simple bridge spans across the lake. Nearby is a stream in which the water has a sweet and refreshing taste. The local Tibetan residents believe that the stream has a supernatural power. They say that the water from the stream can stop diarrhea and quench thirst. A long time ago, a lama from Tibet rode a rhinoceros and arrived here. He was so sick that he couldn't go further. The lama drank the water from the stream, and unexpectedly he was fully recovered and felt rejuvenated. Afterwards the lama led the rhinoceros down to the lake and built a permanent residence near the stream for his Buddhist practice.

Here we are at Nuorilang Waterfall (诺日郎瀑布). It is located between Nuorilang and Shuzheng valleys. The waterfall is 30m in height and 270m in width. It is one of China's largest calcified waterfalls. "Nuorilang" literally means "magnificence".

During the rainly season, the cascading waterfall produces a tremendous noise that ethos repeatedly in the valley. As the water hits the ground, the liquid immediately splashes high up into the air in the form of fine drops. The drops are thrown, blown or projected, forming a splendid water curtain. Visitors often see a rainbow that appears in the curtain when the sun shines upon it. Even at a far distance from the waterfall can be seen and heard an astonishing thundering noise, water mist, and colorful rainbows in the sky forming a wide and dynamic water screen of grandeur. In autumn when the water level is lower, the waterfall presents another wonder. The hanging cliff looks like a colorful silk cloth that matches with the surrounding multi-colored bushes.

KEY WORDS & EXPRESSIONS 关键词汇及表达法

rhinoceros 犀牛
swampland 沼泽地
reef 暗礁
ion 离子
calcium 钙
magnesium 镁

plankton 浮游生物
sediment 沉淀物
deposit 沉淀
observer 观测者
suck 吸，吮
meander 漫延，弯曲
myriad 无数的
cascade 成瀑布落下
diarrhea 腹泻
quench thirst 止渴
feel rejuvenated 感觉恢复活力
astonishing 可惊异的
grandeur 庄严，伟大

Nuorilang Scenic Spots

诺日郎景区

The scenic spot is 9km long and covers a space of 3km. It includes the Pearl Shoal（珍珠滩），the Five-flower Lake（五花海）and others.

Now we are at Jinghai（镜海）. It means the Mirror Lake. The lake is 925m in length and 262m in width. It is encircled by precipitous hills on three sides, and the other side is open rather like an entrance gate. The hills by the lake look green and verdant. In the early morning when there is no wind, the lake is as smooth as a mirror. At this time, the blue sky, white clouds, hills and trees are all reflected in the water. The scenery in and outside the water is closely joined, and it is hard to tell which is the real one or which is a reflection. The scenery has inspired the passion of many artists and poets. A figure of speech is used here to describe the situation. It says, "Inside the water birds fly, and up in the sky fish swim." The depth of the lake is between 10m and 20m, but the water is so clean that you can see soft green algae move, and fish swim at the bottom. Trunks in the water have been fully covered by calcified sediments that look rather like huge corals in pretty shape.

In the bank of the lake, there is a long vine. It is as thick as a bowl. The vine climbs up a towering old tree. The two plants seem to depend upon each other for survival, so local people call them the Trees of Love.

Well, ladies and gentlemen, here we are at Zhenzhutan (珍珠滩, Pearl Shoal). Let's walk around the spot. The slope-shaped shoal is calcified, 160m in width and 200m in length. The water flows freely downwards on the shoal surface that appears quite uneven due to the calcification. As the water unrolls, it splashes numerous tiny drops. They resemble snow-white pearls spraying over the whole shoal. Look at the upper part of the shoal. Poplars, willows and azalea grow all over there. In May as travelers walk through the shoal, the natural beauty is fully displayed by rolling water sprays underneath patches of azalea blossoms and the gentle sound of swaying willows.

Here is Wuhua Lake (五花湖, Five - Flower Lake). It is an ideal place for photographs. The algae and bryophyte thrive in the lake. Sediments stimulate these plants, which give rise to the clusters of multi-colorful ribbons on the lake's surface. When surrounding maple and smoke trees turn red in autumn, their reflection on the water becomes raging flames, encircling ribbons in multi-colors. This lake is also an ideal place to feed the naked carp.

The road near Wuhua Lake spirals up a steep mountain. As it reaches a curve, two lakes will come into sight. One is called Xiongmao Lake (熊猫海, the Panda Lake) and the other Jianzhu Lake (箭竹海, the Arrow Bamboo Lake).

Here we are at the Panda Lake. It is 14m in depth and covers an area of 90,000 square meters. The lake links up with the Arrow Bamboo Lake. Along the bank of the Bamboo Lake, bamboo remains evergreen and firs stand straight. It is said that pandas used to eat arrow bamboo and drink water here. In winter, the Panda Lake is frozen, but the Arrow Bamboo Lake remains unfrozen, and the water in the lake shines brightly. It is an incredible scene.

At the lower end of the Panda Lake is a waterfall. It is the highest waterfall in Jiuzhaigou and is called the Panda Waterfall. The waterfall has a flight of three stages. The first stage is 19m in height and 5m in width; the second is 24m in height and 4m in width; the third is 19m in height and 14m in width. As water rushes down, it leaps at each stage before it cascades into the deep valley. In midwinter, the three stages hang with dripping ice, forming varied-patterns of magnificent scenery as if you found yourselves in a world carved in ice.

Not far from Rizegou Guesthouse is the Swan Lake (天鹅湖). Swans used to reside here. At the present time, the lake remains semi-marsh land; waterweeds fully cover the surface. In spring, the lake resembles a carpet of green grass; in summer, the lake is splendidly decorated with blossomed flowers; in autumn, the yellowness in the lake meets the eye on every side; in winter, the lake remains a world of ice and snow. Near the upper end of the lake is another lake called Fangcaohai (芳草海). It means the Fragrant Grass Lake.

Ladies and gentlemen, the lake leads to the hills. Among the hills there is a peak that towers above the rest. It is named the Sword Rock (剑岩) because it looks sharp on the top and wide at lower part. After we pass by the foot of the towering peak, we will start to walk into a dense primeval forest. In the forest we will find ourselves deep in the boundless expanse of trees and plants, feeling as light as if we had left the world of men and become immortal beings. The forest has an abundance of trees. They are so tall that we can hardly see the sky when looking up. Some of the trees curve down like awnings, some loom up like obelisks, some stand erect like men, and some recline like dragons. Beneath our feet are soft mosses that grow in a thick furry carpet on wet soil. When you walk through the forest, cool greenery soothes your eyes, a gentle breeze whispers in your ears, and the utter quietness refreshes your heart.

KEY WORDS & EXPRESSIONS 关键词汇及表达法

coral 珊瑚
uneven 不平坦的
azalea 杜鹃花
algae 藻类，海藻
bryophyte 苔藓类的植物
thrive 兴旺，繁荣
raging flame 熊熊火焰

primeval forest　原始森林
boundless expanse　无边无际的宽阔区域
awning　天幕
obelisk　方尖石塔
moss　苔，藓
soothe　使(某人，其神经，其情绪)平静
whisper　耳语，密谈

Zechawa Valley Scenic Spots

则查洼沟景区

Zechawa Scenic Spots extend 18km southeastwards from Nuorilang to the Long Lake (长海). They include the Lower Season Lake (下季节海), the Upper Season Lake (上季节海), the Multi-colored Pond (五彩池) and the Long Lake.

Now we are passing the Upper Season Lake and the Lower Season Lake. In rainy summers, water in the lakes rises and turns glossy green; in autumns, the water looks bright blue; in winter, the lakes have no water, and on the lake bottom grasses grow making an extensive pastureland.

Here we are at Wucai Pond (五彩池). It means the Multicolored Pond. It is the smallest lake in Jiuzhaigou, which is 100.8m in length, and 56m in width. The water comes from Changhai Lake, and it neither increases nor diminishes. Its azure translucence below the water stretches to the bottom before your eyes. Wucai Pond has rich sponges, algae, and ferns. In addition, reeds and bushes grow in the pond. As the sun casts lights on the water, sediments at the bottom act on the sense of algae and bryophyte plants, producing the multi-colored clusters.

It is commonly believed that the pond produces more colors than any of the other ponds and lakes in Jiuzhaigou. The colors are light green, milky white, bright yellow and pale blue. Many visitors usually stop to sit by the lake, and the beautiful pond seems to make them feel ease at heart. You may look in amazement at the multi-colored clusters at the bottom, and suspect that they were painted by local people. They are displayed like inexhaustible treasures supplied by the Master Creator of all things.

This is Changhai (the Long Lake). It is located at the top of Zechawa Valley, and is 3,100m above sea level. There are several questions related to the lake. How was the lake formed? Why does the lake have no exit? Are there any fish in the lake? How long is the lake? How deep is it?

The first question still remains a mystery. It is uncertain whether it was formed due to earthquakes, landslides or mud-rock flow. The source of the water comes from springs among the forests and melted snow on the surrounding mountains. The water never overflows in summer and never dries up in winter. The only way for water to drain in the lake is to evaporate and permeate into the ground. The lake has no fish probably because it is too cold. According to a legend a monster ate all the fish a long time ago. The lake is 7.5km in length, and in some parts the lake is 103m in depth.

Changhai is the largest lake in Jiuzhaigou. The natural beauty of the lake strikes you as vast and infinite, presenting a picture of endless imagination. The lake remains unruffled, clouds float by, and water birds frolic across the lake. The sarround green forests grow verdant, casting shadows on the water. Whether or not you believe that a creator exists, this sight will make you feel that there must surely be one. It seems strange that such wonders are set in remote areas like this, where thousands of years may have passed before we come along to appreciate them.

Ladies and gentlemen, our daily tour to Jiuzhaigou is now steadily and serenely approaching the end. Anticipation, curiosity and delight are all held in delicate balance. Reluctantly we must return to the reality of our own everyday world. I hope you have enjoyed my commentaries and the brief glimpses of Jiuzhaigou. I sincerely hope that the cool greenery, running water, the vast scenery and the sweet silence have refreshed your hearts.

KEY WORDS & EXPRESSIONS 关键词汇及表达法

glossy 平滑的，有光泽的
diminish (使)减少，(使)变小
sponge 海绵体，海绵状物
fern 蕨类
inexhaustible 无穷无尽的
dry up 干燥
evaporate (使)蒸发
permeate 弥漫，渗透
infinite 无穷的，无限的
boundless imagination 无限的想象
serenely 安详地，沉着地
anticipation 预期，期望
reluctantly 不情愿地，勉强地

Dazu Stone Sculptures 大足石刻

General Facts

概 说

Ladies and gentlemen, we are on the way to Dazu Stone Sculptures in Dazu county. It is situated in the hills, 160km northwest of Chongqing. Dazu Stone Sculptures ranks first among the most important Buddhist archeological sites in China. They are excellent representative works of stone carvings, produced during the period of the ancient Chinese grotto art. Dazu Stone Sculptures are as great as Mogao Grottoes (莫高窟) in Gansu province, Longmen Grottoes (龙门石窟) in Henan province, and Yungang Grottoes (云岗石窟) in Shanxi province. The four grottoes make up the history of Chinese grotto art.

2,000 years ago, grotto art was introduced to China together with Buddhism. Northern Wei (386 - 534), Sui and Tang dynasties witnessed the development of grotto art when Mogao, Longmen, and Yungang grottoes were constructed. The Yungang Grottoes were built some 1,500 years ago and were greatly influenced by Indian culture. The sculptures of Yungang Grottoes are considered to be the earliest stage of grotto art. The sculptures of Longmen Grottoes began to appear in the fifth century and represented the blending of Chinese and Indian characteristics. Since the late period of Tang Dynasty, grotto art declined in North China. However, the stone sculptures in Dazu continued its development, and displayed religious beliefs from 9th century to the middle of 13th century. Dazu Sculptures established a newstyled art form that evolved from the traditional grotto art in their subjects, artistic forms and aesthetic conceptions.

Mogao, Longmen, and Yungang Grottoes focus on cave sculptures. Most of Dazu Stone Sculptures are cliff-face sculptures. Local artists produce Dazu sculptures based on the three dimensional technology in plastic arts, techniques of realism and artistic exaggeration. The lifelike sculptures display a striking contrast between good and evil. These sculptures, carved out of the rocks at Northern Hill (北山) and Baoding Hill (宝顶山), are the finest in craftsmanship and the richest in contents. Besides, Dazu Stone Sculptures present Buddhist figures as human beings and depict scenes from everyday life.

At the end of Tang Dynasty, Dazu was the principal district of the ancient Changzhou (昌州) area. The sculpture carvings started in the first year of Jingfu period (景福, 892) of Tang Dynasty. It lasted until the end of the Southern Song Dynasty. Only a few figures were added during Ming and Qing dynasties. The numbers of stone sculptures total more than 50,000 pieces, and they are located at some 40 places. Gradually, they are called Dazu Stone Sculptures. Because of Dazu's remote location among the green hill peaks, the sculptures have been fortunately preserved from being destroyed for nearly one thousand years.

Dazu Stone Sculptures are of religious nature. They mainly consist of Buddhist images and Buddhist scripture epochs. Some Confucian and Daoist images are included in separate areas. Visitors may notice that the images of the Confucian, Buddhist and Daoist founders co-exist in the same caves. There are also some statues of historical personages. They include the statue of Lord Wenxuan (honorary title of Confucius), who preserved the system of rites of Han, the statue of Wei Junjing (韦君靖), the military commander of Eastern Sichuan of the Tang Dynasty as well as more than a hundred statues of captains, colonels and generals. One of the statues is Lu Ban (鲁班) accompanied by images of his disciples. Lu Ban was a well-known architect in the period of the Spring and Autumn and Warring States. Chinese laborers loved him through the successive dynasties.

Due to the change of history and the inconvenience of transportation, few scholars of ancient times visited this place, and historical records lack details relating to Dazu Stone Sculptures.

After liberation in 1949, an organization was set up for their preservation and protection. At the same time, the local government set aside money for renovation. Through the joint efforts, a completely new face of the stone sculptures was presented. In 1961, these sculptures were included in the list of the first group of important cultural relics under the state protection. In December 1999, Dazu Stone Sculptures were admitted into the World Cultural Heritage List. The current Northern Hill and Baoding Hill have become well-known scenic spots, which attract many tourists both from home and abroad.

KEY WORDS & EXPRESSIONS 关键词汇及表达法

grotto 洞穴，岩穴
blending 混合，混成
artistic form 艺术形式
aesthetic conception 美学观念
cliff-face sculpture 峭壁面雕刻
plastic arts 造型艺术
techniques of realism 现实主义手法
artistic exaggeration 艺术夸张
striking contrast 显著对比
epoch 时代，时期
historical personage 历史人物
architect 建筑师
inconvenience 麻烦，不方便之处
renovation 革新

Northern Hill Stone Sculptures
北山石刻

Ladies and gentlemen, here we are at the foot of Northern Hill. Please come with me for a tour of the hill.

Northern Hill is 2km north of the county. In ancient times, the hill was known as Longgang Hill (龙岗山), which means the Dragon Hill. By the end of the Tang Dynasty, this area was Yongchang Military Stronghold (永昌寨) used to store grains and station troops. In 892, Wei Junjing had people construct the first Buddhist shrine on the rocks on the site of the present Fowan (佛湾) of the Northern Hill. Fowan means the Buddha Crescent in English. Shortly after that, local officials, gentry and Buddhist monks followed suit, and they donated to carve more images on rocks. The carving work continued for over 250 years up to the Shaoxing Period (绍兴年间) of Southern Song Dynasty. There are nearly 10,000 figure statues spread around the four sides of the hill with Fowan as its center.

As you walk along the hill, you can't help feeling that you're in a museum of stone carvings. Fowan lies on the top of Northern Hill, and the images cover a stretch of over 500m. There are 290 caves and niches, which are grouped in a layered honeycomb pattern. Among them 264 caves or niches contain figure statues. Besides, there are 6 upright stone tablets, 8 Buddhist scripture pillars, and many other carved notes and accounts associated with the construction of the images.

Here we are at the statue of Wei Junjing. A general of the Late Shu carved the statue in memory of Wei Junjing, who started Dazu sculpture-carving program. An inscribed tablet is placed on the left side, and it is generally known as the Inscription of Wei Junjing, which is considered as the earliest written record. It is a record of the origin of the hill sculptures, the peasants' uprising led by Huang Chao (黄巢) by the end of the Tang Dynasty, as well as the situation in Eastern Sichuan during the later period of Tang Dynasty.

Dazu artists developed vividness and grace both in form and content. The caves are filled with delicately carved statues that prominently show their full and stately appearance. The figures are draped in their simple and plain garments, with the light and flowing wrinkles. According to the account from the inscription, Vajra Bodhisattva (北天王) in Cave 3, Vaisravana-devaraja (毗沙门天王) in Cave 5, Thousand-hand Guanyin (千手观音, Avalokitesvara Bodhisattva) in Cave 9, and Sakyamuni Buddha

(释迦牟尼佛) in Cave 10 were all carved in the Later Tang Dynasty. Cave 5 and Cave 10 should be considered as representative works among the stone sculptures.

Here we are at Cave 5. It contains the statue of Vaisravana-devaraja. He is big and tall, and looks heroic. Two men flank him. They are men of unusual strength with fiercely staring faces. The king and two men are all in suits of ancient Chinese armor. The two men are similar to the armored terracotta soldiers excavated in the tomb of Qin Shihuang, 5km east of Lintong (临潼), Shanxi Province. They hold weapons in their hands as if they could march forward irresistibly. The statues are thought to have presented the images of "perfect knights" in the Tang Dynasty. On the left side stand two statues. One is a handsome man, and the other a dignified woman. They are Wei Junjing and his wife. The two statues prominently manifest themselves for their contribution to Dazu Stone Sculptures.

Now we arrive at Cave 10. It contains a statue of Sakyamuni Buddha in the middle. His two closest disciples, Kasyapa and Ananda flank him. The two disciples took charge of all sentient beings after Sakyamuni's death. Kasyapa is usually accepted as the chief disciple of Sakyamuni. The elderly monk has a heavily lined face, and often appears with Ananda in support of Sakyamuni. Ananda was Sakyamuni's cousin. He followed his uncle by about 25 years. It is said that Ananda had a superpower in his hearing and memory.

Look at the two Bodhisattvas in Cave 10. They are carved out of the inside wall. One of them is Guanyin (Goddess of mercy). According to the Buddhist scriptures, Guanyin is able to turn herself into 35 varieties of incarnation to relieve 72 different serious disasters. If sentient beings, when they are in danger, recite her name earnestly, she will appear and rescue them upon hearing their voice.

The fine shaped Guanyin statue in the cave wears a thin full-length skirt, standing on a lotus throne and holding a lotus flower in one hand. She has a full moon shaped face, delicate features and exposed neck and shoulders. People think that the standing Guanyin resembles a fresh lotus flower that has just blossomed out of a water pool.

Ladies and gentlemen, there were many statues on the hill carved during the Five Dynasties, but they have gradually eroded as centuries went by. However, we still can see some well-preserved works carved at that time. They include the Niche of Thousand-hand Guanyin and the Niche of Bhaisajyaguru Buddha. The existing works are small but impressively exquisite for their natural postures in varied ways. Their garments appear beautiful and ornaments complicated, which display the transformation of clothing style from the Tang to the Song dynasties.

Most of the sculptures dated from the Song Dynasty are distributed in the northern area of Fuowan. They are thought to be the best part of the hill stone sculptures.

Here we are at Cave 101. It is one meter in depth and 3m in height. It contains inscriptions engraved on the rocks inside. In the middle is the carved Inscription of Divine Way by Zhao-yi-jian-gong. The calligraphy was written by Cai Jing (蔡京), a well-known calligraphist. So many people name the inscription as the

Inscription of Cai Jing.

Here we are at Cave 125. It contains a Guanyin with Rosary (数珠手观音). Among the images of the hill, Guanyins are made conspicuously beautiful. Guanyin with Rosary and Guanyin Viewing at the Reflection of the Moon (水月观音) in Cave 113 are thought to be the best of the Song-styled hill stone sculptures.

The images of the sculptures dating from Song Dynasty are thought to be close to real life and exhibit a new feature in the development of the ancient stone carvings. The excellent works have lively sentiments merged with realistic techniques and idealistic expression.

Now please look at Guanyin with Rosary. She is particularly attractive. Before Sui Dynasty, the image was a male Bodhisattva. Gradually, Buddhist artists transformed Guanyin into a pretty and kind female Bodhisattva. During Tang Dynasty, great masses of Chinese people worshiped her because she symbolized great mercy and a mother's love. Guanyin with Rosary appears to be a charming young lady standing against stonewalls. She wears a flower corolla and her face slightly downwards. Her gazing is amiable. Her lips are slightly inwards, and the corners of her mouth tilt upwards; her appearance seems to flow out slowly with tenderness and smiles. Her full-length dress is in a sweeping movement as if gentle breezes were caressing her. Guanyin holds her rosary in her right hand with her left hand gently holding her right wrist. Both hands cross down to her abdomen, which suggests that she is generous and completely at ease.

The carved Guanyin image vividly presents the Buddhist

goddess as a charming young lady who has no sacred and fearsome shadows. People have named Guanyin statues as Guanyins with Charming Expressions. This excellent work signals a significant departure from earlier Buddhist art in form and content and reflect to a certain extent the desire of the ancient artists for a happy life.

Here is Cave 136. Its name is the Wheel of the Universe (转轮经藏窟). The cave is considered as the most outstanding and the best preserved among the caves on the Northern Hill. The cave contains in the middle an intricately carved wheel that houses a number of sacred sutras and symbolizes the cycle of man's life and the power of Buddhism. A coiling dragon has a forceful gesture within a circle of clouds, supporting the whole wheel. On the top of the dragon is an Octagonal Dew-Collecting Stone Plate. Along the edge of the plate are carved 40 figures that are lively and innocent children in varied positions. On the plate stand 8 pillars decorated with a motif of dragons. They are either in upward or downward gestures. The artists use the pillars to support the vault of the cave in harmony with about 20 figures. Those figures are carved out of the walls and are arranged in groups. The wall on the east is carved with the images of Sakyamuni, Kasyapa, Ananda, and other two Bodhisattvas. The wall on the south is carved with the images of Wenshu, Yuyin Guanyin (玉印观音) and Ruyizhu Guanyin (如意珠观音). North wall is carved with images of Puxian, Guanyin Holding the Sun and Moon (日月观音) and Guanyin with Rosary. On the other side of the cave gate stands a man of unusual strength.

The artists have endowed the carved divine figures with different lines and rich decoration based on the Buddhist sutras.

Each group appears independent, but remains in perfect harmony with other groups. Most of the figures look like newly carved objects and dress beautifully in dimension proportionate to the importance of the Buddhist power.

Let's have a close look at some of the important figures below:

Wenshu

This is the image of Wenshu. According to Buddhist tradition, Wenshu is a well-learned and eloquent Bodhisattva. He is carved in the shape of a male figure, riding on a blue roaring lion. Wenshu has a calm and stately appearance, looking straightforward. His eyes are full of wisdom, which gives an impression of vim and vigor. Wenshu is the left attendant of Sakyamuni in charge of wisdom. He has five hair buns on his head and holds a Buddhist scripture in his hand. These features symbolize his wisdom.

Puxian

This is Puxian or Bodhisattva of Universal Benevolence. The image is carved as a female Bodhisattva who possesses the features of beautiful Chinese females. He sits cross-legged on a lotus throne. Below the throne are a huge white elephant and an elephant caretaker. Puxian is shown wearing a squared-shaped flower corolla. He has a lump and beautiful face, casting down his eyes, with a faint smile at the corners of his mouth. His chest is fully decorated with jade ornaments and looks delicate in contrast with the vigorous Wenshu.

Riyue Guanyin

This is Riyue Guangin. The translation of the name is Guanyin Holding the Sun and Moon or Guanyin Between the Sun and the Moon. This Guanyin has six hands. Her top two hands support the Sun and the Moon; another two hands at her back hold an axe and a sword; the other two hands hold an alms bowl and a willow branch. Guanyin looks amiable and has a full figure. It seems that she still remains elegant and poised even though she is middle aged.

Yuyin Guanyin

Yuyin Guanyin is shown wearing an 800-year-old flower corolla. Fortunately all the pearls on the corolla still remain intact. The artists have endowed the corolla with changeable carved lines and exquisite decoration. Archaeologists often use the carved corolla to exemplify how well the cave has preserved and what artistic attainments the ancient artists have arrived at.

Outside Cave 136 is a large carved painting. It depicts the story of Wenshu who visits Vimalakirti in sickness. This is the only picture carved in intaglio lines among the stone sculptures in Dazu. It is said that during the Song Dynasty there was a well-known painter. His name was Shi Ke who painted the picture. Its flowing strokes resemble moving clouds or flowing water in a stream. Later a sculptor called Lu Fuming carved the painting on the rock according to the copy of the painting produced by an artist named Li Dalang.

Here is Cave 245. It was made in the late period of the Tang Dynasty. The cave contains over 600 exquisitely carved figures, which tell the story of Amitayus-dhyana-sutra (观无量寿佛经变相). It is commonly thought that it is the highest quality carved work on the hill, dating from the Tang Dynasty. The cave contains the Three Western Sages (西方三圣), who sit crossed-leg on their lotus thrones. This is Amitabha (阿弥陀佛) who is the Buddha of Boundless Splendor and the founder of the Western Paradise. He sits in the middle; the left attendant is Guanyin (Goddess of Mercy), and the right attendant is Mahasthamaprapta (大势至菩萨). The three sages are working to usher the sentient beings up to the Buddhist Western Paradise.

The cave has vividly portrayed the life of the Western Paradise. The four white-colored belts are carved on the top, symbolizing the boundless lights, and making the whole paradise splendid. Buildings are richly decorated; towers and pavilions are dotted here and there. Varied musical instruments automatically sound Buddhist music; green birds fly within colorful clouds. The paradise residents enjoy luxurious transportation. Whenever they go outside, they travel by dragon-drawn carriages or phoenix-rowed boats. They are dressed in silk clothes and eat delicacies produced from land and sea. Usually the residents sit at the paradise tables doing nothing. It suggests that a glimpse at the delicate food will make their stomach full.

The Paradise residents find the scenery pleasant to both their eyes and mind. It is filled with luxurious vegetation. The roads are paved with gold, and they symbolize no days of poverty. The colored glaze represents the sky of the paradise, and it symbolizes freedom from dirt and unwanted matters. Nearby is a lotus pool from which water could relieve people of hunger and sickness.

Below the Three Western Sages are carved figures in three groups. They are classified according to how much kindness and love the figures offer to other people who are in need or in trouble. The top group closest to the lotus flowers consists of Bodhisattvas (菩萨), the center group consists of Arhats (罗汉),

and the lower group consists of all evil persons. Amitabha uses different ways to usher those who are converted to Buddhism up to the paradise.

The cave figure carving also includes clothing, ornaments, and other articles. They all display the highly artistic attainment during the late period of the Tang Dynasty.

Ladies and gentlemen, on Northern Hill, some caves contain a large number of figures that offered financial help to support the religious sculpture development. They include government officials, warriors, commoners as well as Buddhist monks and nuns. The figures' garments, ornaments, utensils, gardens and houses reflect the ancient living conditions during the Tang or the Song dynasties. Attached to their statues are their social ranks, family status and dates of donation. These provide valuable information for research purposes.

The stone carvings on the hill are famous for their gorgeous and delicate craftsmanship. The ancient artists elaborately design the structure and layout of each niche or cave. Their efforts enable the caves or niches to offer visitors the sense of both compactness and variability. Therefore, the artists' names are also inscribed in the caves or niches in an attempt to let their names be known in the history of art sculpture from one generation to another for all times.

KEY WORDS & EXPRESSIONS 关键词汇及表达法

stronghold 要塞，据点
honeycomb 蜂房，蜂巢
fearsome 可怕的
supernatural 超自然的，神奇的

full and stately appearance 丰腴庄严的外观
drape 披盖
wrinkle 皱纹
representative work 代表作
perfect knight 完美武士
thin full-length skirt 轻纱薄长裙
full moon shaped face 面如满月
delicate feature 身段苗条
niche 洞龛，壁龛
transformation 转变
conspicuously 显著地，超群地
amiable 亲切的
tilt （使）倾斜
abdomen 腹部
art in form and content 艺术形式与内容
intricately 复杂地
the octagonal stone dew-collecting plate 八边形露盘
sutra 佛经，经典
proportionate 成比例
well-learned 有学问的
eloquent 雄辩的，有口才的
vim and vigor 充沛活力
caretaker 看管者，看守者
cast down one's eyes 目光向下
changeable 可改变的
artistic attainment 艺术成就
intaglio 凹纹
dragon-drawn carriage 龙拉车
phoenix-rowed boat 凤划船

commoner 平民
layout 规划，设计
compactness 紧密，简洁
variability 可变性

Baoding Hill Stone Sculptures
宝顶石刻

Ladies and gentlemen, we are at Baoding Hill, and it is 15km northeast of Dazu. Take a guess at how many figures have been carved on the hill? If you came close to 10,000 figures, then you are right. Most of the carvings groups gather at the two sides-Xiaofowan (小佛湾) and Dafowan (大佛湾).

The huge carving project lasted about 70 years from 1179 to 1249 during the Southern Song Dynasty. The main project supervisor was Zhao Zhifeng (赵智风). For seventy years he kept collecting funds among the Buddhists in an attempt to financially support the Buddhist carvings on the rocks around the hill.

Zhao Zhifeng was a famous monk and a native of Miliang Village in the Dazu Area. He became a monk when he was young, and at the age of sixteen he traveled west to Hanzhou and Mimu. Three years later, Zhao Zhifeng returned home to spread Tantric Buddhism and establish his sect. He also founded a Buddhist school at Baoding Hill. The center of Tantric Buddhism established by Zhao Zhifeng exerted a great influence on the imperial court as well as on the common people, and Baoding Hill therefore attracted a large number of pilgrims including high-ranking government officials and common people in the Southern Song Dynasty.

The sculptures at Xiaofowan are in Shengshou Monastery (圣

寿院). It was the first group of sculpture carvings under the direction of Zhao Zhifeng. The statues are carved out of stonewalls, beams and pillars. At present, about one thousand images are in existence, and they remind us of the prosperity that occurred before. At Xiaofowan the sculptures and the stone houses seem to have similar patterns with the carvings at Dafowan.

Now we arrive at Dafowan. It is close to Xiaofowan. Look at Dafowan. Actually it is a hill in the shape of a horseshoe, spanning out to a length of about five hundred meters. The surrounding statues vary considerably, including Buddhist images and sages, historical figures, realistic scenes and delicate sculptures. Wind and rains have eroded some of them, and some others have lost layers of paint. Despite of that, there is a remarkable survival rate: 15,000 figures, 31 huge carved works as well as Buddhist towers and stone tablets. All of them stay close to one another, presenting a magnificent sight along the precipitous rock hill.

In China, there are some other important grotto groups. They include Yungang Caves in Datong and Longmen Caves in Luoyang. Buddhist images are the main subject matter, but Dafowan sculptures on Baoding Hill differ from other grottoes. The local carvings here are based on a preconceived plan mainly to depict the stories of Buddhist scriptures. The principle images are carved in nineteen caves or niches, each cave or niche contains some other figures that are further divided into several sub-sections. Each sub-section displays one or more stories that happened at different places and different times as recorded in

Buddhist scriptures. Beside the carved figures, there are inscribed Buddhist texts and explanatory notes that may help visitors understand the carved figures' stories.

Now we are in Dafowan from the middle section of the South Cliff. The first sight is the group of images of Dharma-Protecting Deities (护法神). They have awe-inspiring appearances. Here is the Picture of Transmigration in the Six Ways (六道轮回图) carved in a cave. It is a descriptive picture that shows the reincarnation in six ways after death according to the good and evil behavior during the person's lifetime. As the picture shows, the well-doers may go to the Buddhist Western Paradise, or be reborn as deities, or become again human beings, the evil-doers may be punished in Hell, or be reborn as animals or become hungry ghosts. The 7m tall figure is Yanwang (阎王), the king of Hell. He stands there controlling the six-way reincarnation wheel with his two powerful hands.

The wheel has four circles. In the inner circle sits a Buddhist monk. Next is the circle of the six-way reincarnation. The third circle shows the human beings' happy or bitter life, and the outer circle is the process of reincarnation. The seated monk emits six rays of Buddhist light from his heart, classifying the wheel into six parts. The rays' emission suggests that the heart completely controls good or bad behavior towards other people. Look at each ray. It has many small circles, each small circle has a Buddha sitting inside, and it tells us that all sentient beings have a Buddhist nature and have the possibility of becoming a Buddha.

However, the seated monk has a pig on his left, a pigeon on his right, and a snake below him. The three creatures represent three poisons: greed, anger and sickness. Once the poisons negatively affect the heart of human beings, they will eventually conduct evil deeds. Evil is a predestined reward, and vice versa during the process of reincarnation. Evidently the purpose of the carving is to encourage people to try to accumulate more kindness and love for other people and give help to people in need or in trouble.

Here we are at the Pavilion of Extensive Treasures (广大宝楼阁) behind the Picture of Transmigration. It contains three carved figures sitting cross-legged. Each figure represents Zhao Zhifeng in his youth, middle age and old age. The carved figure has three bamboo trees on the top of his head. What does it mean? It suggests that Zhao practices Buddhism under bamboo trees and is ready to make a trip to the Pavilion of Extensive Treasures in the Buddhist Paradise once he becomes a Buddha.

Now we are at the giant statues. They are called the Three Sages (华严三圣). The three—meter tall sages stand on the lotus thrones and support the top rock edge. They bend a bit and watch passers-by, their huge loose sleeves support their heavy out-stretched arms. Look at the sage in the middle. He is Vairocana Buddha (毗卢佛), and he is considered to be the founder of Tantric Buddhism. On each of his two sides stand Wenshu and Puxian. How could the heavy stone pagoda stand absolutely still on Wenshu's hands for many years? It is because the heavy loose sleeves support the pagoda. Behind the Three Sages are one thousand carved Buddhas. They look much smaller in contrast with the Three Sages.

Here is a lofty hall by the name of Dabei (Mahakaruna) Pavilion (大悲阁). It is the ancient architecture at the east end of the South Cliff, which contains the carved One-Thousand-Hand Guanyin in a seated posture. The 3m high Guanyin has 1,007 hands, and each palm has one eye. All the hands have their own gestures carved out of a 88-square-meter rock. They look like a peacock spreading its colorful tail feathers. The 1,007 hands and eyes respectively symbolize the boundless Buddhist power and wisdom. It is said that the hands could rescue all the sentient beings, and the eyes could discover the minutest detail in everything.

Now we walk into the East Cliff section, and we arrive at the Reclining Buddha. It is a symbol of Sakyamuni entering Nirvana. What is Nirvana? It is the supreme state of the perfect blessedness and the final goal to be attained by those who have achieved Buddhist infinite enlightenment and floated off into the immortal freedom and peace from their life-and-death struggle. Nirvana in Hinayana Buddhism is a symbol of death, and in Mahayana Buddhism a symbol of being reincarnated into a Buddha.

The grottoes in Mogao Caves have portrayed the whole story of Sakyamuni entering Nirvana. The statue of the Reclining Buddha in Dafuowan only depicts the grand occasion as Sakyamuni enters Nirvana. Look at the sculpture. It is 31m in length and 6.8m in height. His right arm is hidden from view, his feet remain uncarved in the rock, the coiling incense smoke comes from an incense burner placed in front of the overwhelming Buddha. About twenty busts of Bodhisattvas respectfully stand around in rows, holding flowers or fruits. They seem to pay their last respects to Sakyamuni who is ready to depart from them. The reclining Sakyamuni gradually closes his eyes. He looks serene and has no sign of pain. According to the Buddhist scripture, as Sakyamuni was about to enter Nirvana, the earth was shaking, and his alarmed followers beat their chests and stamped in deep sorrow. Sakyamuni said to Ananda, "Maybe some of you think my teachings will end soon after I enter Nirvana. No, the Buddhist teachings that I have taught and the disciplines that I have made will be your teacher after my Nirvana."

Now please look at the image in the niche at the northeast corner. The image is called Nine Dragons Bathing the Prince (九龙浴太子). On the top of the rock is a pool. Water in the pool is channeled to the mouth of the nine dragons among clouds. The dragons spout the pool water over the baby who sits in a basin held by the two men of unusual strength. The baby bathing suggests the birth of Sakyamuni. The Buddhist scripture says that when the prince was born, nine dragons flew down from Heaven, spouting out both cold and warm water to bath him.

Ladies and gentlemen, here is a group of stone carvings next to the statue of Nine Dragons Bathing the Prince:

This is the Cave of the Peacock King (孔雀明王). The Peacock King is the principle image. He rides on a peacock with out-stretched wings as if he were about to hover in the clouds. The image is carved in accordance with the story in the Mayurasana-sutra (the Sutra of Peacock King).

Here is the Scene of Vairocana Buddha Preaching the Dharma

(毗卢道场). The scene displays a group of disciples listening to Vairocana Buddha preaching the Dharma. The exquisitely carved figures in the cave are commonly thought as high-quality works among the Buddhist sculptures dating from the Song Dynasty. The carved figures look beautiful with chubby faces and richly ornamented costumes.

This is a group of sculptures by the name of the Story of Scripture on Parental Love (父母恩重经变相). The artists used ingenious skills to create life-like figures and scenes, which constitute a group of sculptures based on the Scripture on Parental Love. It is said that it was composed by a man of the Tang Dynasty. The figures and scenes are divided into two floors. On the upper floor are seven carved Buddhas, and the lower floor consists of a series of ten scenes. The story begins with a young couple in the middle as they stand before the Buddha. The man holds an incense burner, the woman piously puts burning incense sticks into the burner. The two pray before the Buddha and implore the Buddha to bless them to have a son. The story continues in following scenes. The woman is pregnant, she delivers her child, she nurses her baby, she washes diapers, her son gets married, the parent see the child depart. The series of pictures depict the whole process of how parents raise their children and keep worrying about them even when they are grown-up. The final scene displays that parental love is highly respected. There are some more carved figures below the scenes. They warn that those who ill-treat their parents in return will live in misery supervised by evil ghosts in Hell.

Here is a huge cave. The carved figures tell the story from the scripture on Mahopaya Buddha Requiting the Kindness of his Parents (《大方便佛报恩经》). The cave contains a bust of Sakyamuni Buddha. A group of figures on his left side depicts Jataka stories concerning the Buddha's filial piety, and another group on his right side is associated with the events of his filial piety as recorded in his biography. At the lower part of his left side is the third statue group. These statues depict the legend about the followers of the six heretical schools slandering the Buddha as unfilial.

Here is Amitayus-Buddha-Dhyana-Sutra (观无量寿佛经图). The story of Amitayus-Buddha-Dhyana-Sutra carved in this cave is 8m high and 22m wide. Look at the group of figures, and they are exquisitely carved to display the grand scene of Western Paradise. The whole scene looks much like a spacious garden stretching far into the distance. It consists of the upper and lower parts joined by over 30 groups of figures. Children play upon the balustrade, and boys are enwrapped in lotus flowers in full blossom. These lively youngsters have added vitality to the world of the Buddha.

Ladies and gentlemen, Buddhist scriptures display the pictures of Hell and Heaven on purpose to encourage people to perform good deeds and to refrain from doing evil things. Hell is carved on the large face of the rock in the hill. It consists of the upper, middle and lower divisions. The Ten Quarter Buddhas (十方佛) occupy the upper division, and the Ten Hell Kings (十冥王) live in the middle. The lower division displays the horrible scenes of the Eighteen Layers Hell (十八层地狱). Those who have done evil things during their lifetime are supposed to stay there.

Here is Yuanjue Cave（圆觉洞）. Yuanjue means the total awakening in English. The cave is 12m in depth, 6m in height and 9m in width. There are three principle Buddhas, who sit cross-legged and face the cave entrance. The principle figure on the right is Sakyamuni. On either side of the three Buddhas are 6 seated Pratyeka-Buddhas（圆觉菩萨）. They are carved out of the walls and in various postures. Now they take turns asking the principle Buddhas questions that have arisen during their Buddhist practice towards the enlightenment. The Pratyeka scripture（圆觉经）says that there are only 12 Pratyeka-Buddhas, who take turns asking questions. In this cave, there are 13 Pratyeka-Buddhas. The thirteenth Buddha joins the questioning, and he kneels in front of the three principle Buddhas with his palms put together. Why? Well, the artists intentionally added the kneeling Buddha in order to display the scene of how the Pratyeka Buddha asked the questions. The carving of the kneeling Buddha and the 12 Pratyeka-Buddhas is regarded as a unique motif in Buddhist art due to its unity of the carving content and the highest possible perfection of artistic form.

The use of natural light in Yuanjue Cave is worth attention. The inner space of the cave is 12m in length. In the dimly lit cave, the pavilions, cloudy mountains, and other patterns appear indistinct. On the top of the cave entrance is a huge window designed by the artists. The light comes in through the window and illuminates the details of the main carvings, including the scene of the kneeling Buddha. Under the illumination, visitors may feel as if they were in the Buddhist land of peace, far away from the current world, within pavilions, trees, birds, flowers and cloudy mountains. When it rains, visitors in the cave can hear water trickling through invisible pipes. A close look under the clouds, trees and pagodas will reveal a complete system that empties all of the roof water into a cistern located on the head of a dragon where the water disappears underground.

Please follow me to see another group of carvings called the Picture of Cowherds (牧羊道场). This group differs from the scene displayed in Yuanjue Cave. The whole picture seems to be a series of ten scenes recounting the life of a cowherd who is engaged in his daily activities, riding, drinking, sleeping or running. Actually the ten scenes are carved to call up the feeling and influence from the Buddhist world. It suggests that the cowherd's activities are closely related to the process of the Buddhist meditation and practice. Man takes part in Nature but does not dominate it or seek to control it. Man is subordinated to Nature.

Well, so much for the tour of the stone carvings on Baoding Hill and the Northern Hill. Generally speaking, Dazu Stone Sculptures have displayed the splendid achievements in Buddhist art in China. Figures carved on rocks and stones withstand time and stay here in silent testimony to the paot centuries. The marvels of carvings come alive in an expression of art with a glimpse at each figure, where the ancient Buddhist devotees from Tang to Ming Dynasties were patrons to one of the world's finest epochs of art.

I hope as you leave here the scenes of Hell will not give you nightmares, but then I am sure that all of you will be blessed and reincarnated in accordance with your wishes. It has been my pleasure to share these treasures with you.

KEY WORDS & EXPRESSIONS 关键词汇及表达法

exert a great influence on 发挥较大的影响
pilgrim 圣地朝拜者
preconceive 预想
explanatory 解释的
transmigration 轮回
well-doer 善者
evil-doer 恶者
conduct evil deeds 造恶孽
predestined reward 报应
vice versa 反之亦然
accumulate 积聚，堆积
respectively 分别地
minute 微小的，详细的
immortal freedom 不生不灭的彼岸
overwhelming 压倒性的，势不可当的
bust 半身像，胸像
spout out 喷出
out-stretch 伸长
hover 翱翔
in accordance with 与……一致
chubby 丰满的，圆胖的
ornamented costume 装饰的服装
implore 恳求，哀求

pregnant 怀孕的，重要的
diaper 尿布
grown-up 长大的，成年的
ill-treat 虐待
in return 回报
supervise 监督，管理
requite 报答，酬谢
filial piety 孝顺，孝敬
heretical 异教的，异端的
slander 诽谤
unfilial 不孝的
balustrade 栏杆
enwrap 包裹，围绕
motif 主题，主旨
illuminate 照明，照亮
trickle 滴流
marvel 奇迹
nightmare 梦魇，恶梦

Pandas in Sichuan 四川熊猫

Basic Information about Pandas
熊猫的基本情况

Ladies and gentlemen, now we are approaching to Chengdu Giant Panda Breeding Research Base. I'd like to offer you some information about giant pandas before we enter into the panda base.

China is the home of giant pandas. Two thousand years ago,

according to the records of some ancient books, giant pandas were living in many areas in ancient China such as Hunan, Hubei, Shanxi, Gansu, Shaanxi, Sichuan, Yunnan, Guizhou and Guangxi. Because of the constant expansion of human production activities, the habitat of giant pandas gradually shrank, and presently they only inhabit the southern side of Qingling Mountains, the southern part of Gansu province, and the mountain ranges of West Sichuan.

In Sichuan the pleasant climate provides a favorable environment for animals. There are over 1, 000 kinds of vertebrates, accounting for 40 percent of national total amount. Among them are 55 kinds of rare animals. Most pandas inhabit the mountain areas in West Sichuan. They exist as a unique species, which has survived historical evolution and now is of significant value for protection and studies.

The giant panda is the national treasure of China and the world. It is known as the "living fossil" of all animals. Pandas are the earliest known animals that still survive today since the Late Pleistocene Epoch(更新世中期 600,000 years). At that time pandas lived everywhere in China. In the Late Pleistocene Epoch numbers of pandas decreased rapidly due to the change of climate and natural environment. Since pandas are the only survivors from the Pleistocene Epoch, scientists in the world have called attention to the pandas in Sichuan, and have regarded Sichuan as the home of pandas. At the present time, the pandas that are in some domestic and overseas zoos are all from Sichuan province.

In 1876, Père Armand David, a French missionary and naturalist discovered pandas in Sichuan. After David introduced the giant panda to the world, many zoologists, explorers, travelers and hunters came to China from far away, with the purpose of catching a rare giant panda. However, it's very hard to find giant pandas because they usually live alone in the thick forest on mountain areas. Among the cases based on historical records, two Russian got a giant panda fur in an area around Pingwu(平武) and Songpan(松潘) of Sichuan. In 1916, German zoologist Hugo Weigold caught a live giant panda in Wenchuan(文川) of Sichuan and became the first westerner who owned a live panda.

Giant pandas are stoutly built, rather clumsy, and they each have a thick pelt of fine hair, a short tail, and a round white face. Their eyes are set in black-rimmed sockets.

They usually live alone among thick forest and bamboo groves. Pandas like to live in a mountainous forest zone from 2,300m to 3,200m. In spring and winter when snow covers the mountains, the pandas go down to live in much lower areas. In summer and autumn when it gets warmer in the valleys, they return to the higher elevations.

According to reports, zoo pandas can live as long as 35 years old. Scientists aren't sure about the life span of a wild giant panda although they know that pandas in a zoo live longer than wild ones.

Pandas are meat-eaters, but they're too slow to catch animals. So they live mostly on a vegetarian diet of bamboo and sugar cane leaves. Pandas consume enormous amounts of bamboo. An adult panda, for example, usually eats up 15 – 20km of bamboo per day. They also eat sugar cane, rice gruel, a special high-fiber biscuit, carrots, apples and sweet potatoes.

In August 1985, an urgent message reached Beijing from

Wolong Nature Reserve. Arrow bamboo plants in Wolong mountainous areas were beginning to flower in their regular habitat. The arrow bamboo is the pandas' chief food. This flowering happens in cycles every 50 or 60 years. Afterwards the plants quickly die to reseed themselves and start another cycle. At the same time the pandas would go hungry.

Beijing authorities learned of the crisis. Immediately they sent Dong Zhiyong, former vice-minister of Forestry, to take charge of the rescue efforts. He quickly assembled a team of zoologists, botanists and other specialists at Chengdu to work out emergency measures. Vice-Minister Dong said, "We are determined to save these precious animals, no matter what the cost will be."

Soon the emergency team arranged to have local people carry substitute foods up to the mountains. The foods were sugarcane and cooked mutton, and they were carefully distributed in the places where hungry pandas might come. Usually the pandas are shy of human company, so they might not see the distributed food.

Rescue groups searched in the dense forests for starving pandas. The emergency team worked out a more practical plan. They decided to bring starving pandas down to the areas at 1,200 - 2,600m level, where sugarcanes and other bamboo varieties had not been affected by the bamboo cycle period.

All the people stayed out of the food distributed places so that pandas might move downwards. The reserve and two local communes officially sealed off the mountain area, and patrols were organized to prevent people from going up to collect medicinal herbs, or cut down trees for firewood. The reserve then roasted 400 sheep and scattered the meat on the mountains to lure pandas down. A number of feeding posts were also set up where sugarcane, apples, cornmeal and milk were provided to pandas. The emergency team also set up four new mountaintop observation posts. The patrol teams kept searching for pandas and brought ill or starving animals down to the feeding posts for food and medical treatment.

At the same time rescue workers constructed special ponds and lookout stations equipped with chemical fire extinguishers because the dead bamboo groves were highly flammable.

However, the emergency team and research center believed that the long-term solution for the pandas' food was to start sowing more bamboo varieties so that in the future not all the plants would be in blossom at the same time. Later scientists tried a number of new species of bamboo varieties. They collected seeds from flowered bamboo groves in Wolong and other places for experimental testing in an attempt to develop a large-scale sowing project with different varieties.

Giant pandas have their mating season that usually occurs between January and June. During this period, female pandas undergo a "silent heat," which lasts between 12 and 25 days. A female panda may mate with more than one male in a single mating season to ensure successful fertilization. Usually the panda's pregnancy period lasts from 83 to 163 days. In recent years, panda natural mating at centers has been very successful. Scientists realize that the natural environmental factors from no-wall-enclosures might have enhanced the possibility of breeding success.

A newly born baby panda weighs 90 to 130 grams. If the

mother panda delivers two baby pandas at the same time, she usually abandons the weaker one that may die soon after birth. The newly born baby panda's eyes are undeveloped and remain shut until 45 days after her birth. The mother panda usually nurse her child as many as 12 times a day. When the baby panda is born, their skin appears white at the very start. Within 2 weeks, the skin turns gray. Within one month after birth, the baby panda's skin color looks the same with her mother's. Pandas start to eat bamboo when they are five months old, and they get accustomed to food other than their mother's milk when they are 6 months old. Pandas reach sexually maturity when they are 4.5 to 6.5 years old.

China has natural reserves set aside for about 1,000 giant pandas. In 1957, the Third National People's Congress made a decision to establish forest nature reserves. In 1963, China established the first five nature reserves of which four reserves were located in Sichuan to protect giant pandas and other rare animals. The effective panda protection started in 1985. By 1988, more nature reserves had been established mainly for the same objective. In June of 1992, the Chinese Government launched the "Project for the Protection of Giant Panda and its Habitat". The main contents of the project include two items: Strengthening the scientific studies on the ecology and artificial raising and breeding of giant pandas, and establishing a Chinese study center for the protection of giant pandas in a natural panda habitat in Sichuan province.

KEY WORDS & EXPRESSIONS 关键词汇及表达法

breeding 繁殖

habitat 栖息地

evolution 进化
pleistocene 更新世(的)
missionary 传教士
zoologist 动物学家
stoutly 结实地
clumsy 笨拙的
vegetarian 吃素的
consume 消耗
forestry 林业
botanist 植物学家
emergency 紧急情况
cornmeal 玉米粉
extinguisher 灭火器
flammable 易燃的
mating 交配
pregnancy 怀孕
maturity 成熟

Wolong Natural Reserve
卧龙自然保护区

Wolong Natural Reserve covers a space of 200,000 hectares, which abounds with an estimated 3,000 kinds of plants. It is especially rich in arrow bamboo and Chinese pink bamboo the pandas' favorite food. To the northwest rises Mt. Siguniangshan (四姑娘山) at an elevation pf 6240m and to the east the reserve drops as low as 155m.

The United Nations has designated Wolong as an international biosphere reserve. About 100 pandas of the total number of about 1,000 giant pandas live there. The reserve aims to protect 96 species of mammals, including the giant panda, red panda, snow leopard, musk deer and golden monkey. The protection also includes 230 species of birds and scores of rare reptiles and butterflies.

At present, the reserve has turned into a Giant Panda Breeding Centre highlighting research works on panda breeding and bamboo ecology. The reserve scientists and staff have three primary responsibilities. First, they take care of giant pandas that grow up in small enclosures on a daily basis. Second, they take care of some injured pandas or pandas that have lost the ability to survive if people send them back to the wild. Third, they prepare pandas that are ready to return to the wild.

The reserve provides small enclosures or semi-nature enclosures to host giant pandas. Each small enclosure consists of an in-door room and an out-door courtyard with walls around, and the semi-nature enclosures cover an extensive wild areas. Those giant pandas that are on the list of returning to the wild usually inhabit the semi-nature enclosures so that they will gradually adapt themselves to the wild environment. During their stay there, giant pandas have to sleep and eat in the enclosure although food is offered by the reserve staff.

KEY WORDS & EXPRESSIONS 关键词汇及表达法

abound with 充足
biosphere 生物圈
mammal 哺乳动物
ecology 生态学
enclosure 圈地

Chengdu Giant Panda Breeding Research Base

成都大熊猫繁育研究基地

Chengdu Giant Panda Breeding Research Base, located 10km north of Chengdu, is one of the important giant panda conservation and protection centers. The base covers an area of 600 acres where bamboo grows in abundance, and birds fly around. Over thirty giant pandas and some other rare animals share the area. They include red pandas and black-necked cranes.

The base differs from Wolong Natural Reserve. In Chengdu the weather is much warmer and more humid than in Wolong. If the temperature is less than 26°C (78. 8 F), the base staff let pandas stay in the open within enclosures. When the temperature is between 26 and 30°C(78. 8F – 86 F), pandas are kept in rooms, which have facilities like fans, air conditioners, or large blocks of ice. Most enclosures in the base cover a large area, which resembles a landscape painting, decorated with trees, rockery, grass, and water pools.

At the base is a museum called Chengdu Giant Panda Museum established in 1992. It is a comprehensive museum that focuses on multi-programs: giant pandas' up-to-date information, scientific research projects, conservation and rescuing activities. In addition to the Giant Panda Museum, there are butterfly and vertebrate museums. These three museums show more than 800 precious pictures and exhibit over 2,140 different kinds of life-size specimens, including over 100 kinds of animal specimens, 300 kinds of bird specimens, and 240 kinds of reptile specimens. These comprehensive museums highlight the importance of animals' protection by human beings.

Well, so much for my brief introduction of pandas in Sichuan. Here we are at the entrance of Chengdu Giant Panda Breeding Research Base. Please get off the bus and follow me into the base compound.

KEY WORDS & EXPRESSIONS 关键词汇及表达法

Celsius 摄氏的
resemble 类似
comprehensive 综合的
specimen 样品

Appendix 附 录

Pre-Arrival Planning

接团注意事项

On the way to the airport

1. Take your Tour-Guide Certificate, Tour-Guide Professional Rating Card and the local tour schedule for the incoming tour group along with you.
2. Please have a guide banner with you if you are meeting a group of 10 persons or more.
3. Mind your general appearance. You are generally expected to dress compatible with the status of a tour guide. It is generally recommended to dress a little conservatively. Remember not to wear cut-off shorts, tank tops, T-shirts and slippers. Caps should not be worn backwards or sideways in public.
4. It is not acceptable in public to have visible body piercing, tattoos and dirty hair. Dyed hair is inappropriate.
5. You are expected to know as much information as possible about the team, team leader and team members. Besides, you are expected to confirm where to meet the group at the airport reception hall, and how to start the local tour upon arrival of the group.
6. You are expected to let the bus and luggage car drivers know the time when the group arrives. They are supposed to get to the airport ahead of time.

From the airport to the hotel

1. When you meet the group, you are expected to offer each team member a copy of their tour schedule in Sichuan and let the team members know what the local time is.
2. You and the team leader are expected to find out how many pieces of heavy luggage should arrive. The luggage deliveryman should transport all the heavy bags and luggage from the airport to the hotel.
3. On the way to the hotel, you are expected to make a welcome speech. It should include the local weather, your travel agency, the bus driver and yourself. Besides, you should give them a brief introduction of the coming arrangements related to accommodations, food, and local scenic spots.

In a hotel

1. When the team arrives at the hotel, you are expected to help the team leader check in at the hotel reception desk.
2. You are expected to let team members know the hotel facilities, including location of the restaurant, luggage storage room, bar, and swimming pool.
3. The morning call should be confirmed with the team leader based on the local tour schedule the next day.
4. You are expected to watch that all the bags and luggage is safely delivered to the rooms in which the tourists stay.
5. For the team's first meal in Chengdu, you are expected to show the team the way to the restaurant for their meal before or after their settlement in the hotel based on the circumstances. During the mealtime you are expected to offer a general introduction about the meal in an attempt to help them

enjoy dishes. You should be alert and ready to be of service whenever a team member raises suggestions or questions.

6. According to the contract, two persons share a room. If a team member wants a single room, you should ask the reception desk if the hotel has a room available. If the hotel has enough rooms to offer, the team member must pay the extra money to make up the balance. Your patient explanation is necessary and important when the hotel has no vacancy.
7. You are expected to visit each room shortly after each team member moves into his/her room. The purpose of your visit is to remind him/her to check if the room facilities (glasses, cups, lights, or towels) are in good shape. Do let the hotel receptionist know if the room has a shortage of necessities or something is broken when the members move in.
8. When the team arrives at the hotel, and the members find out that the rooms are below their aspiration, and seem to fail to conform to the conditions of the agreement between the travel agency and themselves. At this moment, you are expected to explain what has happened, and the travel agency should return some money if possible.
9. When the team arrives at the hotel, and the members find out that the hotel has transferred their rooms to another team, and they have no rooms to stay in this hotel. Under these circumstances you are expected to help the team look for rooms in another hotel as soon as possible. If the room conditions in the other hotel are below what the agreement requires, the travel agency should return them some money.

In a restaurant

1. At a dinner table in a restaurant you are always ready to do some oral translation. During your oral translation you are not expected to be chewing food or smoking. Do not make noise when you drink soup.
2. For some medical or religious reasons some team members may require food different from the other members. You are expected to satisfy their requirement, and the extra cost will be added to their own expenses.
3. If someone in the team wants some other food rather than the arranged one, you are expected to tell the restaurant manager to change the food three hours in advance before the mealtime. However, when the mealtime is approaching, and someone makes such a request, you are expected to say to him/her that it is too late to change the menu that has been prepared. If he/she insists, the extra cost will be charged to him/her.
4. If someone dislikes eating with the other team members because of an unhappy argument, you are expected to solve their disagreement and try your best to persuade him/her to join the group for meals. It is acceptable if he/she still insists on eating alone. However, he/she must pay for his/her own meal. Some members may like to go to other places for some local food. You are expected to let them know the location of good-food and clean restaurants, designated by the local bureau of the tourism.

Shopping

1. You are expected to show them where to buy good quality objects. Suppose someone has bought an over-100-year-old

item in a store. You are expected to tell the store owner to issue a receipt stamped by an official seal. The buyer should keep the receipt in case the custom official asks for it.

2. Sichuan has rich resources of natural Chinese herbs. Many herb stores are available to overseas tourists. If some members are interested in herbs, you are expected to suggest that they visit a Chinese doctor whose major is traditional Chinese medicine. The purpose of the visit is to get the sound advice of what to buy in a herb store. Perhaps a specific prescription from the doctor is a great idea. Besides, you are expected to show the herb buyers where to buy high quality herbs. A receipt is necessary.
3. Some team members may ask you to buy something and post it for them. In this case you are expected to politely refuse to do so. However, they may have difficulty in buying or posting such items, and your refusal may distress them. So what you are expected to do is to get permission from the travel agency before you help them buy and post the items for the team members. The team members should offer enough money to cover the cost. And a receipt is necessary.

Recreational arrangement

1. Maybe some team members don't want to go to the scheduled recreational program in the evening. Generally speaking, their request is acceptable. However, the fee for the program is not reimbursed. When they want to go to a different program, their choice is covered under their own expenses.
2. According to the arrangement, all the team members will go and watch Sichuan opera in the evening. However there is an

important basketball match, which will be held at the same time. Some young team members plan to go and watch the game; the old members insist on going to Sichuan opera. So you are expected to help the young members purchase admission tickets for the game and arrange their transportation. Afterwards you are expected to go with the old people to Sichuan opera.

Accident

1. Traffic accidents do happen occasionally. In this case you are expected to report the accident to the departments concerned as quickly as possible, hoping that the rescue team will come quickly. You are expected to help the team members get out of danger quickly, arrange people to rescue the victims, and try to keep intact the scene of the accident until traffic policemen arrive.
2. After the traffic accident, you are expected to say something to comfort the tourists and do your best to make them remain stable. Hopefully the arranged trip will continue.
3. When you and the team are on the trip, you are expected to take good care of each member in case an accident might happen. You should let the members know that strangers are not permitted into their hotel rooms, and they are not encouraged to exchange foreign currencies in secret privacy. Their valuable items should be placed in the hotel safety boxes.
4. Robbery, stealing or murder might happen. You are expected to protect travelers' interests and call the police immediately for help if it happens. At the same time, you are expected to report the accident to your travel agency for advice. You are

also expected to say something to comfort the tourists and do your best to make them remain calm.

5. A fire accident usually happens in a hotel. You are expected to say to the members that combustibles and explosives are not permitted to be taken into their hotel rooms; smoking on or in a bed is forbidden. You should show the members how to get to the safety passageway each floor and how to dial the fire alarm phone number. If a fire accident happens, you should first of all call firefighters at the given phone number and help tourists escape through the safety passageway.

Sickness

1. Suppose that one of the team members unexpectedly has a heart sickness. You are expected to help the patient to lie stretched out with his/her head resting a little upwards. Then you should ask the team leader to search the patient's pocket or bag for his/her medicine. You are also expected to contact a hospital nearby for emergency treatment.
2. Some members may have transportation sickness. You are expected to let them know not to eat too much right before a distance trips start. Do remind them to have some pills with them. Besides, you are expected to arrange for those members to sit where they feel more comfortable.
3. If one of the members has a heat stroke in summer, you are expected to help him/her move to a shady place where he/she should lie stretched out for a rest and drink some salty water. At the same time, someone in the team should loosen his/her belt and untie the part of his/her garment that fits too tightly around his/her neck. He/she should be sent to a hospital for

further medical treatment if his/her heat stroke remains or gets worse.

Complaints

1. Some members may make a complaint against the service he/she has during his/her trips. How do you take precautions against this situation?
   - You are expected to provide them high-quality services associated with food, accommodation, transportation, and sightseeings.
   - You are expected to perfect yourself by building up your service experience.
   - You are expected to offer tourists services that conform to the signed agreement between the tourists and the travel agency as well as the rules issued by the local tourism administration.
2. When a complaint does happen, you are expected to handle it carefully with the complainant. Patient explanations and even an apology are necessary. If the complaint sounds serious, and it is beyond your ability to handle it, you should report it to the travel agency for advice. You and the agency should work together to solve the problem.

Loss of a passport

1. The team members are responsible to secure their passports. The loss of a passport is bad news. Getting a new one takes time. Suppose a member has lost his/her passport, you are expected to help him/her look for it. If he/she can't get it back, the following procedure is necessary.

2. The travel agency should produce a letter of the loss of his/her passport.
3. He/she should go to the local police station to report the loss.
4. At the station he/she shows the letter from the travel agency and his/her photo. Accordingly the police station issues him/her an official letter of proof.
5. With the letter of proof he/she can apply for a new passport in the embassy or consulate of his/her country.
6. When he/she receives the new passport from the embassy or consulate, he/she will be able to apply for his/her visa at the local PSB Entry and Exit Department.

KEY WORDS & EXPRESSIONS　关键词汇及表达法

certificate　证书，证明书
handbook　手册，指南
appearance　外貌，外观
inappropriate　不适当的，不相称的
be compatible with　与……谐调的，一致的
conservatively　保守地
cut-off shorts　短裤
tank tops　露肩装
slippers　拖鞋
schedule　日程
luggage-delivery-man　行李员
bar　酒吧
circumstance　环境
make up the balance　补足差额
vacancy　空房
receptionist　接待员，服务员
make a suitable payment　支付适当的费用

extra 额外的，不包括在价目内的
disagreement 意见纷争，不调和
designated 指定的，派定的
stamped 有邮戳的
wax 蜡，石蜡
seal 图章
prescription 处方，药方
receipt 收据，收条
recreational 娱乐性的，供消遣的
accompany 陪伴
rescue 救治
keep intact the scene of an accident 保护事故现场
stranger 陌生人
safeguard 保护
combustible 易燃品
explosive 易爆品
safety passageway 安全通道
lie stretched out 平躺
emergency 急救
bump up and down 颠簸
heat stroke 中暑
garment 衣服
complaint 投诉
complainant 投诉者
take precautions against 预防
official 正式的
embassy 大使馆
consulate 领事馆
PSB Entry and Exit Department 公安局出入境管理局

References

参考文献

笔者在编写这本书时，参考了大量中英文著作和文献，特此致谢。若有遗漏，恳请与笔者联系，以便再版时补正。

1. Beth C. Bauer. *Enjoy China More*. USA: Cain-Lockhart Press

2. D. C. Lau. *Lao Tsu: Tao Te Ching*. Penguin Group, 1963

3. Evelyne Garside. *China Companion*. London: Andre Deutsch Ltd, 1981

4. Michael Buckley. *China*. Australia: Lonely Planet Publications, 1994

5. W. Scott Morton. *China: Its History and Culture*. Lippincott & Crowell Publishers, 1995

6. 杨天庆编著. 四川英文导游应试必备手册. 四川：四川科学技术出版社，2002

7. 段成，贺宗元主编. 四川旅游英语. 四川：西南师范大学出版社，1999

8. 惠长林主编. Si Chuan. 北京：五洲传播出版社，2001

9. 四川省旅游局人事教育处与四川省旅游协会秘书处合编. 四川导游，2000

10. 四川省旅游局人事教育处与四川省旅游协会秘书处合编. 四川导游词汇编(第一分册)，1996

11. 四川省旅游局人事劳动教育处与四川省旅游协会国内旅游分合编. 四川导游词汇编(第二分册)

12. 冷涛，邓成蓉著. 阿坝州旅游大全. 四川：四川人民出版社，1996

13. 齐雯编. 中国概貌. 北京：外文出版社，1984

14. 何志范. 峨眉山·乐山巡礼. 北京:旅游教育出版社,1994.

15. 骆坤琪编著. 峨眉山佛道漫话. 四川:四川人民出版社,1988

16. 龚丹著. *Food and Drink in China*. 北京:新世界出版社,1986

17. 张昌余编. 成都旅游,四川:四川人民出版社,1981

18. 袁祖文. 北京英语导游. 北京:旅游教育出版社,2001

19. 中国手册编辑委员会编. 文学与艺术. 北京:外文出版社,1983

20. 牛华主编. 四川英语导游——景点讲解. 北京:中国旅游出版社,2004

21. 黄友良著. 峨眉山宗教文化旅游. 北京:方志出版社,2001

22. 黄友良著. 乐山宗教文化旅游. 北京:方志出版社,2002